Integrated Services for Children and Families

Opportunities for Psychological Practice

EDITED BY Robert J. Illback
Carolyn T. Cobb
Herbert M. Joseph, Jr.

AMERICAN PSYCHOLOGICAL ASSOCIATION ▪ WASHINGTON, DC

Published by
American Psychological Association
750 First Street, NE
Washington, DC 20002

Copies may be ordered from
American Psychological Association
Order Department
P.O. Box 92984
Washington, DC 20090-2984

In the UK and Europe, copies may be ordered from
American Psychological Association
3 Henrietta Street
Covent Garden, London
WC2E 8LU England

Typeset in Century Schoolbook by EPS Group Inc., Easton, MD

Printer: Data Reproductions Corporation, Auburn Hills, MI
Cover designer: Berg Design, Albany, NY
Technical/Production Editor: Catherine R. Worth

Library of Congress Cataloging-in-Publication Data
Integrated services for children and families : opportunities for
  psychological practice / edited by Robert J. Illback, Carolyn T. Cobb,
  and Herbert M. Joseph, Jr.
     p.   cm.
  Includes bibliographical references and index.
  ISBN 1-55798-431-X
  1. Family services—United States.   2. Family psychotherapy—
United States.   I. Illback, Robert J.   II. Cobb, Carolyn T.
III. Joseph, Herbert M., Jr.
  HV699.I53   1997
  362.2′04256—dc21   97-11282
                                                                                       CIP

British Library Cataloguing-in-Publication Data
A CIP record is available from the British Library

Printed in the United States of America
First edition

Contents

Part I: Description and Rationale for an Integrated Service System

Part II: Implementing Integrated Services: Exemplary Models and Approaches

Contributors

Carolyn T. Cobb, PhD, *North Carolina Department of Public Instruction, Raleigh*

Anna E. Danegger, PhD, *The Finance Project, Washington, DC*

W. David Driscoll, PsyD, *Clinical Assistant Professor of Psychiatry (Psychology), Division of Family Programs, University of Rochester School of Medicine and Dentistry, New York*

Joy G. Dryfoos, MA, *Hastings-on-Hudson, New York, and Columbia University School of Public Health*

Carl J. Dunst, PhD, *Orelena Hanks Puckett Institute, Asheville, North Carolina*

Ellen Foley, PhD, *University of Pennsylvania*

Scott W. Henggeler, PhD, *Family Services Research Center, Medical University of South Carolina*

Robert J. Illback, PsyD, *R.E.A.C.H. of Louisville, Inc., Kentucky*

Herbert M. Joseph, Jr., PhD, *Boston Medical Center*

John Kalafat, PhD, *Rutgers University, New Jersey*

Jane Knitzer, PhD, *National Center for Children in Poverty, Columbia University School of Public Health, New York*

T. Kerby Neill, PhD, *Kentucky Department of Mental Health, Lexington*

George W. Noblit, PhD, *University of North Carolina at Chapel Hill*

Martin E. Orland, PhD, *National Center for Education Statistics, Washington, DC*

Vera S. Paster, PhD, *City University of New York, City College*

Robert J. Resnick, PhD, *Department of Psychology, Randolph Macon College, Virginia*

Victor Romualdi, PhD, *University of California, Davis*

Daniel Sanders, PhD, *R.E.A.C.H. of Louisville, Inc., Kentucky*

Jonathan Sandoval, PhD, *Division of Education, University of California, Davis*

Sonja K. Schoenwald, PhD, *Family Services Research Center, Medical University of South Carolina, Charleston*

Carolyn S. Schroeder, PhD, *Chapel Hill Pediatrics and Chapel Hill Pediatric Psychology, Chapel Hill, North Carolina*

Rick Jay Short, PhD, *Department of Educational and Counseling Psychology, University of Missouri—Columbia*

Donald I. Wagner, EdD, *University of Cincinnati, Ohio*

Joseph E. Zins, EdD, *University of Cincinnati, Ohio*

Acknowledgments

Editing this book has been a great joy and privilege. My coeditors and I wish to thank the contributors for their clarity and timeliness, as well as their patience as the work has progressed. In addition, I would like to acknowledge the unflagging support of the remarkable people at R.E.A.C.H. of Louisville, Incorporated, including Nancy Irvin, Mark Scureman, Jennifer Hakel, Diane Wohlfarth, Charlie Miller, Hope Dittmeier, Dave Rednour, Audrey Newton, John Kalafat, Dan Sanders, Terry Scott, Tonya Young, Ben Birkby, and Caryll Jefferies. Their commitment to integrated, family-friendly services continues to inform my thinking about the subject. Other professional colleagues who have facilitated my growth in this area are too numerous to mention, but I have especially enjoyed collaborating with Carolyn Cobb and Herb Joseph in this endeavor. Finally, I must acknowledge the incalculable and sustaining support of my family, including my mother, Evelyn A. Illback, my children, Anne and Erin Illback, and my sister and nephew, Audrey and Kevin Newton.

Robert J. Illback

Special appreciation is extended to the counties, public schools, agencies, existing collaborative initiatives, and individuals who participated in the North Carolina studies and, in doing so, helped us to better understand collaboration and integrated services. I would also like to thank Delores Brewer on my staff, a colleague and friend, who has consistently encouraged the North Carolina Department of Public Instruction to move toward collaborative services and who continues to integrate principles learned from these studies into our ongoing work.

Carolyn T. Cobb

I would like to express my sincere appreciation for the ongoing support of my colleagues in the Psychiatry and Psychology Department and among the staff and interns at the Center for Multicultural Training in Psychology (CMTP) at Boston Medical Center. I would especially like to thank Drs. Mike Rossi, Pedro Garrido, and Ms. Cynthia Marin. Kudos to Dr. Diana Saal, a friend and colleague, for exposing me to the "cork theory." The CMTP Network has also been a nurturing and sustaining force in my development as a psychologist and as Director of CMTP. My family, beginning with my parents, and including my brothers, sister, aunts, uncles, cousins, and nieces and nephews has sustained me with their love and unqualified support for my dreams and aspirations. Without them, I would not be who I am. The love and patience shown by my wife, Avolon, and children, Felicia and Andrea, while I completed this and other academic pursuits, deserve special acknowledgment. Finally, thanks to my coeditors, particularly Dr. Bob Illback, whose collaborative style kept us focused enough to make this book come to life.

Herbert M. Joseph, Jr.

Introduction

A glance at the alarming statistics displayed on the cover of this book reveals a steady decline in conditions for many American children and families. The indicators of unmet needs of children include unacceptable rates of infant mortality, low birthweight, lack of immunization, child abuse and neglect, psychological disorders, violence and aggression, and substance abuse, to name but a few. Numerous social, demographic, and economic factors have served to weaken the ability of families to provide healthy and developmentally appropriate environments for children. Poverty and economic instability, for example, cause some families to exist in conditions of inadequate nutrition, substandard housing, crime and violence, and social isolation. A growing number of children and youth experience the effects of poverty, along with the related and cumulative risks of poor physical health, low educational attainment, and psychological disorders. More children are also homeless and hungry, and live without appropriate physical and mental health care. Also, changes in family structure associated with increased divorce rates and the emergence of alternative family lifestyles have resulted in more single-parent, step, blended, and foster families, and have decreased access to extended family members. The increase of single-parent families or families in which both parents work, even when not economically disadvantaged, may result in increased stress and diminished functioning of the family system. Many children receive a substantial portion of their primary care from someone other than their parents, and access to adequate, high quality, and affordable child care is limited (Children's Defense Fund, 1992; National Commission on Children, 1991).

Ironically, the very programs designed to support children and families appear overwhelmed by the magnitude of these (and related) problems, and they seem unable to mobilize integrated, effective intervention efforts on behalf of children and families (Children's Defense Fund, 1992). Existing family support systems (e.g., health care, schools, recreation, social services) generally work in isolation and are proving unable to meet the challenges presented by the changing demographics of society (Melaville & Blank, 1993).

There is an emerging consensus among professionals and consumers that the current service delivery system is not effective and that solutions must go beyond adding resources (e.g., more funding, more programs) toward fundamental changes in how the system operates (Knitzer, 1982; Schorr, 1988). In this regard, service delivery is often conceptualized from the point of view of professionals and may not be based on family perceptions of need. Individual service delivery systems for children (e.g., health care, education, social service, mental health) are funded and designed to address isolated and crisis-oriented needs, rather than to promote healthy development for all children and families in a comprehensive fashion. In addition, some parents either have little knowledge of how to access available services, or do not value them. In sum, services provided to children and families frequently are not comprehensive, responsive, or integrated. An integrated service model provides for a more coherent, needs-based response to complex problems (Melaville & Blank, 1991).

To more closely assess the current array of services in regard to the psychological and mental health needs of children ages 0 through 10 years, the Board of Professional Affairs (BPA) of the American Psychological Association established a Task Force on Comprehensive and Coordinated Psychological Services for Children (TFCCPSC) in 1994.[1] The mission of the TFCCPSC was to determine gaps in service delivery, and provide recommendations to BPA on how these gaps should be addressed. After careful study of these issues, the task force determined that organized psychology was well behind many other professional groups relative to the emerging marketplace in child and family services.

This book grew out of the work of the TFCCPSC. In fact, many of the chapter authors are subject matter experts whose exemplary work was reviewed by the task force through its deliberations. As practicing psychologists heavily engaged in systems change, it is our hope that *Integrated Services for Children and Families: Opportunities for Psychological Practice* will serve to organize the best thinking within the profession about how to plan, deliver, and evaluate more responsive psychological services for children and families. Awareness of these concepts and aspirations may also promote discussion within psychology on how to organize for practice in a rapidly changing service system in ways that lead to strengthened, empowered families.

Service Integration: Definition and Description

For the purposes of this book, we have chosen to describe integrated services from the perspective of families. When examined in this light, emphasis is placed upon the nature of service delivery events or episodes that occur and the impact these events have on children and families. Within a well-integrated program,

- services are available in close proximity and are accessible without reference to physical, psychological, social, linguistic, or other barriers;
- services are comprehensive and appropriate in that they possess features that address priority needs the family has identified at a level of service sufficient to meet their need;
- services are formulated and delivered at a high level of quality

---

[1]Members of the Task Force were the editors of this volume, James Paavola (Chair), and Alicia Torruella. Ronda Talley, then a staff member of the APA Practice Directorate, served as liaison between the TFCCPSC and the BPA in addition to contributing to the core work of the Task Force.

such that the family perceives them as an organized whole and can participate in a consistent and effective manner;
- services serve to promote psychological competence and self-sufficiency rather than focuse exclusively on dysfunction and pathology;
- services are oriented toward full participation, partnership, and empowerment of family members;
- services are sensitive to cultural, gender, racial, linguistic, and class issues; and
- interventions are driven by concern for the needs and desires of consumers (i.e., children and families) and emphasize explicit outcomes stated in a positive manner. (Illback, 1994)

Schools and health care settings are two essential social systems with which virtually all children and families have routine, significant contact. The school is an environment wherein children engage in academic learning and growth, and experience social and emotional interactions with adults and peers to build self-esteem and social competence. These experiences can serve to increase later prospects for success in relationships, the workplace, and personal pursuits. Thus, it is vital that schools support the broad developmental needs of children and families. However, schools are being asked to address the needs of children and youth at a time when fundamental transformations of schooling structures and outcome expectations are also being demanded. Restructured schools alone cannot satisfactorily address the multidimensional needs of children and youth. Schools and other child- and family-service organizations must collaborate in an integrated manner to enhance the likelihood of educational and personal success for all children (DeMers, 1995; Illback & Nelson, 1996; Paavola, Hannah, & Nichol, 1989; Talley & Short, 1996).

Similarly, many children and families receive their health care in primary-care settings, such as physician's offices, community-based clinics, and other public-health and mental-health settings. These settings may be viewed as normal points of entry for the prevention, assessment, and treatment of a host of physical and psychological problems. However, health care systems currently are strained and many children access them only on a crisis basis. These systems also require collaboration with other services in order to address the developmental needs of children and families in a comprehensive and preventive manner (Day & Roberts, 1991; Henggeler, 1994; Saxe, Cross, & Silverman, 1988).

There is a continuum of service integration that varies as a function of need, service availability, problem severity, and related dimensions. From the perspective of children and families, many opportunities and services can best be accessed through a single provider and implemented in an integrative manner. When a number of providers are involved (e.g., psychologists, nurses, teachers, social workers, physicians, day-care workers), the need for effective collaboration increases. Timely and responsive interventions on behalf of children and families rely on competent and sustained communication and coordination among service providers, agencies, organizations, and consumers of services (Chaudry, Maurer, Oshinsky, Mackie, 1993; Institute for Educational Leadership, 1992).

Relevance to Psychology

In our view, psychologists have a crucial role to play in the promotion of systems that ensure the healthy development of children and the strengthening and empowerment of families. In primary health care and school settings, psychology can play an integral role in advocacy, prevention, consultation, assessment, and treatment for children and families (DeMers, 1995; Holtzman, 1992). Psychologists employed in other social service, mental health, and related organizational settings can also have considerable impact on the welfare of children and families through early intervention and treatment activities (National Commission on Child Welfare and Family Preservation, 1990). In all settings, psychological services must be integrated with other necessary services and provided in a manner that does not artificially separate physical, emotional, and social needs.

The concept of service integration has several implications for psychology as a profession. On a general level, integrated service models will increase the amount of broad-based services available to children and families, both by generating new funds and by freeing up funds now tied to rigid eligibility criteria. It seems likely that psychologists will remain one of a number of eligible providers to deliver such services, and therefore continue to be in "competition" with practitioners of other professions to demonstrate their relevance and efficacy. Because decisions about service delivery are more likely to be outcome oriented, consumer driven, and cost conscious, the particular strengths of our profession (including its conceptual underpinnings, empirical base, and concern for assessing outcomes) are likely to flourish in integrated service environments.

It must be acknowledged that alternative, less costly approaches to addressing child and family needs will increase within an integrated-services approach. Thus, whereas a child problem might previously have been conceptualized exclusively within a traditional psychotherapeutic approach, in this integrated approach the psychologist might have to collaborate with a "big brother," "big sister," or foster grandparent to meet the needs of the individual.

As integrated services become more prevalent in child and family service systems, a number of implications for psychological training, practice, research, and leadership are apparent. A psychologist serving as the only mental health professional in an elementary school or public health clinic, for example, will need to be competent in a broad number of skills and approaches, ranging from typical developmental concerns and issues to guidelines for monitoring commonly used child psychotropic medications, family interventions, and community consultation. Professionals who are "generalists" in human services will have greater possibilities of employment in an integrated-service system than those whose background is limited specifically to traditional psychological practice specialties. There will, of course, always be some need for specialization, particularly with respect to low-incidence or highly technical problems. Psychologists will need more systematic training in collaborative and consultation-based approaches to practice. Psychological services within an integrated-services framework will also look and feel substantially different. Practitioners will be able to exercise greater flexibility in the range of activities in which they engage, and will not be as constrained in regard to funding-source and eligibility considerations. They will spend more time working as part of a team, in concert with a variety of providers, caregivers, and community members. They are likely to spend more time in home, school, and other community settings, in addition to consulting offices. And, they will routinely work at the interdisciplinary boundaries between various social systems that impinge on children and families to coordinate activities, manage conflict, and ensure focus and quality of services.

Psychologists should be trained and encouraged to assume leadership roles within integrated service programs. In addition to the more traditional aspects of program administration and supervision, leadership activities should focus on establishing an integrative strategic vision for child-serving organizations, building collaborative teams, and facilitating planned organizational change in the direction of more integrated services.

Finally, psychological research on the efficacy of integrated-service-delivery approaches for children and families represents a unique challenge for psychology. Such research is distinct from traditional controlled experimentation in that the array of target problems is vast, treatment programs are diverse and multifaceted, and outcome measurement complicated. Practicing psychologists need to become proficient in a broader range of methods and procedures (e.g., quasi-experimental design, multivariate analysis, program-evaluation techniques, qualitative research) in order to conduct such social policy and program-related investigations. Psychologists are also likely to be in a unique position to help service systems develop and validate information systems to allow for on-going program monitoring and management.

The overall benefit of all of these changes is considerably greater effectiveness in the use of psychology to advance the public interest. There are at present large numbers of children and families whose needs in the area of health, mental health, education, and social welfare are not being met. In addition to the personal cost to these individuals, the prosperity of the country suffers from their resultant inability to contribute fully as citizens. Psychology (in collaboration with other concerned persons and professions) has an opportunity to exercise the leadership necessary to secure for these children and families effective, responsive, and comprehensive services.

Organization of the Book

Integrated Services for Children and Families: Opportunities for Psychological Practice is organized around three broad themes: (a) What are integrated services and why do we need them? (b) How has the integrated services model been implemented in a variety of organizations and contexts? and (c) What implications does the approach have for the practice of professional psychology?

In the opening chapter, Jane Knitzer, an acclaimed leader in the integrated-service movement since the publication of her seminal report *Unclaimed Children* (1982), provides an insightful update on the challenges and opportunities within the field. The concept of integrated-service delivery is no longer novel to child-serving professionals and organizations, and it continues to hold much promise as a means of transforming how people are served. However, changing complex systems remains difficult and perplexing. Knitzer reviews what has been learned to date and raises thought-provoking questions about what will be required in the future.

Joy G. Dryfoos, another visionary leader, then provides a highly engaging tour of school-based services to youth who confront the "new morbidities" in adolescent health (e.g., violence, suicide, substance abuse, sexual behavior). The chapter is replete with examples and insights into successful development and implementation, and an appendix provides details on exemplary school-based and school-linked service programs around the country.

Victor Romualdi and Jonathan Sandoval provide an alternative, complementary perspective. Following a historical analysis of community services, the authors contrast community-based with school-based models, and examine conceptual issues and challenges in community-based service delivery. Special consideration is given to the challenges and opportunities within minority communities, with emphasis on the potential role that informal parent networks can play (to the extent that professionals recognize and capitalize on these). Salient examples are provided in programs such as Black churches, community centers, and family resource centers.

Carl J. Dunst, one of the most prolific scholars in the area of family support, enablement, and empowerment, provides an in-depth conceptual and empirical overview of family-oriented help-giving practices. He relies heavily on research on interventions that have been shown to enhance family capacity and strength (much of which has been generated by Dunst and his colleagues), and teases out a set of elegant principles and practices that are central to his concept of family-centered practice. In many ways, Dunst's empirical findings provide the basis for much of the integrated-services movement, and are therefore central to an understanding of how psychologists must think and behave differently if they are to adopt a family-centered orientation. The author concludes by contrasting this perspective with other family therapy paradigms with which practicing psychologists will be familiar.

In the final chapter in the initial section of the book, Martin E. Orland, Anna E. Danegger, and Ellen Foley provide a primer on the funding of children's services. This is an area in which practitioners are notoriously weak, but also one in which there is mounting interest due to recent and anticipated changes in many venues. Some of the themes that may provide opportunities (as well as challenges) and that will be of special interest include (a) results-based budgeting and accountability, (b) decategorization, (c) refinancing, and (d) fund redeployment.

Implementing Integrated Services: Exemplary Models and Approaches

Sonja K. Schoenwald and Scott W. Henggeler furnish a thoughtful discussion of the integration of traditional forms of child mental health with more innovative famly preservation models in the form of a set of strategies they call multisystemic therapy (MST). MST features a core set of beliefs about families and the influence of the environment, and is both ecologically and empirically driven. The approach has great promise as a conceptual framework for the design of integrated service "packages" and as a model for how psychological theory and research can inform practice.

Joseph E. Zins and Donald I. Wagner then present an overview of integrated, prevention-oriented strategies to enhance the psychological competence of children and youth. The authors describe the social, emotional, and health challenges faced by young persons and make a compelling argument for the inclusion of competence-enhancement approaches within the integrated-service-delivery system. In particular, the chapter provides a fascinating discussion of several promising school-based approaches.

T. Kerby Neill is a pioneer in the development of integrated services for children with serious emotional disabilities through his role as a primary planner for *Kentucky IMPACT* (and its forerunner, the Robert Wood Johnson *Bluegrass IMPACT* demonstration program). This is one of the most extensive, successful, and long-standing initiatives in the nation, and at its core are the dual concepts of service coordination and interagency collaboration. Neill's chapter serves as a comprehensive primer for complex activities suggested by the service-coordination/case-management model, and highlights how psychologists can be involved in this growing field of endeavor. It also provides a thoughtful analysis of implementation issues and challenges in service coordination, and examines what can be gleaned from available research.

The concepts and strategies of integrated services are, in essence, descriptors of desirable features of a new system of care. Although it is useful to describe how this system should look and feel optimally, the challenge of changing long-standing organizational patterns remains. George W. Noblit and Carolyn T. Cobb present an in-depth analysis of interagency collaboration within an organizational context. They show, using rich descriptions of field research in North Carolina, the complexity of setting collaborative efforts in motion and assessing those efforts. Practitioners will undoubtedly resonate to their perceptive descriptions of organizational facilitators and barriers to collaboration.

Carolyn S. Schroeder, a leader in the field of pediatric psychology contributes a final application of the integrated service paradigm. Based on her own clinical practice, Schroeder portrays the range of useful work psychologists can perform in community primary-care settings, and she reflects on the kinds of preparation that are most salient in this emerging (and rapidly growing) marketplace. She discusses different models of collaboration with pediatricians, outlines several examples of psychology practices in this regard, and reviews a number of professional issues.

Implications for Professional Psychology

Vera S. Paster provides a comprehensive historical overview of the child mental health system (a troubled "nonsystem"), and proceeds to outline the features of the emerging system of care in this field, with special reference to the federal Child and Adolescent Service System Program (CASSP), which now drives system development. Psychologists who work in this rapidly changing area need to be familiar with the concepts and program elements that are being implemented throughout the nation. Additionally, the chapter considers the various funding streams that shape child mental health practice. The discussion of opportunities within Medicaid and managed care environments will be especially useful for practitioners.

Robert J. Illback considers the professional and organizational challenges ahead, based primarily on his experience as program evaluator for Kentucky IMPACT, a statewide system of care initiative enacted in 1990. Five emergent themes are discussed: (a) diversity and complexity of child and family needs, (b) delineating and integrating expanded service arrays, (c) maintaining and sustaining outcomes, (d) strengthening organizational capacity, and (e) family support and community building.

Many practicing psychologists work in independent or small group practice settings in which third-party reimbursement generates the bulk of revenue. Providing integrated services within these narrow strictures can be frustrating and challenging, to say the least. W. David Driscoll articulates how creative and determined effort can result in more integrated approaches, in the context of a systems-oriented independent-practice model. The chapter provides a comprehensive conceptual framework for thinking about systems practice, reviews the difficulties inherent in the strategy (with suggestions for overcoming these), and illustrates the approach through a highly engaging case study.

Robert J. Illback, John Kalafat, and Daniel Sanders then reflect on the need for evaluation of integrated service programs. Their chapter summarizes essential concepts and strategies in the area of program planning and evaluation, delineates the major conceptual and methodological problems that face evaluators of integrated service programs, and provides a case study to demonstrate a creative response to the need for management-oriented evaluation research.

Training for integrated practice is the subject of Rick Jay Short's chapter. It examines the assumptions underlying interprofessional practice, outlines what several writers consider to be the most central elements of successful training programs, reviews obstacles to such education and training within universities and other preparation programs, considers the relatively limited research base, and delineates unresolved issues. The chapter will be especially useful for those responsible to train or supervise practicing professionals.

Finally, Robert J. Resnick, a recent president of the American Psychological Association and a long-time leader and practitioner in child mental health, provides an afterword that enjoins practitioners to recognize the historical, political, and societal forces that contribute to the evolving practice environment and challenges practitioners to become part of the solution.

Whether you are a professional psychologist, social worker, educator, program administrator, or other human services professional, we feel confident you will find material in this volume that will both challenge you to think about change and provide guidance to promote it.

ROBERT J. ILLBACK
CAROLYN T. COBB
HERBERT M. JOSEPH, JR.

References

American Psychological Association. (1994). *Comprehensive and coordinated psychological services for children: A call for service integration. Report of the Task Force on Comprehensive and Coordinated Services for Children: Ages 0–10*. Washington, DC: Author.

Chaudry, A., Maurer, K. E., Oshinsky, C., & Mackie, J. (1993). *Service integration: An annotated bibliography*. New York: National Center for Service Integration, Columbia University.

Children's Defense Fund. (1992). *The state of America's children: 1992*. Washington, DC: Children's Defense Fund.

Day, C., & Roberts, M. C. (1991). Activities of the child and adolescent service system program for improving mental health services for children and families. *Journal of Clinical Child Psychology, 20*, 340–350.

DeMers, S. T. (Ed.). (1995). School psychology and health care: Emerging perspectives on the role of psychologists in the delivery of health and mental health services [Special issue]. *School Psychology Quarterly, 10*, 179–270.

Henggeler, S. W. (Ed.). (1994). Task force report on innovative models of mental health services for children, adolescents, and their families. [Special issue] *Journal of Clinical Child Psychology, 23*, 2–58.

Holtzman, W. H. (Ed.). (1992). *School of the future*. Washington, DC and Austin, TX: American Psychological Association and Hogg Foundation for Mental Health.

Illback, R. J. (1994). Poverty and the crisis in children's services: The need for services integration. *Journal of Clinical Child Psychology, 23*, 413–425.

Illback, R. J., & Nelson, C. M. (1996). *Emerging school-based approaches for children with emotional and behavioral problems: Research and practice in service integration*. Binghamton, NY: Haworth Press.

Institute for Educational Leadership. (1992). *Developing collaborative leaders: A selected bibliography of resources*. Washington, DC: Institute for Educational Leadership.

Knitzer, J. (1982). *Unclaimed children: The failure of public responsibility to children and adolescents in need of mental health services*. Washington, DC: Children's Defense Fund.

Melaville, A. I., & Blank, M. J. (1991). *What it takes: Structuring interagency partnerships to connect children and families with comprehensive services*. Washington, DC: Institute for Educational Leadership.

Melaville, A. I., & Blank, M. J. (1993) *Together we can: A guide for crafting a profamily system of education and human services*. U.S. Office of Education, Office of Educational Research and Improvement, and U.S. Department of Health and Human Services, Office of Assistant Secretary for Planning and Evaluation (EDRS No. ED 357856). Washington, DC: U.S. Government Printing Office.

National Commission on Child Welfare and Family Preservation. (1990). *A commitment to change*. Washington, DC: American Public Welfare Association.

National Commission on Children (Final report). (1991). *Beyond rhetoric: A new American agenda for children and families* (Publication No. 91-22834). Washington, DC: U.S. Government Printing Office.

Paavola, J. C., Hannah, F. P., & Nichol, G. T. (1989). The Memphis City Schools Mental Health Center: A program description. *Professional School Psychology, 4*, 61–74.

Saxe, L., Cross, T., & Silverman, N. (1988). Children's mental health: The gap between what we know and what we do. *American Psychologist, 43*, 800–807.

Schorr, L. B., & Schorr, D. (1988). *Within our reach: Breaking the cycle of disadvantage*. New York: Anchor.

Talley, R. C., & Short, R. J. (Eds.). (1996). Future of psychological practice in schools [Special issue]. *Professional psychology: Research and practice, 27*, 5–40.

Part I

Description and Rationale for an Integrated Service System

1 ———————————————————————————

Service Integration for Children and Families: Lessons and Questions

Jane Knitzer

The past decade has been a time of tremendous ferment and activity with respect to services for children and families, particularly publicly supported services. Calls for changing paradigms, services integration, cross-system collaboration, and systemic reform have spread across traditional service domains—children's mental health, child welfare, juvenile justice, and education—as well as emerging domains, largely reflected in the growth of family support programs and early intervention initiatives (Chaudry, Maurer, Oshinsky, & Mackie, 1993). Slowly, these initiatives have begun to transform not just the response to individual children and families, but the ways services are organized and funded. They have also begun to transform notions of professional practice for psychologists and other helping professionals. The purpose of this chapter is to place these developments in context, examining their assumptions, their scope, and some of the dilemmas and opportunities that the next decade is likely to bring.

Defining the Concept of Service Integration

During the past decade, efforts to conceptualize, implement, and examine service integration efforts have been marked by a remarkable consensus about the core characteristics of such efforts (Bishop, Woll, & Arango, 1993; Boyd, 1992; Burnim et al., 1991; Kagan, Goffin, Golub, & Pritchard, 1995; Kahn & Kamerman, 1992; Lewis, Carr, South, & Reed, 1995; McCart, 1993; Melaville & Blank, 1993; Stroul & Friedman, 1986; Task Force on Comprehensive and Coordinated Psychological Services for Children: Ages 0–10, 1994). Five value orientations have been particularly clearly and repeatedly identified.

First, service-integration efforts are characterized by a strong emphasis on the family. Service-integration language is replete with variations and nuances that call on service providers and policy makers to ensure a family perspective in service delivery: Families are described as *partners*, services are to be family-centered, service plans are to be built around family strengths, and governance and policy-making structures are to include families (Kagan & Weissbourd, 1994; Knitzer, 1993). A focus on family strengths and voices marks a clear reaction to the traditional services paradigm. In that paradigm, parents are the passive recipients of professional expertise and, thus, are often made to feel mistreated, scrutinized, or advised by the "experts" without recognition of their own strengths, ideas, or questions. Typically, this imbalance of respect and power is most visible in exchanges among low-income families and professionals, but it has also been noted and felt by families across the economic spectrum, particularly among those whose children have special health care needs or disabilities or face other special circumstances. New kinds of relationships are easy to call for in rhetoric, but in reality, although efforts to encourage practitioners, researchers, evaluators, and policy makers to be more responsive to a family perspective has been a focus of much activity, results have been mixed. This in turn has significant implications for the future.

A second theme that pervades the literature of service integration is a call for cross-system collaboration (Kagan, 1991; McCart, 1993; Stroul & Friedman, 1986). This too is a reaction to the ways in which services have often been delivered. Each program, agency, or public system has typically functioned in isolation from all others, even when multiple agencies work with the same family. This has also resulted in service inefficiencies and costs—multiple home visitors or case managers for one family, for example, and no services for others. More important, the lack of collaboration has fed into ineffective services, with families often confused about who was doing what and why. This in turn has fueled interest in service integration initiatives designed to build better connections across multiple programs, agencies, and public systems.

A third value that is reflected in service-integration efforts is a commitment to services grounded in a neighborhood/community-based context. In part, the perspective follows from a commitment to build on family strengths. Families live in neighborhoods. The more formal and informal supports that exist in neighborhoods, the more they will be able to draw on these supports to help their children. In part, the community emphasis also reflects a recognition that if communities do not take responsibility for children and families who need access to basic and specialized services, those needs are easily ignored. And increasingly, there is interest—particularly in low-income communities—in returning the economic benefits of a community-based service delivery system back to the community, thus viewing it as a form of economic development as well as a service provision.

The fourth value that is reflected in service-integration efforts is an important one, but it is also one that is difficult to operationalize. It marks a commitment to what has been called *cultural competence*—delivering services in a way that is respectful of the cultural values and traditions that families bring with them (Chang, Salazar, & Leong, 1994; Cross, Barzon, Dennis, & Issacs, 1989; McAdoo, 1993). In part, the growing recognition of the importance of attention to cultural issues is a response to the changing demographic face of America; growing numbers of families with children, particularly low-income families, reflect recent waves of immigration or are people of color. In part, the emphasis on cultural competence also reflects the recognition that unless services are sensitive to the culture and traditions of consumers, they are unlikely to be effective. Providers of service must be able to make sense out of the subtleties and assess the strengths that families bring to their childrearing and related tasks (Stevenson, 1994; Stevenson & Abdul-Kabir, 1995).

The fifth value that is increasingly reflected in service integration efforts is a pragmatic one: the commitment to link service integration efforts to concrete outcomes and positive change in the lives of children and families. In this context, one of the objectives of service integration efforts is to create an outcome-oriented system of services with decisions guided not just by shared goals, but by performance indicators, sometimes called *benchmarks*. This interest in outcomes is rooted in sound management practice. However, it also may be a corrective to what has been perceived as an overemphasis on due process (that is, procedural fairness) and an underemphasis on substantive process (that is, attention to the quality of services). The focus on outcomes may also be a corrective to a great emphasis on the processes of collaboration, rather than the results, in early framing of service-integration initiatives. And, it may also be a mark of a maturing social-intervention strategy, reflecting a willingness to be tested against hard child- and family-outcome data and fiscal data (Hayes, Lipoff, & Danegger, 1995).

What is particularly interesting about the identification of these five sets of values across systems and foci is that they speak to a general philosophical framework for service delivery rather than to "nuts and bolts." In other words, although the term *service integration* suggests a more limited focus on the mechanics of how services are organized and funded, in fact, the term is actually used as a shorthand for both a broad critique of past service-delivery approaches and a framework for reorganizing those approaches.

Service Integration Then and Now

Early Roots

The concept of service integration has its roots in the early settlement-house movement at the turn of the century. During the 1960s, interest in service integration resurfaced, this time around creating structures and mechanisms for the war on poverty (Kahn & Kamerman, 1992). To that end, for example, the concept of neighborhood centers, or *multiservice centers*, as they were sometimes called, took hold, pieced together with multiple federal funding streams (Illback, 1994; Kagan & Neville, 1993). The interest in service integration was furthered by Kennedy administration officials who became alarmed at the many different funding streams (largely federal) for services and supported a series of service-integration experiments. These, however, did not yield the kind of usable knowledge or affect the larger services-delivery system in ways that their proponents had hoped, and high-level interest waned (Edelman & Radin, 1991).

The service integration experiments of the 1960s were focused on generic services for the poor. The service integration movement of the 1990s, in contrast, is focused on services for children and families, particularly those who are poor or those who have special needs, such as children with disabilities. This shift in focus is an important difference in three ways: It puts families squarely in the center, shifting the focus from service delivery technicalities to the value orientations highlighted previously. It links interest in service integration with knowledge about how children develop, thus opening the pathways for clear goal-driven services and for more attention to links between services and developmental outcomes. It also permits a large group of practitioners, researchers, advocates, and families to frame a common agenda and, potentially, form a significant constituency around children and families.

Current Catalysts

Three sets of forces during the past decade combined to rekindle interest in service integration on behalf of children and families: changing family and child demographics coupled with the complex and multiple needs of many children and families; ecologically grounded theories of child development and increased scientific knowledge about how risk and protective factors affect development; and the emergence and use of shared family-focused practices and policies across individual service sectors (i.e., the schools, child welfare, mental health, etc.).

Consider first the impact of changing demographics and changing family needs. Much has been written about the dramatic changes in the American family in general and low-income families in particular (Hernandez, 1993; National Commission on Children, 1991; Zill & Nord, 1994). The increase in the numbers of children growing up for part or all of their childhood in single-parent homes has been particularly significant, as has the high percentage of working women—including over 50% of women with infants and toddlers. For low-income families, poverty has become more concentrated geographically and more intense economically (Haveman & Wolfe, 1994). A recent report, for example, found that over one half of children under 6 living in poverty were in families with incomes that were 50% or less than the poverty level. Moreover, the gap between the poor and the nonpoor is increasing, causing strain on the middle class also (Children's Defense Fund, 1996; U.S. Bureau of the Census, 1992). Empirical data support the obvious. The stresses and strains of low-income parenting take an enormous toll on both children and families (Culbertson, 1994; Illback, 1994; McLloyd, 1990). In addition, across all classes, but particularly among the low-income families, children and families are increasingly diverse, representing many ethnicities and cultures. These families often bring different cultural expectations about child rearing, unfamiliar traditions, and unfamiliar values to service providers and institutions.

Taken together, these demographic and family patterns have challenged traditional service providers and agencies, whose "help" has often been found wanting. Sometimes the complaint is that service providers and agencies are disrespectful to families, particularly families with different traditions and from different cultures than their own. Sometimes the complaint is that services are unfriendly and hard to access, requiring long trips, long waits, complex forms, and unclear explanations of what is going on. Sometimes the complaint is that appropriate services simply do not exist. Often the complaint is all of the above and more, setting the stage for interest in service integration as a solution.

At one level, the most basic tenet of service integration—that services and supports ought to be available to families in a way that makes it easy for them to recognize and "own" their own strengths and address their own problems—is nothing more than a common-sense view. But the research world also provides support and a second catalyst for service integration. From a theoretical perspective, the ecological constructs first articulated by Bronfenbrenner (1979) have clearly had an impact on the service sectors, resulting in growing attention to community and even larger systemic forces on children and families. Similarly, a decade of research on risk and protective factors (often, although not exclusively, carried out by psychologists) points to a very important finding that has significant service-related implications. Research suggests it is the number of risk factors that place a child "in harm's way" for poor school- and life-related outcomes, not any one single risk factor (Rutter, 1979; Sameroff & Seifer, 1983; Werner & Smith, 1992). Therefore, program strategies that address multiple risk factors at once are likely to be most effective in producing positive outcomes. This in turn translates into both program-design and service-delivery principles. Put most directly, it suggests the payoff of focusing on strategies that address multiple aspects of a child and family's life to reduce risk factors and strengthen protective factors, whether in the context of single-program design or service-system design (Yoshikawa, 1994).

The third catalyst for the current interest in service integration has been the emergence of program and policy strategies that embody the core values of service integration. Most significant from a program perspective has been the development of both family-preservation and family-support strategies. The former originally were a response to evidence in the child welfare system that very few efforts were made to keep children in their own families (Kinney, Madsen, & Fleming, 1977). Designed to challenge the "antifamily" bias in the child welfare systems (Knitzer, Allen, & McGowan, 1978), and to gain some control over the high cost of out-of-home placement, intensive in-home services have become an important cross-system service strategy that embodies the changing service-value orientation toward families. Although the evaluation data on these programs vary, as do the programs themselves, family-preservation programs clearly embody a strong family focus and attend to multiple risk factors and the ecology of a child and family's world (Wells & Biegel, 1992). They have also, in a parallel process, developed and expanded under the auspices of the child welfare system, the mental health system, and the juvenile justice system (Culbertson, 1994).

Family-preservation programs generally serve children at risk of, or returning from, out-of-home placement. Family support, another family-focused program strategy, emerged in response to a need felt in many communities for nonjudgmental, nonstigmatizing support to all families. Built on a concept of universal (or at least neighborhood-based) eligibility, family support programs offer an informal alternative to the increasingly problem-driven formal service delivery system. Families can get help without being defined as deficient in some way, for example, at risk of abusing or neglecting their child. They also can learn from and connect with other parents, thus reducing the loneliness and difficulties of parenting (Kagan & Weissbourd, 1994).

At the same time that these family-focused service and support strategies were emerging, so too were three federal policy paradigms. These paradigms also challenge the typical ways of "helping" families. One emerged from efforts to address the needs of children with emotional and behavioral disorders involved with multiple systems (Knitzer, 1982, 1993); one came from efforts to develop a systemic early intervention strategy for very young children with developmental delays (Miesels, 1989); and one grew out of a decade of efforts to strengthen child welfare and child protection services.

For children with emotional and behavioral disorders, the agenda was shaped by three defining events: the publication of a monograph on integrated service delivery for this population (Stroul & Friedman, 1986); passage of the federal Child and Adolescent Service System Program (CASSP), a small federal initiative that provided incentive monies to states to develop a family constituency and to build partnerships among mental health professionals and others involved in serving children with emotional and behavioral disorders; and development of the Robert Wood Johnson Foundation's Mental Health Services Program for Youth, which provided support for six system-of-care efforts across the country (Beachler, 1990). These all shared commitments to develop a cross-system governance structure for children with emotional and behavioral disabilities, to deliver family friendly services, and to blend funds to maximize the impact of federal and state dollars for flexible services responsive to family need (Knitzer, 1997).

For young children with developmental disabilities, landmark legislation was enacted in 1986 as part of the Individuals With Disabilities Education Act. Growing out of a Congressional belief that early intervention would improve opportunities for young children and reduce later costs, the law created "Part H," a new program for infants and toddlers, and required states to serve preschoolers with disabilities (Kahn & Kamerman, 1992; Meisels, 1989). As with CASSP, there were two central foci: ensuring that families had a strong voice in the development of service plans for their own children and in the design and implementation of the overall program at both the state and community levels and building an infrastructure to support cross-system service delivery and integration through the use of blended funds, professional development strategies, and public awareness campaigns. Although there has been no overall assessment of the impact of the Part H program, it has generated a strong core of parental leadership and clear service gains for very young children in many states, despite significant implementation and resource challenges (Bryant & Graham, 1993).

The third catalyst for policy-level services-system reform and integration is reflected in over a decade of efforts to transform child welfare laws to be more family friendly. Thus, the 1980 Adoption Assistance and Child Welfare Act was, in part, a response to a spate of research highlighting unfriendly system practices that were tantamount to system neglect of families of children in foster care settings (Knitzer, Allen, & McGowan, 1978). This in turn paved the way for the 1990 amendments to the child welfare federal legislation known as the Family Support and Family Preservation Act. Although a what's-in-a-name approach to policy analysis is limited, the fact is that the names of two pieces of federal legislation passed a decade apart speak eloquently to the growing recognition that families themselves must be in the center of at least most efforts to help children and families, even those at risk. Equally important, the Family Support and Family Preservation Act included a major effort to bring systems and families together to reinvent child-serving systems within the context of a family-friendly, collaborative framework through a major community-driven planning process (Center for the Study of Social Policy & Children's Defense Fund, 1994). Taken together, these policy efforts turned the spotlight on processes to build a vision of an integrated system of services for children and families; on infrastructure mechanisms, including financing strategies; and on improving the quality of actual frontline practice.

Service Integration in Practice

Efforts to create systems of services and supports for children and families have, to date, clustered in four ways. First, there have been efforts targeted to the most high-risk and costly group of children and adolescents—troubled children or other children in or at risk of out-of-home placement (Cole & Poe, 1993; Hayes, Lipoff, & Danegger, 1995; Nelson, Rutherford, & Wolford, 1996). Second, there have been efforts to create a family-centered early-intervention system for young children with disabilities, enacted largely, as just highlighted, through the impetus of Part H. Third, there have been efforts to increase access to social and health services and supports for school-aged children and youth, particularly those who are at risk of poor school outcomes. Finally, there have been some halting efforts to develop systems of services for young children and their families, largely through state initiatives (Kagen et al., 1995; Kagan & Neville, 1993; Knitzer & Page, 1996).

The systems to be integrated vary depending on the focus of the efforts. The systems integration, cross-system collaboration efforts targeted to children in or at risk of out-of-home placement typically involve the four major systems with which these children are involved either concurrently or sequentially: child welfare, mental health, juvenile justice, and special education. The systems integration, cross-system collaboration efforts focused on young children with special needs typically include the public and private health care system; professionals and agencies involved in the delivery of specialized therapeutic services (i.e. occupational therapy, speech therapy); early intervention programs; and sometimes the child welfare system, the preschool special education system, and the mental health system. At their best, they also reach out to child-care and other settings, seeking to include children with special needs in natural environments. School-linked or school-based service integration efforts take a variety of forms: full-service schools, school-linked family resource centers, co-located services, or combinations of these (Center for the Future of Children, 1992; Dryfoos, 1994; Lewis et al., 1995). Service integration efforts focused on young children and families reach across the early-care and education community to link Head Start, child care, and preschool programs, and, at their best, health and social services agencies also. Documented and anecdotal experience suggests that in practice, whatever the focus, the strategies of choice have much in common at the family level, the program level, and the policy level.

Service Integration at the Family Level

The most crucial test of service integration is how the family experiences the help offered. As suggested earlier, fundamental to a service integration approach is a family-centered orientation, a commitment to connect with the family by attending to what they view as their needs. Given that one of the difficulties of the traditional service delivery system is the fragmentation of direct service efforts at the family level, the most obvious example of service integration is in the increasing interest in the role of *care coordinators, family advocates,* or even *case managers* (although when faced with the latter term, families often note that they are not "cases" and they do not like to be "managed"). This function is particularly likely to be part of a service "package" for families with special needs. Part H of the Individuals With Disabilities Education Act requires, for example, that there be care coordinators for infants and toddlers with developmental disorders or delays. But other programs serving low-income families experiencing both concrete needs (for housing or food, for example) coupled with other kinds of crises often have at their core some kind of care-coordinating function (Marks, Maurer, & Simkin, 1994). Similarly, programs for new or at-risk parents of infants and toddlers often include some kind of coordinating function. In these programs, as in many others, the effort to ensure families access to the range of needed services is coupled with the supportive function of relationship building (U.S. General Accounting Office, 1990).

Other tools for tailoring a service package to individual children and families include the development of a service plan that reflects simultaneous input from service providers. This has proven to be a particularly valuable strategy in the mental health reform efforts of the past decade. Known as *wrap-around* services, multiple services are "packaged" to meet the particular set of circumstances of children with serious emotional or behavioral disorders and their families at a particular point in time and then refined or modified as need requires. For example, for one particular family a wrap-around package might include a special training program in behavior management paid for by the schools, medication management by a psychiatrist, and daily contact with a teacher (Burchard & Clark, 1990). For another, it might include a home respite worker, coupled with a care coordinator and an in-home therapist. The integration of a mix of services at the family level is particularly challenging in that it requires a blending of a clinical with a concrete perspective, a mix for which clinicians are not always trained.

Service Integration at the Program Level

At the program level, there are myriad examples of service integration strategies that either ensure the capacity within an individual program to respond to the range of issues families and children face or ensure links with other agencies and providers. In either instance, the key is to see that services are delivered in a family-friendly, responsive manner across agencies, so it is "seamless" for an individual family. For the infants and toddlers, for example, there are home-based home-visiting programs designed primarily to help families nurture their young children (Wallach & Lister, 1995). These programs typically use trained aides from the same community or background and have friendly visitors as the lynchpin of the effort to help families access services that they want or need. Although the primary focus of these programs is on helping parents enjoy their babies and become more knowledgeable about what to expect as development unfolds, it is also to help parents deal with their own issues and needs. The beneficiaries of these programs are families deemed at risk of child abuse or neglect or families perceived as needing special supports to access appropriate maternal and child health care.

For preschoolers, a commitment to the integrated services is increasingly reflected in the development of prekindergarten programs that require or strongly encourage that children have access to a range of support services, including nutritional and social services and health care, and that offer parents opportunities to meet their own needs or help their children more effectively. This growing trend (Adams & Sandfort, 1994; Knitzer & Page, 1996) in many ways reflects an important legacy of Head Start, one of the earliest examples of an integrated services framework within a program context.

For school-aged children, school-based or school-linked types of service are emerging. These range from efforts to co-locate services on school grounds (with or without modifying the services) to the development of family resource centers. These family resource centers take many forms, but are typically designed to reduce the alienation from the schools that many families, particularly low-income or ethnically diverse families, feel. These programs provide informal and sometimes formal support to families in culturally sensitive ways and often access to needed services, such as health or mental health care (Illback, 1994). Not all efforts, however, focus on bringing services to the school. Some, such as Fast Track—a multisite, multistrategy effort to demonstrate the power of reducing later conduct disorders by an intensive, largely school-based early-intervention effort (Conduct Problems Prevention Research Group, 1992), focus on weaving a rich tapestry of strategies within and beyond the classroom.

Service Integration at the Policy Level

At the policy level, recognition of the importance of service integration is reflected in at least three key ways. First, it is reflected in the framing of federal or state legislation that encourages or requires service integration. Landmark federal efforts fostering service integration for children and families (i.e., CASSP and Part H) have already been described in this chapter. Examples of state efforts are also visible. In California, for example, the Healthy Start legislation set the context for the development of school-linked support programs across that state (Wagner et al., 1994). In Kentucky, the state government created a structure to support state, regional, and local interagency planning and service delivery strategies, which grew out of the Robert Wood Johnson Project and a parallel planning process. In general, this legislation might be characterized as enabling, rather than prescriptive. It turns back to local decision makers, including families, decisions about service structure and approaches, but requires only that a wide range of people be involved in shaping the service delivery system. Similarly, Kentucky has also enacted legislation to build a network of family resource centers in schools serving high-risk populations in an effort to maximize the impact of scarce public resources and to enhance learning outcomes (Kalafat & Illback, 1993).

   Second, a policy-level commitment to service integration is reflected in the growth of mechanisms to generate support for high-level policy attention to children and families and development of administrative mechanisms to engage state managers in solving bureaucratic complexities and barriers that interfere with service integration efforts. For example, some states have established cabinets for children in an effort to bring all key decision makers to the table. This can sometimes lead to positive and unexpected results. For example, Ohio, as part of its comprehensive Family and Children First Initiative, enlisted the aid of agencies not known for involvement with children. As a result, the medical corps of the Ohio National Guard now provides immunizations and well-child care to young Ohio children. This strategy only emerged because the guard leaders were part of discussions about how to meet the goals of Ohio Families and Children First, which included improving the health of young children (S. Ignelzi, personal communication, December 1995). In addition, in Ohio, state-level managers are engaged in efforts to solve cross-system challenges such as unlinked administrative databases, overlapping or inconsistent eligibility requirements, funding inconsistencies, and nonstrategic training. The same is happening in other states as well. For example, a recent report on state initiatives for young children and families identified five states with explicit administrative strategies to link early care and education efforts through such mechanisms as shared standards, shared training, and new fiscal strategies (Knitzer & Page, 1996). The underlying message of these efforts is clear: System integration is often a prerequisite for institutionalized service integration at the family and community level.

Third, there seems to be a growing interest across the country in seeding and growing community-based planning efforts to ensure that services provided to children and families "fit" well with family and community needs and expectations. Known by many names (*planning efforts, governance initiatives, system reform strategies*), all seem intended to provide a forum to operationalize the core values of service integration. Thus Knitzer and Page (1996) also found that at least two fifths of the states have significant state-level or state- and community-level planning initiatives designed to improve services and, often explicitly, outcomes for children and families. These take many different forms. Sometimes, the emphasis is on state-level planning and management. Most typically, however, efforts are oriented toward building a community-owned agenda, incorporating not only families and service providers, but also the local business community and other decision makers.

Lessons From the Field

Service integration is a code word for a major paradigm shift in the delivery of services to children and families. Thus, service integration is both a framework for highlighting important values related to helping children for shaping specific family interventions, program design and implementation, regulatory and fiscal administrative procedures, and policies that cut across and govern multiple systems, and the training strategies across and within "helping" disciplines. Although many of the efforts are relatively recent, there are a number of important lessons that have implications for the next generation of research, in both training and practice, particularly for psychologists.

1. *Integrated services is a means to an end, not an end in and of itself.* The end is improved outcomes for young children and families, preferably coupled with the more efficient use of public (and private, in some instances) resources. It is against this standard that the efficacy of integrated services for children and families should be judged. Do integrated services result in greater family satisfaction with services? Do integrated services result in young chil-

dren being better prepared to enter school? Do integrated services improve outcomes for children and adolescents at risk of out-of-home placement? In what ways do integrated service projects affect frontline practice (Kinney, Strand, Hagerup, & Bruner, 1994)?

2. *The integration of services is not necessarily automatically linked to improved quality. It is a facilitator of improved quality—a necessary but not sufficient condition.* For example, in the Robert Wood Johnson Mental Health Services Program for Youth sites, there were two fundamental agendas: integrating services and fiscal streams and providing innovative and more family-responsive clinical services. Although there are no hard data, there are some indications that in some sites, there was administrative integration of services, but the services were still fairly traditional. In some other sites, the services were more innovative, regardless of whether there was administrative integration.

3. *Integrated service strategies in one project does not necessarily lead to widespread institutionalization of service integration.* In the absence of larger political leadership and solid infrastructure support, integrated service delivery projects can be isolated pockets of excellence in the same way that strong program initiatives can be isolated pockets of excellence. Indeed, this is the current picture—scattered integrated service efforts (of remarkable form, variety, and target populations) embedded within a context of still largely categorical state and federal policies. As of this writing, however, there are clear signs that many of these categorical programs will be replaced with either federal or state block grants.

4. *Service integration presumes that there are resources and services to be integrated.* The movement for service integration for children and families during the last decade has emerged out of frustration with multiple categorical programs. These have largely been organized around single issues, such as child abuse, runaway youth, serious emotional disturbance, out-of-home placement, and so forth. Yet the children and youth often fit many of these categories, both in terms of needs and experiences (Knitzer, 1982). To correct this single-issue approach, many of the service integration reforms have been driven by efforts to blend categorical dollars, often using federal entitlement monies as the basis. This has particularly been the case with Medicaid dollars, as well as child welfare entitlement dollars. (Under an entitlement framework, all children who meet specified criteria must receive services, benefits, or protections.) It is not known what the current move to replace entitlement federal dollars with block grants (i.e., capped sums of monies) will do to the efforts to blend previously categorical dollars.

5. *The vision of integrated services needs to be articulated for different age groups and different systems.* As with services that must be tailored to fit the needs of children and families, one size, one strategy does not fit all. Integrating services for children at risk of out-of-home placement largely involves collaborations among

one set of systems—child welfare, juvenile justice, special education, and mental health—those systems through which such children often move, either currently or sequentially. Service integration for young children in the context of child care and education involves a different set of systems. For example, states are currently struggling to create "seamless" regulations and pooled dollars among Head Start, prekindergarten, and child care programs. This effort itself is so fraught with symbolic land mines that only in a few places has the effort stretched to include a more comprehensive set of systems, such as health, substance abuse, and mental health.

6. *Implementing integrated services is hard work.* It is not easy to address the attitudinal, regulatory, fiscal, and service paradigm barriers all at once or, indeed, at all. This means that leadership, relationship building, and the authority to change regulations and procedures are all crucial. Put differently, effective service integration projects appear to have several critical elements, including a level of trust among the participants, shared vision or common goals, and concrete incentives such as new program dollars or regulation-free zones (Bruner, 1991; McCart, 1993).

Facing the Future: Risks and Opportunities

Integrated service experiments have played an important role in shaping a new vision of service delivery. But they remain embedded in a larger human service and political context that is not necessarily supportive. Although forecasting the future is no less treacherous for psychologists than for economists, two sets of realities are likely to have a major impact on whether interest in service integration reflects a short-lived, partially implemented reform or whether the spirit and values it embodies flourish and spread. One of these types of hurdles that must be overcome is related to generic and long-standing issues, the other to the recent and dramatic changes in the political and policy landscape.

The more generic issues include finding and nurturing elected officials who understand that *how* services are delivered is as important as *what* services are delivered; overcoming the politics within and across human service agencies that make change so difficult; training the next generation of helping professionals, researchers, and policy makers to understand new approaches to service delivery; and building the kind of research knowledge that will make it possible to correct and fine-tune the next generation of initiatives.

The issues related to electoral and interagency politics are fairly straightforward and obvious. The issues related to training and research require some comment. With respect to training, one of the most interesting phenomena of the integrated service movement for children and families is that it is largely the invention of the field—of those struggling to better meet the needs of children and families. The impetus for service integration has emerged from what one close observer of early social service reform strategies has called *practice worries* (Rein, 1983). As a result, universities and those involved in professional training have often not been a part of the process of implementation or even evaluation (Knitzer, 1993; Lewis et al., 1995; Pires, 1992). Cross-disciplinary training, using families as faculty, providing rotating internships in different systems, and other tools to orient students to service integration are the exception (Jivanjee, Moore, Schultze, & Friesen, 1995; Newell, Jivanjee, Schultze, Friesen, & Hunter, 1994). Thus, it is difficult for the academic community to provide its students with the theoretical, research, and field-based grounding that would enable them to help shape the next iteration of integrated services.

With respect to building a research base, there is much to be done. The research data on integrated services is still in its infancy. Some signs are promising, but the overall verdict is still out. To quote the pithy assessment of Kahn and Kamerman (1992), "What is not in dispute is the problem. What is in dispute is just how good a solution services integration is" (p. 9). Thus, at the very least there is a need for empirical (and comparable) data across projects and disciplines focused on some of the key questions. What difference do service integration experiments make to children and their families, both in terms of perceived satisfaction and concrete outcomes? How do different constellations of service integration strategies affect outcomes? Is the investment in service integration cost effective? If a family has access to a skilled, caring professional or paraprofessional provider, is service integration necessary? How does involvement in service integration projects affect the service delivery system itself, the service providers, and other decision makers? Answering these questions will not be a simple task. Indeed, as has been noted by others, the complexity and interrelatedness of these questions suggests that new research methodologies and paradigms will be required (Connell, Kubisch, Schorr, & Weiss, 1995; Stroul, 1993).

There are also two major unanticipated realities that are likely to have a significant impact on the trajectory of service integration efforts. One is the rapid and pervasive support for the concept of managed care, not just within health care, but across other sectors also. On the negative side, there is concern that, within the context of managed care, children and families will simply be denied access to the range of services that are needed or that supporting cross-system collaboration either at the individual family level or the policy/system level will become more difficult. Put most bluntly, notwithstanding a decade of work to challenge the medical mental-health model, there are signs that the managed-care single-system approach may take reformers backward. Absent a major effort to convince managed-care providers of the fiscal efficacy of integrated services and systems and states to require integrated services in contract provisions, there may be a return to a single-system, categorical, medical-model approach.

On the other hand, managed care also holds out the promise of a more positive outcome, particularly as a vehicle for building family-supportive early-intervention services. Theoretically, it should be possible to make a strong case for prevention and early intervention as part of a cost-effective strategy, instead of the more typical high-cost crisis-oriented system that prevails. However, the extent to which this will occur as managed care unfolds remains to be seen.

The second unanticipated political reality that will affect service integration is a dramatically reshaped view of federal and state responsibility. Recent Congressional action has resulted in the elimination of the Aid To Families With Dependent Children entitlement program and the substitution of a time-limited block grant to states to develop their own plans for welfare. This sweeping change in the framework of federal support to children and families is part of a larger transformation, known loosely as "devolution," the transfer of responsibility to the states for shaping and implementing programs of federal aid with a minimum of federal requirements through block grants. From one perspective, block grants could serve as an incentive to service integration, removing many alleged federal restrictions. However, given the reality that federal resources will grow at significantly reduced rates and that states will have to assume a greater responsibility for ensuring that basic needs for income support, housing, health care, and probably food are met, there will be new pressure on those supporting integrated services. As with managed care, however, there is also a more promising possibility. The "glass-is-half-full" argument suggests that proponents of integrated services use this time to create the kind of support structure that can help to sustain integrated services, even as efforts to enhance resources continue.

The Implications of Service Integration for Psychologists

No one discipline is responsible for service integration. However, there do seem to be some functions for which psychologists seem particularly suited. For example, the formation of a shared vision, a shared decision-making forum, and a shared framework for problem solving are key to the development of integrated services. Psychologists are well qualified to take a leadership role in facilitating all these processes. Second, psychologists bring substantive clinical and developmental understandings to the table. Thus, they have a significant role to play in sharing the development of programs that reflect the principles of service integration and are consonant with the best psychological theories of child and family development and tenets of effective practice. Third, psychologists are in a strong position to take an active, if not a leadership, role in framing the kind of focused research agenda that needs to be formulated, linking outcomes for children and families with service-delivery mechanisms.

These roles are in fact familiar to many psychologists, including those represented in this book. The real challenge, however, is one of training. The most critical need is for a dialogue between those in the field and those training the next generation of psychologists to examine the implications of service integration strategies for university-based training within psychology and across disciplines. This is not a small challenge in the best of times. These are not the best of times, with much training energy invested in building survival skills for students in the context of managed care. At the same time, the premises and promises of integrated services on behalf of children and families represent a potentially important vehicle for psychology to strengthen and expand its understanding of and commitment to an informed psychology in the public interest.

References

Adams, G., & Sandfort, J. (1994). *First steps, promising futures: State prekindergarten initiatives in the early 1990s.* Washington, DC: Children's Defense Fund.

Beachler, M. (1990). The mental health services program for youth. *Journal of Mental Health Administration, 17,* 115–121.

Bishop, K. K., Woll, J., & Arango, P. (1993). *Family/professional collaboration for children with special health needs and their families.* Burlington, VT: Family/Professional Collaboration Project.

Boyd, L. A. (1992). *Integrating systems of care for children and families: An overview of values, methods and characteristics of developing models, with examples and recommendations.* Tampa: University of South Florida, Florida Mental Health Institute.

Bronfenbrenner, U. (1979). *The ecology of human development: Experiments by nature and design.* Cambridge, MA: Harvard University Press.

Bruner, C. (1991). *Thinking collaboratively: Ten questions and answers to help policy makers improve children's services.* Washington, DC: Education and Human Services Consortium.

Bryant, D. M., & Graham, M. A. (Eds.). (1993). *Implementing early intervention: From research to effective practice.* New York: Guilford Press.

Burchard, J. D., & Clark, R. T. (1990). The role of individualized care in a service delivery system for children and adolescents with severely maladjusted behavior. *Journal of Mental Health Administration 17,* 48–98.

Burnim, I., Jackson, R., Schoen, J., Turner, O., Johnson, E., & Cohen, R. (1991). *The R. C. case: Creating a new system of care for children in the child protection and foster care systems.* Washington, DC: The Mental Health Law Project.

Center for the Future of Children. (1992). School-linked services. In R. E. Behrman (Ed.), *The Future of Children, 2*(1), 4–143. Los Altos, CA: The David and Lucille Packard Foundation, Center for the Future of Children.

Center for the Study of Social Policy & Children's Defense Fund. (1994). *A guide for planning: Making strategic use of the family preservation and support services program.* Washington, DC: Authors.

Chang, H. N., Salazar, D. D., & Leong, C. (1994). *Drawing strength from diversity: Effective services for children, youth and families.* San Francisco: California Tomorrow.

Chaudry, A., Maurer, K. E., Oshinsky, C. J., & Mackie, J. (1993). *Service integration: An annotated bibliography.* New York: National Center for Service Integration, Child and Family Policy Center, Des Moines, IA.

Children's Defense Fund. (1996). *The state of America's children: Yearbook 1996.* Washington, DC: Author.

Cole, R., & Poe, S. (1993). *Partnerships for care: Systems of care for children with serious emotional disturbances and their families.* Washington, DC: Washington Business Group on Health.

Conduct Problems Prevention Research Group. (1992). A developmental and clinical model for the prevention of conduct disorder: The FAST Track Program. *Developmental and Psychopathology, 4,* 509–527.

Connell, J. P., Kubisch, A. C., Schorr, L. B., & Weiss, C. H. (Eds.). (1995). *New approaches to evaluating community initiatives: Concepts, methods, and contexts.* New York: The Aspen Institute, Roundtable on Comprehensive Community Initiatives for Children and Families.

Cross, T., Barzon, B., Dennis, K., & Isaacs, M. (1989). *Towards a culturally competent system of care.* Washington, DC: CASSP Technical Assistance Center, Georgetown University Child Development Center.

Culbertson, J. L. (1994). Task force report on innovative models of mental health services for children, adolescents, and their families. *Journal of Clinical Child Psychology, 23* (Suppl.), 2–55.

Dryfoos, J. G. (1994). *Full-service schools: A revolution in health and social services for children, youth and families.* San Francisco, CA: Jossey-Bass.

Edelman, P. B., & Radin, B. A. (1991). *Serving children and families effectively: How the past can help chart the future.* Washington, DC: Education and Human Services Consortium.

Haveman, R., & Wolfe, B. (1994). *Succeeding generations: On the effects of investments in children.* New York: Russell Sage Foundation.

Hayes, C. D., Lipoff, E., & Danegger, A. E. (1995). *Compendium of comprehensive, community based initiatives: A look at costs, benefits, and financing strategies.* Washington, DC: The Finance Project.

Hernandez, D J. (1993). *America's children: Resources from family, government, and the economy.* New York: Russell Sage Foundation.

Illback, R. J. (1994). Poverty and the crisis in children's services: The need for services integration. *Journal of Clinical Child Psychology, 23,* 413–424.

Jivanjee, P. R., Moore, K. R., Schultze, K. H., & Friesen, B. J. (1995). *Interprofessional education for family-centered services: A survey of interprofessional/interdisciplinary training programs.* Portland, OR: Portland State University, Research and Training Center on Family Support and Children's Mental Health.

Kagan, S. L. (1991). *United we stand: Collaboration for child care and early education services.* New York: Teachers College Press.

Kagan, S. L., Goffin, S. G., Golub, S. A., & Pritchard, E. (1995). *Toward systemic reform: Service integration for young children and their families.* Des Moines, IA: National Center for Service Integration, Child and Family Policy Center.

Kagan, S. L., & Neville, P. R. (1993). *Integrating human services: Understanding the past to shape the future.* New Haven, CT: Yale University Press.

Kagan, S. L., & Weissbourd, B. (Eds.). (1994). *Putting families first: America's family support movement and the challenge of change.* San Francisco: Jossey-Bass.

Kahn, A. J., & Kamerman, S. B. (1992). *Integrating services integration: An overview of initiatives, issues, and possibilities.* New York: National Center for Children in Poverty, Columbia University School of Public Health.

Kalafat, J., & Illback, R. J. (1993). *Implementation evaluation of the family resource and youth service centers: A qualitative analysis.* Louisville, KY: R.E.A.C.H. of Louisville, Inc.

Kinney, J. M., Madsen, B., & Fleming, T. (1977). Homebuilders: Keeping families together. *Journal of Consulting and Clinical Psychology, 45,* 667–673.

Kinney, J., Strand, K., Hagerup, M., & Bruner, C. (1994). *Beyond the buzzwords: Key principles in effective frontline practice* (Working paper). Falls Church, VA: National Center for Service Integration.

Knitzer, J. (1982). *Unclaimed children: The failure of public responsibility to children and adolescents in need of mental health services.* Washington, DC: The Children's Defense Fund.

Knitzer, J. (1993). Children's mental health policy: Challenging the future. *Journal of Emotional and Behavioral Disorders, 1*(1), 8–16.

Knitzer, J. (1997). Children's mental health: Changing paradigms and policies. In E. Sigler, S. L. Kagan, & N. W. Hall (Eds.), *Children, families and government: Preparing for the 21st century* (pp. 207–232). New York: Cambridge University Press.

Knitzer, J., Allen, M. L., & McGowan, B. (1978). *Children without homes: An examination of public responsibility to children in out-of-home care.* Washington, DC: Children's Defense Fund.

Knitzer, J., & Page, S. (1996). *Map and track: State initiatives for young children and families.* New York: National Center for Children in Poverty, Columbia University School of Public Health.

Lewis, A., Carr, B., South, L. A., & Reed, T. (1995). *School-linked comprehensive services for children and families: What we know and what we need to know.* Washington, DC: U.S. Department of Education, Office of Educational Research and Improvement, & American Educational Research Association.

Marks, E. L., Maurer, K. E., & Simkin, L. S. (1994). *Case management in service integration: An annotated bibliography.* New York: National Center for Children in Poverty, Columbia University School of Public Health.

McAdoo, H. P. (Ed.). (1993). *Family ethnicity: Strength in diversity.* Newbury Park, CA: Sage.

McCart, L. (1993). *Changing systems for children and families.* Washington, DC: National Governors' Association.

McLoyd, V. C. (1990). The impact of economic hardship on Black families and children: Psychological distress, parenting and socioemotional development. *Child Development, 61*, 311–346.

Meisels, S. J. (1989). Meeting the mandate of Public Law 99-457: Early childhood intervention in the nineties. *American Journal of Orthopsychiatry, 59*(3), 451–460.

Melaville, A. I., & Blank, M. J. (1993). *Together we can: A guide for crafting a profamily system of education and human services.* Washington, DC: U.S. Government Printing Office.

National Center for Children in Poverty. (1996). *One in four: America's youngest poor.* New York: Author.

National Commission on Children. (1991). *Beyond rhetoric: A new American agenda for children and families.* Washington, DC: U.S. Government Printing Office.

Nelson, C. M., Rutherford, R. B., Jr., & Wolford, B. I. (1996). *Comprehensive and collaborative systems that work for troubled youth: A national agenda.* Richmond, KY: Eastern Kentucky University, University College of Law Enforcement, National Juvenile Detention Association.

Newell, S. S., Jivanjee, P., Schultze, K. H., Friesen, B. J., & Hunter, R. W. (1994). *Collaboration in interprofessional practice and training: An annotated bibliography.* Portland, OR: Portland State University, Research and Training Center on Family Support and Children's Mental Health.

Pires, S. A. (1992). *Staffing systems of care for children and families.* Washington, DC: Human Service Collaborative.

Rein, M. (1983). *From policy to practice.* New York: Macmillan.

Rutter, M. (1979). Protective factors in children's responses to stress and disadvantage. In K. A. Dodge (Ed.), *Social competence in children* (pp. 49–74). Hanover, NH: University of New England.

Sameroff, A. J., & Seifer, R. (1983). Familial risk and child competence. *Child Development, 54*, 1254–1268.

Stevenson, H. C., Jr. (1994). Racial socialization in African American families: The art of balancing intolerance and survival. *The Family Journal: Counseling and Therapy for Couples and Families, 2*(3), 190–198.

Stevenson, H. C., & Abdul-Kabir, S. (1995, November). Reflections of hope from the "bottom": Cultural strengths and coping among low-income African-American mothers. In *Proceedings of the Roundtable on Cross-Cultural Psychotherapy.* New York: Teachers College, Columbia University.

Stroul, B. A. (1993). *Systems of care for children and adolescents with severe emotional disturbances: What are the results?* Washington, DC: Georgetown University Child Development Center.

Stroul, B., & Friedman, R. (1986). *A system of care for severely emotionally disturbed children and youth.* Tampa: University of South Florida, Florida Mental Health Institute.

Task Force on Comprehensive and Coordinated Psychological Services for Children: Ages 0–10. (1994). *Comprehensive and coordinated psychological services for children: A call for service integration*. Washington, DC: American Psychological Association.

U.S. Bureau of the Census. (1992). *Income, poverty, and wealth in the United States: A chart book*. Pittsburgh, PA: U.S. Government Printing Office.

U.S. General Accounting Office. (1990). *Home visiting: A promising early intervention strategy for at-risk families*. Washington, DC: Author.

Wagner, M., Golan, S., Shaver, D., Newman, L., Weschler, M., & Kelley, F. (1994). *A healthy start for California's children and families: Early findings from a statewide evaluation of school-linked services*. Menlo Park, CA: SRI International.

Wallach, V. A., & Lister, L. (1995). Stages in the delivery of home-based services to parents at risk of child abuse: A Healthy Start experience. *Scholarly Inquiry for Nursing Practice: An International Journal, 9*(2), 159–173.

Wells, K., & Biegel, D. (1992). Intensive family preservation services research: Current status and future agenda. *Social Work Research & Abstracts, 28*, 21–25.

Werner, E. E., & Smith, R. S. (1992). *Overcoming the odds: High risk children from birth to adulthood*. Ithaca, NY: Cornell University Press.

Yoshikawa, H. (1994). Prevention as cumulative protection: Effects of early family support and education on chronic delinquency and its risks. *Psychological Bulletin, 115*(1), 28–54.

Zill, N., & Nord, C. W. (1994). *Running in place: How American families are faring in a changing economy and an individualistic society*. Washington, DC: Child Trends, Inc.

2

School-Based Youth Programs: Exemplary Models and Emerging Opportunities

Joy G. Dryfoos

The idea of offering services in schools is as old as the history of public education in the United States. For over a century, the pendulum has swung back and forth: In some years, the movement has been toward maintaining schools as "pure" educational "three-R's" places, whereas in other years the movement has been toward adding to schools whatever "extras" were needed by changing populations. During the Progressive Era in the early 1900s, rapid urbanization and massive immigration forced schools to let in medical and social welfare "do-gooders" from local clinics and settlement houses to deal with communicable and chronic diseases, family problems, and the effects of poverty (Dryfoos, 1994).

After World War I, primary health services in schools were portrayed as socialistic and were eliminated under pressure from the American Medical Association, which feared competition from school doctors (Kort, 1984). Eventually, school systems institutionalized pieces of what started out as extras such as health screening, driver education, physical education, health education, and psychological testing. Most of the "add-ons" were components that were attractive to the growing number of middle-class families who controlled school boards in suburban areas. In 1975, Congress enacted the Education for All Handicapped Children Act (now the Individuals With Disabilities Education Act) requiring schools to create and implement individual education plans for all students with physical and mental disorders (Dryfoos, 1994). Special education was laid on school systems, bringing in a whole new cadre of remediators and therapists.

As we move into the 21st century, a consensus is building around the concept of using the school as the place for locating health, mental health, and social services for all children and families. Social conditions in this highly complex and troubled society are generating a new movement for integrating services. As is obvious, school buildings are where the children are supposed to be from early years (increasingly as prekindergartners) to adolescence. Advocates of school-based services believe that if more support services were provided in schools, high-risk teenagers would be more

24   JOY G. DRYFOOS

likely to stay there and graduate. Educators are eager to obtain all the help they can get, as long as it does not come out of their budgets.

This chapter primarily focuses on school-based services for adolescents in middle schools and high schools. I will address the following questions: Why school-based now? What is actually going on in these school programs? Do we have any evidence that they make a difference in outcomes? What are the issues in replication? Of what specific interest are these new developments to psychologists? And finally, do school-based programs have a future?

What Is Driving the Movement?

At least three major social developments are leading public policy analysts, program administrators, and family advocates to consider new kinds of institutional arrangements that involve schools and community agencies. First, there is rising concern about the vulnerabilities of youth as they confront the consequences of early sexual activity, drugs, violence, and other behavioral problems. At the same time, schools are trying to compete in a new technological world that requires more rigor and discipline. And finally, although many social and educational programs have been promulgated to deal with these needs, they are fragmented and not successfully achieving the goals of helping young people become responsible adults.

The "New Morbidities"

When I was young, parents worried about acne, overweight, head lice, and contagious diseases like scarlet fever. Today's parents worry about the *new morbidities*—the negative consequences of drugs, sex, violence, and stress. Young people worry also because they are confronted daily with decisions about whether to experiment with drugs, have sexual intercourse, buy a gun, cut school, and engage in other potentially hazardous choices.

The indicators of problem behaviors among adolescents are familiar to youth workers. In the United States almost three fourths of all deaths among school-age youth and young adults can be attributed to preventable causes: motor vehicle crashes, other unintentional injuries, homicide, and suicide (National Center for Education Statistics, 1993). Beginning in 1990, documentation of potential morbidities among young people has been available through a National Youth Risk Behavior Survey, conducted annually by the Centers for Disease Control and Prevention in Atlanta (Centers for Disease Control, 1995).

Table 1 presents the latest findings about self-reported youth behavior for high-school aged females and males. Adolescent health issues are not what they used to be. As these data show, many students practice behaviors that increase their vulnerability. More than a third have ridden with a driver who had been drinking alcohol, one in five had carried weapons, more

Table 1. Findings From the National Youth Risk Behavior Survey, 1995. Self-reported behaviors (%)

Behavior	Female	Male
Violence		
Carried a weapon (gun, knife, or club) within past 30 days	8.3	31.1
Carried a weapon on school property	5.1	17.9
Carried a gun	2.5	12.3
In a physical fight this year	30.6	46.1
Suicidal ideation this year		
Thought seriously about attempting suicide	30.4	18.3
Made a suicide plan	21.3	14.4
Attempted suicide	11.9	5.6
Substance use in past 30 days		
Current cigarette use	34.3	29.8
Current alcohol use	49.9	53.2
Current marijuana use	22.0	28.4
Current cocaine use	1.8	4.3
Rode with a driver who had been drinking	37.8	39.5
Offered, sold, or gave illegal drug on school property this year	24.8	38.8
Sexual activity		
Ever had sexual intercourse	52.1	54.0
Currently sexually active	40.4	35.5
Condom use last intercourse	48.6	60.5

Source: Youth Risk Behavior Surveillance—United States, 1995, *Morbidity and Mortality Weekly Report*, Center for Disease Control and Prevention Surveillance Summaries, September 27, 1996, Vol. 45, No. SS-4. $N = 10,904$.

than half had even been sexually active, and close to half were not using condoms during sexual intercourse. More than one third of the respondents smoked cigarettes, half used alcohol, and more than 25% had used marijuana within the previous month. Use of hard drugs, such as cocaine, was reported by very few students—under 2%—but these are currently enrolled students, not dropouts.

Perhaps the most striking findings are that nearly one fourth of the students nationwide had seriously considered suicide during the previous year. Female students were much more likely than male students to report this strong indicator of depression. Even more distressing, almost 18% of the respondents had actually made a plan to attempt suicide, and almost 9% had tried to do away with themselves. Suicide attempts were more likely to be reported among Hispanic students than among White or African American students. Of Hispanic female students, 21% reported that they had attempted suicide within a 1-year period.

What these selected findings about adolescents fail to convey is the overlap in high-risk behaviors. I have previously estimated that about one in four adolescents "do it all": They are failing in school, are getting in trouble with the law, abuse substances, have unprotected sexual intercourse, and are in grave jeopardy of never making it without immediate intense interventions (Dryfoos, 1990). Another one in four are on the brink and need a lot of help to straighten out their lives. About half of all young people are relatively risk free, as long as they continue to have access to strong families, good schools, and safe communities. Since the time those estimates were made, new data about the incidence of depression and stress have become available, strongly linking mental health problems to high-risk behaviors (Benson, 1990).

Traditional health professionals have not been trained to deal with these kinds of social and behavioral problems. Adolescents who have access to health care generally go to pediatricians or family doctors, who are reticent about discussing drugs or sex or feelings of depression and rarely raise such issues in the course of annual examinations. In any case, many high-risk adolescents do not have access to private medical care, and few other resources are available to them. As a result, if a crisis occurs, or even an illness, teenagers are likely to show up at hospital emergency rooms.

Concern about the rising tide of adolescent behavioral problems has led practitioners in the field of adolescent medicine to the concept of placing services in schools. A number of commissions and task forces support this conclusion, which is summed up in a report of Congress's Office of Technology Assessment (OTA). In 1991, OTA documented the consequences of the new morbidities and called for greatly expanded access to comprehensive health care (OTA, 1991). They concluded that school-based health clinics were a most promising recent innovation, providing excellent access points for young people to receive confidential primary health and social services, although they noted insufficient evaluation. Both the American Medical Association and the American Academy of Pediatrics have become strong supporters of comprehensive services for adolescents located in schools or community sites.

High-Risk Students Are Hard to Teach

Although the national dropout rates have stabilized, test scores have continued to lag, and some schools, in particular those in disadvantaged communities, are considered to be educational disasters (National Education Goals Panel, 1996). School systems are under a lot of pressure to raise those scores and produce graduates who are able to enter the competitive, technologically advanced labor force of the future. School administrators often acknowledge that they cannot deal with the hordes of ill-prepared, stressed-out, hungry children who arrive at their doorsteps every morning to learn. Many of these young people are coming from homes where the parents have extreme difficulty holding the family together because of lack of employment, inadequate housing, dangerous streets, and personal problems of their own. Numerous parents are involved in alcohol and drug abuse, and are neglectful and sometimes abusive of their offspring. Poverty rates are on the rise, putting even more pressure on young people who are trying to make a transition to an adulthood that offers little in the way of opportunity or hope.

Although the proportion of school staff categorized as pupil personnel other than teachers has increased over the years, the growing demand for help cannot be met by the current number of school nurses, guidance counselors, social workers, and psychologists (Tyack, 1992). Few were trained to deal with either the psychosocial problems of today's teens or the therapeutic and social welfare needs of their parents. The demand for support services in the schools with the highest-risk students would overwhelm most school systems (National Commission on Children, 1991).

As in the health domain, many reports have been issued documenting the problems that schools face in trying to carry out their traditional missions of educating youngsters who suffer as a result of devastating family and community problems. In the opinion of the Committee for Economic Development (CED), schools are not social service institutions and should not be asked to solve the nation's social ills and cultural conflicts (Committee for Economic Development, 1994). Nevertheless, CED supports the placement of social services in schools or delivered through schools, but under no circumstances should they be funded by educational systems.

Many in the educational establishment agree with CED. School policy makers and administrators would like to have some of the care-taking burden, and particularly the cost of service provision, lifted off of their backs. Therefore, the idea of relocating services generated by community agencies in schools is very attractive to them as long as they do not have to cover the programs in their school budgets.

The concept of school-based programs also fits in well with movements toward school reform. The nation's educational goals for the year 2000 encompass several objectives that are especially relevant here: readiness for school, safe learning environments, adult literacy, and parental participation (National Educational Goals Panel, 1996). None of these objectives can be accomplished without greatly expanding the scope of services offered in and around the school—for preschool children and adults—after school, in evenings, and on weekends, in addition to during the school day (Lavin, Shapiro, & Weill, 1992). As an indicator of the emerging consensus around integrating services in schools, Title 1 (formerly Chapter 1), the federal program that supports learning opportunities for disadvantaged children, has been revised to address the total school community rather than just the funding of individual children who are being pulled out of classrooms for occasional remediation.

Service Integration for Adolescents

The need to integrate services for children and families has been well documented in other chapters of this book. Indeed, integration is the main theme of other recent works that touch on school-based services (Melaville, Blank, & Asayesh, 1993; National Center for Service Integration, 1993). For generations, the response to crises has been to create new categorical programs for adolescents. Thus, each of the new morbidities has its own stream of funding, with different Congressional supporters, grant requirements, administrative housing, and academic gurus. Every epidemic seems to generate its own prevention curriculum for teaching basic skills that further cuts into classroom time. Few of these drug, pregnancy, AIDS, suicide, or violence interventions have been proven to impact on vulnerability in the long run. It has been documented that these categorical programs are not powerful enough to change high-risk behaviors and should be combined with other interventions such as individual attention, organized support services, enriched educational settings, career training, and parent involvement (Dryfoos, 1990). One argument for "one-stop" coordinated interventions stems from the negative experiences that young people have when they are required to shop around for services. This fragmentation—the patchwork quilt of unrelated programs—does not solve their problems.

The Rationale for School-Based Services

Connecting these movements (prevention of the new morbidities, improvement of educational outcomes, and the thrust toward more comprehensive service delivery systems) is at the center of school-based service development efforts. Schools are where most young people can be found. Schools are where most families can establish contact with the people who educate their children and where they can obtain the help they need to be effective parents. Providing quality education along with access to requisite health, mental health, and social and cultural services for children and families at one site should improve both educational and psychosocial outcomes. Of course, accomplishing this will require major changes in both the educational and human services establishments in the way they relate to each other and conduct their business.

Different Kinds of School-Based Initiatives

As a long-time observer of program and policy development in the field of adolescence, I have been fascinated by the apparent simultaneous innovation that has occurred. In the far corners of this country, caring individuals have concluded independently that the best way to help young people succeed is to create programs in middle and high schools that should enhance potential outcomes of students. These models vary considerably depending on their origin. If the practitioner starts with an orientation toward health services, then the model is frequently a school-based clinic. Mental health workers have created school-based centers providing individual and group counseling, family counseling, and even treatment (Catron & Weiss, 1994). Educators are more likely to devise an approach to school reorganization that starts with curricular reform, but also relies on partnerships to bring in outside support services. This model may result in a community school. Community-based youth advocates bring services to "light up" schoolhouses after hours in models that have been called Beacons (Dryfoos, 1995).

Each version of school-based services packages the components in different ways, moving along a continuum from simple to complex administrative arrangements. Relocation of a contract service from one site (a public health, mental health, or social service agency) to another (a school building) is much less complicated than the creation of a new type of community school in which the educational system and the support interventions are completely integrated and operated collaboratively by several agencies. In this chapter, and other work, I use the phrase *full service school* to define a broad framework that encompasses both school reform and the support services necessary to ensure that the school reform is effective (Dryfoos, 1994).

In addition to school-based services, another form of increasing access is *school-linked services*—referral locations to which school personnel send students or families for needed services. One example would be an adolescent health center located near a school where students could go for reproductive health care or primary health care and counseling. Almost any community agency, such as the local health department, community mental health center, or drug treatment program, could be designated as school-linked if school personnel ever referred students or families to that source. In terms of the goals of service integration, the success of the linkage would depend on the strength of the relationship—whether the ties were formal and intensive or informal and weak. If a referral is made without follow-up, the student may not use the resource, or if the provider does not offer high quality care, the linkage may be ineffective. For the purposes of this discussion, I concentrate primarily on services provided directly at school sites, reflecting my own strong bias toward the co-location, one-stop programs.

School-Based Primary Health Care Clinics

The simplest model is the *school-based clinic* (SBC), a designated center within a school building that delivers comprehensive health, mental health, and social services to the student body. The provider typically is a local health department, community health center, medical facility, or a youth-serving agency. Staff includes nurse practitioners, social workers, clinic aides, and part-time physicians, as well as after-hours medical back-up assured by the provider agency. In a few school systems, the Board of Education directly operates the medical services, but this is rarely feasible because of insurance, personnel, and back-up emergency care requirements.

After a slow start, SBCs are proliferating rapidly, increasing over the past decade from 10 locations to more than 900 (Making the Grade, 1996). Although the earlier models were in urban high schools, the growing recognition of the importance of early intervention has generated replication in middle and elementary schools. School districts and community agency partners are responding eagerly to requests for proposals. These requests are promulgated by states using Maternal and Child Health Block grant funds and other state initiatives, foundations, and most recently, the Bureau of Primary Health Care, which awarded the first 25 direct federal grants to SBCs in 1995. As these school centers open, students crowd in with a profusion of complaints ranging from respiratory diseases and menstrual cramps and accidents and injuries to personal crises and family problems (McKinney & Peak, 1994). The school-based clinic protocol generally includes a medical history and routine lab tests of hematocrit, hemoglobin, and urinalysis. Enrolled students may be asked to complete a psychosocial assessment that reveals risk levels for substance abuse, violence, suicide, pregnancy, sexually transmitted diseases (STDs), accidents, and family conflict. Depending on indications from the health history and assessment tool, the student is scheduled for a visit with the nurse practitioner or counselor. Most clinics are open from 8:00 a.m. to 5:00 p.m. for scheduled appointments and walk-in visits for emergency care and crisis intervention.

At the clinic, students receive physical examinations, immunizations, pregnancy and STD tests, and individual counseling. More than half of the clinics dispense medications, diagnose and treat sexually transmitted diseases, and perform gynecological exams. Most provide reproductive health counseling and exams, about one third give out condoms, and 15% distribute oral contraceptives on site. States, school districts, and sponsoring agencies set policies regarding the provision of contraceptives and other medical practices. SBC staff run group counseling workshops in the school on relevant subjects such as living with asthma, substance use, bereavement, sexual abuse, weight control, pregnancy prevention, and family relationships. SBC staff may also offer health education and health promotion curricula in the classroom. Parental consent is required for enrollment in these programs, and families are involved when appropriate.

School-Based Mental Health Centers

When school-based-clinic providers are asked what the largest unmet need is among their clients, they most frequently mention mental health counseling. Students come in to the medical clinics with an array of stress and depression, their typical adolescent problems exacerbated seriously by the deteriorating and unsafe social environment in which they live. As one provider described it, "as soon as we opened our doors, kids walked past the counselor's office, past the school nurse, past the principal, and came into our clinic to tell us that they have been sexually abused or that their parents are drug users." The fact that the clinic staff are outsiders and provide confidential services probably explains why students will bring their problems to the clinic rather than disclosing to school staff. The demand for mental health counseling has led to the development of school clinics that have a primary function of screening and treating for psychosocial problems. Mental health interventions in schools take many forms, however. In some communities, a mental health worker, such as a psychologist or a social worker, is outstationed by a community mental health agency in a school usually under a contractual relationship. A number of universities have collaborative arrangements with schools for internship experiences in mental health counseling. Within a broader framework of training young people to enhance their social skills, many university-based psychologists have been busy designing and implementing school-based curricula.

A mental health center in a school transfers the functions of a community mental health center to a school building. In this model, a room or group of rooms in a school building is designated as a services center. This center is not usually labeled as a mental health facility, but is presented as a place where students can go for all kinds of support and remediation. Staff typically includes psychologists and social workers. Depending on the range of additional services, other staff might be youth workers, tutors, and mentors. The goals of school-based mental health centers are to improve the social adjustment of students and help them deal with personal and family crises. Outcomes are measured in terms of improved classroom behavior, school attendance, self-reported reduction in suicidal ideation, and improvement in feeling "good."

A group of practitioners centered in Los Angeles have created a network of school-based mental health programs. The work of carving out this subset of activities is being refined by the School Mental Health Project at the University of California, Los Angeles, a national clearinghouse that offers training, research, and technical assistance. This project works in conjunction with the Los Angeles Unified Schools District's School Mental Health Center (Adelman & Taylor, in press).

Perhaps the most complete mental health program in a school system is operated by the Memphis City Schools (Nichol, 1993; Hannah & Nichol, 1994). Since 1970, a nonprofit corporation has administered a whole array of mental health services in the local school system, using two centers as a base and outstationing a staff of 160 psychologists, social workers, drug counselors, and homemakers throughout the school system. This program is described in the appendix to this chapter.

The state of New Jersey Department of Human Resources pioneered the one-stop concept with their School-Based Youth Services Program that began in 1987. Grants have been awarded to 29 communities to develop joint school–community agency partnerships to bring core services into school centers. As the programs have evolved, each has a different configuration reflecting the needs in the schools and the skills of the community agencies. Of these programs, five are operated by community mental health centers. An exemplary school-based mental health program located in New Brunswick High School is described in the appendix to this chapter.

The Pulaski County (Virginia) school system has established a School Family Counseling Center in cooperation with Radford University's program in counseling and human development (R. Whytal, personal communication, October 1994). In a building on the high school campus, rehabilitated by vocational students from the school, the school system has set up a mental health center that is staffed with two professional counselors and student interns from the university who are available to work with children and their families. The project provides a comprehensive approach to identification and assessment of at-risk students in the local schools, and individual and group counseling, testing, tutoring, family counseling, and training at the center. The Family School Center is also used by the Chamber of Commerce, the Office on Youth, a community college, job-training programs, and other agencies.

The Schools of the Future project is a large-scale foundation effort to help schools evolve into primary neighborhood institutions for promoting child and family development (Holtzman, 1992). The Texas-based Hogg Foundation for Mental Health supports efforts in four major cities (Austin, Dallas, Houston, and San Antonio) with 5-year grants for using elementary and middle schools as the locus of delivery of services. An equal amount of funding has been set aside for evaluation and monitoring. The foundation is interested in creating and testing an intervention that combines multiple approaches—the Comer School Development Program, Edward Zigler's Schools of the 21st Century, school-based clinics, programs for community renewal, and family preservation. The model places a full-time project coordinator (a social worker) in a community to establish links and partnerships between the schools and health, mental health, and human services providers and to involve parents and teachers in program activities. For example, at San Antonio's three school sites, family, group, and individual therapy are being provided by psychology graduate-student interns; and social work graduate students are providing crisis intervention, home visits, and welfare and food stamp certifications, and are working with child-protective services (Holtzman, 1992). Parent education, parent volunteer activities, after-school recreation, gang prevention programs, and other efforts involved many local organizations.

In a unique outreach effort, the Orange County (California) Health Care Agency relocated all of its children's mental health clinics to school-based facilities and expended almost all of its budget for children's services in those programs (Orange County Health Care Agency, 1989). This public agency model is of great interest because of its design and dimensions, but the future of the Orange County program is uncertain given the county's catastrophic fiscal crisis. A similar effort is underway in Dallas. Beginning in 1993, the Dallas County Mental Health and Mental Retardation agency established its mental health clinics in 5 schools, with 10 additional sites in the planning stages (Dallas Public Schools, n.d.). The plan calls for integrating the mental health services with school-based primary health care designed around a high school cluster, including all the feeder schools.

School-Based Youth Service Centers

Some centers focus more on coordination and referral than colocation of services in schools. Kentucky's significant school reform initiative in 1988 called for the development of youth service centers in high schools with more than 20% of the students eligible for free school meals (an indicator of economic disadvantage). In this case, small grants were given to school systems to set up a designated room in the school with a full-time coordinator to oversee referrals to community agencies for health and social services and to provide on-site counseling related to employment, substance abuse, and mental health (Dryfoos, 1994).

In New York City, the Beacons program, which was created by the city youth agency, supports community-based agencies to develop "lighted school houses" that are open from early morning until late at night, on weekends, and throughout summers (Annie E. Casey Foundation, 1993). These Beacons offer a wide range of activities, depending on the neighborhood needs, including after-school recreation, educational remediation, community events, and health services. One impressive program attracts 400 participants to meetings of Narcotics Anonymous several evenings each week in the school. Another has organized students to clean up the neighborhood, plant trees, and run their own newsstand at the corner. Beacons were used as the prototype for the Family and Community Endeavors part of the 1994 Crime Bill, on the belief that offering after-school activities in high-risk communities would help prevent delinquency.

Family Service/Resource Centers

The Kentucky legislation also called for family resource centers in elementary schools, which would offer parent education and refer parents to infant and child care, health services, and other community agencies. In other states, family resource centers are being supported through various state initiatives and federal grants that deliver comprehensive services on school sites, including parent education, child care, counseling, health services, home visiting, and career training. (See Romualdi & Sandoval, this volume.)

Community Schools

In the past, the phrase *community school* has been applied mainly to adult education classes in school buildings. The new generation of community schools begins to follow the broader construct of full-service schools, the integration of quality education with support services. Several schools have been identified as potential models (i.e., IS 218, PS 5, and Children's Aid Society in New York City; Robertson and Hanshaw in Modesta, California; Farrell School System in Pennsylvania; Turner School in Philadelphia). What these community schools have in common are restructured academic programs integrated with parent involvement and services for parents, health centers and family resource rooms, after-school activities, cultural and community activities, and 24-hour access. Mental health services are provided through contracted services with community mental health agencies and interns from social work schools. Each of these community schools is striving in different ways to become a village hub, with joint efforts from school and community agencies to create as rich an environment as possible for the children and their families. IS 218 is described in the appendix to this chapter.

School Reorganization

School-based services, most broadly defined, include interventions at the district, school-building, or classroom level that change the way the school functions. These programs are typically brought into schools by university groups or youth-serving organizations with the intent of training existing school personnel to create a different school climate. The goal is institutionalization of the program, with the outside agency removing itself when the school has proven that it can function on its own.

The School Development Program is a school-based management mental health approach to making school a more productive environment for poor minority children. In this case, outsiders come into the school to conduct training in a process developed by James Comer from the Yale University Child Study Center (Millsap et al., 1995). This program was successfully implemented in several inner city elementary schools in New Haven and is being replicated widely throughout the country in at least 382 schools in 65 districts. The School Development Program is the core component of a Rockefeller Foundation $15 million 5-year effort to improve education. The program attempts to transfer mental health skills to schools where change agents must be created by strengthening and redefining the relationships between principals, teachers, parents, and students. The sharply defined process sets up three parallel and interrelated structures: a school advisory council, a mental health team, and a parent participation program. According to Comer, the strength of this project is its focus on the entire school rather than any one particular aspect, its attention to institutional change rather than individual change, and its ability to successfully engage parents in school programs (Comer, 1984).

Psychosocial Counseling Programs

The models just described offer an array of comprehensive services and are typically located in a designated area such as a center or a clinic. However, many social workers and psychologists who are employed by community agencies and placed in schools focus on specific categorical issues such as substance abuse, teen pregnancy, and even school failure. Usually one outside practitioner is assigned to a school. These efforts generally augment pupil personnel services in school systems that want or need additional staff resources for dealing with psychosocial problems. In Westchester County, New York, the Student Assistance Program, which is partially supported by state and federal grants, covers 28 local school districts, with a focus on prevention of substance abuse. In Pennsylvania, the Department of Education has developed and disseminated a student assistance model with a focus specifically on reduction in absenteeism. Typically, student assistance counselors are placed in schools at the invitation of the principal, are given an office, and work along with the school personnel as part of a team. They provide individual counseling to students referred to them by guidance counselors and teachers and organize group counseling sessions on subjects of particular importance in the school population, such as alcoholic parents, families experiencing divorce, and coping with stress and depression. Student assistance workers train teachers and other school personnel to recognize the signs of stress and other problem behaviors among students.

The Options program of the Youth and Family Counseling Service in Lexington, North Carolina, was created to prevent juvenile delinquency by combining in-home family therapy with an alternative school setting (Community Research Associates, undated). It is currently being replicated in at least 10 school districts, with funding from the state juvenile justice and delinquency prevention program. Program goals include helping families resolve problems that contribute to undisciplined behavior, connecting parents to the school, and encouraging children to bond to the school and behave responsibly. A small group of targeted students who are in middle or high school spend their day in an alternative classroom within their regular school environment with specially trained teachers and a family therapist from the counseling agency. The staff family therapist visits with each family at least once a week but is on call at all times. Follow-up therapy begins immediately upon each school year's completion, with evaluations continuing for a year after the transition back to the conventional school setting. Repeated evaluations demonstrate success in truancy reduction and improved school behavior and achievement.

Many school systems have been used as research laboratories for developing new curricula in the area of prevention of substance abuse, teen pregnancy, suicide, and conduct disorders. The new wave of prevention programs relies heavily on contemporary psychological theory about building resistance skills and assertiveness training. The process typically involves a university-based researcher who designs a prevention curriculum, does field tests within a school system, and conducts evaluation in a sample of classrooms or schools, either within one system or across systems. The testing of a curriculum is conducted under the auspices of the university, usually the psychology department, or a research organization (e.g., Rand Corporation), supported with a foundation or government grant (e.g., National Institutes of Health). After the curriculum is tested, the researchers develop training materials, and rather than administering the curricula themselves they train school personnel to implement the program.

Initiatives That Created School-Based Services

It is difficult to create a typology of school-based youth services because of the many models, and even models within models (e.g., clinics and resource centers within community schools). Foundation and state initiatives have shaped these various structures. In some states, including Florida, California, and Kentucky, competitive grants have been awarded to school districts who must then seek partners in collaboration. In other states, such as New Jersey, a community-based agency may be the lead grantee and seek partnerships with a school. More than $30 million is being spent each year in Florida on their innovative Full Service Schools program, supporting collaborative school-based projects of varying service mixes, including family resource centers, case management, recreational programs, and school-based clinics. The expectation is that all schools will be full service in a few years, gradually bringing in child care, vocational education, and mental health services.

California's Healthy Start Support Services for Children Act was launched in 1991 with high ideals: "to be a catalyst in a revolution that will fundamentally change for the better the way organizations work together, the way resources are allocated for children and families, the nature and location of services provided, and ultimately, the outcomes experienced by children and families" (Wagner et al., 1994, p. 1.1). The $40 million initiative directly funds 40 service projects and 200 planning projects. School districts have created four types of collaborative programs: school-site family resource centers, satellite school-linked family-service centers, family-service coordination teams involving school personnel with project staff, and youth service programs that include school-based clinics. New Jersey's Department of Human Resources has committed more than $6 million annually for its School-Based Youth Services Program, beginning in 1987.

Foundations have played major roles in creating demonstration models. The Robert Wood Johnson Foundation first supported 23 school-based clinics and recently organized Making the Grade, an initiative in 10 states selected to develop district-wide comprehensive school health programs through the departments of health and education. Dewitt-Wallace Readers Digest is supporting a cohort of university-assisted community schools, using the University of Pennsylvania program as the lead agency. The Carnegie Corporation's Turning Point initiative in states is directed toward the reorganization of middle schools, including arrangements for access to health and social services in the school or in the community. Annie Casey, Kaufman, Kellogg, and Stuart foundations also support school-based services in various forms as well as research and evaluation efforts.

Research About School-Based Services

Support for the concept of services in schools is strong, but even the most ardent advocates want to be assured that centralizing services in restructured schools will make a difference in the lives of the children and their families. Evaluation results are spotty, which is not surprising given the early stages of program development and the difficulties inherent in program research (Cook, Anson, & Walchli, 1993). Much of the research has been on school-based clinics. About 400 of the programs are using a special management information system—On Line—designed and managed by

David Kaplan at Children's Hospital in Denver. Several years ago, the Robert Wood Johnson Foundation commissioned an evaluation of its school-based adolescent health care program (23 clinics) (Kisker, Brown, & Hill, 1994). The preliminary report expressed great frustration with the methodological problems inherent in school-based program outcome research. Researchers were prohibited from using similar schools in each area as controls because of fear of raising controversy over the use of too personal questions on the student surveys. They resorted to a comparison of a relatively small sample of students from the program schools (a mix of users and nonusers) with a small national sample of high school students. Although they found a high level of use of the clinics for health services, no evidence was found that the health centers led to reductions in high-risk behaviors in those schools. The researchers recommended that "future research should be based on a well-matched comparison group design to obtain valid, dependable estimates of program effects" (p. 174).

Several states (e.g., Florida, Kentucky, California) are beginning to produce reports on more comprehensive programs in those states, and grantees are mandated to participate in evaluation (Berger & Hetrick, 1994; Illback, 1993; Kalafat & Illback, 1993; Wagner et al., 1994). Individual researchers around the country have published papers, with some positive results (Brindis, Morales, McCarter, & Wolfe, 1994; Dryfoos, Brindis, & Kaplan, 1996; Godin, Woodhouse, Livingwood, & Jacobs, 1993; Kirby, 1994; Santelli, Kouzis & Newcomer, 1996; Rienzo & Button, 1993), and several government publications have included summaries of preliminary research findings (Bureau of Primary Health Care, 1953; Government Accounting Office, 1994).

In general, programs have been successfully implemented in the communities and schools with the greatest needs and are enrolling high percentages of the student body. School clinics are most heavily used by the highest risk students with the greatest number of problems and no other source of medical care. More than half a million students are receiving free primary health care that is convenient, confidential, and caring. In centers with mental health personnel, substantial numbers of students and their families are gaining access to psychosocial counseling (Wolk & Kaplan, 1993). The demand is overwhelming, especially for mental health services, substance abuse treatment, and dentistry.

Use of emergency rooms has declined in a few areas, with school clinics and hospitalization rates decreased in others. Because minor illnesses such as headaches, menstrual cramps, and accidents on school property can be treated in school, absences and excuses to go home have decreased (Emihovich & Herrington, 1993). School-based clinics have demonstrated the capacity to respond to emergencies, for example, conducting immunization campaigns and doing tuberculosis screening (Bosker, 1992).

Scattered evidence suggests that a few school-based clinics have had an impact on delaying the initiation of sexual intercourse, upgrading the quality of contraceptive use, and lowering pregnancy rates, but only in programs that offer comprehensive family-planning services (Dryfoos, Brindis, & Kaplan, 1996). Large numbers of students are being diagnosed and treated for sexually transmitted diseases. In a few places, school-based program users have reported decreased substance use and improved classroom performance and school attendance and the school has shown higher retention rates. Having a clinic in a school has no proven effect on non-enrollees, and rates of problem behaviors in the total school have not changed significantly. Comprehensive school-based programs for pregnant and parenting teens have demonstrated earlier access to prenatal care and higher birth weights, lower repeat pregnancy rates, and better school retention (Bureau of Primary Health Care, 1993).

Reports from Florida's Full Service Schools are encouraging (Florida Department of Education). Students, parents, teachers, and school personnel report a high level of satisfaction with school clinics and service centers, and particularly appreciate their accessibility, convenience, confidentiality, and caring attitudes. In family resource centers with health clinics, preventive medical care and treatment of minor illnesses are the major services sought and used. In some programs, school staff also receive health screening, nutrition, and other services. Youth service centers that have focused on student behaviors report an improvement in classroom performance.

Early reports from the more comprehensive community schools are encouraging (Children's Aid Society, 1993; Farrell Avenue School District, 1993). Attendance and graduation rates are significantly higher than in comparable schools, and reading and math scores have shown some improvement. Students are eager to come to schools that are stimulating, nurturing, and respectful of cultural values. Parents are heavily involved in classrooms as aides, on advisory boards, in classes and cultural events, and with case managers and support services.

Although the models mentioned here—clinics, centers, and community schools—have many differences, a review of the "state of the art" yields a number of common components of successful programs (Dryfoos, 1994; Melaville et al., 1993). School and community people (e.g., local agencies, parents, leaders) join together to develop a shared vision of new institutional arrangements. An extended planning process starts off with a needs assessment to ensure that the design is responsive to the requirements of students and their families.

The configuration of support services brought in from the outside is dependent on what already exists in the school in the way of health, mental health, social services, and counseling. The building principal is instrumental in the implementation and smooth operation of school-based services. Principals not only act as the leaders in school restructuring, they must also be the prime facilitators for assuring smooth integration of outside partners into the school environment. Active visible support of the program is essential. Adequate space must be made available, with security, maintenance, and assurance of confidentiality.

Successful programs rely on a full-time coordinator or program director in addition to the principal. This person must be flexible, persistent, and patient, and be able to handle management decisions and relate well to both school and community situations. In the most effective programs, personnel are trained to be sensitive to issues related to youth development, cultural diversity, and community empowerment. Bilingual staff are essential. A designated space such as a clinic or a center in a school acts as a magnet for bringing in other services from the community. Perhaps the most important effect of entering into the partnership process is the capability of the new entity to bring new resources into the school building.

Issues in Replication

This brief overview of school-based services cannot possibly capture the amount of activity going on that involves partnerships between schools and a vast array of community agencies. At one point, I counted 40 different categories of outside personnel going into schools under various arrangements to perform services or offer enrichment. But these partnerships do not evolve out of thin air, and they are not easily developed or maintained. Broadscale replication requires enormous fortitude, commitment, and determination on the part of these diverse practitioners.

Governance

As would be expected, the more complex the model, the more demanding the administrative arrangements. The mounting rhetoric calls for sophisticated collaborative organizations. School systems and community agencies are expected to leave behind their parochial loyalties and pitch in together to form a new kind of union with a common vision and shared decision making. In reality, most of the emerging models have one designated lead agency. If it is the school system, as in Modesta, California, it dispenses its Healthy Start grant to a whole array of public and voluntary agencies through contractual relationships. In other places, such as New Jersey, community agencies may be direct grantees and enter schools through a memorandum of agreement. But in neither case is governance changed. This is not surprising. According to one anonymous observer, "collaboration is an unnatural act between two or more nonconsenting adults."

The first evaluation of New Beginnings in San Diego (a multi-agency program that operates a family resource center in Hamilton School) warns that it is "difficult to overestimate the amount of time collaboration takes" (New Beginnings Evaluation Team, 1994). The participants discovered that it was easier to get agencies to make "deals" (sign contracts to relocate workers) than to achieve major changes in delivery systems. Staff turnover, family mobility, fiscal problems, and personality issues were cited as some of the barriers to change.

Turf

When a whole new staff working for an outside agency moves on to school property, many territorial concerns arise. One issue that complicates the collaboration process, which is related to governance, is *turf*: Who owns the school building? What role does the school nurse play in the school-based clinic? Why not hire more school social workers if case management is needed? Why not hire more school psychologists if individual and family counseling is required? Issues arise over confidentiality, space, releasing students from classes, and discipline. It takes time and energy, and particularly, skilled principals and program coordinators to work through appropriate policies and practices.

Adelman and Taylor (in press), seasoned observers of school-based initiatives, believe that the major challenge for school-based mental health centers is to identify and collaborate with what is already going on in the school district. Many schools have programs focused on substance abuse and teen pregnancy prevention, crisis and suicide intervention, violence reduction, self-esteem enhancement, and other kinds of support groups. However, these efforts lack cohesiveness in theory and implementation, often stigmatize students by targeting them, and suffer from the common bureaucratic problem of poor coordination between programs. One of the most demanding roles for the mental health center is to establish working relationships with key school staff members.

Staff turnover is endemic, especially in schools in disadvantaged areas. Many school-based practitioners have the experience that just as they have achieved a good working relationship with the principal, and the turf problems begin to dissipate, the principal leaves. The effort has to be undertaken all over again to orient the new principal to the partnership's purposes, policies, and practices.

Controversy

In the earlier years, communities and school boards expressed resistance even to the idea of school-based clinics; in some places, any proposal to use the school building for any purpose other than education was perceived as controversial. Still, in some parts of the country, the suggestion of mental health services in schools is considered to be just as threatening as reproductive health care. When school-based clinics with mental health counseling were first proposed in Arkansas, state health department personnel were accused of being "child snatchers." Militant opposition groups who loudly claim they are protecting the sanctity of the family almost never include parents of the children in the school ("Fate of School," 1995).

On the whole, my experience in looking at programs throughout the country has shown me that controversy has dwindled with the availability of state and foundation grants for comprehensive school health and social services. Hundreds of schools and agencies jointly apply for these grants. At the local level, the requirement for extensive needs assessments and planning prior to program development has equipped parents and school personnel with the data necessary to convince decision makers and educate the media about the importance of integrating services in the school (Rienzo & Button, 1993). Parents are the most articulate and credible advocates for these programs.

School-Based Versus Community-Based

Questions have also been raised about placing the locus of health, mental health, and social service programs in schools in communities that are distrustful of the educational establishment (Chaskin & Richman, 1992). Some school systems are so resistant to change that community leaders have little confidence that the quality education part of the full-service vision will ever materialize. Human resource planners have proposed an alternative model that places services in buildings run by community-based organizations, in which families feel comfortable and are assured larger roles in decision making. The service-integration theory still holds, but the locus of services is placed firmly in the neighborhood, and directly operated under local control. The school board has no place in this model, obviating the difficult negotiations that can be stressful and time-consuming.

Michigan's experience with its 19 teen health centers (11 school-based or school-linked and 8 community-based) suggested that community-based centers had greater flexibility, especially in regard to the provision of family planning; could more easily assure confidentiality; served more dropouts; were free to set their own parental consent protocols; and avoided the (unfounded) suspicion that school funds were being used for nonacademic services (Anthony, 1991). However, the school-based centers were found to reduce the necessity for outreach, involved school personnel more readily, served students on site, were perceived to have more direct access to teens, were more likely to obtain foundation support, took on the function of health promotion in the schools, and were able to garner in-kind resources from the school system such as space, maintenance, utilities, and supplies.

I do not know of any research about the location of mental health services, but it appears, on the basis of observations in New Brunswick, New Jersey, that students are much more likely to obtain psychosocial counseling in a school-based clinic than at the local community mental health center (see appendix to this chapter). Virtually none of the students or their families had ever used the mental health center because they were rarely referred, were convinced they could not afford it, or were unaware of its existence. Brindis, Kapphanhn, McCarter, and Wolfe (1995) documented a high level of use of mental health services in school-based clinics in San Francisco among students with HMO and private insurance. The extensive use of the school clinic by students with other health care options was attributed to the ability of the clinic

> to provide mental health services in a manner that is more acceptable to the adolescents, and that the integration of this service with a comprehensive array of health services may help diminish the stigma often associated with this kind of service ... [and it] may also reflect the relative unavailability ... of these services as provided through HMO or private insurance coverage. (p. 24)

Catron and Weiss (1994) made a very strong case for locating mental health services in schools based on their experiences in Nashville elementary schools:

> In community mental health centers, services are specialized and fragmented. Different . . . services are . . . provided by different professionals . . . and the therapist treating a child must coordinate the various services to provide a full multi-level intervention. . . . [This] results in multiple visits to the clinic and separate locations for different services. (p. 248)

In the Nashville program, services are integrated within the school and coordinated by a case manager.

Concern has been raised about the viability of using schools as sites for dealing with young people who no longer attend school. Some of the existing school-based centers do serve out-of-school youth as well as siblings and parents of current students, whereas others do not. Two major community-based youth-serving organizations in New York City (El Puente and The Door) transformed into community schools by adding to their rosters basic educational components of services and obtaining certification as part of the public school system. This community youth center school model offers an approach for working with school dropouts who are often youth-agency clients. The disaffected youth are drawn back into the school system through the efforts of trusted youth-service-agency staff.

Funding

The annual cost for these school-based service models ranges from $75,000 for Kentucky's Youth and Family Service Centers to $800,000 for the most comprehensive community school. School-based clinics average about $150,000 per year, not including large amounts of in-kind and donated goods and services. The cost for a clinic user is about $100 per year, while the incremental cost for a student in a community school might be about $1,000. As has been discussed, states are major funders of these initiatives and, even with looming budget cuts, are moving ahead to support more comprehensive school-based programs (Dryfoos, in press).

Except for a recent initiative in the Bureau of Primary Health Care, no federal grants go directly to communities and schools for integrated services. However, the school-based-services concept has been recognized in significant new legislative endeavors, including the Crime Bill, Title 1, versions of health reform, and empowerment zone grants. Federal regulations could be changed to facilitate the increased use of categorical dollars, for example, from special education, HIV prevention, substance abuse, and mental health programs. Medicaid is already being accessed in many schools, although providers experience difficulties both with eligibility determination and reimbursement procedures. The advent of managed care adds to the complexity, with providers struggling to establish either fee-for-service or capitation contracts with managed care providers.

State and federal health care reform legislation should guarantee that school-based centers can become essential community providers and that enrollees in managed care plans can obtain mental health, health education, and other preventive services within these plans.

One federal agency that has heavily influenced the development of comprehensive health services in schools is the Division of Adolescent and School Health (DASH) in the Centers for Disease Control and Prevention. Although DASH does not give direct service grants to local school-based programs, it supports many state education agencies, national organizations, and training centers to promote health education. DASH has funded 12 states to develop comprehensive school health programs through collaborative efforts between the health and education departments. It also supports evaluation research and conducts the National Youth Risk Behavior Survey (see Table 1).

Technical Assistance

Many of the school-based programs cited here were initiated by outside experts who work with schools under various arrangements. Some of these experiences may be useful to those attempting to replicate these models, or even to implement new ones. Abt Associates is tracking the dissemination of the Comer School Development Program in a number of schools, a process that is believed to take at least 5 years to bring about school change (Millsap et al., 1995). Millsap et al.'s preliminary report documents the differences between schools that had access to officially designated partners from universities or state departments of education who were trained to offer technical assistance and those who only had access to a video on the process. The partnerships were quite successful at moving along the development of the three-part program, but little change was observed in the schools that only had access to the video. The participation of the partners included acting as facilitators, attending team meetings, giving technical assistance, and helping schools overcome obstacles and persist in these efforts. Apparently the continuing presence of these outsiders in the schools had a significant impact. Few schools could make progress without support from their systems, including some financial backing for in-service training and other aspects of the program.

The Accelerated Schools project reported a similar finding: after working with schools for more than 8 years, the researchers determined that the role of the trainer (whom they call a *coach*) was crucial in implementing the systematic schoolwide change required of this model (Accelerated Schools Project, 1995). According to the project report, "Without ongoing support, changes tend to be isolated and/or short-lived" (p. 1). The coach's primary responsibility is to foster the conditions for a school community to effectively implement the model and build capacity for institutionalization. For this purpose, the National Center on Accelerated Schools has selected and trained outside individuals from state departments of education, universities, and schools who can provide objective and unbiased assistance to the school site personnel. As one coach reported, "the greatest challenge is keeping my mouth shut. There are things you hear that you want to react to very badly, but you can't because of your role" (Accelerated Schools Project, 1995, p. 14).

Implications for Psychologists

The proliferation of school-based youth services in many different versions creates an array of new opportunities for the field of psychology. Conoley and Conoley (1991) spell out many diverse roles for psychologists in schools, including individual and group counseling, enhancing affective education, and implementing social-problem-solving and coping skills curricula, in addition to traditional testing. A recent publication of the American Psychological Association (APA) lists 29 discrete activities for psychologists in schools in terms of health education (behavioral skills), public health (working with families), school-based services (individual assessment), and traditional activities such as crisis intervention, consultation, and staff training (Talley, Short, & Kolbe, 1995). In 1994, the APA established a Center for Psychology in Schools and Education to raise consciousness among psychologists about issues in school reform, school health, educational practice, research opportunities, and training.

For those who are interested in practice that deals with individuals, being able to work with young people in their own settings provides huge benefits. First of all, if mental health services are delivered as part of a comprehensive package of school-based services, the possible stigma is removed. Young people receive assessments, counseling, and treatment for personal problems in the same context that they receive physical examinations and dental care, obtain tests for pregnancies and sexually transmitted diseases, and are given medications or treatment for minor illnesses and injuries. Psychologists have the opportunity to work with many high-risk young people who would never appear at mental health clinics, but yet are deeply troubled with depression and stress.

Practitioners working in these new kinds of school-based settings report an overwhelming demand for personal attention to the life situations of troubled youngsters. Some youth need the most basic nurturing, which involves close one-on-one experiences with a caring adult. This attention must be concentrated and sustained, requiring both deep commitment and tireless patience from the worker. This is not necessarily traditional psychotherapy, but rather an extension of warmth and caring that is not being given by missing parents. This experience can be very rewarding for practitioners as they watch young people begin to function better. It can also be quite frustrating when the clients fail to show up for appointments, do not follow through, get discouraged, or land in jail.

Although there are parents who are hard to reach, most are available if properly approached. Programs that provide parents with tangible benefits like the services provided at family resource centers can be successful. Practitioners need to understand the home environments from which their clients come and work with families to establish trust. Psychologists have a very important role in acting as liaison between the family and the school, but the family must be empowered to articulate their expectations that their children succeed in school. School personnel need help in dealing with difficult family situations. Psychologists can conduct specific training sessions for these different clusters, with a view toward creating an agreeable and responsive school environment for all.

Psychologists who are engaged in preventive interventions such as social-skills training and self-competency enhancement can work with groups within the school and use the group experience as outreach for follow-up with individuals. Psychologists can contribute to research on the prevalence and nature of risk factors, especially in light of the new morbidities, and help school systems deal with these problems. Visiting psychologists can form teams with teachers and school-pupil personnel to address the holistic needs of the child, and together they can develop appropriate means for involving families in counseling and parent education. Working in comprehensive systems rather than isolated offices will give practitioners much more flexibility in terms of modalities of care and treatment and a wider range of resources for support (Illback, 1994).

In the past, a wall of separation tended to isolate pupil-personnel issues from educational reform movements. Psychologists were not included in school restructuring dialogues. Comer (1984) and others have raised awareness about the mental health implications of the total school environment: how children feel in the school, whether parents feel comfortable coming to the school, how teachers feel about their roles, and whether teachers and administrators have the skills to make the school a welcoming place for children and their families. Mental health workers are beginning to evaluate the impact of traditional school practices such as tracking, grade retention, suspension, and other disciplinary measures on the well-being of youngsters. These kinds of issues are rapidly moving to the front burner in the process of making schools more responsive to contemporary concerns. The whole concept of full-service schools is predicated on the fact that children who are burdened with social, psychological, and health problems cannot be educated, and children who are in schools that are dysfunctional cannot be educated either.

The creation of new arrangements such as community schools implies greater involvement with the outlying community—the people, the other agencies, businesses, churches, media, and the police. Community psychologists can offer leadership in the design of these new kinds of institutions, helping planners to overcome resistance in the community and to deal with controversy as it arises. Advocates for school-based youth services are often frustrated when they are attacked by extremist groups. They need help in devising strategies that will appeal to the broader public and approaches to get the community to understand that it is to their interest to improve the outcomes for all children. One approach is the conduct of a local study using the protocol of the National Youth Risk Behavior survey (see Table 1). Communities are often shocked to discover that local students are just like those elsewhere: More than one fourth carry weapons and more than half are sexually active. Survey results carefully presented and interpreted can be helpful for stimulating support for prevention programs in schools.

Psychologists and other categories of professionals need to establish their own credibility with disadvantaged and alienated community groups. Today's families come in many different configurations, colors, ethnic identities, language groups, and value systems. Practitioners must be sensitive to all of these factors and develop appropriate skills. They must also offer leadership and support in arenas that relate to the broader social environment such as gun control, immigration, poverty, and racial discrimination.

The delineation of these various roles for psychologists in schools implies attention to training issues. The list of expected competencies is greatly extended as psychologists take on personal nurturing, collaborative programming, school reform, and community development. The traditional curriculum of graduate education has to move out of its categorical mode and adapt to the movement toward comprehensive interventions. Contemporary psychology students need exposure to educational theory, public health, and social science, as well as skills that will make them more effective working with diverse community groups. For those who are interested in directing programs as coordinators of school-based youth services, the whole complex world of program financing has to be explored. The era of managed care puts increasing demands on program operators who must understand how schools can capture funding through these mechanisms.

The Future

The emerging field of school-based services is a home-grown product with many variants, developed at the local level by committed individuals who come together from diverse domains to try to build more responsive institutions. It is not known how many schools now have established partnerships with human services agencies, but the number is clearly growing. Relatively small investments by state governments and foundations enable innovative leaders to better use existing categorical resources to relocate personnel and devise more integrated delivery systems. Broadly replicating full-service schools in disadvantaged communities will require more federal resources, a challenging goal in a period of budget tightening. Advocacy groups are forming at the state and national level to push for this new movement and to give the concept of full-service community schools greater visibility.

Research will confirm that combining prevention interventions with school restructuring creates stronger institutions and that schools will become neighborhood hubs—places where children's lives are enhanced and families want to go. The school's role is to educate and the family's responsibility is to raise the children, and many of today's parents need assistance in accomplishing that task. Full-service schools may be an effective arrangement for achieving school, family, and societal goals. Psychologists can offer leadership to this emerging movement, bringing their interpersonal skills, knowledge of healthy family and community functioning, and commitment to human values to the organization of new prototypes of institutional settings.

Exemplary Programs

School-Based Youth Services Program, New Brunswick (NJ) Public Schools

This mental health program was initiated in New Brunswick High School in 1988, is funded by the New Jersey School Based Youth Services Program, and is operated by the Community Mental Health Center of the University of Medicine and Dentistry of New Jersey. The program was stimulated by New Brunswick Tomorrow, a local business-sponsored effort that is trying to revitalize New Brunswick. In 1991, the New Brunswick School-Based Youth Services Program (SBYSP) was awarded new state funds to expand services into five local elementary schools.

The SBYSP is a centralized service delivery system that integrates existing school programs, creates new services within the schools, and links a network of youth service providers. Although its primary thrust is mental health promotion and treatment, it "looks like" a comprehensive youth center in a school setting. Currently, the program has 10 full-time core staff members, including 8 clinicians (psychologists and social workers), one of whom serves as the director. Staff members conduct individual, group, and family therapy and serve as consultants to school personnel and other agencies involved with adolescents. An activities/outreach worker plans and supervises recreational activities and outreach contacts at the high school. Specialized part-time staff include a pregnancy and parenting counselor, substance abuse counselor, and consultants in suicide prevention, social problems, and medical care. A number of student interns from Rutgers University Graduate Schools have field placements in this program, and there are also some volunteers.

The facility at New Brunswick High School is located in the old band room, which has been attractively fixed up to resemble a game room in a settlement house, with television, ping-pong, and other active games; comfortable furniture; and books and tapes on loan. Private offices where students can go for individual psychological counseling ring the main room. The center offers tutoring, mentoring, group activities, recreational outings, and educational trips. A number of therapeutic groups have been organized: social problem solving, substance abuse, Children of Alcoholics, and coping skills for the gifted and talented. Students are referred to the local neighborhood health center for health services and treatment. Children of teen parents are offered transportation to child care centers.

Of the 650 students in the New Brunswick High School, 91% are enrolled in the program and have parental consent statements on file. During the past 2 years, one in four of the enrolled students have been involved in active mental health counseling with one of the clinicians. Many of the students, especially the girls, appear to be clinically depressed. According to Gail Reynolds, the director, the demand for services is overwhelming. Many of the problems require immediate and time-consuming interventions with the family, school, and other social agencies. After a student has made three visits, parents must come in for counseling sessions. Staff make home visits in order to involve parents.

In the process of setting up the program within the school, the superintendent was a key player and was supportive from the start. The first summer was spent overcoming the resistance of people in the school, preparing the school staff, and working out referral procedures with the school's four guidance counselors and the teachers. Reynolds meets with the counselors once a month and with the principal and vice-principal weekly. Relationships with school staff are complex and vitally important to the functioning of the center. One problem that had to be overcome was convincing the maintenance staff to allow the premises to stay open after 3:00 p.m. The center is open all day and into the evening, and all summer.

Memphis City Schools Mental Health Center

The oldest running mental health center in a school has been operating within the Memphis City Schools since 1970. The Memphis City School Mental Health Center (MCSMCH) is a private, nonprofit corporation that also acts as an administrative arm of the school system. It is funded largely through contracts with the Tennessee Department of Human Services, the State Department of Health, and a grant from Drug Free Schools and Communities. MCSMHC, a state-licensed center, has a staff of 161, including psychologists, social workers, alcohol and drug counselors, and homemakers.

The focus of the program is to affect the school environment through many different components with powerful preventive interventions that affect all children and their families, rather than concentrating on individuals. The core program consists of 36 mental health teams housed in two school centers, which rotate through all 160 schools, providing assessments, consultation, faculty in-service, crisis intervention, and counseling. The teams work closely with school support teams, who make sure that interventions are actually carried out in the classroom, with families, and with individual students. The center organizes prevention groups in areas such as social skills, divorced families, grief issues, and anger control. In 1992–1993, the teams provided over 9,000 hours of treatment to students and their families and 7,500 hours of consultation.

The mental health center also takes responsibility for implementing drug abuse prevention, including training teachers in a K–12 curriculum. MCSMHC counselors are assigned to the schools and coordinate the programs, including student leadership training, just-say-no clubs, and parent-to-parent training. The mental health staff train school teams to work with community groups to address neighborhood issues. A student assistance program specially trains teachers to identify high-risk students. School students suspended for a drug incident are required to attend an early intervention group of nine sessions, which has resulted in a decline in school problems.

The most recent initiatives have sought to reduce conflict and violence. Center staff have organized prevention groups in conflict resolution, using officers from the Memphis police department as cofacilitators. One school is involved in a firearms eradication program. Students who have received firearms suspensions and their parents are seen by a center psychologist and receive more in-depth services if appropriate.

One mental health team is located at the adolescent parenting program and works on this issue throughout the school system. Counseling is available and workshops offered on stress management, personal goal setting, and African American issues. MCSMHC also offers services for abused and neglected children, including a homemaker program for families with abuse problems.

The MCSMHC is well positioned to offer leadership in the school and the community to coordinate a wide range of services and programs to enhance the quality of life for the students and their families.

IS 218 Children's Aid Society Intermediate School

In New York City, the Children's Aid Society (CAS), in conjunction with Community School District 6, has created a true settlement house in a school. IS 218 is located in a new building in Washington Heights and was designed to be a community school, with air-conditioning for summer programs, outside lights on the playground, and an unusually attractive setting indicative of a different kind of school. It offers students a choice of five self-contained "academies": business; community service; expressive arts; ethics and law; or mathematics, science, and technology. The school opens at 7:00 a.m. for breakfast and classes in dance, Latin band, and sports and stays open after school for educational enrichment, mentoring, sports, computer lab, music, arts, trips, and entrepreneurial workshops. In the evening, teenagers are welcomed to use the sports and arts facilities and take classes along with adults who come for English, computer work, parenting skills, and other workshops. A family resource center provides social services to parents, including immigration, employment, and housing consultations. A group of 25 mothers have been recruited to work in the center as family advocates. They receive a small stipend for their services. In addition, a primary health and dental clinic and a store that sells student products are arrayed around the attractive lobby of the school. School-supported and CAS-supported social workers and mental health counselors work together to serve students and families. The school stays open weekends and summers, offering the Dominican community many opportunities for cultural enrichment and family participation.

50   JOY G. DRYFOOS

References

Accelerated Schools Project (1997). The role of the coach in accelerated schools. *Accelerated Schools, 6*(1), 19–25.

Adelman, H., & Taylor, L. (in press). Mental health facets of the school-based health center movement: Need and opportunity for research and development. *Journal of Mental Health Administration.*

Annie E. Casey Foundation. (1993). The Beacons: A school-based approach to neighborhood revitalization. *AEC Focus.* Greenwich, CT: Author.

Anthony, D. (October, 1991). *Remarks to Support Center for School Based Clinics Annual Meeting.* Speech presented to Michigan Department of Public Health, Dearborn, MI.

Benson, P. (1990). *The troubled journey: A portrait of 6th–12th grade youth.* Minneapolis, MN: Search Institute.

Berger, N., & Hetrick, M. (1994). *The evaluation of Florida's full service schools: The 1992–1993 evaluative report and the future.* Paper presented at Conference on School Health and Full Service Schools, St. Petersburg, Florida.

Bosker, I. (1992). *A school-based clinic immunization outreach project targeting measles in New York City.* Paper presented at the Annual Meeting of the American Public Health Association, Washington, DC.

Brindis, C., Kapphanhn, C., McCarter, V., & Wolfe, A. (1995). The impact of health insurance status on adolescents' utilization of school-based clinic services: Implications for health reform. *Journal of Adolescent Health Care, 16,* 18–25.

Brindis, C., Morales, S., McCarter, V., Dobrin, C., & Wolfe, A. (1994). *An evaluation study of school-based clinics in California: Major findings, 1986–1991.* San Francisco: Center for Reproductive Health Policy Research, University of California.

Bureau of Primary Health Care. (1993). *School-based clinics that work.* Washington, DC: DHHS Public Health Services, Health Resources and Services Administration.

Catron, T., & Weiss, B. (1994). The Vanderbilt school-based counseling program: An inter-agency, primary-care model of mental health services. *Journal of Emotional and Behavioral Disorders, 2*(4), 247–253.

Centers for Disease Control. (1995). Youth risk behavior surveillance—United States, 1993. *Morbidity and Mortality Weekly Report, CDC Surveillance Summaries, 44,* SS-1.

Chaskin, R., & Richman, H. (1992). Concerns about school-linked services: Institution-based versus community-based models. In Center for the Future of Children (Ed.), *The future of children: School-linked services* (Vol. 2, pp. 107–117). Los Altos, CA: David and Lucille Packard Foundation.

Children's Aid Society. (1993). *Building a community school: A revolutionary design in public education.* New York: Author.

Comer, J. (1984). *Improving American education: Roles for parents. Hearing before the Select Committee on Children Youth and Families, June 7, 1984* (pp. 55–60). Washington, DC: U.S. Government Printing Office.

Committee for Economic Development. (1994). *Putting learning first: Governing and managing the schools for high achievement.* New York: Research and Policy Committee, CED.

Community Research Associates. (n.d.). *Profile, Juvenile Justice and Delinquency Prevention* [pamphlet], *4*(6).

Conoley, J., & Conoley C. (1991). Collaboration for child adjustment: Issues for school- and clinic-based child psychologists. *Journal of Consulting and Clinical Psychology, 59*(6), 821–829.

Cook, T., Anson, A., & Walchli, S. (1993). From causal description to causal explanation: Improving three already good evaluations of adolescent health programs. In S. Millstein, A. Peterson, & E. Nightengale (Eds.), *Promoting the health of adolescents: New directions for the twenty-first century* (pp. 339–374). New York: Oxford University Press.

Dallas Public Schools. (n.d.). *School based mental health clinics.* [Handout at National Assembly on School-Based Health Care, Washington, DC, June 29, 1995.]

Dryfoos, J. (1990). *Adolescents-at-risk: Prevalence and prevention.* New York: Oxford University Press.

Dryfoos, J. (1994). *Full service schools: A revolution in health and social services for children, youth, and families.* San Francisco: Jossey-Bass.

Dryfoos, J. (1995). *Full service schools: Schools and community-based organizations finally get together to address the crisis in disadvantaged communities.* Paper presented at 1995 Annual Meeting of the American Educational Research Association, San Francisco, CA.

Dryfoos, J. (in press). *Safe passage: Making it through adolescence in a risky society.* New York: Oxford University Press.

Dryfoos, J., Brindis, C., & Kaplan, D. (1996). Research and evaluation in school-based health care. In Juszcak, L., & Fisher, M. (Eds.), *Adolescent medicine: State of the art. Health Care In Schools.* Philadelphia: Hanley & Belfus, Inc.

Emihovich, C., & Herrington, C. (1993). *Florida's supplemental school health services projects: An evaluation.* Tallahassee, FL: Florida State University.

Farrell Avenue School District. (1993). *A tradition of care and education for all: Prescription for America* [Flyer]. Farrell Avenue School District.

Fate of school clinics rests with state. (1995, May 29). *Times Picayune,* B1.

Florida Department of Education. (1995). *Full service schools: Samples of evaluation highlights* [Information sheet distributed by Florida Department of Education]. Tallahassee, FL: Author.

Godin, S., Woodhouse, L., Livingwood, W., & Jacobs, H. (1993). Key factors in successful school-based clinics. *NMHA Prevention Update, 4*(1), 3.

Government Accounting Office. (1994). *School-based health center can expand access for children* (Publication No. GAO/HEHS-95-35). Washington, DC: U.S. Government Accounting Office.

Hannah, F., & Nichol, G. (1994). Model programs in service delivery in child and family mental health: Memphis City Schools Mental Health Center. In M. Roberts (Ed.), *Model programs in service delivery.* Hillsdale, NJ: Erlbaum.

Holtzman, W. (1992). *School of the future.* Austin, TX: American Psychological Association and Hogg Foundation for Mental Health.

Illback, R. (1993). *Formative evaluation of the Kentucky Family Resource and Youth Service Centers: A descriptive analysis of program trends.* Louisville, KY: REACH of Louisville.

Illback, R. (1994). Poverty and the crisis in children's services: The need for services integration. *Journal of Clinical Child Psychology, 23,* 413–424.

Kalafat, J., & Illback R. (1993). *Implementation evaluation of the Family Resource and Youth Service Centers: A qualitative analysis.* Louisville, KY: REACH of Louisville.

Kirby, D. (1994, September 23). *Findings from other studies of school-based clinics.* Presentation given at meeting on evaluation sponsored by the Robert Wood Johnson Foundation, Washington, DC.

Kisker, E., Brown, R., & Hill, J. (1994). *Healthy caring: Outcomes of the Robert Wood Johnson Foundation's school-based adolescent health care program.* Princeton, NJ: Mathematics Policy Research.

Kort, M. (1984). The delivery of primary health care in American public schools: 1890–1980. *Journal of School Health, 54*(11), 455.

Lavin, A., Shapiro, G., & Weill, K. (1992). *Creating an agenda for school-based health promotion: A review of selected reports.* Cambridge, MA: Harvard School of Public Health.

Making the Grade. (1996). *Access.* Washington, DC: The George Washington University.

Melaville, A., Blank, M., & Asayesh, G. (1993). *Together we can: A guide for crafting a profamily system of education and human services.* Washington, DC: U.S. Government Printing Office.

McKinney, D., & Peak, G. (1994). *School-based and school-linked health centers: Update 1993.* Washington, DC: Center for Population Options.

Millsap, M., Gamse, B., Beckford, I., Johnston, K., Chase, A., Hailey, L., Brigham, N., & Goodson, B. (1995). *The School Development program and implementation: Preliminary evaluation evidence.* Paper presented at American Educational Research Association, San Francisco, CA.

National Center for Education Statistics. (1993). *Youth indicators 1993: Trends in the well-being of American youth* (Publication No. NCES 93-242). Washington, DC: U.S. Department of Education.

National Center for Service Integration. (1993). *Service integration: An annotated bibliog-*

raphy [Report from National Center for Children in Poverty]. New York: Information Clearinghouse.

National Commission on Children. (1991). *Beyond rhetoric: A new American agenda for children and families*. Washington, DC: National Commission on Children.

National Educational Goals Panel. (1994). *1994 goals report*. Washington, DC: U.S. Government Printing Office.

National Education Goals Panel. (1996). *The national education goals report 1995*. Washington, DC: U.S. Government Printing Office.

New Beginnings Evaluation Team. (1994). *The evaluation of New Beginnings*. San Diego, CA: San Diego City Schools.

Nichol, G. (1993, November). Model programs: Memphis City Schools Mental Health Center. *Communique/National Association of School Psychologists*, 1–2.

Office of Technology Assessment, U.S. Congress. (1991). *Adolescent health—volume I: Summary and policy options* (Publication No. OTA-H-468) Washington, DC: U.S. Government Printing Office.

Orange County Health Care Agency. (1989). [Brochure describing Children's Mental Health Program, South Orange County, California, May, 1989.]

Rienzo, B., & Button, J. (1993). The politics of school-based clinics: A community-level analysis. *Journal of School Health, 63*(6), 266–272.

Santelli, J., Kouzis, A., & Newcomer, S. (1996). School-based health center and adolescent use of primary care and hospital care. *Journal of Adolescent Health, 19*(4), 267–273.

Talley, R., Short, R., & Kolbe, L. (1995). *School health: Psychology's role*. Washington, DC: American Psychological Association.

Tyack, M. (1992). Health and social services in public schools: Historical perspectives. *The Future of the Children, 2*(1), 19–31.

Wagner, M., Golan, S., Shaver, L., Wechsler, M., & Kelley, F. (1994). *A healthy start for California's children and families: Early findings from a statewide evaluation of school-linked services*. Menlo Park, CA: SRI International.

Wolk, L., & Kaplan D. (1993). Frequent school-based clinic utilization: A comparative profile of problems and service needs. *Journal of Adolescent Health, 14*, 458–463.

3

Community-Based Service Integration: Family Resource Center Initiatives

Victor Romualdi and Jonathan Sandoval

Family Resource Centers in Community Settings

The impetus for integrated and comprehensive services delivered to families need not be the public schools or other governmental agencies. Grassroots community-based organizations may also organize to provide both a location and an administrative umbrella for the delivery of a wide range of services to children and families. An attempt to conceptualize and clarify emerging initiatives in service integration has led Marzke, Chimerine, Morrill, and Marks (1992) to describe four types of service-integration efforts at the local level: (a) community-based multiservice centers, (b) targeted programs in community settings, (c) institution-based programs in community settings, and (d) school-based programs.

Marzke et al.'s classification groups local initiatives on the basis of the relative role that community-based organizations (e.g., a Free Clinic) and private and public institutions (e.g., hospitals or schools) play in the collaborative structure and on the range of available services targeting either specific populations or needs, or more general areas of concern. This chapter describes the functioning of *family resource centers*, a generic term we shall use for community-based service providers, but particularly community-based multiservice centers. The major advantage of family resource centers is that they empower community members to shape their own futures. Community members may organize services they perceive themselves to require, and arrange for the delivery of services in a manner with which they are comfortable.

The definitions of *neighborhood* and *community* have been discussed extensively in the sociological literature and conceptualized variously, depending on the aspect of community life that is emphasized (Froland, Pancoast, Chapman, & Kimboko, 1981). There is general agreement, however, that community is a geographical entity within which neighborhoods represent distinct subunits, also defined by proximity (Garbarino & Kostelny, 1994). Within this general frame, Unger and Wandersman (1985) identified

three major components of the neighborhood construct: a social component, a cognitive component, and an affective component.

Social interactions among neighbors are a source of emotional, instrumental, and informational support. Social networks established by neighbors involve linkages with key individuals for personal benefit or linkages
developed collectively to improve neighborhood quality of life. The social
network component is especially important in understanding the viability
of a neighborhood as it strives to develop and maintain linkages to resources in the larger community (Warren, 1981).

Neighbors also develop thoughts and ideas about their physical and
social environment. Cognitive strategies, such as the mental mapping of
safe and unsafe areas and the adoption of self-imposed curfew rules,
clearly interact with social strategies.

The social and cognitive dimensions of neighboring are further associated with the development of affective states that characterize resident
relationships to neighbors and the neighborhood. Development of a sense
of community (perceived feelings of membership and belongingness) influences individual capacity for participation in collective problem solving
and resourcefulness (Sarason, 1974). Communities and neighborhoods,
then, are a logical starting point and locus for the establishment of family
service centers.

Historical Perspectives

Early Efforts

The neighborhood and local community have historically been central to
efforts to address the negative consequences of poverty in American society (Halpern, 1995). In her brief history of family support programs,
Weissbourd (1987) discussed three traditional programmatic efforts: parent education, self-help, and settlement houses. Each of these efforts has
continued to evolve throughout the twentieth century.

Parent education. Since the turn of the century, parent education has
been the primary means to shape parenting practices toward societal
norms and expectations. Its potential relevance for the well being of educationally and financially underprivileged children became more evident
in the years following the economic depression of the late 1920s. During
this period, social programs were created to ease widespread social breakdown. In the 1960s, parent education, in the context of public education,
was viewed as a method to redress discrimination against minorities by
increasing opportunity and equality. At this time, government involvement
and assistance assumed a central role in the promotion of parent education initiatives. Head Start is the most prominent example.

Self-help groups. Similarly, self-help groups have a long history in the
United States, dating back at least to the 1930s when Alcoholics Anony-

mous was founded. Similar groups with a self-help focus include the American Association of Retarded Children, the United Cerebral Palsy Foundation, and the Mothers' March of Dimes, to name just a few. These groups tend to adopt a relatively structured and problem-specific approach based on common issues and a need for mutual help. Self-help groups started with people sharing common issues and with the purpose of providing mutual help. By the 1960s, the self-help movement spawned an endless variety of programs designed to address issues and conditions such as drug dependency and spousal abuse.

Weissbourd (1987) noted that reasons for the growth of self-help groups parallel those motivating parents to contact resource programs: "a lack of services for the problems and concerns parents have; barriers such as expense, logistics, or red tape that make existing services hard to utilize; and the simple need to belong to a group of people with similar concerns" (p. 43). An additional similarity between self-help groups and current community-based organizations relates to parental distrust of professional involvement in their community.

Settlement houses. The settlement house experiment began at the turn of the century as a response to the stressful circumstances affecting large groups of individuals relocating to urban areas. Settlement houses were located in poor neighborhoods and were staffed by workers who could do local outreach. Settlement houses had a neighborhood focus and were concerned primarily with families and the quality of life. Their emphasis was on helping families use existing services, rather than replacing or duplicating them. Focus on the family, connection to a particular community, and reliance on existing community resources is clearly consistent with the ecological perspective central to present day efforts.

Reformers have historically called for improved social services to prevent or remedy ill health, crime, child neglect, poverty, addiction, hunger, and unemployment (Tyack, 1992). The merit of the settlement house movement included an increased awareness of the living conditions among poor children and an attempt to address basic needs through social reform (Schorr, 1988). Such philanthropic efforts, however, often originated from the assumption that poor parents were too ignorant to provide adequately for their children, thus requiring the intervention of professionals who could fix problems (e.g., Terman, 1929, quoted in Tyack, 1992). In the late twentieth century many functions, including child care and education, have been progressively transferred from the family to institutions, thus diminishing family control and autonomy (Kagan & Shelley, 1987). Solutions were often simplistic (e.g., playgrounds to eliminate juvenile delinquency), and immigrants were the most likely targets. Cultural resistance to professional practices also emerged historically (e.g., Italian mothers rioted in New York against any medical treatment at school in 1906). But by the 1940s, some form of public health service became a common feature in schools, and school-based professional roles (e.g., psychologists, social workers) became more prominent.

Recent History

Between the 1920s and the 1960s, school-based health and mental health services became institutionalized. Over time, institutionalization resulted in a shift from an interest in social justice to the objective of treating individual maladjustment (Tyack, 1992). Community agendas were often lost.

By mid-century, funding based on local property taxes resulted in service disparities between rich and poor, especially in schools. To address this pattern, reformers in the 1960s targeted disadvantaged populations (poor and minority) directly, and emphasis again shifted toward the whole family as the focus of intervention (Sedlak & Church, 1982). Head Start and Title I legislation exemplified this family-focused intervention model. However, critics of this approach decried its centralized and bureaucratic features, in addition to its treatment of clients as passive recipients (Tyack, Lowe, & Hansot, 1984).

In the 1970s and 1980s preoccupation about academic standards tended to replace concerns about poverty and inequality. The dissolution of the family, poverty, drugs, and violence became headline news, however, and the pressure for schools to become multipurpose agencies persisted. Academic instruction came to be considered just one in a broad range of services that might be delivered in this surviving primary institution.

School-Based Versus Community-Based Efforts

At present, there is general agreement about the need to serve children and families, but a dichotomy exists between those who want educational reform to focus on a *nation* at risk (school-based) and those who emphasize a concern for *children* at risk, especially low-income minority students (often community-based). The emphasis in this chapter is on community-based multiservice centers, but let us first contrast school-based with community-based efforts.[1]

School-Based Services

Although the recent momentum toward service integration has emphasized the role that schools can play as the locus of delivery and as facilitators of collaborative alliances, concerns have been expressed regarding the possibility that school-linked initiatives may "grow to reflect, primarily the operational desires and needs of the school" (Chaskin & Richman, 1992, p. 108). Having schools involved has the advantage of helping to assure that the educational needs of children are met and that children develop cognitive and social skills. Nevertheless, with the involvement of schools comes the possibility that educational priorities will dominate collaborative efforts.

---

[1]For an extensive discussion of school-based efforts, see chapter 2, this volume.

Chaskin and Richman (1992) have also pointed out that disenfranchised students and parents may view schools as antagonistic settings associated with feelings of failure and rejection. On the other hand, compared with other institutions housed in the communities, the school may also be perceived quite favorably, or at least neutrally.

An additional difficulty with school-based programs is that not all schools are truly local schools. Some school catchment areas may not correspond to the resident community that provides the context for children's social lives. Access to services located at magnet schools, for example, may be more difficult for some children than access to services provided within their primary communal context. When schools are neighborhood schools, they are more convenient for those who rely on public transportation.

Schools have an advantage as locations for multiple service centers in that staff often know and serve a minority community surrounding the school. However, because many schools work with a diverse population of children and families, they may be ill equipped to address specific cultural needs of each group. A small geographical area may concentrate several linguistic and cultural groups attracted to affordable housing. As a result, community-based organizations (e.g., Black churches) may be more effective in providing an access point for African American residents, who may represent a minority in a given school.

A final difficulty with basing services in schools is the heavy burden these institutions carry. It may not be feasible to expect schools to take on additional functions when they are often overwhelmed with existing responsibilities and inadequate funding.

Despite reservations about locating services in schools, little evidence exists to support the relative superiority of a community-based approach over a school-based approach. Ideally, growing attention to evaluation of integrated-services initiatives will address this issue (see chapter 14, this volume). In the meantime, we believe that a *goodness-of-fit* approach—matching service provision models to specific community needs—justifies a serious examination of community-based models as alternatives to the dominant trend toward school-linked initiatives.

Advantages of the Community-Based Focus

Family resource centers based in community settings have advantages not enjoyed by other approaches. Community-based centers do not carry the institutional stigma that schools may have, and they often are culturally specialized. Basing a center in a community setting also allows the center to address controversial issues that public agencies often cannot. The schools, for example, have had difficulty dealing with family planning and sexuality issues.

Family resource centers not associated with schools or other governmental agencies are free from some of the bureaucratic constraints imposed by formal organizations. The absence of union contracts, tenure rights, and the compartmentalization of knowledge within role, permit freedom of action and innovation in small, community-based agencies. Public funding always comes with strings attached, and community-based centers, although often less well-funded, can more easily avoid these "strings."

Perhaps the primary virtue of family service centers has more to do with sociopolitical factors than with these practical matters. Community-based family-services centers may be more likely to reflect local control and involvement than school-based centers, which often are constrained by the need to carry out institutional mandates. As a result, neighborhood centers may be perceived by clients as more responsive to grass-root voices and specific community needs.

Conceptual Issues and Challenges in Community-Based Service Delivery

A number of conceptual issues and challenges confront the developers of community-based family-services centers.

Knowledge of Resources

In reporting findings from a study on child maltreatment Garbarino and Kostelny (1992) pointed out that high-risk community residents knew less about community services and agencies that were available and showed little evidence of a network or support system (either formal or informal). In contrast, within low-risk neighborhoods there were more services available, respondents knew more about what was available, and there were strong informal and formal social support networks. Of particular interest was the finding that social service agencies staff reflected the attitudes and perceptions characterized by isolation and depression typically reported by resident families. Garbarino and Kostelny (1994) concluded that "social service agencies in a community mirror the problems faced by the community" (p. 311).

Social Integration

Garbarino and Kostelny (1994) emphasized the importance that social integration plays in understanding the meaning of social impoverishment. The construct of *social integration*, or connection among individuals on a social level and lack of isolation, is reflected by indicators related to levels of unemployment, stability of residence, possession of a telephone, and vacancy rates. There is evidence, for example, that differences in levels of child maltreatment between two economically similar neighborhoods are associated with differences in levels of social integration (Garbarino & Kostelny, 1994).

The implications of Garbarino and Kostelny's analysis are relevant for the development of community-based interventions. On the one hand, their discussion indicates that although community-based efforts have the potential to enhance social support and nurturance, the simple introduction or reintroduction of direct services is not likely to be effective unless the need for renewed economic opportunities is also addressed. On the other hand, community-based efforts need to address neighborhood patterns, particularly those related to increasing violence, that limit access to services even when services do exist and create work conditions for project staff that are likely to generate feelings of inadequacy. This conclusion speaks directly to the issues of comprehensiveness understood not only as a broad spectrum of professional family services but also as inclusive of efforts toward socioeconomic development and peace keeping as well as ongoing support for community-based workers.

For example, the impact of growing community violence is especially critical in affecting the ability of residents and professionals to make a commitment to social support programs (Garbarino, 1992). Community violence affects parental willingness to attend night meetings and professionals' safety in conducting necessary home visits. If violence is not directly addressed, other community-based programs will wither and die.

Deficit Orientation

There is a tendency in recent family support literature to consider a deficit orientation (i.e., placing emphasis on disease and lack of ability) as outmoded and associated with massive categorical assistance programs such as Aid to Families With Dependent Children (AFDC; see, for example, Moroney, 1987; Weissbourd, 1987, 1994). Deficit-based programs feature eligibility criteria that emphasize sickness or inadequacy, prescriptive practices for families, and expert advice by health, educational, and mental health professionals.

Many assume the deficit orientation has disappeared; however, elements of this "old fashioned" approach may still be found in recent efforts, especially when the intended target includes minority and bilingual families. Typically, such programs require economically disadvantaged parents (and especially mothers) to attend child development and family management workshops and lectures (Bowman, 1994).

Moroney (1980) reviewed professional practices in medicine, psychiatry, psychology, and social work and concluded that most professionals tended to view families as less than capable caregivers. Even when family members were considered part of the helping team, they were characterized as secondary to professionals. The author concluded that professionals were socialized to such a perspective through their training, commonly based on the pathology-oriented medical model subsequently reinforced by organizational and institutional practices. In this context, Pinker (1973) argued that traditionally the interaction between families and government social services has been based on the principle of *unilateral exchange*, ruling out any reciprocity among equals and fostering continued dependency on providers.

The central question raised, for example, by Powell (1982), is whether programs are imposing middle-class child and family values on non-middle-class groups. Sigel (1983) contended that expert knowledge on child development and parenting developed largely from White middle-class samples has limited construct validity when applied across populations. Although all may not agree with Sigel, minimizing a deficit orientation reduces the likelihood of the imposition of unfair standards and practices on a minority community.

Ecological Perspectives

Recent legislation promoting comprehensive and collaborative service provision (e.g., Healthy Start in California) has explicitly emphasized the need to expand the area of intervention to address school problems, such as low attendance, in the context of social factors affecting family functioning and community trends. This emphasis is consistent with an ecological view of human development (Bronfenbrenner, 1979a) as an alternative to a narrowly defined medical model of intervention and a deficit-based orientation in service provision. Bronfenbrenner's (1979b) ecological perspective is based on the assumption that "behavior evolves as a function of the interplay between person and environment" (p. 16). He concluded that psychological research and practice in the 1970s concentrated to a large degree on the properties of the person and relied on simplistic characterizations of environmental factors. Bronfenbrenner conceptualized the ecological environment as a set of nested and interacting structures including the school, the home, and other systems that do not necessarily involve a person as an active participant but that nonetheless affect his or her development. In Bronfenbrenner's view, family functioning can only be understood as a function of cultural, racial, and socioeconomic characteristics of the community, as well as of the policies of the nation. The ecological perspective, then, may be differentiated from behavioral research suggesting that changes in child behavior can be accomplished through changes in parent behavior. Whereas the latter emphasizes standardized practices (e.g., child management) leading to desired outcomes (e.g., compliance), the ecological view stresses that the meaning of a certain behavior varies across social groupings and must be viewed (and altered) in context (Bowman, 1994).

Thus Bronfenbrenner (1979b) suggested that deteriorating developmental outcomes among children are better viewed by focusing on the adverse circumstances families are struggling against. Broadening the focus from family dynamics to the sources of stress and support in the external environment allows professionals to uncover family strengths and to identify new goals for public policy. He wrote, "Most families are doing the best they can under the circumstances; our task is to try to change the circumstances and not the families themselves" (p. 103).

A clear implication of an ecological perspective for family support efforts is that considering children and families in context involves understanding diversity, including individual, family, racial, sociocultural, ethnic, and socioeconomic characteristics. However, many family support programs that subscribe to an ecological perspective tend to reduce such a consideration to an emphasis on the family as the primary socializing institution, excluding from consideration factors external to the family but clearly related to its functioning (Weiss, 1987), such as economic opportunities, discriminatory practices, political climate, and availability of resources. By virtue of their comprehensive and collaborative nature, multidisciplinary family centers, both in schools and in the community, have the potential to bring about interventions based on an ecological perspective. However, ecologically valid interventions cannot be based solely on professional practices. The next section addresses the need to revisit family–professional interactions as an essential element in developing a democratic alternative to deficit-oriented approaches.

Diversity and Parent–Professional Interactions

Improving parent–professional interactions is central to the success of community-based programs. Harry's (1992a, 1992b) study of Latino families served by the special education system provides an excellent example of issues involved in parent–professional discourse. Special education evidences a prevalent concern for documentation rather than information sharing and decision making. Furthermore, the system appears to function under the assumption of a linear, hierarchical model of organizational structure and decision making. Clear authority lines and step-by-step problem solving may stifle, rather than promote, parent participation. In addition, professional discourse within this system is characterized by low-context, abstract language (often technical terms and acronyms). Parents from high-context cultures (such as Latinos), who tend to value personal and informal exchanges, may find it hard to function in low-context structures (Delgado-Gaitan, 1994b). The professional tools that have been developed to ensure objectivity and accountability (such as standardized tests) thus interfere with communication.

Institutional practices that are likely to create and maintain a status (and power) differential between professionals and parents include reliance on written communication, use of professional jargon, and exclusive use of English. The barriers created by the abstract and often obscure nature of professional discourse within the school system has been widely documented in the ethnographic literature (e.g., Mehan, Hertweck, & Meihls, 1986) and appear to be representative of practices typical of most social services.

One way to address the issue of diversity in the family-support movement has been to examine the knowledge base of a particular culture and to amend professional practices accordingly. In this regard, *cultural scripts* (culture-specific patterns of communication and social interaction uncovered by ethnographic research), may be used to help understand family functioning, parenting practices, and informal support network systems.

In the case of Latinos the following constructs have emerged from research (Delgado-Gaitan, 1994a; Greenfield, 1994; Harry, 1992a, 1992b): high-context communication, interdependence orientation (concern for collectivity); focus on immigrant generation socialization for survival (i.e., practices that are adaptive in the country of origin but less effective in taking advantage of new opportunities); apprenticeship approach to teaching and learning; emphasis on respect for elders; and deference toward experts (e.g., teachers, physicians). Cultural scripts can be useful to improve professional understanding of a specific community. Reluctance to approach professionals, for example, may be better understood as a result of deference rather than as a sign of low interest or unconditional agreement. Interdependence orientation may be valued as a strength facilitating community organization and mutual support rather than seen as a lack of individual initiative.

Guidelines for professional behavior based on this knowledge base have been developed (e.g., Barona, Santos de Barona, Flores, & Gutierrez, 1990), and bilingual/bicultural competency requirements have only recently begun to be built into accreditation, credentialing, and licensing standards. Attention has been given in mental health literature, for example, to the level of acculturation of a particular family or person and to the role that external factors such as economic hardship and discrimination may have in increasing stress (Sue & Sue, 1990). By understanding the adaptive value of parents' "everyday cognition" (Tharp & Gallimore, 1988), professionals can increase the validity of consultation and move away from the often abstract and unilateral teaching of parent-training efforts. A parent–professional collaboration model that emphasizes knowledge in context would be consistent, for example, with the previously mentioned apprenticeship model of learning (Tharp & Gallimore, 1988).

In the course of advocating professional sensitivity to diversity, concern has arisen regarding the danger of applying cultural concepts in stereotypical fashion, ignoring important between- and within-group differences among Latino populations. Thus, Garcia (1994) stressed that professionals may benefit from understanding the cultural orientations that are widely held in a person's ethnic community. However, he concluded that "this inventory of knowledge should be viewed only as background information. The question of its applicability to the particular person should be treated as inherently problematic" (p. 256).

Delgado-Gaitan (1993) discussed how she came to reconcile her roles of researcher and facilitator among the Spanish-speaking parents she studied who were attempting to gain influence in their local schools. The same kind of reflective work could be beneficial among professionals interested in reconciling their role as experts with new roles shaped around facilitating empowerment. Professionals, including health, mental health, and community-based and school-based practitioners, may benefit from critical reflection on the knowledge model that traditionally has shaped their work (e.g., passive transmission), to embrace a perspective that is more consistent with a new role (e.g., facilitator). The possibility of developing a consultation model for parent–professional interactions that can

eliminate hierarchical distinctions and that is based on reciprocal negotiation should be considered. This shift seems consistent with the goal
expressed by researchers (Delgado-Gaitan, 1995; Lareau, 1989) to increase
minority and working-class parents' opportunities to shape their child's
school (as well as other institutions).

The task of reconfiguring family–expert interactions, however, cannot
rely solely on new training and updated professional guidelines. An emerging issue in the comprehensive services movement has been the opportunity for shared governance of local initiatives, to involve community members beyond the role of mere service recipients. The family aspiration
toward a more meaningful participation in human-service delivery has
been reflected by the recurring theme of empowerment.

Empowerment

A more radical perspective on diversity and institutional behavior has
emerged around the idea of empowerment. The concept of empowerment
has unfortunately been widely used (and abused) in a variety of contexts
and with varying meanings. On one hand, empowerment has come to represent the type of behavioral and attitudinal changes that are associated
with the psychological constructs of self-efficacy and self-esteem. An example of this orientation is found in Williams (1987): "Family support
programs should seek to empower parents, help family members feel better about themselves, and look for strengths within families to help them
gain some control over their environment" (p. 299). This conceptualization
emphasizes changes at the personal level (e.g., increased self-concept and
economic self-sufficiency) and at the family functioning level (e.g.,
parent–child interactions) resulting from expert interventions (e.g. Seitz,
Rosenbaum, & Apfel, 1985). The notion of empowerment as a set of specific
outcomes continues to be popular in recent family support programs.

An alternate view of empowerment developed independently of the
family support movement is Freire's critical pedagogy (Freire, 1972).
Within this perspective, Delgado-Gaitan (1994a) characterized empowerment as a process of collective critical reflection through which "people
lacking an equal share of valued resources gain greater access to and control over those resources" (p. 7). Although such a process does include steps
to increase one's personal efficacy, it is the collective realizations of concerns and strengths that is emphasized here. Delgado-Gaitan (1990) has
documented the empowerment process as it was generated among Latino
families in Carpinteria, California, by family literacy activities.

Although the collective empowerment process has not developed in
connection to intervention programs and, in fact, explicitly differentiated
itself from interventionist thinking (Delgado-Gaitan, 1995), some family
support initiatives have attempted to translate it into practice. For example, Cochran and Woolever (1983) reported on a program (Family Matters) that originated from a critical view of research on families as excessively focused on the micro-level. Cochran and Woolever argued that social

and structural systems may hold the key for a better understanding of family functioning and that meaningful changes cannot be limited to individual self-perceptions and spousal interaction patterns. Neighboring behavior (informal networking) and institutional behavior (organizational change) serve as crucial target variables.

Consistent with this formulation, Family Matters was based on certain assumptions: (a) all families have strengths, (b) folkways provide a relevant perspective on child rearing, (c) various family forms are legitimate and can be effective, and (d) cultural differences are both valid and valuable. These assumptions result in practices including open eligibility for services (rather than eligibility based on evidence of incompetence), respect for nonexpert knowledge that becomes collective knowledge through community linking, belief that successful child rearing depends on the resources a parent can marshal rather than on any single parent characteristic, and the conviction that cultural and ethnic heritage are part of the family's resources and strengths. Although Family Matters did attempt to change self-perceptions, the goal was not expressed exclusively in psychological terms and included developing the confidence to fill new roles such as change facilitator in the community and child advocate. Implicit in Cochran's view was an attempt to address parents' needs as adults rather than parents, thus focusing on external stressors rather than on personal inadequacy. Accordingly, program workers, who were members of the community, had a facilitative, rather than prescriptive, role.

Informal Parent Networks

In discussing the relevance of community-based initiatives, it is essential to understand the potential that informal parent networks offer. These networks have been discussed from the inception of the family-support movement, although their use has often been narrowly restricted or made secondary to essential program goals (Weiss, 1987). Recent ethnographic studies provide examples of naturally occurring (parent generated) informal networks through which parents "collectively learn ways of talking about and drawing upon knowledge and understandings that are outside of their individual experience" (Vasquez, Pease-Alvarez, & Shannon, 1994, p. 112). Spontaneously occurring networks offer a building block for identifying needs that are relevant to a community of families and a catalyst for addressing them. However, as Vasquez et al. (1994) pointed out, the negotiation of institutional and professional discourse requires a level of education, technical knowledge, and understanding of the norms of the dominant Anglo culture that are not immediately available to parents recently immigrated from other countries. Access to specialized knowledge is one of the crucial factors limiting the bargaining positions that minority parents have with institutions. Although Vasquez et al. (1994) believe that schools can play an important role in facilitating the development of knowledge and skills necessary for active participation in society, such a role might more naturally be extended to community-based agencies.

Professional Strategies and Informal Networks

Thus, an essential issue for community-based initiatives is the role of informal helping networks and the strategies that human service agencies may adopt to ensure productive connections with these naturally occurring support systems. *Helping networks* are here defined as "that set of social relationships which provide care, support, and other forms of assistance for people who experience social and health related problems of the sort which might also be of concern to human service agencies" (Froland, Pancoast, Chapman, & Kimboko, 1981, p. 20). Helping networks present a vantage point in understanding the strengths of a specific community. Furthermore, they provide a model of expertise based on common background and experience, overcoming the dichotomy between helpers and clients often found in organized agency interventions. It is evident that not all the complex needs of contemporary communities can be met through informal networks. Demographic and societal trends (e.g., violence, poverty) associated with the previously described progressive decline of disenfranchised neighborhoods have critically impaired network functioning. Nevertheless, an understanding of actual and potential sources of social capital (Coleman, 1987) at the community level is imperative for the promotion of complementarity between professional services and informal support (Froland et al., 1981).

Increasingly, professionals have begun to emphasize informal networks in their interventions (e.g. Trimble, 1980), a practice that may become problematic in light of formal and procedural practices of professionals and agencies (Froland, 1980). In their study of 30 programs within agencies that were working with informal support systems, Froland et al. (1981) identified three different types of relationships underlying the spectrum of linkages between staff and helpers: coordinative, collegial, and directive. The typology was developed on the basis of characteristics indicating how authority and responsibility for selecting and carrying out tasks were divided.

The *coordinative* type of relationship was characterized by a high degree of independence among helpers, who were primarily responsible for activities and received minimal supervision from agency staff. An example of this model may be agency involvement with existing volunteer "clothes closet" efforts throughout a community to increase promotion and coordination. The *collegial* relationship was characterized by less independence and more interdependence than the coordinative relationship. Staff and helpers developed more exclusive, one-to-one relationships that closely resembled the egalitarian interaction often described in collaborative consultation. Agency staff working with neighborhood leaders to contact families with specific needs in the community is an example of this approach. The *directive* relationship involved systematic recruitment of helpers and often required a formal commitment from those selected. The helpers worked on staff-determined tasks under supervision and monitoring. Bilingual and bicultural community members selected to work as outreach workers exemplify such an approach.

Froland et al. (1981) also identified five different strategies, which are detailed throughout the remainder of this section, that agencies used in their collaboration with helping networks. The *personal networks strategy* focuses on an individual client support system. Consultation and assistance provided to family members in supporting a child's mental health needs is an example of this strategy, which primarily involves a collegial relationship.

Volunteer linking relates to the use of citizen volunteers, usually with experience, skills, and interests relevant to the client's case. An example of this strategy includes helping disabled clients develop independent living skills by linking them to other disabled residents who have made a successful adjustment. This strategy may rely on primarily directive relationships, depending on the helper's level of formal involvement.

Mutual aid networks are similar to self-help organizations and provide mutual support among individuals facing similar issues. Agencies may help establish peer support groups (e.g., young mothers) or may consult with existing groups and support their activities (e.g., church-sponsored bereavement support groups). Collaborative relationships associated with this strategy tend to be collegial with existing networks and coordinative with created networks. Two additional strategies have a more marked neighborhood focus. The *neighborhood helper* strategy entails providing collegial assistance to local leaders identified by reputation such as bicultural residents helping new immigrants with translation and advocacy. The *community empowerment* strategy focuses on identifying community opinion leaders and providing coordinative assistance in their task of representing a range of local interest groups. Support to local and informal efforts to organize against neighborhood violence and gang activities is an example of this strategy.

Froland and his colleagues (1981) pointed out that although these strategies can be conceptualized as separate approaches, most of the agencies they surveyed combined strategies to maximize the number of resources and relationships mobilized around a supportive task. When working with a client's personal network, for example, the use of the mutual aid strategy may help in broadening an otherwise limited supported system. Likewise, while using the community empowerment approach, agencies may rely on other client-related strategies to address specific needs identified within the community during the service-planning phase.

Program Models

Having discussed some of the conceptual issues relevant to the development of community-based service integration, we now want to provide examples of specific initiatives. The following section is not meant to provide a comprehensive review of programs but rather a description of selected efforts chosen to demonstrate the range of interventions and the variety of organizational approaches. Selection of programs was based on availability of documentation and on our personal experience.

Black Churches as Community Centers

Historically Black churches have not only provided religious and spiritual guidance to their parishioners, but have acted as centers of emotional, economic, and social support for families (Lincoln & Mamiya, 1990). A recent poll showed that the great majority of African Americans viewed Black churches as effective in representing the interests of African American communities ("Who speaks for Black America?", 1992). Caldwell and her colleagues (Caldwell, Greene, & Billingsley, 1994) reported on a longitudinal study on the interactions between family and church within African American communities. Their sample included 635 churches in the north and northeastern region of the states. They reported that 67% of the churches sponsored at least one outreach program targeting the wider community, with a total of 1,804 community-outreach programs. The majority of the programs were family-support programs including interventions such as family counseling, food and clothing distribution, adult literacy, and support programs for men and women. Basic needs assistance was the most frequently featured intervention.

Of particular interest from a service-integration perspective was the finding that churches often acted as mediators between the African American family and the formal system of service delivery. Churches performed this function by providing referrals and being involved in active collaboration with local police; welfare, health, housing, and recreation departments; and schools, hospitals, and prisons. Most churches helped their members in making effective contacts with community agencies and sometimes provided a site for the delivery of services such as immunization clinics. Occasionally, churches functioned as centralized referral centers.

In an effort to promote the identification of churches that might be more responsive to outreach efforts, Caldwell et al. (1994) described church characteristics that were associated with the provision of family support programs. These churches tended to be older and more well established (e.g., were able to purchase their church building and had a large congregation), to have a high percentage of female members, to employ paid clergy, and to be more willing to let community groups use church facilities.

Caldwell et al. (1994) concluded that Black churches had a "great unrealized potential . . . to provide an infrastructure for coordinating and furnishing an array of family support services within African American communities" (p. 136). By relying largely on volunteers, Black churches have a better chance to establish contacts with families than formal service providers and may help efforts to work with hard-to-reach families. Obstacles to a greater church involvement included a reluctance to abide by intrusive government regulations and the inability to negotiate the grantsmanship process. The development of information centers and clearinghouses within the church network may help in overcoming such barriers.

Community Centers Resulting From System Change

An example of a community center approach to services delivery is the Center for Integrated Services for Families and Neighborhoods (1994). This approach emphasizes the need to replace bureaucratic control over local initiatives with a system of neighborhood-based governance, given that resident participation in service initiatives is relegated to the role of advocate or advisor (Bolton, 1994). The recommended approach includes and involves residents and their elected representatives, and creates opportunities to consolidate various functions and budgets within a unified system. According to Bolton (1994), "*Consolidation* of governance and program functions is a more ambitious goal than *collaboration* among the providers of various services" (p. 11), which enables better control over program outcomes and a more accurate understanding of cost-effectiveness issues as they relate to local interventions. In locally controlled programs, problems are addressed as they are perceived and experienced at the neighborhood level, rather than being reshaped around bureaucratic constraints.

This center has worked on identifying initiatives in California that share this ambitious goal and that have thoroughly addressed the need to develop interventions that are ecologically sound. One of these exemplary programs is based in North Richmond, a small urban community in Contra Costa County, California. The first step to systemic restructuring in this program was the creation of the North Richmond Municipal Advisory Council (MAC) in 1992 as a result of resident pressure for community redevelopment. MAC was representative of various constituent groups, including youth, seniors, homeowners, and renters, and various cultural communities, such as African American, Latino, and Laotian men and women. After completing an extensive resource assessment to account for all existing intervention in the community, MAC received foundation support to build a partnership with the county, city, and nonprofit organizations to develop a comprehensive plan of intervention. By surveying each household and community group, the County Board of Supervisors avoided making any *a priori* decision on who should be included in the Council, thus fostering the development of a truly representative team. Council membership was also left free to grow incrementally as new needs arose. Although this was not presented as an optimal strategy because it often led to a dispersion of efforts and resources, it constituted a valid attempt to deal with the inevitable conflict emerging among different perspectives on community needs. By choosing the difficult and time-consuming road of democratic consensus building, rather than a stifled problem-solving process based on convenience, MAC has functioned as an arena for discussion that has resulted in wide community support and commitment. An additional and irreplaceable component of the North Richmond initiative has been the substantial commitment of public agencies to relocate a number of workers under the direction and supervision of the community-based council, thus avoiding an unfair weighting of institutional representatives in the conflict-resolution process.

Family Service Centers

Formal family service centers represent a form of collaborative action that brings together staff and programs from various agencies into one location to serve a community (Kadel, 1992). These centers usually incorporate case management, collaborative councils, and colocation of services. Although such an approach may have system-wide policy implications, its major focus is on improved service provision (sometimes this model is referred to as "one-stop shopping").

Compared with initiatives deliberately promoting increased political participation within a community, these centers represent a more traditional approach to community revitalization and human services reform. This strategy is exemplified by three pilot projects in the Sacramento, California, urban area promoted by the County Board of Supervisors and the City Council (Scott & Gatten, 1994). The three projects originated after a survey of over 50,000 service recipients, interviews with agency staff at different levels, and dialogue with community organizations. Rather than focusing on generating participation leading to political action, these projects focus on increasing service accessibility and effectiveness by increasing coordination, decentralizing executive decision making, and increasing preventive activities through reduced caseloads.

Each project was developed by a separate planning team including mid-level managers, line staff, client representatives, and community-based organizations. The teams identified community needs and developed appropriate service components. The staff composition at each pilot project included several public assistance workers (AFDC, Medi-Cal, General Assistance, and Food Stamps), family maintenance or family reunification social workers, alcohol and drug counselors, GAIN employment workers and probation officers, and when available, law enforcement, and community-based organization workers. Staff cross-training was provided in an attempt to (a) foster mutual awareness across representatives of different fields, (b) promote common practices and procedures, and (c) develop consistent policies. Multidisciplinary teams that handle case management and provide direct service meet daily to discuss new and ongoing cases, assess progress, and decide on interventions. Once service plans are developed, they are offered to and discussed with individual families. The adoption of a single, inclusive plan aims at avoiding duplication of effort and increasing accountability. As policy issues arise, team suggestions for possible resolution are forwarded to a higher level human services cabinet. Feedback from service recipients occurs throughout planning and implementation of a service plan in an attempt to respond to client needs.

Evidence of the effectiveness of these models and of service-integration initiatives in general are still sketchy and anecdotal (Knapp, 1995). In fact, little agreement exists on how to define effectiveness for comprehensive programs as competing views emphasize alternatively cost containment, individual client outcomes, family empowerment, and extent of systemic change. We can hope, however, that an ongoing clarification of the challenges these initiatives face may help in guiding future evaluation research.

Conclusions

As Halpern (1995) pointed out

> [n]eighborhood-based services have always embodied multiple purposes—to assist poor people in coping with the hardships of poverty and economic insecurity, to guide and monitor them in their roles as parents, to teach them middle-class ways and link them to mainstream opportunities, to provide basic health care, to counsel, encourage, organize, advocate for. (p. 192)

As past efforts have often been characterized by an acculturation bias that favored mainstream and professional knowledge over the diversity of families' adaptive strategies (as is implicit in Halpern's description), the recent wave of initiatives faces the challenge of reconciling expert contribution with a growing demand for family empowerment. Current efforts represent a renewed interest in responding to the increasingly deteriorating fabric of poor neighborhoods through initiatives involving comprehensive approaches, committed partnerships, and multilevel interventions.

The widespread emergence of school- and community-based initiatives offering comprehensive and integrated human services reflects a growing recognition that developmental and educational outcomes are fundamentally affected by factors that are often external to the family. Consequently, the focus for intervention is essentially directed at the surrounding community.

The community-based family service center model has advantages over the school-based approach. It has potentially fewer institutional constraints and more direct contacts with naturally occurring networks that represent the building blocks of community organization. The organizational and programmatic flexibility of community-based centers may also facilitate a more intimate connection with specific community needs. On the other hand, community-based centers may lack the resources that schools are able to muster and may be less able than school-based centers to have direct access to children.

As school-based initiatives are often characterized by a strong community focus and community-based initiatives often cannot survive without the committed involvement of neighborhood schools, the distinction between these two models may decrease in the future. However, to the extent that model differences are still identifiable they should be conceptualized and researched in regard to their relative effectiveness. This appears to the next step in family-support-movement research.

References

Barona, A., Santos de Barona, M., Flores, A., & Gutierrez, M. (1990). Critical issues in training school psychologists to serve minority school children. In A. Barona & E. Garcia (Eds.), *Children at risk: Poverty, minority status and other issues in educational equity* (pp. 187–200). Washington, DC: National Association of School Psychologists.

Bolton, A. (1994). A strategy for distressed neighborhoods. In The Center for Integrated Services for Families and Neighborhoods (Ed.), *Strategies for distressed neighborhoods* (pp. 5–29). Sacramento, CA: Author.

Bowman, B. (1994). Home and school: The unresolved relationship. In S. L. Kagan & B. Weissbourd (Eds.), *Putting families first* (pp. 51–72). San Francisco: Jossey-Bass.

Bronfenbrenner, U. (1979a). Beyond the deficit model in child and family policy. *Teacher's College Record, 81,* 95–104.

Bronfenbrenner, U. (1979b). *The ecology of human development: Experiments by nature and design.* Cambridge, MA: Harvard University Press.

Caldwell, C. H., Greene, A. D., & Billingsley, A. (1994). Family support programs in Black churches. In S. Kagan & B. Weissbourd (Eds.), *Putting families first: America's family support movement and the challenge of change* (pp. 137–160). San Francisco: Jossey-Bass.

Center for Integrated Services for Families and Neighborhoods. (1994). *Strategies for distressed neighborhoods.* Sacramento, CA: Author.

Chaskin, R. J., & Richman, H. A. (1992). Concerns about school-linked services: Institution-based versus community-based models. *The Future of Children, 2,* 107–117.

Cochran, M., & Woolever, F. (1983). Beyond the deficit model: The empowerment of parents with information and information supports. In I. E. Sigel & L. M. Laosa (Eds.), *Changing families* (pp. 225–245). New York: Plenum Press.

Coleman, J. S. (1987). Families and schools. *Educational Researcher, 16*(6), 32–38.

Delgado-Gaitan, C. (1990). *Literacy for empowerment: The role of parents in children's education.* London: Falmer Press.

Delgado-Gaitan, C. (1993). Researching change and changing the researcher. *Harvard Educational Review, 63,* 389–411.

Delgado-Gaitan, C. (1994a). Socializing young children in Mexican-American families: An intergenerational perspective. In P. Greenfield & R. Cocking (Eds.), *Cross-cultural roots of minority child development* (pp. 55–86). Hillsdale, NJ: Lawrence Erlbaum Associates.

Delgado-Gaitan, C. (1994b). Spanish-speaking families' involvement in schools. In C. L. Fagnano & B. Z. Werber (Eds.), *School, family and community interaction* (pp. 85–98). San Francisco: Westview Press.

Delgado-Gaitan, C. (1995). *Protean literacy: Extending the discourse on empowerment.* London: The Falmer Press.

Freire, P. (1972). *Pedagogy of the oppressed.* New York: Herder & Herder.

Froland, C. (1980). Formal and informal care: Discontinuities in a continuum. *Social Service Review, 54,* 572–587.

Froland, C., Pancoast, D. L., Chapman, N. J., & Kimboko, P. J. (1981). *Helping networks and human services.* Newbury Park, CA: Sage.

Garbarino, J. (1992). *Children and families in the social environment* (2nd ed.). Hawthorne, NY: Aldine.

Garbarino, J., & Kostelny, K. (1992). Child maltreatment as a community problem. *International Journal of Child Abuse and Neglect, 16,* 455–464.

Garbarino, J., & Kostelny, K. (1994). Family support and community development. In S. L. Kagan & B. Weissbourd (Eds.), *Putting families first: America's family support movement and the challenge of change.* San Francisco: Jossey-Bass.

Garcia, E. E. (1994). Addressing the challenges of diversity. In S. L. Kagan & B. Weissbourd (Eds.), *Putting families first* (pp. 243–275). San Francisco: Jossey-Bass.

Greenfield, P. (1994). Independence and interdependence as developmental scripts: Implications for theory, research and practice. In P. Greenfield & R. Cocking (Eds.), *Cross-cultural roots of minority child development* (pp. 1–37). Hillsdale, NJ: Erlbaum.

Halpern, R. (1995). *Rebuilding the inner city: A history of neighborhood initiatives to address poverty in the United States*. New York: Columbia University Press.

Harry, B. (1992a). *Cultural diversity, families, and the special education system*. New York: The Teachers College Press.

Harry, B. (1992b). An ethnographic study of cross-cultural communication with Puerto Rican-American Families in the special education system. *American Educational Research Journal, 29*, 471–494.

Kadel, S. (1992). *Interagency collaboration: Improving the delivery of service to children and families*. Tallahassee, FL: SouthEastern Regional Vision for Education (SERVE).

Kagan, S. L., & Shelley, A. (1987). The promise and problems of family support programs. In S. Kagan, D. Powell, B. Weissbourd, & E. Zigler (Eds.), *America's family support programs* (pp. 3–18). New Haven: Yale University Press.

Knapp, M. (1995). How shall we study comprehensive, collaborative services for children and families? *Educational Researcher, 24*, 5–10.

Lareau, A. (1989). *Home advantage: Social class and parental intervention in elementary education*. New York: Falmer.

Lincoln, C. E., & Mamiya, L. (1990). *The Black church in the African American experience*. Durham, NC: Duke University Press.

Marzke, C., Chimerine, C., Morrill, W., & Marks, E. (1992). *Service integration programs in community settings* (Contract No. LC 89089001). Washington, DC: U.S. Department of Education and U.S. Department of Health and Human Services.

Mehan, H., Hertweck, A., & Meihls, J. L. (1986). *Handicapping the handicapped*. Stanford, CA: Stanford University Press.

Moroney, R. (1980). *Families, social services and social policy*. Washington DC: U.S. Government Printing Office.

Moroney, R. (1987). Social support systems: Families and social policy. In S. Kagan, D. Powell, B. Weissbourd, & E. Zigler (Eds.), *America's family support programs* (pp. 21–37). New Haven: Yale University Press.

Pinker, R. (1973). *Social theory and social policy*. London: Heinemann.

Powell, D. (1982). From child to parent: Changing conceptions of early childhood intervention. In W. M. Bridgeland & E. A. Duane (Eds.), *The Annals of the American Academy of Political and Social Science, 461*, 135–144.

Sarason, S. B. (1974). *The psychological sense of community: Prospects for a community psychology*. San Francisco: Jossey-Bass.

Schorr, L. B. (1988). *Within our reach*. New York: Double Day.

Scott T., III, & Gatten, C. (1994). An early perspective on human services reform in Sacramento, California. In The Center for Integrated Services for Families and Neighborhoods (Ed.), *Strategies for distressed neighborhoods* (59–67). Sacramento, CA: Author.

Sedlak, M., & Church, R. (1982). *A history of social services delivered to youth 1980–1977*. Final report to the National Institute of Education. Washington, DC: NIE.

Seitz, V., Rosenbaum, L., & Apfel, N. (1985). Effects of family support intervention: A ten-year follow-up. *Child Development, 54*, 376–391.

Sigel, I. E. (1983). The ethics of intervention. In I. E. Sigel & L. M. Laosa (Eds.), *Changing families* (pp. 1–21). New York: Plenum Press.

Sue, D. W., & Sue, D. (1990). *Counseling the culturally different: Theory and practice*. New York: Wiley.

Tharp, R. G., & Gallimore, R. (1988). *Rousing minds to life*. NY: Cambridge University Press.

Trimble, D. (1980). A guide to the network therapies. *Connections, 3*, 9–21.

Tyack, D. (1992). Health and social services in public schools: Historical perspectives. *Future of Children, 2*(1), 19–31.

Tyack, D. H., Lowe, J., & Hansot, E. (1984). *Public schools in hard times: The Great Depression and recent years*. Cambridge, MA: Harvard University Press.

Unger, D. G., & Wandersman, A. (1985). The importance of neighbors: The social, cognitive, and affective components of neighboring. *American Journal of Community Psychology, 13*, 139–169.

Vasquez, O. A., Pease-Alvarez, L., & Shannon, S. (1994). *Pushing boundaries: Language and culture in a Mexicano community*. New York: Cambridge University Press.

Warren, D. I. (1981). *Helping networks*. Notre Dame, IN: University of Notre Dame Press.

Weiss, H. (1987). Family support and education in early childhood programs. In S. Kagan, D. Powell, B. Weissbourd, & E. Zigler (Eds.), *America's family support programs* (pp. 133–160). New Haven, CT: Yale University Press.

Weissbourd, B. (1987). A brief history of social support programs. In S. L. Kagan, D. R. Powell, B. Weissbourd, & E. Zigler (Eds.), *America's family support programs: Perspectives and prospects*. New Haven, CT: Yale University Press.

Weissbourd, B. (1994). The evolution of the family resource movement. In S. L. Kagan & B. Weissbourd (Eds.). *Putting families first* (pp. 28–47). San Francisco: Jossey-Bass.

Who speaks for Black America? (1992, February 9). *Detroit News and Free Press*, 23–25.

Williams, K. (1987). Cultural diversity in family support. In S. L. Kagan, D. R. Powell, B. Weissbourd, & E. Zigler (Eds.), *America's family support programs: Perspectives and prospects* (pp. 295–307). New Haven, CT: Yale University Press.

4

Conceptual and Empirical Foundations of Family-Centered Practice

Carl J. Dunst

Although the use of the term *family centered* can be traced historically to the 1950s and 1960s (e.g., Birt, 1956; Hungerford, 1964; Scherz, 1953; Wiedenbach, 1967), it was only a decade ago that the operational features of family-centered practices began to be articulated (Kopp, 1987; Shelton, Jeppson, & Johnson, 1987). Whereas *family centered* was first used to simply refer to intervention practices that emphasized the family rather than an individual as the focus of intervention, its use took on added meaning as practitioners grappled with its implications for practice. It is now generally recognized that the term *family centered* refers to a particular approach to intervention that aims to support and strengthen parents' abilities to nurture and enhance child well-being and development (see Dunst, 1995).

A family-centered approach to intervention evolved from two separate but complementary perspectives: one conceptual and the other philosophical. Conceptually, a family-centered approach recognizes the facts that the family is an important source of influence affecting the physical and emotional well-being of individual family members and that when practitioners support families, parents are in a better position to have time, energy, knowledge and skills to beneficially parent a developing child (Bronfenbrenner, 1979, 1992). Philosophically, a family-centered approach evolved from the fact that more traditional professionally centered intervention practices often usurped families' rightful role to be meaningfully involved in important decisions as part of their involvement in help-seeking–help-giving relationships (Midmer, 1992; Shelton et al., 1987).

The purpose of this chapter is to describe and illustrate both the characteristics and benefits of a family-centered approach for psychology practice. The call for adoption of a family-centered approach by psychologists is not new. It can be found in pediatric psychology (M. Roberts & Wallander, 1992; Rodrigue, 1994), community psychology (Friedman, 1994),

Appreciation is extended to Eileen Byrnes for typing the manuscript and compiling and verifying the references.

school psychology (Epps & Jackson, 1991), family therapy (Rodway & Trute, 1993b), and early-childhood intervention (R. N. Roberts, & Magrab, 1991). This chapter, however, differs from previous work describing family-centered practices in one very important way. In this chapter family-centered practices are considered a special case of participatory and empowering help giving that places families in central and pivotal roles in decisions and actions involving both the family as a whole and individual family members (Dunst & Trivette, 1996). This particular perspective suggests the kinds of help-giving behaviors that professionals need to adopt to become family-centered.

The chapter is divided into four sections. The first section describes the meaning of a family-centered philosophy and both the principles and practices of a family-centered approach to intervention. The second section illustrates the relationship between family-centered practices and effective help giving, placing both within the context of several paradigm shifts discussed in the psychological literature and in this book. The third section summarizes evidence concerning the value-added benefits of family-centered help-giving practices.[1] The fourth section includes a brief discussion of the similarities and differences between a family-centered approach and other kinds of family-oriented intervention practices.

The family-centered help-giving perspective described in the chapter has specific application to service coordination and integration as there is evidence that different approaches to mobilizing supports and resources are likely to have different kinds of effects (see Dunst & Trivette, 1994). For example, service integration that is not consumer-driven is more likely to have dependency-forming rather than competency-enhancing consequences. Thus, it is important that efforts to mobilize resources, supports, and services for children and families explicitly recognize the fact that how something is done is as important as what is done if optimal positive benefits are to be realized. A number of investigators, for example, found that service-integration efforts often backfired and had negative effects when families were not meaningfully involved in decisions about needed services and the conditions under which services were rendered (Marcenko, Herman, & Hazel, 1992; Marcenko & Smith, 1992; Trivette, Dunst, & Deal, 1997; Weller, 1991).

What Is a Family-Centered Approach?

A family-centered approach to intervention is a philosophy of care characterized by generally agreed upon principles and elements that uniquely define a coherent set of family-centered practices. Inasmuch as the elements and principles form the foundation of these practices, examination

---

[1]The term *value-added* is used in this chapter to refer to the benefits of an intervention beyond those that would occur as a result of generally accepted practices. These aspects of an intervention having value-added benefits are ones that operationally differentiate different models and sets of practices (see especially Brickman et al., 1982; Dunst et al., 1993, Chapters 20 and 21).

of both should help place family-centered practices in perspective (Dunst, Trivette, & Deal, 1988, 1994).

Family-Centered Philosophy

Efforts to capture the meaning of a family-centered approach have proliferated in recent years (see, e.g., Allen & Petr, 1996; Dunst, 1995; Duwa, Wells, & Lalinde, 1993). A representative definition follows:

> Family-centered care results . . . in practices in which the pivotal role of the family is recognized and respected. Families are supported in their caregiving roles by building on their unique strengths as individuals and families. Opportunities are created for families to make informed choices for their children, and more importantly, these choices are respected. Family-centered . . . practices promote normalized patterns of living . . . where family/professional partnerships are clearly evident. (Shelton & Stepanek, 1994, p. 4)

Common features that uniquely define the meaning of a family-centered approach include (a) recognition that families are the primary and principal context for promoting child health and well-being, (b) respect for family choice and decision making, (c) emphasis on child and family strengths and resources needed for normalized patterns of living, (d) family–professional partnerships as the catalyst for matching resources to desired choices and actualizing choices, and (e) mutual respect between families and professionals as they work together to achieve desired outcomes. Collectively, these features both constitute a family-centered philosophy and define the meaning of a family-centered approach to intervention.

Family-Centered Principles and Practices

A family-centered philosophy consists of both family-centered principles (Dunst, 1990) and practices (Dunst, 1995). *Principles* are statements of beliefs and values about how supports and resources ought to be rendered to families, whereas practices are particular ways of behaving derived from the principles.

Exhibit 1 lists the eight principles and elements of family-centered care articulated by Shelton and Stepanek (1994). Inspection of these elements of care illustrates how each "fleshes out" the philosophy of family-centeredness, and how collectively they contribute to a unique approach to supporting and strengthening families. The principles and elements reflect a family- and social-systems perspective with emphasis on both intrafamily (e.g., child–family strengths, coping styles, and cultural and ethnic values and beliefs) and extrafamily (e.g., informal, formal, community, and family-to-family supports) factors affecting child/family behavior and development. They also reflect the use of collaborative professional help giver

78   CARL J. DUNST

Exhibit 1.   Some Key Elements of Family-Centered Care

Incorporating into policy and practice the recognition that *the family is the constant* in a child's life, whereas the service systems and support personnel within those systems fluctuate.

Facilitating *family–professional collaboration* at all levels of hospital, home, and community care:
• care of an individual child;
• program development, implementation, evaluation, and evolution; and
• policy formation.

Exchanging complete and unbiased information between families and professionals in a supportive manner at all times.

Incorporating into policy and practice the recognition and *honoring of cultural diversity,* strengths, and individuality within and across all families, including *ethnic, racial, spiritual, social, economic, educational, and geographic diversity.*

Recognizing and respecting *different methods of coping* and implementing comprehensive policies and programs that provide *developmental, educational, emotional, environmental, and financial supports* to meet the diverse needs of families.

Encouraging and facilitating *family-to-family support* and networking.

Ensuring that *hospital, home, and community service and support systems* for children needing specialized health and developmental care and their families are *flexible, accessible, and comprehensive* in responding to diverse family-identified needs.

Appreciating families as families and children as children, recognizing that they possess a wide range of strengths, concerns, emotions, and aspirations beyond their need for specialized health and developmental services and support.

From T. L. Shelton & J. S. Stepanek. (1994). *Family-Centered Care for Children Needing Specialized Health and Developmental Services,* Association for the Care of Children's Health, 7910 Woodmont Avenue, Suite 300, Bethesda, Maryland 20814. Reprinted by permission of the publisher.

roles in promoting the flow of resources to families. Additionally, these principles and elements emphasize that how interventions are conducted matters as much as what is done. As Karuza and Rabinowitz (1986) noted, "the effects of help not only depend on what is done but also on how it's done, and is a matter of helping style . . . and [practitioner] approach" (p. 380).

Exhibit 2 lists core practices most often described as key features of a family-centered approach to practice (Dunst, 1995; Family Resource Coalition, 1996). Not surprisingly, they parallel the principles and elements listed in Exhibit 1, but are more explicit behaviorally. Individually, the practices provide standards against which to judge whether family–practitioner transactions are family-centered.

Exhibit 2.   Core Practices of a Family-Centered Approach to Intervention

- Families and family members are treated with dignity and respect at all times.
- Practitioners are sensitive and responsive to family cultural, ethnic, and socio-economic diversity.
- Family choice and decision making occurs at all levels of family involvement in the intervention process.
- Information necessary for families to make informed choices is shared in a complete and unbiased manner.
- The focus of intervention practices is based on family-identified desires, priorities, and needs.
- Supports, resources, and services are provided in a flexible, responsive, and individualized manner.
- A broad range of informal, community, and formal supports and resources are used for achieving family-identified outcomes.
- The strengths and capabilities of families and individual family members are used as resources for meeting family-identified needs and as competencies for procuring extrafamily resources.
- Practitioner–family relationships are characterized by partnerships and collaboration based on mutual trust and respect.
- Practitioners employ competency-enhancing and empowering help-giving styles that promote and enhance family functioning and have family strengthening influences.

Sources: Dunst (1995), Dunst and Trivette (1996), Dunst et al. (1988, 1990, 1994).

The core practices listed in Exhibit 2 have been used by a number of persons to develop and conduct interventions that support and strengthen family functioning. For example, Dunst, Trivette, and Deal (1988, 1994) have developed an intervention framework that emphasizes (a) identification of family desires, priorities, aspirations, needs, and choices; (b) identification of informal, community, and formal supports and resources for meeting family-identified needs, and their mobilization; (c) identification and use of family strengths as intrafamily resources for attaining desired outcomes and as competencies for promoting the flow of desired supports and resources to families; and (d) use of help-giving practices that have competency-enhancing and family-strengthening influences.

Paradigmatic Bases of a Family-Centered Approach

Family-centered approaches include characteristics found in the promotion (Dunst, Trivette, & Thompson, 1990), competency-enhancing (Dunst, Trivette, & Deal, 1988), strengths-based (Dunst, Trivette, & Deal, 1994), empowerment (Dunst, Trivette, & LaPointe, 1992), and community building (Dunst, Trivette, Starnes, Hamby, & Gordon, 1993) literature, all of which place major emphasis on help-giving and intervention practices that enhance help-receiver competence, well-being, self-efficacy appraisals, and other aspects of psychological empowerment (Cochran, 1992; Skinner, 1995; Zimmerman, 1990a, 1990b). When placed in this wider web of psychological theory, a family-centered approach constitutes an intervention strategy that aims to support and strengthen family functioning in ways that have empowering consequences (Dunst, Trivette, & Deal, 1988, 1994; Dunst, Trivette, & Thompson, 1990).

Empowerment and Effective Help Giving

The relationship between a family-centered approach and both empowerment and effective help giving has constituted a major focus of my research and that of my colleagues for more than a decade (Dunst & Trivette, 1987, 1988, 1989). This research began with an extensive review of the help-giving literature, with particular emphasis on the identification of competency-enhancing and empowering practices (Dunst, Trivette, Davis, & Cornwell, 1988, 1994). The literature review identified some 20 different kinds of attitudes, behaviors, and practices that met these criteria. These included characteristics typically considered critical and desirable, including a helpgiver's sincere sense of caring, warmth, honesty, and empathy; active and reflective listening; and the maintenance of confidentiality. In addition, a variety of less typical help-giving practices were identified, including help-giver assumptions about the presumed capabilities of help receivers, practices that build on strengths rather than correct weaknesses, and emphasis on solutions rather than causes to people's problems. Effective practices also included (a) the active, participatory involvement of help receivers in the help-giving process, (b) focus on the process on receiver-identified needs and concerns, (c) provision of information necessary to make informed choices, (d) emphasis on decisions about courses of action to meet needs or achieve desired goals, and (e) enhancement and promotion of knowledge and skills needed to take action in ways that are competency producing. Additionally, help-giving practices associated with empowerment outcomes included making suggestions and offering advice that were normative and ecologically relevant to the receiver; acknowledging, accepting, and supporting help-receiver decisions; and affirming the role help receivers played in achieving positive outcomes. Collectively, it was found that these characteristics constituted the kinds of help-giving practices that increase the likelihood of positive, empowering effects from help-giver–help-receiver exchanges.

These beliefs, attitudes, and behaviors formed the basis for the development of the Helpgiving Practices Scale (Trivette & Dunst, 1994) and the subsequent determination of its psychometric properties (Dunst, Trivette, & Hamby, 1996). Factor analysis of the scale items administered to a sample of 220 parents of young children involved in a number of different kinds of human services programs yielded two interpretable solutions. The first factor, labeled *participatory involvement*, includes a preponderance of helpgiving behaviors that Maple (1977) described as the essential components of shared decision-making and what Rappaport (1981, 1987) described as the kinds of experiences that are likely to have empowering consequences. The items are action oriented and emphasize strengthening of existing capabilities and promotion of new help-receiver competencies. Participatory involvement items have been described as practices that meaningfully involve people in help-giver–help-receiver exchanges and are most likely to result in positive control appraisals about one's existing and emerging capabilities (Bandura, 1977, 1986; Brickman et al., 1982; Rappaport, 1981, 1987; Swift & Levin, 1987; Zimmerman, 1990a, 1990b; Zimmerman, Israel, Schulz, & Checkoway, 1992; Zimmerman & Rappaport, 1988).

The second factor, labeled *help-giver–help-receiver attributions*, includes items focusing on help-receiver attributions about the help giver and assessment of the presumed beliefs of the help giver toward the help receiver. They included behaviors typically associated with "good" clinical practice (e.g., compassion, active listening) and attributions about the help-giver's beliefs concerning help-receiver capabilities (Brammer, 1993).

Effective Help Giving and Family-Centered Practices

Table 1 shows some commonalities between help-giving characteristics from the scale (Trivette & Dunst, 1994) and family-centered principles and elements and practices detailed previously. It appears that family-centered principles and practices can be conveniently organized according to those that are either relational (help-giver traits and attributions) or participatory in focus and emphasis. Also, a family-centered approach may be considered a special case of effective help giving, at least at the practitioner level of intervention. Characterizing family-centered intervention as a special case of effective help giving provides guidance about particular kinds of practices one would adopt in order to become a family-centered, empowering help-giving professional.

These analyses suggest that what makes a family-centered approach different from "good clinical practice" is principally participatory involvement of the family. The extent to which families participating in different kinds of family-oriented programs differentially assessed help-giving practices of the professionals in these programs was recently tested in a study by Dunst, Boyd, Trivette, and Hamby (1996). Participants were 46 mothers of children, birth to 3 years of age, with or at-risk for poor outcomes. Mothers completed both the Family-Centered Practices Scale (FCS; Dunst & Trivette, 1996) and a short-form version of the Helpgiving Practices Scale (HPS; Dunst et al., 1996). The FCS includes 10 items asking a respondent to indicate the extent to which a program in which he or she is involved experiences different kinds of family-centered practices. The scored FCS sample was divided into three groups, experiencing low, medium, and high degrees of family-centeredness. A factor analysis of the HPS produced participatory involvement and help-giver traits and attributions factors, which were used as the dependent measures in the analysis of the relationship between family-centered and help-giving practices.

A 3 × 2 (Between Levels of Family-Centeredness × Within Help-Giving

Table 1. Some Common Features of Effective Help-Giving and Family-Centered Principles and Practices

Help-giving component	Common practices and elements	
	Help-giving practices	Family-centered elements and practices
Help-giver traits/attributions	Listens to help-receiver concerns and bases interventions on help-receiver needs	Is responsive to family concerns and priorities
	Is honest, sincere, and supportive	Is supportive at all times
	Is warm and caring	Is respectful of family individuality
	Treats help-receiver as capable	Recognizes family strengths and diversity
	Acknowledges help-receiver's role in achieving desired outcomes	Promotes mutual respect
Participatory involvement	Provides help-receiver information needed to make informed choices	Exchanges complete and unbiased information between families and professional
	Works collaboratively with help receiver	Facilitates family–professional collaboration
	Encourages help-receiver decision-making	Facilitates family choice
	Builds on help-receiver strengths	Honors family strengths and respects family coping strategies
	Promotes help-receiver capabilities	Builds parenting confidence

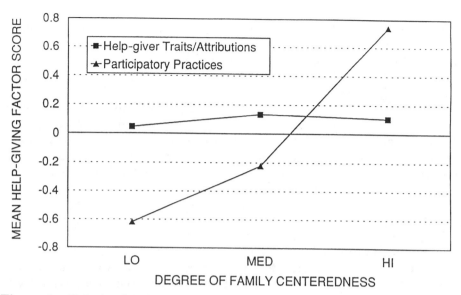

Figure 1. Relationship between the degree of family centeredness of early intervention programs and practices and two types of help-giving practices.

Type) analysis of variance produced the interaction effect displayed in Figure 1. As can be seen, participatory practices, but not help-giver traits and attributions, differed as a function of the degree of family-centered practices experienced by the respondents, thus confirming the expectation that participatory involvement is what makes family-centered practices unique.

Benefits of a Family-Centered Approach

The manner in which family-centered help-giving practices influence the outcomes of help-receiver–help-giver interactions has been the focus of both quantitative (Boyd & Dunst, 1993; Dunst, Boyd, & Trivette, 1994; Dunst, Trivette, Boyd, & Brookfield, 1994; Dunst, Trivette, & LaPointe, 1992; Trivette, Dunst, & Hamby, 1996a, 1996b; Trivette, Dunst, Boyd, & Hamby, 1996; Trivette, Dunst, Hamby, & LaPointe, 1996) and qualitative (Boyd & Dunst, 1995; Dunst, Trivette, Gordon, & Starnes, 1993; Dunst, Trivette, Starnes, Hamby, & Gordon, 1993) investigations that my colleagues and I have conducted. The independent variables in these studies included parent characteristics (e.g., age, education level, marital and work status); family characteristics (socioeconomic status and income); child characteristics (e.g., age, child at-risk status, developmental quotients); and background characteristics (e.g., age, education level, years of experience, discipline) of a target help giver; program type (e.g., early intervention, public health, rehabilitation) of the target help giver; degree of family-centeredness of the target helpgiver's program; practices (help giver traits and attributions and participatory involvement practices of the target help giver); and frequency of contact and length of involvement of the target helpgiver with the help-receiver. Outcomes have included help-receiver empowerment (e.g., efficacy expectations, control appraisals, efficacy attributions), help-receiver well-being, family quality of life, and other outcomes resulting from effective help-giving practices as reported and experienced by help receivers.

The findings as a whole indicate that neither parent–family characteristics nor child characteristics are generally related to the majority of outcomes examined. In contrast, help-giving practices and program type, and degree of family centeredness of a help-giver's program have been found to be related to a number of outcomes. To a lesser degree, help givers with family-level-practice backgrounds and more frequent contact with help receivers have also been found related to certain outcomes. The particular help-giver and program measures associated with positive benefits, however, depends on the outcomes being considered.

Whether family-centered help-giving is related to various empowerment outcomes has been the focus of a number of investigations (Dunst, Trivette, & LaPointe, 1992; Trivette, Dunst, Boyd, et al., 1996; Trivette et al., 1996a; Trivette, Dunst, Hamby, & LaPointe, 1996). For example, in two separate studies, Trivette, Dunst, Boyd, et al. (1996) found that help-giving practices accounted for 24% and 39% of the variance in the degree to which families indicated they had control over resources for a target help-giver and a specific program. This variance is *beyond* that attributable to parent, family, and child characteristics, as well as *beyond* that attributable to program type and frequency of contact with a target help-giver.

A subsequent set of studies by Trivette, Dunst, and Hamby (1996b) examined specifically whether help-giver traits and attributions, participatory-involvement help-giving practices, or both were related to a number of different empowerment outcomes. In these studies, regardless of the empowerment outcome measure, participatory involvement, but not help-giver traits and attributions, was found to be the component of help-giver practices associated with control appraisals. This demonstrates the value-added benefits of family-centered help-giving. Moreover, the findings indicate that practitioners must use, in addition to good clinical skills, participatory involvement practices if empowerment outcomes are to be realized.

In a series of yet-to-be-published studies by Dunst, Trivette, and their colleagues, a somewhat different pattern of findings emerges when parent psychological health is the outcome. Results indicate that parent–family and child characteristics are related to well-being, but beyond these influences, help-giver traits and attributions account for significant amounts of variance in psychological health and, beyond this influence, participatory involvement practices account for even more variance in well-being. The fact that help-giver traits and attributions are related to well-being is not surprising given what is known about the relationship between good clinical practices and mental health status (Brammer, 1993). Perhaps more important, however, is the value-added benefits of participatory involvement practices, indicating that when such practices are used (in addition to good clinical practices) the influences of family-centered help-giving are enhanced considerably.

The evidence briefly presented here indicates that family-centered helpgiving is related to a number of domains of family functioning and that there are value-added benefits of participatory help giving practices. The findings are consistent with results from both experimental (Ozer & Bandura, 1990) and applied (Zimmerman & Rappaport, 1988; Zimmerman et al., 1992) research indicating that active involvement of people in help-giving–help-receiving relationships is an important factor contributing to positive outcomes. Additionally, the evidence makes explicit which component of family-centered help giving (i.e., participatory involvement) must be adopted if positive benefits are to be maximized.

Similarities and Differences Between Contrasting Family-Oriented Intervention Approaches

The family-centered approach described in this chapter is one of many family-oriented approaches to intervention. According to Dunst, Johanson, et al. (1991), there are four kinds of family-oriented intervention models: professionally centered, family-allied, family-focused, and family-centered. All four approaches consider the family as the focus of intervention and, to varying degrees, use family-systems frameworks for conceptualizing and conducting interventions. The models differ, however, in terms of any number of features, including, but not limited to, assumptions about family capabilities and the roles families play in the intervention process, decisions about the focus of intervention practices, and the kinds of supports and resources used to influence child, parent, and family functioning.

Proponents of *professionally centered models* view professionals as experts who determine child and family needs from their own as opposed to a family's perspective. In *family-allied models*, families are seen as the agents of professionals and are enlisted to implement interventions that professionals deem important and necessary for optimal child and family functioning. Advocates of *family-focused models* view families as consumers of professional services and assist families in choosing among options that professionals consider necessary for best meeting child and family needs. Proponents of *family-centered models* view professionals as instruments of families and conduct interventions in ways consistent with family-centered principles and elements (Exhibit 1) and practices (Exhibit 2). Thus, whereas all four models are family-oriented, they differ in their help-giving assumptions and approaches to working with families.

A number of studies (Dunst, Trivette, Boyd, & Brookfield, 1994; Dunst, Trivette, & Hamby, 1996; Trivette, Dunst, Boyd, & Hamby, 1996; Trivette, Dunst, & Hamby, 1996a) confirm the hypothesis that programs using different family-oriented models are related to differences in the help-giving practices used by staff in these programs. In each of these investigations, program model (professionally centered to family-centered) was used as a blocking variable. Findings indicated that families assessed the help-giving practices of staff in these programs as more effective and empowering when the practitioners were from programs using models found toward the family-centered end of the paradigmatic continuum. Consequently, whereas the four models are similar in their emphasis on family, they differ considerably in terms of how help-givers practice their crafts.

The family-centered approach to intervention described in this chapter also shows both similarities and differences with family therapy (e.g., Minuchin & Fishman, 1981). Family-centered interventions differ from family therapy in three significant ways. First, family therapy tends to pathologize. According to Karpel (1986a), "[family therapy, as] currently practiced on a daily basis, even with the best of intentions, is characterized by assessing damage done, assigning blame, and looking for outside resources (primary among which is the therapist)" (p. 9). In contrast, family-centered interventions are best characterized as consumer driven, proactive, strengths based, and health-promotion oriented (Dunst, Trivette, & Thompson, 1990). Second, in family therapy, the primary focus of interventions is changing the nature of relationships among family members (Karpel, 1986a), whereas family-centered interventions are responsive to both the individual and collective needs of family members beyond those pertaining to interactional patterns (Dunst, Trivette, & Deal, 1988, 1994). Third, in family therapy, the interventionist takes primary responsibility for bringing expertise to bear on determining family problems and solutions to them (Karpel, 1986b), whereas in a family-centered approach, a family is seen as possessing existing capabilities as well as the capacity to decide the focus of the intervention process and methods to achieve desired outcomes (Shelton & Stepanek, 1994). Family therapy, at least as characterized here, is primarily of a professionally centered approach to intervention.

Recent advances in family therapy have led to an expanded perspective of this approach to intervention called *ecological family-centered therapy* (Rodway & Trute, 1993b). This approach has many commonalities with a family-centered approach to intervention (e.g., systems perspective, emphasis on intrafamily and extrafamily resources and supports), but still differs in one fundamentally important way. According to Rodway and Trute (1993a), ecological family therapy takes a "view which appreciates that *human behavioral dysfunctions* can be reflective of disruptions [not only] in interpersonal transactions and patterns of relationships [but also disruptions] in the interrelationships between person, family, and environment" (p. 15, emphasis added). Thus, whereas ecological family-centered therapy uses a wider lens for viewing sources of problems and solutions to them, the focus is nonetheless on poor functioning as the target of change.

Comparing and contrasting the family-centered approach to intervention described in this chapter with other family-oriented approaches helps clarify the meaning of family-centered practices, makes its defining characteristics more explicit, and helps differentiate it from other approaches to working with families. Not surprisingly, however, all family-centered approaches are "not created equal." Proponents of family-centered approaches, while generally agreeing on the defining characteristics of this kind of intervention, often differ with regard to the meaning and inter-pretation of the term and its operational features. For example, one such characteristic pertains to the meaning of the family as a unit of interven-tion. According to Allen and Petr (1996), "although professionals may con-sider the entire family as the unit of attention, in actual practice, involve-ment and collaboration may be limited to the parents, to a parent–child dyad, or even solely to the primary caregiver, who is usually the mother" (p. 67). However, it was never intended that the principle or practice of the family as a unit of intervention meant that interventions be directed at all family members or that the family be brought together to come to agreement about desired outcomes and intervention strategies. The intent of this characteristic was that interventions be responsive to the concerns and desires of all family members and the family unit; that family dynam-ics, choices, and values be taken into consideration as part of the inter-ventions involving individual family members; and that interventions be supportive rather than disruptive of family life. When considered and de-fined in this way, conceptualizing the family as the unit of intervention is not fraught with difficulties, as Allen and Petr (1996) and others have argued. Further advances in defining the meaning and characteristics of family-centered intervention practices and family-centered help giving will require this kind of clarification and elaboration.

Conclusion

This chapter defined the meaning of a family-centered approach to inter-vention and enumerated its key features and characteristics. It argued that a family-centered approach was a special case of effective help-giving practices emphasizing the participatory involvement of family members in helping relationships and the empowerment of families as a primary way of supporting and strengthening family functioning. Emerging evidence indicates that conceptualizing a family-centered approach in this way helps make explicit those aspects of family-centered practices that have value-added benefits. As noted earlier, the value-added benefits of an intervention are those consequences realized beyond the influences of generally accepted practices. Participatory involvement of families in help-receiving–help-giving relationships have such influences at least in terms of the psychosocial health and empowerment outcomes we have studied.

Family-centered help-giving seems especially applicable for psycholo-gists who work with children, their siblings, and parents. This is the case because psychologists have traditionally viewed their activities and efforts from a help-giving perspective, and family-centered help-giving seems to provide a wider lens for defining the meaning of effective help-giving, its operational characteristics, and expected benefits. Consequently, the value of this chapter for a family-centered approach in psychology practice de-rives from the fact that psychologists can use the operational lists of family-centered principles, elements, and practices for judging the areas in which they are already family-centered and deciding which aspects of a family-centered approach they desire to incorporate in future work with families. The value of the chapter in terms of service integration and co-ordination is indicated by the fact that how families are involved in these efforts matters as much as what is done or provided. Indeed, if service integration and coordination explicitly consider and incorporate family-centered help-giving practices into program development and implementation, the likelihood of there being positive effects are increased considerably.

Interventions with families must be considered successful only to the extent that family functioning is promoted and improved as a result of the kinds of practices used by psychologists and other helping professionals. The approach described in this chapter holds special promise for accomplishing this goal.

References

Allen, R. I., & Petr, C. G. (1996). Toward developing standards and measurements for family-centered practice in family support programs. In G. H. Singer, L. E. Powers, & A. L. Olson (Eds.), *Redefining family support: Innovation in public-private partnerships* (pp. 57–78). Baltimore: Paul Brookes Publishing Co.

Bandura, A. (1977). Self-efficacy: Toward a unifying theory of behavioral change. *Psychological Review, 84,* 191–215.

Bandura, A. (1986). *Social foundations of thought and action: A social theory.* Englewood Cliffs, NJ: Prentice Hall.

Birt, C. J. (1956). Family-centered project of St. Paul. *Social Work, 1,* 41–47.

Boyd, K. A., & Dunst, C. J. (1993, December). *Effects of helpgiving behavior on a family's sense of control and well-being.* Presentation made at the 20th International Early Childhood Conference on Children with Special Needs, Council for Exceptional Children, Division for Early Childhood, San Diego, CA.

Boyd, K. A., & Dunst, C. J. (1995). Providing help to families of young children with disabilities. *Network, 4*(3), 39–45.

Brammer, L. (1993). *The helping relationship: Process and skills* (5th ed.). Boston: Allyn and Bacon.

Brickman, P., Rabinowitz, V., Karuza, J., Coates, D., Cohn, E., & Kidder, L. (1982). Models of helping and coping. *American Psychologist, 37,* 368–384.

Bronfenbrenner, U. (1979). *The ecology of human development: Experimental by nature and design.* Cambridge, MA: Harvard University Press.

Bronfenbrenner, U. (1992). Ecological systems theory. In R. Vasta (Ed.), *Six theories of child development* (pp. 187–249). London: Kingsley Publishers.

Cochran, M. (1992). Parent empowerment: Developing a conceptual framework. *Family Science Review, 5,* 3–21.

Dunst, C. J. (1990). Family support principles: Checklists for program builders and practitioners. *Family Systems Intervention Monograph, 2* (No. 5.). Morganton, NC: Family, Infant and Preschool Program, Western Carolina Center.

Dunst, C. J. (1995). *Key characteristics and features of community-based family support programs.* Chicago: Family Resource Coalition.

Dunst, C. J., Boyd, K., & Trivette, C. M. (1994, May). *Tracing the effects of professional beliefs and practices on family empowerment.* Presentation made at the Family Resource Coalition National Conference, Chicago, IL.

Dunst, C. J., Boyd, K., Trivette, C. M., & Hamby, D. W. (1996). *Relationship between family-oriented program models and early intervention practitioner helpgiving*. Manuscript in preparation.

Dunst, C. J., Johanson, C., Trivette, C. M., & Hamby, D. (1991). Family-oriented early intervention policies and practices: Family-centered or not? *Exceptional Children, 58,* 115–126.

Dunst, C. J., & Trivette, C. M. (1987). Enabling and empowering families: Conceptual and intervention issues. *School Psychology Review, 16,* 443–456.

Dunst, C. J., & Trivette, C. M. (1988). Helping, helplessness, and harm. In J. Witt, S. Elliott, & F. Gesham (Eds.), *Handbook of behavior therapy in education* (pp. 343–376). New York: Plenum Press.

Dunst, C. J., & Trivette, C. M. (1989). An enablement and empowerment perspective of case management. *Topics in Early Childhood Special Education, 8*(4), 87–102.

Dunst, C. J., & Trivette, C. M. (1994). Empowering case management practices: A family-centered perspective. In C. J. Dunst, C. M. Trivette, & A. G. Deal (Eds.), *Supporting and strengthening families* (pp. 187–196). Cambridge, MA: Brookline Books.

Dunst, C. J., & Trivette, C. M. (1996). Empowerment, effective helpgiving practices, and family-centered care. *Pediatric Nursing, 24,* 283–290.

Dunst, C. J., Trivette, C. M., Boyd, K. & Brookfield, J. (1994). Helpgiving practices and the self-efficacy appraisals of parents. In C. J. Dunst, C. M. Trivette, & A. G. Deal (Eds.), *Supporting and strengthening families: Vol 1. Methods, strategies, and practice* (pp. 212–220). Cambridge, MA: Brookline Books.

Dunst, C. J., Trivette, C. M., Davis, M., & Cornwell, J. (1988). Enabling and empowering families of children with health impairments. *Children's Health Care, 17*(2), 71–81.

Dunst, C. J., Trivette, C. M., Davis, M., & Cornwell, J. (1994). Characteristics of effective helpgiving practices. In C. J. Dunst, C. M. Trivette, & A. G. Deal (Eds.), *Supporting and strengthening families: Vol.1, Methods, strategies and practices* (pp. 171–186). Cambridge, MA: Brookline Books.

Dunst, C. J., Trivette, C. M., & Deal, A. G. (1988). *Enabling and empowering families: Principles and guidelines for practice.* Cambridge, MA: Brookline Books.

Dunst, C. J., Trivette, C. M., & Deal, A. G. (Eds.). (1994). *Supporting and strengthening families: Vol. 1: Methods, strategies and practices.* Cambridge, MA: Brookline Books.

Dunst, C. J., Trivette, C. M., Gordon, N., & Starnes, L. (1993). Family-centered case management practices: Characteristics and consequences. In G. S. Singer & L. E. Powers (Eds.), *Families, disabilities, and empowerment: Active coping skills and strategies for family interventions.* Baltimore: Paul Brookes Publishing Co.

Dunst, C. J., Trivette, C. M, & Hamby, D. W. (1996). Measuring the helpgiving practices of human services program practitioners. *Human Relations, 49,* 815–835.

Dunst, C. J., Trivette, C. M., & LaPointe, N. (1992). Toward clarification of the meaning and key elements of empowerment. *Family Science Review, 5,* 111–130.

Dunst, C. J., Trivette, C. M., Starnes, A. L., Hamby, D. W., & Gordon, N. (1993). *Building and evaluating family support programs.* Baltimore: Paul Brookes Publishing Co.

Dunst, C. J., Trivette, C. M., & Thompson, R. L. (1990). Supporting and strengthening family functioning: Toward a congruence between principles and practice. *Prevention in Human Services, 9,* 19–43.

Duwa, S. M., Wells, C., & Lalinde, P. (1993). Creating family-centered programs and policies. In D. M. Bryant, & M. A. Graham (Eds.), *Implementing early intervention: From research to effective practice* (pp. 92–123). New York: Guilford.

Epps, S., & Jackson, B. J. (1991). Professional preparation of psychologists for family-centered service delivery to at-risk infants and toddlers. *School Psychology Review, 20*(4), 498–509.

Family Resource Coalition. (1996). *Guidelines for family support practice.* Chicago: Author.

Friedman, R. M. (1994). Restructuring of systems to emphasize prevention and family support. *Journal of Clinical Child Psychology, 23*(Suppl.), 40–47.

Hungerford, M. J. (1964). Nutritional education in family-centered maternity care. *Journal of Applied Nutrition, 17*(2), 114–125.

Karpel, M. (1986a). Questions, obstacles, contributions. In M. Karpel (Ed.), *Family resources: The hidden partner in family therapy* (pp. 3–61). New York: Guilford Press.

Karpel, M. (1986b). Testing, promoting, and preserving family resources: Beyond pathology and powers. In M. Karpel (Ed.), *Family resources: The hidden partner in family therapy* (pp. 175–234). New York: Guilford Press.

Karuza, J., & Rabinowitz, V. (1986). Implications of control & responsibility on helping the aged. In M. Baltes & P. Baltes (Eds.), *The psychology of control and aging* (pp. 373–396), Hillsdale, NJ: Erlbaum Associates.

Kopp, C. E. (1987). *Surgeon General's report: Children with special health care needs—Commitment to family-centered, coordinated care for children with special health care needs.* Washington, DC: U.S. General Printing Office.

Maple, F. F. (1977). *Shared decision making.* Beverly Hills, CA: Sage.

Marcenko, M. O., Herman, S. E., & Hazel, K. L. (1992). A comparison of how families and their service providers rate family generated quality of service factors. *Community Mental Health Journal, 28*(5), 441–449.

Marcenko, M. O., & Smith, L. K. (1992). The impact of a family-centered case management approach. *Social Work in Health Care, 17*(1), 87–100.

Midmer, D. K. (1992). Does a family-centered maternity care empower women? The development of the women-centered childbirth model. *Family Medicine, 24*(3), 216–221.

Minuchin, S., & Fishman, H. (1981). *Family therapy techniques.* Cambridge, MA: Harvard University Press.

Ozer, E., & Bandura, A. (1990). Mechanisms governing empowerment effects: A self-efficacy analysis. *Journal of Personality and Social Psychology, 58,* 472–486.

Rappaport, J. (1981). In praise of paradox: A social policy of empowerment over prevention. *American Journal of Community Psychology, 9,* 1–25.

Rappaport, J. (1987). Terms of empowerment/exemplars of prevention: Toward a theory for community psychology. *American Journal of Community Psychology, 15,* 121–148.

Roberts, M., & Wallander, J. (Eds.). (1992). *Family issues in pediatric psychology.* Hillsdale, NJ: Erlbaum Associates.

Roberts, R. N., & Magrab, P. R. (1991). Psychologists' role in a family-centered approach to practice, training, and research with young children. *American Psychologist, 46*(2), 144–148.

Rodrigue, J. R. (1994). Beyond the individual child: Innovative systems approaches to service delivery in pediatric psychology. *Journal of Clinical Child Psychology, 23*(Suppl. 2), 32–39.

Rodway, M. R., & Trute, B. (1993a). Ecological family therapy. In M. R. Rodway & B. Trute (Eds.), *The ecological perspective in family-centered therapy* (pp. 3–16). Lewiston, NY: Edwin Mellen Press.

Rodway, M. R., & Trute, B. (1993b). *The ecological perspective in family-centered therapy.* Lewiston, NY: Edwin Mellen Press.

Scherz, F. H. (1953). What is family-centered case work? *Social Casework, 34,* 343–349.

Shelton, T. L., Jeppson, E. S., & Johnson, B. (1987). *Family-centered care for children with special health care needs.* Washington, DC: Association for the Care of Children's Health.

Shelton, T. L., & Stepanek, J. S. (1994). *Family-centered care for children needing specialized health and developmental services* (2nd ed.). Bethesda, MD: Association for the Care of Children's Health.

Skinner, E. (1995). *Perceived control, motivation, and coping.* Thousand Oaks, CA: Sage Publications.

Swift, C., & Levin, G. (1987). Empowerment: An emerging mental health technology. *Journal of Primary Prevention, 8*(1/2), 71–94.

Trivette, C. M., & Dunst, C. J. (1994). *Helpgiving Practices Scale.* Unpublished scale, Center for Family Studies, Western Carolina Center, Morganton, NC.

Trivette, C. M., Dunst, C. J., Boyd, K., & Hamby, D. W. (1996). Family-oriented program models, helpgiving practices, and parental control appraisals. *Exceptional Children, 62,* 237–248.

Trivette, C. M., Dunst, C. J., & Deal, A. G. (1997). Resource-based early intervention practices. In S. K. Thurman, J. R. Cornwell, & S. R. Gottwald (Eds.), *The contexts of early intervention: Systems and settings.* Baltimore: Brookes Publishing Co.

Trivette, C. M., Dunst, C. J., & Hamby, D. W. (1996a). Characteristics and consequences of helpgiving practices in human services programs. *American Journal of Community Psychology, 24,* 273–293.

Trivette, C. M., Dunst, C. J., & Hamby, D. W. (1996b). Factors associated with perceived control appraisals in a family-centered early intervention program. *Journal of Early Intervention, 20*(2), 165–178.

Trivette, C. M., Dunst, C. J., Hamby, D. W., & LaPointe, N. (1996). Key elements of empowerment and their implications for early intervention. *Infant-Toddler Intervention: The Transdisciplinary Journal, 6,* 59–73.

Weller, B. (1991). Client satisfaction with developmental disabilities services. *Population and Environment: A Journal of Interdisciplinary Studies, 13*(2), 121–139.

Wiedenbach, E. (1967). *Family-centered maternity nursing.* New York: Putnam.

Zimmerman, M. A. (1990a). Toward a theory of learned hopefulness: A structural model analysis of participation and empowerment. *Journal of Research in Personality, 24,* 71–86.

Zimmerman, M. A. (1990b). Taking aim on empowerment research: On the distinction between individual and psychological concepts. *American Journal of Community Psychology, 18,* 169–177.

Zimmerman, M. A., Israel, B., Schulz, A., & Checkoway, B. (1992). Further explorations in empowerment theory: An empirical analysis of psychological empowerment. *American Journal of Community Psychology, 20,* 707–727.

Zimmerman, M. A., & Rappaport, J. (1988). Citizen participation, perceived control, and psychological empowerment. *American Journal of Community Psychology, 16,* 725–750.

5

The Critical Role of Finance in Creating Comprehensive Support Systems

Martin E. Orland, Anna E. Danegger, and Ellen Foley

Programs serving children and families are funded through countless federal, state, and local governmental channels, as well as through private sources. The federal government alone currently funds nearly 500 distinct programs for children, their families, and their communities, ranging from health to education services, and from child protection and support to youth centers. In addition, state and local governments and private individuals and corporations fund their own series of initiatives for children and their families. By one count, there are some 238 separate programs for "at-risk" youth operating within the Los Angeles Unified School District alone (Gardner, 1995, p. 4). Each of these programs was no doubt initiated with the best of intentions, among them to ensure that politically and economically vulnerable constituencies (e.g., low-income children and families, children with disabilities) actually benefit from public expenditures. However, such guarantees come at a price.

Every one of these programs contains a unique set of standard rules and requirements about how funds may be used, and who is eligible to receive them. For example, the requirements for compensatory education programs differ from those for health awareness, which, in turn, are separate from those for family preservation, and so on. These programs are each run independently and managed separately, following procedural requirements typically set by federal, state, or local government officials. "Street-level" children's-service providers (e.g., teachers, social workers, nurse practitioners) are likely to be quite knowledgeable about the particular rules and regulations connected with serving the children or families for whom they are responsible. However, it would not be surprising if they

The views of the authors are their own. No official support or endorsement by the National Center for Education Statistics, the U.S. Department of Education, The Finance Project, or the University of Pennsylvania is intended or should be inferred. All three authors wrote this while serving at The Finance Project.

were unaware of even the existence of many of the other special program services that these same children or families also receive.

Increasingly, policy makers, educators, professional service providers, and advocates have begun to recognize the limitations of such fragmented, functionally based approaches to the delivery of children's services. As currently constituted, the dizzying array of separate rules, regulations, and administrative structures makes it all but impossible to design and implement strategies that are responsive to the needs of the children and families who are the objects of such assistance. Current arrangements ignore two fundamental tenets of effective service provision for children: (a) children with multiple needs require comprehensive and coordinated service strategies, and (b) local communities represent an indispensable asset for effectively linking programs and resources across agencies and public and private institutions (Hayes, Lipoff, & Danegger, 1995).

In response to these limitations, researchers and program developers have begun to outline new systems of children's support that integrate programs across service sectors and involve communities as centerpieces of program design and operation. Ideally, such comprehensive, community-based support systems (CCBSS) have a number of features that distinguish them from traditional children's service arrangements (Farrow & Bruner, 1993; Hayes et al., 1995; Schorr, 1988). These include

- *A focus on prevention-oriented services and supports.* In traditional children's service programs, most resources are made available for treating a problem (such as juvenile delinquency) rather than for trying to prevent it in the first place. A CCBSS aims to prevent problematic outcomes for children from the start.
- *Flexibility in supporting the needs of children within the context of their families and communities.* Traditional children's service programs target the use of funds to narrowly delineated purposes (e.g., hiring substance abuse professionals) and place detailed restrictions on how resources may and may not be used. A CCBSS blends resources and coordinates services and supports across professional domains (such as health, social welfare, education, and neighborhood development) as well as public, private, and nonprofit institutions in order to make the most worthwhile investments for children. Such investments need not focus solely on the child, but can also include supports to his or her family and community.
- *A strong community role in program design, implementation, and governance.* In most children's programs, service and funding decisions are made centrally by federal, state, or local bureaucracies. Ideally, in a CCBSS, community members exercise substantial decision making authority in defining their high-priority needs and then marshaling the resource and program strategies for meeting them.
- *A focus on accountability for outcomes.* Most traditional program-accountability systems measure narrow service inputs (e.g., the

number of teacher workshops the school system offers on classroom disruption). In a CCBSS, the accountability system is performance-driven, with community members defining desirable child, family, and community outcomes (e.g., reducing the rate of violent incidents in and around neighborhood schools), periodically monitoring their attainment, and adjusting program strategies accordingly.

Today, there are numerous local efforts around the nation that attempt to initiate program strategies for children and families that are consistent with these characteristics.[1]

Despite the fact that the number of comprehensive, community-based systems has been growing, the children's-service landscape continues to be dominated by fragmented, uncoordinated, and bureaucratically driven program strategies. Why do such arrangements persist in light of their commonly acknowledged limitations? It is the central thesis of this chapter that their continued presence is intimately related to the way in which most children's services are now financed. That is, the current financing system—grounded in narrow and functionally based requirements for how public resources may be obtained, used, and reported—discourages the development of comprehensive, community-based support systems for children and their families. However compelling the arguments for more integrated service delivery approaches might be, as long as these basic financing systems remain more or less intact, efforts to develop and sustain these new structures will only have marginal success.

Because finance and service delivery are so closely related, it is essential to carefully examine the links between the vision for children's service delivery and the financing strategies that are needed to see this vision fulfilled. The purpose of this chapter is to conduct such an examination, which is done by addressing two critical questions. First, how do current financing arrangements present obstacles to implementing comprehensive, community-based children's service approaches? Second, what types of financing reforms hold particular promise in overcoming these obstacles, and what is the likelihood that such reforms will become more prevalent?

The chapter begins by describing the current system of children's financing and documenting the number, types, and funding levels of major federal programs for children. Next, it examines how these financing structures inhibit the creation, effective implementation, and institutionalization of more comprehensive, community-based program designs. This chapter then describes and analyzes significant efforts (both proposed and under way) to reform children's financing arrangements so as to encourage more integrated, community-driven service approaches. Finally, it concludes with a discussion of the prospects for furthering such reforms in the months and years ahead.

---

[1]A summary of more than 50 such programs can be found in The Finance Project's *Compendium of Comprehensive, Community-Based Initiatives* (Hayes et al., 1995).

The Current Financing of Children's Services and Supports

Children need "decent education, health care, and safe neighborhood environments where they can play, parents can work, and people of all ages can socialize and develop personal relationships" (Hayes et al., 1995, p. 1). These needs traditionally have been met by families and communities; however, changing demographics and family–community dynamics have meant that, in many cases, the necessity for organized supports that meet some or all of the needs of children and families has grown. More and more, children grow up in single-parent families, generations of families live farther away from one another, and communities are less cohesive because of increased personal mobility. Individuals, private organizations, and the public sector have attempted to fill the resulting social gaps through financing organized supports and services. However, the services that currently support children and their families are delivered by a range of providers and financed in myriad ways, with little coordination among them.

The following section relies heavily on The Finance Project's Database of Federal Allocations and Tax Expenditures Benefiting Children and Families[2] and highlights both the magnitude of spending on, and the principal mechanisms for financing, services and supports for children and families. The Finance Project is an independent, nonprofit organization established in 1994 as a national initiative to improve the effectiveness, efficiency, and equity of public financing for education and other children's services.

The Magnitude of Public Expenditures

The primary financing source of organized support for children and families is public expenditures—specifically, revenues from federal, state, and local governments. While there are overlapping responsibilities among the different levels of government, distinct differences exist in the focuses of funding. For example the federal government plays the most significant role in financing human services for children and their families (e.g., health, nutrition, housing, and welfare programs). State and local governments play the primary role in financing education expenditures.

As defined for The Finance Project's database, federal allocations for children fare rather poorly in relation to many other categories of federal expenditures. In fiscal year (FY) 1994, direct federal allocations supporting education and other services for children and their families totaled ap-

---

[2]The Finance Project's Database of Allocations and Tax Expenditures Benefiting Children, Families, and Communities tracks approximately 500 programs that benefit children broadly. A significant portion of these programs benefit children and families indirectly (e.g., through community-development grants) or assist others in addition to children and their families (e.g., low-income housing assistance grants). Of the approximately 500 programs in the database, about 150 are targeted exclusively to supports and services for children and their families.

proximately $104 billion. As a reference point for comparison, federal allocations for discretionary defense spending in the same year totaled more than twice that, at $280.6 billion. Allocations for seniors were also dramatically higher than those for children and families with children. The federal government allocated $63 billion for federal retirement, $140.8 billion for Medicare, and $317.7 billion for Social Security (Budget for the United States Government, 1994), totaling $521.5 billion directed to the nation's senior populations, more than five times its $104 billion allocation for children and their families.

Of the $104 billion allocated by the federal government to children and families, 56% ($58 billion) goes to only four large programs: Food Stamps, Aid to Families with Dependent Children (AFDC), Medicaid, and Children's Old Age Survivors and Disability Insurance (OASDI).[3] Each of these programs either transfers income directly to individuals or provides payment waivers for expenses such as food and medical care. The balance of federal funds—$46 billion—benefits children and families through numerous categorical programs, the great majority of which were smaller than $100 million in FY 1994.

Federal spending for children and families with children pales in comparison not only to other categories of federal spending, but also in relation to overall state investments in children and families. This is because state and local governments finance the lion's share of educational services, the only children's service area where eligibility for government support is universal and the costs are fully subsidized by public funds. In the 1992–1993 school year, states provided $115.2 billion, and localities and other nonfederal sources $114.1 billion, of the approximately $253.8 billion spent on elementary and secondary education (Gold & Ellwood, 1994). States also make significant contributions to funding other services for children and families, including providing federally required matching funds for AFDC and Medicaid. In 1992, states spent $21.5 billion on matching federal investments in noneducation supports for children and their families. Of this amount, $17.3 billion (or approximately 80%) was spent on matching federal AFDC and Medicaid expenditures.

State investments in children vary greatly, however. Education spending per pupil in 1992 was three times greater in New Jersey than in Utah. In that same year, Massachusetts spent about 10 times more per poor child than Mississippi on noneducation children's programs (Orland & Cohen, 1995).

State and local funding has been affected in recent years by citizen tax revolts, waning economic growth, and increasing numbers of children, particularly children in poverty. From 1980 to 1992, state and local AFDC spending per poor family has declined 19% in real terms, whereas spending data from 1990 to 1994 reveals that state and local education spending per pupil appears to have slowed, following two decades of relatively uninterrupted growth (Orland & Cohen, 1995).

[3]OASDI is a part of Social Security.

Public Financing Mechanisms

Whatever the relative size of investments in children and their families, it is clear that governments in general, and the federal government in particular, have enormous influence on how services for children and families are delivered. Federal influence is attributable to two related factors. First, although states and localities may spend more overall on children and families, the federal government has come to shoulder unique responsibilities in supporting children and families with high levels of need. Programs such as Head Start, Title I of the Elementary and Secondary Education Act, and the Special Supplemental Food Program for Women, Infants, and Children (WIC) are three prominent examples of large-scale federal initiatives designed to meet the unique needs of at-risk children and families. Second, even in instances when the financing responsibilities for serving high-need children and families is shared among levels of government (such as the AFDC, Medicaid, and special education programs), the federal government establishes the rules by which its financial assistance is granted, thus driving the basic design of services and supports.

The federal government provides financial support to children and their families in two basic ways: (a) by transferring income directly to individuals, and (b) by funding special programs and services. The principal mechanisms used to deliver these resources are as follows: Family incomes are generally subsidized through entitlement programs, tax expenditures, and loans. Competitive grants-in-aid and formula grants are the primary financing mechanism for delivering special program services.

Entitlements are the largest source of public funds for children and their families. An entitlement guarantees a financial subsidy or service to an individual—provided that a specific eligibility standard is met—and the funds are used for the clearly defined purposes specified by government rules and regulations. As the name implies, eligible individuals are automatically entitled to receive these funds, and services are based on one or more defining characteristics, such as age, occupation, disability, or income.

The federal government funded $79.2 billion of FY 1994's $104 billion of allocations for children and their families through entitlements,[4] making this by far the most prevalent means by which the federal government invests in children and families (*Database of Federal Allocations*, 1995). Food Stamps, AFDC, Medicaid, and OASDI payments make up the majority of these funds. Every person meeting the eligibility requirements may receive such subsidies, provided that they comply with the program's rules and regulations (such as AFDC beneficiaries participating in job-training programs, as stipulated in the 1988 Family Support Act).

When entitlement eligibility requirements are not met—no matter how small the margin of difference—it is illegal for an individual to access the funds and services. Nor can the monies be used for purposes other than those that are federally designated. For example, only medical care

---

[4]This figure includes allocations for both capped and uncapped entitlements.

is to be provided with Medicaid funds, and food stamps can only be used to purchase food. So, although entitlements represent a major source of funds for needy children and families, their broad use is severely circumscribed.[5]

Tax expenditures are another method by which financial investments in children and families are encouraged. Like entitlements, tax expenditures are a way to invest in general family needs and support, rather than in the delivery of specific services. They differ from entitlements, however, in two significant ways. First, tax expenditures are not direct government allocations; rather, they reduce individuals' income tax liabilities. They are thus ordinarily of limited value to low-income individuals paying little or no income tax.[6] Second, unlike entitlements, tax expenditures not only transfer income and services to a particular category of individuals (such as the poor), but also encourage private investment in activities deemed to be socially desirable.

Overall, $3.4 billion was forfeited by the federal government in 1994 through four tax expenditures expressly targeted to increasing the after-tax incomes of families with children (*Database of Federal Allocations*, 1995).[7] The child and dependent care tax credit was the largest single tax expenditure of this kind, totaling $2.8 billion dollars.[8]

Like tax expenditures, *loans* are another form of public subsidy providing both direct and indirect benefits to children and families. Because loans must be repaid and are commonly considered a tool of the private sector, they are often not counted as a public support mechanism. However, government loans are usually offered to fulfill a public purpose that is not being met by private financial markets. Thus, the government undertakes a financial obligation—for example, by underwriting high-risk ventures (and absorbing the financial losses that are more likely to come with such ventures), subsidizing interest rates, or extending loan repayment periods.

In 1994, the federal government provided approximately $79 billion in loans to support families and their communities (*Database of Federal Allocations*, 1995). These loans subsidized purchases of housing, home

---

[5]However, as will be pointed out later, resourceful local administrators have in recent years developed practices to enhance the flexibility of entitlement funds, particularly Medicaid, by aggressively seeking federal entitlement matches for activities previously supported through state and local funds, and using the resulting revenue savings to fund other programs and services.

[6]The exceptions to this are the few tax expenditures that are refundable, such as the Earned Income Tax Credit. In these cases, government payments to individuals may exceed their level of income tax liability, thus benefiting many low-income people with little or no income tax obligations.

[7]This $3.4 billion is not included in the $104 billion figure cited earlier as the total federal allocation for children and their families. It would be misleading to imply that tax expenditures are direct investments parallel to allocations.

[8]In addition to those described, there are other significant tax expenditures, such as a deduction for the mortgage of a house and the exemption for charitable contributions, which both directly and indirectly benefit families, but that also benefit adult individuals without children, and thus have not been included in the $3.4 billion figure.

heating, and educational services, as well as the start-up costs for business ventures.

Aside from individual income transfers, the federal government supports children and families through grant-in-aid programs to state and local governments and private organizations. Such grant programs fall into two broad categories: competitive and formula grants.

Competitive grants-in-aid, commonly called categorical grants, are the most common form of federal grants serving children and families. They began to proliferate in the 1960s as a means for the federal government to encourage states and localities to serve disadvantaged or disenfranchised groups and deliver particular types of program services.

In a categorical grant arrangement, the federal government carefully details the designated purposes, eligibility requirements, and permissible uses of funds. Recipients (known as *grantees*) are typically selected through a competitive application review process, and are usually state and local governments agreeing to administer a program consistent with the grant-in-aid guidelines. The grants are monitored by federal officials to check compliance with the prescribed requirements. Many grants are designed to ensure that the program will benefit the intended target population and that the grant will supplement existing state and local commitments to these beneficiaries rather than merely replacing state and local resources with federal funds. Using categorical grants for purposes other than those that are designated can make the grantee financially liable.

In 1994, the federal government delivered approximately $5.5 billion of services for children and families through 82 competitive grant-in-aid supports. Large numbers of grant programs exist in every children's service area, including education (47 programs), health (19 programs), and juvenile justice (6 programs; *Database of Federal Allocations,* 1995). In addition to federal competitive grants, each state runs its own series of competitive categorical grant-in-aid programs for children and families.

Formula grants are a less prescribed form of federal grant-in-aid support. While they too are created and authorized for a definitive purpose, it is usually broader than that of the competitive categorical grant.[9] For example, a formula grant may be provided for school reform, while a categorical grant might fund a program for staff training to meet the needs of learning disabled children. Formula grants are allocated to states and localities based on legislated formulas rather than being awarded through a grants competition. In 1994, the federal government transferred approximately $15 billion (in the form of supports and services) to children and families through formula grants.

Block grants are a type of formula grant that historically has been created by merging numerous smaller competitive and formula grant pro-

---

[9]The Catalog of Federal Domestic Assistance (OMB and USGSA, 1994) defines a *formula grant* as an "allocation of money to states or their subdivisions in accordance with a distribution formula prescribed by law or administrative regulation, for activities of a continuing nature not confined to a specific project" (pp. 6–94).

grams. Under block grants, the grantee (usually the state) is given much greater discretion than in either categorical or more prescribed formula grant arrangements in deciding how to use the funds. Federal compliance and reporting requirements are also less stringent. In 1994, four major block grants directly served children and families: the Maternal and Child Health Services Block Grant, the Child Care and Dependent Block Grant, the Social Services Block Grant, and the Chapter 2 Education Block Grant. These four grants accounted for $5.6 billion of 1994 allocations for children and families.

In 1996, The Personal Responsibility and Work Opportunity Reconciliation Act was passed. This act consolidates numerous categorical public welfare programs and provides aid to states in the form of block grants. It drastically increases the size of block grant allocations in the children and family service arena (and in general). Four implications of the changes are surfacing: (a) the entitlement status of some federal programs has been eliminated, (b) the federal role in financing social services has been greatly reduced, (c) states have more authority to design, administer, and finance programs benefiting their children and families, and (d) states are expected to place much more attention on workforce development and the creation of new jobs. These changes generate both challenges and opportunities for financing more comprehensive, community-based support systems for children and families.

Summary

This section outlined the magnitude of government spending on children and families and highlighted the principal mechanisms by which public resources are allocated to provide them with supports and services. All told, the federal government directly allocated about $104 billion for children and families in FY 1994, a figure considerably lower than that for both federal defense expenditures and spending on the elderly. It is also much lower than state and local expenditures on children and families, primarily because the single most heavily funded service for children—education—is almost exclusively supported by state and local dollars. Nevertheless, federal funds exert influence on children and family services that is belied by these relatively modest resource levels—both because of the targeting of much of the assistance on needy populations and the leverage exerted through setting the conditions by which funds will be received.

The current major funding mechanisms for children's services—entitlements, tax expenditures, loans, categorical grants-in-aid, and formula grants—can be said to drive the current support systems for children and families. As described in the following section, with the present situation of funding from so many different sources and so many varying regulations, "families' needs usually have to be fitted to available services, rather than the reverse" (Farrow & Bruner, 1993, p. 7).

The Current Financing System: Implications for Service Delivery

The amalgamation of categorical grants, formula grants, and entitlement programs that is called the public financing "system" is more than just a fund-disbursement mechanism. It also has enormous implications for how social services are delivered. Imagine that paychecks came with purchasing rules and that getting paid each week was contingent on proving that the previous week's salary was spent accordingly. Imagine further that raises were granted not based on job performance but according to how well employees documented their weekly expenditures. Some employees would no doubt find that the purchasing rules prevented them from getting what they really needed. Even so, most would take pains to show that they had followed the rules, even perhaps letting their work suffer in the process. In essence, this is how the social service financing system works. Funds that flow from the public treasury typically are neither easy to get nor easy to use, and are generally accompanied by very strict and specific spending requirements. The following section specifically describes how the current financing system inhibits the development of comprehensive, community-based services for children and families. Particular attention is placed on the ways in which the financing system is centrally governed (rather than community-based), treatment- (rather than prevention-) focused, process- (rather than outcome-) oriented, and fragmented (rather than comprehensive).

Centralized Governance

A central tenet of successful business is staying "close to the customer" (Peters & Waterman, 1982, p. 156). Osborne and Gaebler (1992) and many adherents of their book, *Reinventing Government*, suggest that this philosophy should be transferred to the public sphere in order for government to be efficient and effective. The current system for financing social services, however, is governed centrally, either at the federal or state levels. Localities are consequently far removed from the decision making process. Many federal allocations go directly to individuals, but officials at the federal and state levels determine what kinds of services are to be provided, who is eligible to receive services, and how funds will be allocated. This decision making authority is also centralized and institutionalized through federal and state rules and regulations governing the use of funds. For example, there are 27 federal programs focused on substance-abuse prevention and treatment for high-risk communities, families, and children. At least 10 different federal agencies administer these programs and control allocations through categorical and formula grants. The federal agencies distribute these grants primarily to state agencies, which then can further restrict or regulate the use of funds (Office of Management and Budget [OMB] and U.S. General Services Administration [USGSA], 1994). By the time the funds reach communities, there is scant flexibility left for social service professionals to use them creatively to meet local needs.

As Gardner (1995) noted, under the current highly prescriptive system, local policy makers find it difficult to shift resources from any public sources to meet their community's specific needs. For instance, one-quarter of the funds provided for substance-abuse prevention and treatment comes from competitive grants, which specifically delineate the types of programs that will be funded. In order to be awarded a compatible grant, a community must design a program according to grant stipulations, regardless of its own priorities. These stipulations can be constraining; for example, the Catalog of Federal Domestic Assistance (OMB & USGSA, 1994) lists 13 different federally defined objectives for a single program, the Comprehensive Residential Drug Prevention and Treatment for Substance Abusing Women and Their Children, a $15 million grant program. The objectives specify exactly what kind of services are to be provided and how they are to be administered. Only programs designed specifically to fulfill these federally defined goals can be funded. Although programs like this one were developed with the good intention of helping communities respond to a growing need, the federal government determined how this need was to be met, leaving little room for localities to determine their own courses of action.

Treatment Orientation

Although many people pay lip service to the adage that an ounce of prevention is worth a pound of cure, few dollars are earmarked for the former. The most well-funded federal programs are treatment oriented. Treatment allocated funds are *only* delivered to programs for persons who exhibit particular problems, such as drug abuse, or poverty, or some combination of defining factors. Disbursed in this manner, categorical and other public funds play an important role in alleviating some of problems, but they do little to prevent them from occurring in the first place. For example, in FY 1994, from $104 billion dollars earmarked for children and families, the federal government allocated only $3.2 billion to primary prevention services, while nearly 10 times that amount was spent on crisis intervention and support and maintenance programs (*Database of Federal Allocations*, 1995). Spending patterns like these signal a focus on treatment of specific problems, rather than an investment in prevention.

This treatment orientation is further exacerbated by a lack of flexibility in the use of public funds. Even if, for example, a community-based organization wanted to shift some of its drug-treatment monies to prevention-oriented services, strict spending requirements would inhibit its efforts. Dollars generated from entitlement and other grant programs at both the federal and state levels must by law be earmarked for the provision of mandated services and their administration.[10] Additionally, all

---

[10]Formula grants, which include block grants, are more flexible than categorical/competitive grants. But the history of block grants demonstrates that the longer they exist, the more regulated they become (Hayes, 1995), so they, too, are restricted in their use.

funds distributed require an "audit trail"—that is, it must be possible to track money as it moves through the system to a particular client or for a specific function. All but the most exceptional and creative local administrators who attempt to shift monies from remediation to prevention find it nearly impossible.

Fragmentation

When a child acts out, this behavior is often a reaction to difficult conditions in the family. The child's parents may need job training, substance abuse counseling, and parenting education, or the child may need better nutrition or parental attention. Families—particularly economically disadvantaged families living in distressed areas—often have complex, interconnected problems. However, frequently in the current system, treatment is fragmented: Each problem is treated individually, without regard for a client's other issues, or family circumstances. This is due in part to the way that funds are appropriated and to the regulations that guide them.[11] For example, there are substance-abuse prevention and treatment programs for juveniles, pregnant women, the homeless, and Native Americans, among others. There are also family support services for these same groups. Little documentation exists on the interaction of the providers of these services, but program administrators report that relationships between them are limited or nonexistent (Orland & Foley, 1996). There is little incentive to collaborate, because resources are tight and because social service programs are not reimbursed for service provision outside their narrowly defined domains.

Additionally, because receiving public funds relies in part on showing compliance with regulation, programs need to be able to demonstrate exactly what services the funding provides and to whom. This results in rigid procedural adherence, and can lead to a file, a case manager, and a counselor for treating and providing for each individual. Administratively, this makes tracing funds easier, but it is difficult for multiple discrete service providers to address the complexity of a clients' problems, and it increases the fragmentation of service delivery. People within the same family or even one individual may interact with a multiplicity of providers, with each provider focusing on a different aspect of their lives and acting autonomously, not in concert. Imber-Black (1988) described a family "served" by 14 different "helpers," each unaware of the others' existence. In this environment, providers duplicate effort, working at odds with each other, and, in many cases, wasting resources.

---

[11]Farrow and Joe (1992) also noted that both categorical training and the categorical structure of public agencies also play a role in creating social services that treat problems in isolation.

Process Orientation

Funding for many public programs, particularly entitlement programs, is determined by caseload. Logically, the greater the number of people who need services, the larger the fund allocation. However, this seemingly rational system supplies social service staff with perverse incentives. When services succeed by removing individuals from the ranks of those needing support and getting them on their own two feet, funding is reduced. If finances are managed well and savings accrue, the savings must often be returned to the treasury at the end of the fiscal year, and the following year's allocation is cut accordingly. Because annual program audits ignore outcomes, staff tend to focus on compliance with rules and regulations rather than results. The goal of many categorically funded programs then becomes to maintain caseloads, spend every dime allocated, and focus on procedures not progress.

Contributing to this process orientation is one of the ongoing frustrations of the public financing system: the existence of varying eligibility requirements. At the federal, state, and local levels, separate programs intended for the same population have differing participation guidelines. This is particularly true of categorical grant programs. For example, three competitive grant programs administered by the U.S. Department of Health and Human Services have been established to benefit substance-abusing women. The first program focuses on pregnant or postpartum women and includes their infants up to the age of 5 and other children ages 6 to 15. The target of the second program is low-income pregnant or postpartum women and their infants only. The third program targets the women and their infants and children, but is not limited to pregnant or postpartum women (OMB & USGSA, 1994). One woman might qualify for the services funded through the first program but may not meet the income requirement of the second program, while an older child may be eligible for services through the third program. Social service providers and administrators must sort out this morass. If they are awarded all three grants to support service delivery for overlapping populations, they must fill out different paperwork for each program and separately prove eligibility for each individual. They also must provide services only to those who meet the requirements of each program.

The paperwork is not limited to eligibility determination and grant applications. Publicly funded programs often are required to submit numerous reports to the government. To continue receiving funds, many recipients of competitive grants must provide to federal officials quarterly progress reports, yearly financial status reports, and an overall final report, and be subjected to annual fiscal audits (OMB & USGSA, 1994). For a 3-year grant, this totals no less than 16 reports and three audits. Fiscal accountability is important, but no equivalent emphasis is placed on a program's impact on social service recipients. Most accountability audits of categorical programs virtually ignore outcomes. Because compliance with regulations rather than outcomes is stressed, most current social services focus on process, not results.

Implications for Financing Comprehensive, Community-Based Support Systems

The current categorical financing structure has, in part, fostered a service-delivery system that social service professionals and other decision makers increasingly recognize as contrary to best practice (Farrow & Bruner, 1993). Its centralized governance, fragmentation, process orientation, and remediation focus inhibit the development of more family-centered, locally controlled prevention services, which are considered primary elements of model service delivery (see, for example, Schorr, 1988).

Comprehensive, community-based support systems attempt to incorporate all of these best practices, but they are inhibited by the problems of the current financing system. In fact, the current financing system is often cited as the primary barrier to developing comprehensive community-based support systems for children and families (see, for example, Feister, 1994; Gardner, 1995; Sipe & Batten, 1994; U.S. Department of Education and American Educational Research Association, 1995). The characteristics that the system fosters in social service programs are almost entirely at odds with the goals of integrated service initiatives. Where comprehensive initiatives focus on prevention and early intervention services, most public programs respond only after problems become acute (Hayes et al., 1995). Where comprehensive initiatives acknowledge the complexity and interconnectedness of social issues, public systems define eligibility narrowly and focus treatment on individuals. Where comprehensive initiatives recognize the assets of individuals and communities, programs funded from the public treasury focus on their liabilities. And where comprehensive initiatives seek an outcomes focus, public systems reward process and compliance rather than results (Farrow & Joe, 1992). Other barriers to developing comprehensive, community-based support systems exist, but the structure of the current public financing system and its impact on service delivery significantly hinder their growth.

Fortunately, efforts are being made to align practice with theory. The following section describes several innovative efforts to develop and maintain comprehensive, community-based support systems.

Innovations in Financing Integrated Services

In response to the financing challenges described in the previous section, several strategies have been developed and tested to encourage and sustain comprehensive, community-based support systems. Advocates of integrated service initiatives are looking to nonpublic revenues for fiscal backing in areas where public monies are lacking. Also, several alternative public financing methods—which incorporate prevention-oriented, family-centered, and locally controlled services—have been developed or adapted to support comprehensive initiatives. From policy reform efforts that include decategorization and block grants, to intrasystem reform strategies (e.g., funding coordination, fund redeployment, and results-based budgeting), financing innovations supporting comprehensive initiatives are being piloted nationwide. The following section illustrates financing options for comprehensive, community-based support systems and provides examples of initiatives using these strategies.

Private Expenditures

Private expenditures have played a significant role in the development of more comprehensive services for children and families. Government funding for social services limits resource use to a standard array of categorical services and supports, but private citizens, corporations, and foundations who provide philanthropic gifts and grants can afford more cutting-edge approaches. These expenditures often have fewer reporting requirements and other constraints, so they can provide the flexibility that comprehensive initiatives need. They also can fill in the gaps that other expenditures often do not cover, including funds for planning, demonstration, or evaluation costs.

However, private funds have their limitations, with the most problematic being their availability. There are limited private funds for which comprehensive initiatives and other social service providers must compete. Large amounts of resources can be invested in grant applications with no results. Additionally, nearly all private benefactors are loathe to finance ongoing operating costs, preferring instead to invest in time-limited, supplementary projects that might advance the field but do not commit the benefactors over the long term. Finally, the flexibility of private expenditures can be a bane as well as a boon. Private funds can often be withdrawn as easily as they are granted. For these reasons, private funds—whether individual, corporate, or foundation grants, gifts, or loans—must be used in conjunction with other funds in order to finance a comprehensive initiative over the long term. For example,

> *New Futures*: The New Futures Initiative of the Annie E. Casey Foundation was initiated in 1988 to help communities develop school-based, integrated services for at-risk youth. Savannah, Georgia, received a $10 million grant from the Foundation for a five-year project. The Foundation required the community to put up an equal amount in matching funds to ensure local commitment during the project, as well as at the conclusion of the grant period. (Hayes et al., 1995)

To generate some of their own revenue, independent of public or private largesse, some comprehensive initiatives have begun to experiment with user fees as a funding source. Although they have shown promise in helping to develop community "buy-in,"[12] user fees have yet to become a

---

[12]User fees are also frequently a symbolic gesture, rather than a mechanism for fundraising. For instance, if a CCBSS is serving a low-income population, a user fee may be instigated in order for the client population to feel as though they are paying for the services that are being received, to feel inclusion and membership, or to get them to buy-in to a certain program. However, these fees may only cover a very small fraction of the actual costs of service delivery.

stable source of revenue for comprehensive initiatives. They rarely cover the entire cost of integrated-service provision, because they neglect both administrative and start-up costs. They also may be burdensome to economically disadvantaged persons, who often are a target of comprehensive service initiatives. For example, Family Focus Centers, operating in the Chicago area since 1976, provide families with support through a variety of services, including child care, parent support groups, case management, family literacy, and counseling. Ten percent of Family Focus Centers' FY 1995 budget came from user fees (Hayes et al., 1995).

Public Financing Strategies

Private expenditures can supplement some activities, but the broad-based development of comprehensive, community-based support systems will require changes in the public finance system, the largest organized source of revenue for children and family services. Used in conjunction with each other or alone, many innovative approaches for garnering and using public funds are being piloted nationwide. Highlighted below are existing strategies that can be reapplied, as well as new techniques that are being developed to support comprehensive initiatives.

Results-based budgeting and accountability. Results-based budgeting (also known as *outcomes-based budgeting*) and results-based accountability bring business principles to the social service arena. Used together, these strategies link program planning and resource allocation, providing rewards and sanctions to programs on the basis of their progress toward achieving desired outcomes (Brizius & The Design Team, 1994). Desired outcomes can include removing people from the welfare roles, preventing teen pregnancy, or any other social service goal that a community agrees upon in the planning process. Commonly practiced in the business community, these strategies give managers the tools to understand program costs and to allocate funds on the basis of sound financial investments rather than on changing economic or political situations. Outcomes of services also can be tracked to determine whether or not goals were achieved (Bruner, 1994). Many states and local agencies are making strides toward using desired results to influence their planning and budgeting processes. As an example, consider the following:

> *Oregon Benchmarks*: In 1988, the state of Oregon developed a 20-year strategic plan called Oregon Shines. To measure progress toward the goals outlined in Oregon Shines, 272 benchmarks were developed. Oregon Shines has since been renewed, and the benchmarks rewritten—the state's now 92 benchmarks serve as goals and measures around which agencies and organizations can collaborate and direct fund allocations to work toward desired results.

> *Cleveland Works, Inc.*: Cleveland Works is a program designed primarily to move Cleveland, Ohio AFDC recipients from welfare to work. To

facilitate this transition, the program provides comprehensive services, including day care, health and mental health services, and legal aid, in addition to job training and job placement services. About 50 percent of the Cleveland Works budget comes from a performance-based contract, in which the organization is paid for every person it removes from the welfare roles, with payment based on the expected savings to the city and state governments. (Hayes et al., 1995)

One of the reasons these methods previously were not used extensively in the public sector stems from the difficulty of measuring outcomes in social programs. In order to use results-based budgeting and accountability, one must be able to assess results. In the private sector, profit is a natural measure of performance; in the public sector, there is not always a parallel measure. Placing a dollar value on prevention services is very difficult. What is the value of fewer runaways or reduced infant mortality, for example? What are the costs of failing to prevent vagrant teens or unhealthy babies? The development of a credible performance measurement system is necessary in order to use results-based strategies effectively.

Decategorization methods. Decategorization methods, such as funding coordination and block grants, are techniques that emphasize greater efficiency and coordination in the use of public funds (Friedman, 1994). Whereas new funds may be appropriated for results-based planning and budgeting and other refinancing efforts, decategorization methods typically rely on the more efficient use of existing monies. *Funding coordination*, for example, does not change the way that funds flow to programs: They are still disbursed categorically, but are coordinated to finance prevention-oriented services and other activities essential to comprehensive service provision. Developing the structure for funding coordination is often a long process, done through waivers or in conjunction with legislation that allows participating initiatives to receive exemptions from conventional categorical restrictions on the uses of funds. This technique can promote services that have the flexibility to respond holistically to the needs of children and families.

> *Child Welfare Decategorization Project*: In Iowa, the Child Welfare Decategorization Project coordinates more than 30 separate state funding streams at the county level. Legislation was developed that allows the participating counties funding flexibility and increased authority over their resources. (Hayes et al., 1995)

Broader decategorization strategies, which actually change the fund-disbursement mechanism, are related to funding coordination. With *blending* or *pooling*, funds are no longer distributed categorically. Funds once directed toward specific services are freed from the categorical disbursement mechanism and can be blended across agencies and applied in less restricted ways. This strategy is often used to coordinate service delivery and eliminate duplicative efforts by social service providers. Again, this strategy usually requires legislation or new administrative structures at state and local levels before it can be accomplished. Consider this example,

> *California Assembly Bill 1741 (The Youth Pilot Program)*: California Assembly Bill 1741 provides allowances for five pilot counties to blend monies from at least four categorical programs to fund services for children and families. No new money was appropriated for this effort. All the funds utilized are simply freed up from categorical restrictions and redirected as the counties see fit. The state exchanges control through compliance monitoring for an outcomes-based strategic plan from each county. If results are successful, these counties will serve as models for future statewide adaptation of decategorized, comprehensive, prevention-oriented services. (Hayes et al., 1995)

> *West Virginia Governor's Cabinet on Children and Families*: The West Virginia Governor's Cabinet on Children and Families—with members from social service, education, and labor agencies—was created in 1990 to create closer ties among agencies providing services to children and families. The relationship that developed spawned an effort to set aside one-third of one percent of expenditures on the thirteen largest federal categorical programs, including Medicaid, AFDC, and the Job Training Partnership Act funds. The pooled funds will be utilized to plan and coordinate comprehensive services. (Hayes et al., 1995)

Block grants are another type of decategorization measure. Block grants have the potential to fully fund a comprehensive initiative, but they are politically controversial. They consolidate disparate grant programs into a few unified funding streams, usually with the exchange of autonomy for reduced fiscal responsibility. In August 1996, Congress passed and the President signed the Personal Responsibility and Work Opportunity Reconciliation Act. This law overhauls the nation's welfare system and consolidates numerous categorical public welfare programs to provide aid to states in the form of block grants. States are thus granted greater autonomy to design and operate programs to meet the needs of their low-income families with children. In turn, they will have to provide for their ever-changing welfare populations with defined and potentially constraining federal aid.

> *Lafayette Courts Family Development Center*: The Lafayette Courts Family Development Center receives about 90 percent of its funds through the Community Development Block Grant administered by the Baltimore Housing Authority. On-site services—including child care, adult education, job training, and family support services—are available to the 2,400 residents of the Lafayette Courts public housing facility. (Hayes et al., 1995)

If they are developed correctly, block grants and other decategorization methods could become opportunities for policy makers interested in reforming the categorical system and could help make comprehensive service initiatives a widespread reality (Hayes, 1995). However, critics warn that inadequate funding could negate the potential benefits expected from the reduction of federal regulation and the devolution of authority (Hayes, 1995). As block grant policy is formed and re-formed, what is needed is model legislation that will guide decision makers in developing block grant or decategorization policy that bolsters comprehensive, community-based support systems. Informed by lessons from the history of block grant reforms (Hayes, 1995), future legislation should describe the full complement of federal programs available for communities to access and include incentives for developing comprehensive initiatives.

Refinancing. Refinancing[13] is another tool that social service administrators use to fund comprehensive service initiatives. Refinancing entails aggressively pursuing monies from uncapped federal appropriations such as entitlement funds, using these new federal funds to pay for standard services, and then applying the freed-up local and state funds to pay for alternative programs, including, perhaps, comprehensive service initiatives.[14] At this writing, there are five primary programs that can be used in refinancing efforts: Title IV-E Foster Care and Subsidized Adoption, Title IV-A Emergency Assistance, Title XIX Medicaid, Title IV-D Child Support, and Title XVI SSI Benefits (Farrow & Bruner, 1993; Friedman, 1994). Although a detailed account of the ways in which programs acquire more federal funds is beyond the scope of this chapter, it should be emphasized that most refinancing is achieved by increasing program eligibility rates and expanding coverage to additional service areas. For example,

> *Healthy Start*: Another California-based initiative, Healthy Start is a school-linked, comprehensive support program. One of its primary financing strategies has been to aggressively pursue federal Medicaid funds by claiming reimbursement for services provided at school sites, particularly therapeutic services. School districts can be reimbursed for speech and physical therapy, and health screenings provided to Medicaid-eligible children. (Hayes et al., 1995)

Refinancing, however, would be a much more effective financing tool if funds were appropriated over time periods greater than 1 year. Annual funding uncertainty is the bane of several comprehensive service initia-

---

[13]Refinancing is not a viable financing strategy when the entitlement status of federal programs is eliminated. And entitlement programs are increasingly facing scrutiny and criticism as taxpayers and voters urge lawmakers to devolve authority to lower levels of government, balance budgets, and produce tangible results with fiscal investments. The 1996 Personal Responsibility and Work Opportunity Reconciliation Act reforms welfare, ending its federal entitlement status and devolving authority for its provision to the states. This is a good example of how variations to traditional financing systems can create challenges to using creative financing mechanisms and tools.

[14]According to Friedman (1994), the chance that the freed-up local money will not be used for services for children and families is the greatest risk of using refinancing strategies.

tives. Each year, many programs must devote energy to lobbying for support in their communities and state legislatures in the face of budget cuts and staff pressures. This constant uncertainty makes developing collaborative relationships among public agencies and other service providers difficult. The promise of multi-year funding has helped some current initiatives create longer term plans, which is an activity appropriate to an intervention designed to make a lasting impact on a community.

Fund redeployment. Another technique being used to support the development of comprehensive initiatives is *fund redeployment.* When redeploying funds, social service providers emphasize movement from restrictive and expensive services to cheaper, more humane, community-based supports and services. Nonviolent mentally ill persons, for example, may be transferred from institutions to group homes, or juvenile delinquents may be sent to an alternate sentencing program rather than a detention center. Friedman (1994) identified four methods of redeployment: (a) investment-based, (b) capitation-based, (c) cut-based, and (d) material. Material redeployment is probably the easiest type to achieve. Staff and other nonfiscal resources are shifted from one place to another, which is more conducive to the development of integrated services. School-linked comprehensive initiatives often use this technique when co-locating family support, juvenile justice, and other services at the school site.

Cut-based redeployment is very straightforward: It involves cutting one type of service in order to fund another. Although social service budgets are very tight, it is widely agreed that money often is not used efficiently (Friedman, 1994). Cutting can be conducted discriminantly, and the savings can be invested in integrated service efforts. Kagan, Goffin, Golub, and Pritchard (1995) noted that by "decreasing bureaucracy and duplication of efforts, integrated services and service delivery systems can become more cost efficient, with portions of monies funneled back into service delivery" (pp. 83–84).

Other types of redeployment are more complicated. Capitation-based redeployment, for example, entails charging one fixed cost for groups of services. Health maintenance organizations use this type of financing strategy. Investment-based redeployment, on the other hand, is founded on the idea that short-term investments will reap long-term gains. Savings anticipated from the use of preventive services, for example, can be used up front to fund those services. This method is more easily discussed than done, however. Although many believe that investing in prevention-oriented services is more efficient than investing in remediation, there is little information on the short- and long-term costs and benefits of such investments.

> *Kansas City's Local Investment Commission (LINC)*: LINC is an initiative to reform Kansas City's human services system and devolve responsibility for the design and operation of services to neighborhood leaders. LINC serves as a catalyst for reallocating current resources

from highly formalized categorical services to more flexible responses to community needs. For example, some LINC communities are redesigning their schools to be the hubs of neighborhood social services. LINC also sponsors a program which converts AFDC and Food Stamp benefits to grants to local employers who hire welfare recipients. (Hayes et al., 1995)

Fund redeployment and the other techniques described often rely on the availability and accessibility of valid data on program participation and the use of funds. The development of a model management information system (MIS) for comprehensive service initiatives would help support these endeavors. Many comprehensive initiatives have already had to modify their existing MIS, or create a new one to support the data demands of redeployment, refinancing, evaluation, and other collaborative work. A thorough review of these MISs is presented in the National Center on Service Integration report by Marzke, Both, and Focht (1994). Building on some of this work and creating user-friendly, easily modifiable software would help support the development of comprehensive, community-based support systems.

Investments in Interprofessional Development

Even if all of these promising strategies for reform were implemented and all of the needed policies were adopted, one challenge to the development of comprehensive, community-based support systems would remain.[15] The impact of the existing inflexible, treatment-oriented, process-focused, hierarchical financing system will persist unless the relationships among providers and the attitudes and skills of social service professionals are addressed (Orland & Foley, 1996). Research and anecdotal evidence has shown that the public financing structure not only affects the way in which social services are delivered, it also affects the attitudes and competencies of social service professionals (Orland & Foley, 1996; Kirst et al., 1994). The fallout from the current public financing system makes it difficult for professionals to establish and maintain relationships across disciplines and contributes to a deficit orientation. Combined with specific professional training and agencies organized around particular areas (Farrow & Joe, 1992), specialized funding causes many social service professionals and staff to "think" categorically. The message they receive when, for example, funding for substance abuse treatment is provided separately from funding for family support and other services, is that these are distinct issues that must be dealt with separately.

Public funds are primarily obtained by identifying the weaknesses of

---

[15]In a joint report, the U.S. Department of Education and the American Educational Research Association suggested that investment in interprofessional development was needed. *Interprofessional development* was defined as preparation to support "the ability of professionals to integrate and connect services for children and youth with their potential problems" (p.19).

clients in need of social services. Clients must present a specific problem or be classified as disadvantaged in some way in order to qualify for services. Because the focus is on liabilities, social service providers often think of their clients as deficient rather than as individuals with the capabilities to solve their own problems with support and guidance.

Even in initiatives that have developed a substantially different financing structure, administrators described the pervasiveness of these attitudes as one of their primary challenges (Orland & Foley, 1996). However, some comprehensive initiatives have attempted to address this issue through interagency planning and collaboration, as well as efforts at creating interprofessional development opportunities. For example, *New Beginnings*, A San Diego county collaborative, seeks to use existing resources more efficiently and to develop family-centered integrated services for children and families. In the project's initial year, an Institute for Collaborative Management was developed "to institutionalize collaboration among the partner agencies" (Barfield et al., 1994, p. 11) and to develop professionals' collaborative skills. Interagency conferences and training activities have been held (Barfield et al., 1994).

But interprofessional development cannot be achieved by comprehensive initiatives alone. Universities and other institutions that provide training to social workers, psychologists, educators, and other service professionals must revamp their curricula, and governing agencies must reorganize to provide opportunities for collaboration. Using strategies like results-based planning and budgeting, decategorization, fund redeployment, and refinancing to change the financing system is a necessary step to improving services for children and families. But these strategies will be insufficient unless social service professionals concurrently promote decategorized training and service. One of the current financing system's unfortunate legacies is its negative impact on service delivery; undoing its effects is one of the primary obstacles threatening the development of comprehensive, community-based support systems. The following section highlights this and other challenges that lie ahead.

The Challenges Ahead

Three major areas were analyzed in the previous sections. The magnitude and nature of current public financing efforts on behalf of children and families were described. The difficulties caused by such arrangements were then outlined from the perspective of delivering integrated and community-centered services and supports. Finally, specific attempts to better align the goals of more comprehensive, community-based support systems for children and families with the financing arrangements needed to create and sustain them were presented.

Implicit throughout this chapter is the belief that more integrated and community-based approaches have considerable potential to enhance positive outcomes for children. However, despite the numerous initiatives launched over the last decade, significant changes in the current institutional techniques for financing services for children and their families are required in order for this service delivery paradigm to become both large-scale and sustainable.

The necessary changes are primarily in three areas: (a) management systems, (b) external grant mechanisms, and (c) professional development activities. Because the areas are interrelated, reforms in each area are critical for bringing about widespread systemic change consistent with a comprehensive community-based service-delivery paradigm.

First, new public-sector management systems need to be developed and used in the public sector in order to design, budget, and evaluate services for children and families. The new systems must articulate across traditional functionally organized service sectors (education, health, social services, juvenile justice, and community development) by focusing attention on the contributions from each that are needed to achieve high-priority children's outcomes. Management reforms should also encourage greater resource investment in prevention services, as well as the use of new accountability systems for monitoring and reporting progress in achieving desired children's outcome objectives.

Second, new intergovernmental grant arrangements must be developed that empower local communities to allocate resources consistent with their children's outcome goals. The current system of fragmented, prescriptive, and detailed service mandates needs to be replaced with more flexible outcomes-based grant policies as a condition for external financial support. Furthermore, explicit incentives should be built into new grants for interagency cooperation, as well as the leveraging of private-sector resources.

Finally, there must be dramatic changes in how child and family service administrators and service providers are trained to perform their jobs. As noted earlier, the current financing system has reinforced professional training that underemphasizes interservice cooperation and often conflicts outright with the objectives of integrated, community-based approaches. New management and structural reforms can be expected to have marginal impact on service arrangements as long as the attitudes and skills of front-line workers reflect traditional categorical arrangements.

These needed system changes are, of course, not trivial, and the challenges ahead are made even more daunting by the fact that they are both technical and political in nature. Put simply, there is a need for new financing and related service delivery structures that alter both horizontal relationships among service providers and vertical relationships among the federal, state, and local governments. Is it realistic to expect changes of this magnitude?

External factors may create unprecedented opportunities for such restructuring to occur. It is significant that virtually no one defends the existing children's financing and service delivery system anymore.[16] In part, this reflects the near-universal belief that public investments to date

---

[16]See Gardner (1995), however, for a description of both the pros and the cons of a categorical financing structure.

have not yielded favorable child and family outcomes. It also reflects the recognition among officials of all political persuasions that governments cannot continue to make such inefficient resource investments in the years ahead. Budget deficits, stagnant real incomes, and increasing children's service demands driven by demographic factors such as increased school enrollments and higher child-poverty rates, are all expected to increase the level of fiscal stress on government in the foreseeable future (Orland & Cohen, 1995). Cuts in federal aid will make this condition particularly acute in some states and localities. These circumstances could lead political officials, policy leaders, and program managers to rally around fundamental changes in management and service delivery arrangements offering the promise of increased efficiency and enhanced outcomes. The unprecedented recent level of reform activity exemplified by Oregon Benchmarks and California's Assembly Bill 1741 at the state level and federal initiatives such as empowerment zones and block grants can be partly attributed to this challenging fiscal context.

Of course, this is not the only possible scenario, or even the most likely one. Having a heightened receptivity to new ways of doing things is not the same as redesigning financing and service delivery structures so that they are more comprehensive, community-based, and results-driven. From this perspective, the future fiscal and political climate includes at least as many dangers as opportunities. Scarce resources could as easily (perhaps more easily) lead to further politicization of children's services as to increased intergovernmental and service-sector cooperation. Funding limitations may also preclude the resource investments needed to redesign government management systems and interprofessional development.

Even structural reforms like block grants may have little impact on traditional service arrangements. Bureaucratic inertia and political pressures may result in the persistence of preexisting local categorical service structures long after they are required by federal or state governments. Even worse, given heightened fiscal stress, the increased flexibility afforded states and communities could be used not to further integrate services, but to divert scarce public resources from needy to more affluent constituents.

Helping to ensure that new financing arrangements such as block grants further the objectives embodied in an integrated community-based service delivery paradigm will be the major policy challenge facing reform advocates in the months and years ahead. Opportunities to devise alternative programs will abound as states develop their own structures to replace federal requirements and mandates.

The providers of social services, particularly program administrators, are uniquely suited to lead these endeavors. Armed with an understanding of both the strengths and limitations of current financing arrangements, they can promote new financing mechanisms that will avoid the negative implications of the categorical system while ensuring support for poor children and families. For example, practitioners can encourage the inclusion of strategies like results-based budgeting to alter the service-delivery focus from process to outcomes. They can also support activities such as fund blending and resource redeployment that allow for the acknowledgment of the complexity of the problems that children and their families face and encourage the development of coordinated service delivery. Finally, social service providers—particularly those with strong professional associations, such as psychologists, teachers, and health care providers—can press credentialing institutions to provide more opportunities for interprofessional instruction and development.

A vast improvement of social service delivery is indeed possible. Even with the expected reductions in funding that accompany them, block grants have the potential to promote this improvement. However, one should not underestimate the degree of perseverance, political leadership, technical know-how, and good fortune that will be necessary in order to succeed with this ambitious service-restructuring agenda. Social service professionals and other advocates must seize the moment and play a lead role in efforts to reshape financing mechanisms so that they facilitate, rather than inhibit, the development of comprehensive, community-based support systems for children and families.

References

Barfield, D., Brindis, C., Guthrie, L., McDonald, W., Philliber, S., & Scott, B. (1994). *The evaluation of new beginnings: First report.* San Diego, CA: New Beginnings.

Brizius, J., & The Design Team (1994). *Deciding for investment: Getting returns on tax dollars.* Washington, DC: Alliance for Redesigning Government, National Academy of Public Administration.

Bruner, C. (1994). *Investment based budgeting: The principles in converting from a remediation/response to a prevention/investment budget.* Washington, DC: Child and Family Policy Center.

Database of Federal Allocations and Tax Expenditures Benefiting Children and Families [database]. (1995). Washington, DC: The Finance Project [Internal Product].

Farrow, F., & Bruner, C. (1993). *Getting to the bottom line: State and community strategies for financing comprehensive community service systems* (Resource Brief 4). New York: National Center for Service Integration.

Farrow, F., & Joe, T. (1992). Financing school-linked, integrated services. *The Future of Children, 2*(1), 56–67.

Feister, L. (1994, July). *Comprehensive strategies for children and families: The role of schools and community-based organizations.* (Report of the July 15, 1994, White House Meeting). Washington, DC: The White House.

Friedman, M. (1994). *Financing reform of family and children's services: An approach to the systematic consideration of financing options, or "The cosmology of financing."* [Draft manuscript] Washington, DC: The Center for the Study of Social Policy.

Gardner, S. (1995). *Reform options for the intergovernmental funding system: Decategorization policy issues.* Washington, DC: The Finance Project.

Hayes, C. D. (1995). *Rethinking block grants: Toward improved intergovernmental financing for education and other children's services.* Washington, DC: The Finance Project.

Hayes, C. D., Lipoff, E., & Danegger, A. (1995). *Comprehensive service initiatives: A compendium of innovative programs.* Washington, DC: The Finance Project.

Imber-Black, E. (1988). *Families and larger systems: A family therapist's guide through the labyrinth.* New York: Guilford Press.

Kagan, S. L., Goffin, S. G., Golub, S. A., & Pritchard, E. (1995). *Toward systemic reform: Service integration for young children and their families.* Falls Church, VA: National Center for Service Integration.

Kirst, M. W., Koppich, J. E., & Kelley, C. (1994). School-linked services and Chapter I: A new approach to improving outcomes for children. In K. K. Wong & M. C. Wang (Eds.), *Rethinking policy for at-risk students* (pp. 197–220). Berkeley, CA: McCutchan.

Marzke, C., Both, D., & Focht, J. (1994). *Information systems to support comprehensive human services delivery: Emerging approaches, issues, and opportunities.* Falls Church, VA: National Center for Service Integration.

Office of Management and Budget, Executive Office of the President. (1994). *Budget of the United States Government, Fiscal Year 1995.* Washington, DC: U.S. Government Printing Office.

Office of Management and Budget and U.S. General Services Administration. (1994). *Catalog of federal domestic assistance.* Washington, DC: U.S. Government Printing Office.

Orland, M. E., & Cohen, C. E. (1995). *State investments in education and other children's services: The fiscal challenges ahead.* Washington, DC: The Finance Project.

Orland, M. E., & Foley, E. (1996). *Beyond decategorization: Defining barriers and potential solutions to creating effective comprehensive, community-based support systems for children and families.* Washington, DC: The Finance Project.

Osborne, D., & Gaebler, T. (1992). *Reinventing government: How the entrepreneurial spirit is transforming the public sector.* New York: Plume.

Peters, T. J., & Waterman, R. H. (1982). *In search of excellence: Lessons from America's best-run companies.* New York: Warner.

Schorr, L. B. (1988). *Within our reach: Breaking the cycle of disadvantage.* New York: Doubleday.

Sipe, C. L., & Batten, S. T. (1994). *School-based programs for adolescent parents and their young children: Overcoming barriers and challenges to implementing comprehensive school-based services.* Bala Cynwyd, PA: Center for Assessment and Policy Development.

United States Department of Education and the American Educational Research Association. (1995). *School-linked comprehensive services for children and families: What we know and what we need to know.* Washington, DC: Author.

Part II

Implementing Integrated Services: Exemplary Models and Approaches

6

Combining Effective Treatment Strategies With Family-Preservation Models of Service Delivery

Sonja K. Schoenwald and Scott W. Henggeler

Within the past decade, family-preservation programs have proliferated under the auspices of federal, state, and foundation-sponsored initiatives to stem the tide of out-of-home placements of children (Adams, 1994). Consistent with their origins in the social work disciplines, the proliferation of programs has occurred primarily within the domains of public child-protective service–child welfare systems (Farrow, 1991; K. Nelson, 1994a; K. Nelson & Landsman, 1992). Recently, however, family-preservation programs have been adopted by mental health (Stroul & Goldman, 1990) and juvenile justice (K. Nelson, 1990) systems in some states. In addition, mental health services researchers and advocates of mental health reform have described family-preservation services as desirable alternatives to the use of restrictive and expensive placements for children and adolescents with serious emotional disturbances (Burns & Friedman, 1990; Stroul & Friedman, 1994).

The primary aims of this chapter are to familiarize psychologists with the family-preservation services literature and to illuminate the important role that psychologists and child and adolescent psychotherapy researchers can play in the development, evaluation, and dissemination of effective family-preservation services for youth with serious clinical problems. Several tools are used to accomplish these aims. First, the philosophical and programmatic features that distinguish family preservation services from traditional (e.g., inpatient, residential, traditional outpatient) models of service delivery are described, as are the most prevalent "practice models" of family preservation services (K. Nelson, 1994b). Next, research on the effectiveness of family-preservation programs with child welfare, juvenile justice, and "mixed" populations is reviewed, and the implications of these findings for the development of effective family-preservation services for child mental health populations are discussed. Emerging practice models

Preparation of this manuscript was supported in part by National Institute on Drug Abuse Grant DA-08029 and by National Institute of Mental Health Grants MH-51852 and R24MH53558-01.

designed specifically for youth with serious clinical problems are de-scribed. One of these models, multisystemic therapy (MST; Henggeler & Borduin, 1990), has been empirically validated in several clinical trials (Santos, Henggeler, Burns, Arana, & Meisler, 1995) and provides a good example of the type of theory- and research-driven approaches that may advance the family-preservation field.

Core Philosophical and Service Delivery Characteristics

While initially conceptualized as "a programmatic intervention" to prevent out-of-home placements of children deemed at risk of maltreatment (D. Nelson, 1990), family preservation is more accurately described as a model of service delivery through which a variety of counseling and concrete ser-vice interventions are implemented in the homes and communities of re-ferred families.

Underlying Philosophy

A basic assumption underlying most programs is that children are better off being raised in their natural families than in surrogate families or institutions (Farrow, 1991; Kinney, Madsen, Haapala, & Fleming, 1977; Knitzer & Cole, 1989; K. Nelson & Landsman, 1992). Consistent with this assumption, philosophical principles common to most programs are (a) the family is the focus of interventions; (b) interventions should capitalize on family strengths, which can be identified even in families challenged by multiple and serious needs; and (c) interventions should be designed to enhance the capacities of family members to meet, or garner the resources to meet, their own needs, thus empowering rather than "doing for" fami-lies (Farrow, 1991).

Service Delivery Characteristics

Several structural features distinguish the family-preservation model of service delivery from traditional models of mental health service delivery (e.g., residential treatment, inpatient treatment, outpatient clinic treat-ment). Family preservation services are (a) delivered in the home; (b) in-tense (ranging from 2 to 15 hours per week); (c) flexible (workers are gen-erally available 24 hours per day, 7 days a week); (d) time-limited (4–6 weeks to 4–6 months); and (d) characterized by low caseloads (2 to 10 families per worker).

Interventions

The interventions most commonly used by family-preservation workers are informed by a broadly generic, multiproblem orientation based on the assumption "that a multiplicity of interaction and different problems most frequently disable family functioning" (D. Nelson, 1990, p. 24). That is, it is assumed that families referred for family preservation are characterized by problems meeting basic needs (e.g., housing, adequate income, health care) and by problems with family interaction (e.g., parent–child conflict, poor communication, inadequate parenting skills). It is this multiproblem focus that presumably necessitates implementation of a combination of concrete services and practical problem solving combined with counseling and instructional assistance (D. Nelson, 1990; K. Nelson & Landsman, 1992). On the other hand, as suggested later in this chapter, it appears that a broadly generic or multiproblem approach alone is not sufficient to address the problems that prompted referral, and therefore, to produce positive outcomes. The treatment orientation of family-preservation programs is or should be ecological in nature, viewing children in the context of their families and families in the context of their community (Farrow, 1991; D. Nelson, 1990; K. Nelson, Landsman, & Deutelbaum, 1990). It appears that in many states, this feature of family-preservation programs "remains more rhetorical than real" (Farrow, 1991, p. 270).

Program Typologies

Within the context of the aforementioned philosophical assumptions and structural characteristics, programs vary substantially with respect to objectives, program structure, relative emphasis on treatment vs. concrete services, theoretical orientation, and nature of treatment (K. Nelson & Landsman, 1992; Pecora, Haapala, & Fraser, 1990). Program typologies have been developed by several reviewers (Barth, 1990; Frankel, 1988; K. Nelson & Landsman, 1992; K. Nelson et al., 1990; Pecora et al., 1990), and some consensus has emerged with respect to the features that distinguish family-preservation programs from other models of service delivery and from other "family-based service programs" (K. Nelson & Landsman, 1992; Pecora et al., 1990). For example, K. Nelson and her colleagues (K. Nelson, 1994b; K. Nelson et al., 1990) have identified three distinct practice models, described subsequently, that can be differentiated on the basis of their objectives, theoretical orientation, and program structure.

Crisis intervention model. Crisis intervention theory (see Barth, 1990) underlies the entire program, suggesting that families are most likely to be motivated to change in times of crisis. Program objectives are relatively limited (Haapala, 1996; Kinney, Haapala, Booth, & Leavitt, 1990), though often stated quite broadly, and include increasing family safety, improving child and family functioning, and averting out-of-home placement. Thus, while improvement in aspects of family functioning presumed related to the precipitation of the referral is expected, it is also expected that families will continue to have problems and will require additional help once the crisis has passed and the service has ended (Haapala, 1996; Kinney et al., 1990). Structural features of the crisis intervention model, of which

Homebuilders has become a national prototype, include very brief duration (4–8 weeks), caseloads of 2–4 families per worker, and intensive family contact (8–10 hours per week, with 24-hour availability).

Interventions combine counseling and concrete services, with emphasis on helping clients meet needs such as food, clothing, shelter, and transportation (Haapala, 1996). Most counseling interventions are informed by social learning theory, and, as such, emphasize the enhancement of a range of communication skills, behavior management practices, and problem-solving skills through the use of teaching and behavioral reinforcement strategies. However, crisis-intervention programs also borrow from other treatment models such as client centered, rational–emotive, and cognitive–behavioral therapy (Kinney et al., 1990).

Home-based model. The home-based model of family-preservation services was developed in the Midwest at the same time that the crisis-intervention model was being developed in Washington State. The prototype of the home-based model is the FAMILIES program, which originated in Iowa (K. Nelson et al., 1990). Family-systems theory underlies the treatment approach, and the focus of treatment is both on interactions between family members and on the family's interaction with its community (Lloyd & Bryce, 1984). Using more complex clinical procedures than used in the crisis intervention model, a range of structural, strategic, and communications techniques are implemented to alter problematic patterns of interaction: Behavioral interventions such as parent training are provided as needed. Concrete and supportive services (e.g., transportation, coordination with providers of day care, housing) are also provided directly by the therapist. Caseloads are 10 to 12 families per therapist, and the duration of treatment averages 4.5 months to provide more time to make clinical changes in family relations.

Family treatment model. The family treatment model shares a similar theoretical orientation with the home-based model, but concrete services are generally provided by case managers rather than therapists, and services are as likely to be provided in an office-based setting as in the family home. Thus, core service delivery characteristics of family-preservation programs (e.g., home-based, low caseloads) are absent in this practice model.

Research on the Effects of Family-Preservation Programs

Quasi-Experimental Studies

Reviewers (K. Nelson & Landsman, 1992; Rossi, 1992; Rzepnicki, Schuerman, & Littell, 1991; Schuerman, Rzepnicki, & Littell, 1994; Wells & Biegel, 1991) have observed that the family-preservation services literature consists largely of nonexperimental program evaluations (e.g., single-group posttest-only designs) and quasi-experimental studies. Some of the quasi-experimental studies involved equivalent comparison groups, whereas others did not. Thus, for example, three of the five quasi-experimental studies reviewed by Schuerman and colleagues (Schuerman et al., 1994) that focused on child welfare populations (Mitchell, Tovar, & Knitzer, 1989; Pecora, Fraser, & Haapala, 1992; Schwartz, AuClaire, & Harris, 1991; Wood, Barton, & Schroeder, 1988) and the two quasi-experimental studies of samples that included juvenile offenders (Gordon, Arbuthnot, Gustafson, & McGreen, 1988; Schwartz, AuClaire, & Harris, 1991) are characterized by such significant problems with sample selection, attrition (Schwartz et al., 1991), or nonequivalent control groups (Gordon et al., 1988) as to seriously compromise the validity of the findings. Findings from the studies that included more appropriate comparison groups (e.g., Mitchell et al., 1989; Wood et al., 1988) did not support the effectiveness of family-preservation services in preventing out-of-home placement. Essentially, findings of the few quasi-experimental studies that have not been characterized by serious methodological flaws have failed to support the effectiveness of family preservation in preventing placement, regardless of the population (child welfare or combinations of child welfare, juvenile justice, and mental health) targeted for services.

Experimental Studies

Child welfare. Schuerman and his colleagues (Schuerman et al., 1994) recently completed a review of all experimental studies of placement prevention in the family-preservation literature. Of the randomized trials, 9 of 10 focused on families referred by child welfare or child protection agencies because of perceived risk—imminent in some studies, more distal in others—of out-of-home placement of a child due to abuse or neglect. Early studies (conducted in the 1970s and 1980s) involved very small samples and included some programs that were precursors of family-preservation programs. More recent studies focused on well-established family-preservation programs and included larger samples. Findings from the 10 randomized trials were mixed, with no effect on placement in 5 studies, and slight, but not lasting, reductions in placement in others. In all studies, the number of placements in the control group families was relatively low, suggesting that the samples were generally not composed of families at imminent risk of child placement (K. Nelson & Landsman, 1992; Schuerman et al., 1994).

In the largest-scale (1,564 families across 6 sites) experimental test of family-preservation services with child welfare populations completed to date (Rzepnicki et al., 1991; Schuerman et al., 1994), families were randomly assigned to receive family-preservation services through the Families First program or traditional services. Providers at each site were encouraged to develop their own programs within guidelines on caseload size, initial response time, and duration of service (3–6 months). Although no specific treatment model or theoretical orientation was imposed, training predicated on Cimmarusti's (1989) "Multi-Systems Approach to Family Preservation" was provided to workers at all sites. Based on descriptions of that training provided by Schuerman and colleagues and on data regarding the nature of services implemented by workers at all sites, it appears that this approach is a hybrid between the home-based and crisis-intervention practice models identified by Nelson and colleagues. That is, whereas the case conceptualization appears to draw heavily on family systems approaches and treatment techniques, the counseling techniques and concrete services workers implemented were similar to those provided by Homebuilders workers (Kinney et al., 1990).

Findings indicated that while families in the family-preservation condition received a wider range of services and were more satisfied with services than families in the traditional services condition, the former families had a statistically significant higher rate of placement than families who received traditional services. As found in the early randomized trials, the placement rate was low for families in both conditions, a finding that again raises issues regarding the process by which "imminent risk" of the target population is defined. In addition, no between-groups differences emerged with respect to risk for future maltreatment. Thus, Schuerman and his colleagues concluded that "there is little evidence that family preservation programs result in substantial reductions in the placement of children" (Schuerman et al., 1994, p. 33) or that they prevent child maltreatment.

Juvenile justice and mixed populations. Until recently, studies of the use of family-preservation services targeted specifically for juvenile offender populations have been non- or quasi-experimental. (For reviews see Borduin, 1994; K. Nelson, 1990; K. Nelson & Landsman, 1992; Schoenwald, Scherer, & Brondino, 1997). As noted previously, some quasi-experimental investigations (AuClaire & Schwartz, 1986; Schwartz et al., 1991) have included youth referred by juvenile justice agencies in samples composed of referrals from multiple child-serving agencies, whereas others have focused on samples composed of both adjudicated juveniles and status offenders (Gordon et al., 1988).

In the one truly randomized trial published in the family-preservation literature, Feldman (1991) contrasted the effects of the New Jersey Family Preservation Services (FPS) program, modeled after Homebuilders, with traditional preventive services (e.g., less intensive counseling interventions, referral to mental health services, youth advocacy, agency monitoring of youth, family court intervention). The sample consisted of youth and families referred by juvenile justice, child welfare (family court or crisis intervention), and regional community mental health crisis centers. The study objectives were (a) to determine whether the Homebuilders model actually had been implemented, (b) to test the effectiveness of the model in preventing placement over time, (c) to test the effectiveness in improving family functioning, and (d) to examine whether client characteristics and selected ecological variables (e.g., stress level, social support, a community risk variable) mediated outcome.

Results indicated that FPS achieved better placement results than traditional services up to 9 months after completion of services, after which the effects of FPS dissipated. Families in the FPS group appeared to function at higher levels at case closure on some measures of family functioning and stress, but they generally did not experience greater improvement than families that received traditional services. The results of this study, which documented implementation of the Homebuilders model with a mixed population of youth referred by mental health, juvenile justice, and child-welfare services, are somewhat more encouraging than the "no difference" findings of experimental studies of child welfare populations in that placement prevention was achieved up to 9 months after treatment.

Implications for Family Preservation in Child Mental Health

Apparently, extant practice models of family preservation have not been successful in preventing placement or child maltreatment in child welfare populations or in maintaining placement prevention over time with mixed populations of youth that include youthful offenders. Discussions of these discouraging findings have often focused on design issues (for a review see Rossi, 1992); problems with sample definition (e.g., defining *imminent risk*," reducing the heterogeneity of samples; Tracy, 1991); and the extent to which family-preservation research is constrained by the policies and practices of the public agencies that support and refer clients to family-preservation programs (Rossi, 1992; Rzepnicki et al., 1991).

Equally important, but relatively underemphasized in the family-preservation literature, are issues related to the construct validity of the treatment models themselves. Although crisis intervention, social learning theory, family systems, and ecological theories presumably underlie the crisis intervention and home-based practice models, the relationship of these broad theories to the correlates and causes of child abuse, delinquency, and serious emotional disturbances in youth is not clearly specified. Crisis-intervention theory, for example, holds that people are most open to change in times of crisis and provides the rationale for the Homebuilders model, in which immediate, intensive, and flexible services are delivered (Haapala, 1996). Crisis-intervention theory does not, however, specify what needs to change or how to change it. To answer these questions, a thorough understanding of the causes of the behaviors that precipitate the crisis is required. Such understanding, conceptualized as a *treatment theory* (Lipsey, 1988) in the psychological literature, should incorporate what is known about the correlates and causes of the problems that prompted the referral (e.g., child maltreatment, juvenile delinquency, youth presenting with psychiatric emergencies). Interventions flowing from such a treatment theory would, in turn, target the known correlates and causes of the problems, presumably with techniques that have demonstrated efficacy.

Developing Empirically Informed Treatment Theories

Serious problems are multidetermined. Comprehensive reviews of empirical research on child and adolescent psychotherapy (Kazdin, 1994; Weisz & Weiss, 1993; Weisz, Donenberg, Han, & Weiss, 1995); on the treatment of child abuse and neglect (Becker et al., 1995); and on treatments for juvenile delinquents (Borduin, 1994; Lipsey, 1992) provide excellent starting points for the development of empirically based treatment theories and interventions for practice models of family-preservation services. Research has demonstrated that virtually all types of serious problems are multidetermined (e.g., Belsky, 1993; Elliott, Huizinga, & Ageton, 1985; Henggeler, in press). Causal-modeling literature in the areas of delinquency (for a review, see Henggeler, 1991) and adolescent substance abuse (Brook, Nomura, & Cohen, 1989; Dishion, Reid, & Patterson, 1988; Oetting & Beauvais, 1987) indicates that characteristics of individual family members; family relations (low affection, high conflict); parenting practices (harsh or inconsistent discipline, poor monitoring); peer relations (association with deviant peers); school functioning (poor academic performance, low family–school bonding); and neighborhood functioning (disorganization, transience, criminal subculture) predict serious antisocial behavior in youth. Such behavior represents a major focus of child mental health and juvenile justice systems (Melton & Pagliocca, 1992; Quay, 1987). Similarly, reviews of the determinants of child abuse and neglect (Belsky, 1993; Cicchetti & Carlson, 1989) suggested that characteristics of individuals (including abuse history), marital relations (e.g., conflict), parent–child relations, social networks, neighborhoods, and factors in the broader ecology (e.g., unemployment; Cohn & Daro, 1987) all contribute to child maltreatment, which, in turn, has been correlated with diverse and pervasive symptomatology in children and adolescents.

Traditional treatment approaches. Despite the abundance of evidence supporting the multidetermined nature of serious clinical problems in youth, reviews of the child and adolescent psychotherapy literature (Kazdin, 1994; Weisz & Weiss, 1993) indicate that treatment approaches demonstrated to be effective in university-based studies (e.g., behavioral and cognitive–behavioral treatments for youth, parent management, and behavioral parent training) have typically focused on fairly circumscribed domains or aspects of youth and family functioning. Although such approaches have demonstrated efficacy in university-based settings, such settings differ significantly from community-based settings in regard to the youth treated, clinic conditions, and treatment orientations employed (Weisz et al., 1995), with the result that outcomes are not as efficacious. Clinicians in community-based settings have higher caseloads, serve more severe clinical populations, and use treatment approaches that are less behavioral and more eclectic than those implemented in university-based studies (Kazdin, Siegel, & Bass, 1990; Weisz et al., 1995). Recently, authors have recommended vehicles through which the apparent gap between treatment as practiced in university and community-based settings might be bridged (Henggeler, Schoenwald, & Pickrel, 1995; Weisz et al., 1995). Evidence from clinical trials of multisystemic therapy, described subsequently, suggests that combining the family-preservation model of service delivery with empirically informed treatment approaches is one such vehicle.

Emergent Models of Family Preservation for Child Mental Health

In this section, we describe research on practice models of family-preservation services designed specifically for use with youth with serious clinical problems. One line of research examines the effectiveness of modified versions of extant models (Evans & Boothroyd, 1997). The other examines the effectiveness of an alternative practice model—multisystemic therapy (MST; Henggeler & Borduin, 1990)—which was initially developed in the context of child and adolescent psychotherapy research on the treatment of serious antisocial behavior (e.g., delinquency, adolescent substance abuse, and dependence).

Modified Crisis Intervention Models

Home-based crisis intervention. In a controlled three-group study design, Mary Evans and her colleagues (Evans & Boothroyd, 1997) examined the effectiveness of three in-home crisis-intervention programs with youth whose families are seeking emergency psychiatric assistance. The programs being compared are Home-Based Crisis Intervention (HBCI); an enhanced version of HBCI, the HBCI+; and Crisis Case Management (CCM). HBCI, which has been operating in the Bronx since 1987, was modeled on the Homebuilders program (Kinney et al., 1977) but incorporated modifications thought to be useful to families of youth with serious emotional disturbances (SED; e.g., availability of a psychiatrist for in-home assessment, treatment, and consultation to counselors). HBCI+ is characterized by enhancements to the HBCI model that provide additional support services for families (e.g., respite care, flexible service dollars, a bilingual parent advocate) and additional training for counselors (i.e., technical assistance in cultural competence and family and community violence issues). The third program, Crisis Case Management (CCM), is a time-limited variant of a longer-term intensive case management program through which families receive long-term (average of 34.8 months) services from a case manager (Evans & Boothroyd, 1997). In contrast with the HBCI programs, however, CCM emphasizes coordination of service delivery and linkage to other services and supports rather than direct provision of services by the case worker. The respite care enhancement is also available to families in CCM.

Research in progress. Measures of child and family characteristics and functioning are assessed at enrollment, at discharge, and 6 months after discharge. Measures of program implementation (e.g., Services Checklist, Activity Log, Program Implementation/Fidelity Questionnaire; Evans & Boothroyd, 1997) and of personnel perceptions of, satisfaction with, and burn-out on the job are also being collected. Finally, systems changes are being measured. As of August 1995, 251 of 1,019 children assessed in emergency settings were admitted and randomized to the in-home service programs, and the remainder were admitted to hospitals because of the seriousness of the clinical condition.

Pre–post data on the first 80 youth enrolled in the study showed significant gains across all three conditions in child self-concept on the Piers-Harris scale, and data on the first 85 families show that they experienced significant gains in cohesion and adaptability. Between-group differences in treatment effects do not appear to be emerging, however. Parent satisfaction with services, staff, and interventions was very high for all three programs, though slightly (but not significantly) higher in the HBCI+ program.

Multisystemic Therapy

Multisystemic therapy is an intensive, time-limited, in-home treatment approach that has demonstrated effectiveness in randomized trials with chronic and violent juvenile offenders and their families (Borduin et al., 1995; Henggeler, Melton, & Smith, 1992; Henggeler, Melton, Smith, Schoenwald, & Hanley, 1993; Scherer, Brondino, Henggeler, Melton, & Hanley, 1994). In these studies, MST has been equally effective with families of different cultural backgrounds (African American and White) and socioeconomic status. Current projects are examining its effectiveness with diagnosed substance-abusing and substance-dependent juvenile offenders (Henggeler, Pickrel, & Brondino, 1995); with gang-affiliated juvenile offenders, many of whom are Hispanic (Thomas, 1994); and as an alternative for youth about to be hospitalized for homicidal, suicidal, and psychotic behavior (Henggeler & Rowland, in press). MST has also been effective with small samples of maltreating parents (Brunk, Henggeler, & Whelan, 1987) and adolescent sex offenders (Borduin, Henggeler, Blaske, & Stein, 1990).

Treatment theory. The treatment theory (Lipsey, 1988) underlying MST draws on causal modeling studies of serious antisocial behavior and social–ecological (Bronfenbrenner, 1979) and family systems (Haley, 1976; Minuchin, 1974) models of behavior. Consistent with Bronfenbrenner's (1979) theory of social ecology, MST views individuals as being nested within a complex of interconnected systems that encompass individual (e.g., biological, cognitive), family, and extrafamilial (peer, school, neighborhood) factors. Importantly, this ecological view of child behavior problems is strongly supported by the causal modeling studies cited previously in this chapter. To recap, these studies indicate that a combination of family (low warmth, high conflict, harsh or inconsistent discipline, low monitoring of youth whereabouts, parental problems, low social support); peer (association with deviant peers); school (low family–school bonding, problems with academic and social performance); and neighborhood (transiency, disorganization, criminal subculture) factors predict the development of serious antisocial behavior in adolescents. Thus, consistent with both the empirically established determinants of serious antisocial behavior and with socioecological theory, MST directly targets for change those factors within the youth's family, peer group, school, and neighborhood that are contributing to his or her antisocial behavior (Henggeler & Borduin, 1990). MST targets identified child and family problems within and between the multiple systems in which family members are embedded. Interventions are designed in accordance with nine treatment principles (Henggeler, Schoenwald, Pickrel, Brondino, & Hall, 1994) and incorporate treatment techniques with empirically demonstrated efficacy. A clinically oriented volume describes MST in detail (Henggeler & Borduin, 1990; Henggeler, Schoenwald, Borduin, Rowland, & Cunningham, in press) and gives specific guidelines for implementing MST for youth presenting serious clinical problems and their families.

Service delivery characteristics. Consistent with the core philosophical and service delivery characteristics of family-preservation services, MST assumes that the most ethical and effective way to help children is through helping their families. Thus, families are seen as valuable resources, even when they are challenged by multiple needs. Structural characteristics include low caseloads (4–6 families), delivery of services in community settings (e.g., home, school, neighborhood center), time-limited duration of treatment (3–5 months), 24-hour-per-day and 7-day-per-week availability of therapists, and provision of comprehensive services. Depending on the stage of treatment and extant crises, sessions may be held every day or as infrequently as once a week. Emphasis is placed on the efficient use of treatment sessions, each typically lasting 30–75 minutes and concluding with the assignment of explicit tasks related to the identified goals.

Using MST to treat psychiatric emergencies. Currently, a National Institute of Mental Health-funded research project is being conducted in South Carolina to determine whether MST is a more clinically effective and less costly strategy than psychiatric hospitalization for addressing the mental health emergencies of adolescents with SED (Henggeler & Rowland, in press). The treatment portion of this 5-year study is underway and will continue over a 3-year period, during which time 252 11- to 17-year-old youth presenting with suicidal ideation, homicidal ideation, psychosis, or threat of harm to self or others will be randomly assigned to receive psychiatric hospitalization or MST. Thus, in contrast with the New York project described above, there is no front-end assessment process during which youth currently in psychiatric crisis are removed from the pool eligible for in-home services. The South Carolina study is therefore the first randomized trial in which psychiatric hospitalization is a treatment condition.

Future Directions

The success of MST in treating serious antisocial behavior, adolescent substance abuse, and small samples of juvenile sex offenders and maltreating families is instructive with respect to the treatment and service delivery issues that should be considered in the development and validation of effective, community-based treatment for youth with serious clinical problems. Consistent with the family-preservation model of service delivery, MST is characterized by a philosophical commitment to the empowerment of families and by service-delivery characteristics that reduce the barriers to access and effectiveness that often characterize more traditional models of service delivery (e.g., traditional outpatient, residential treatment, inpatient). In contrast with dominant practice models of family preservation, however, the treatment theory guiding MST is specified not only in accordance with a broad theory (e.g., social ecology), but also in terms of the specific factors in the youth's ecology shown to cause or maintain the problems being targeted for treatment. Although the crisis-intervention and home-based practice models appear to acknowledge the multiproblem aspects of the families they serve, it may be that the treatment theories they invoke to address those problems are not sufficiently specified or informed by empirical knowledge to facilitate the development and implementation of appropriately targeted, sufficiently complex, clinical conceptualizations and treatment plans to yield positive outcomes.

As suggested elsewhere (Henggeler et al., 1995; Henggeler, Smith, & Schoenwald, 1994), combining treatment models characterized by construct validity with models of service delivery characterized by ecological validity may be essential to providing effective community-based services to youth with serious clinical problems and their families. We suggest that efforts to develop effective family-preservation services for such youth are more likely to be successful if the development incorporates certain characteristics of the modus operandus of treatment research. These are

1. Articulation of clearly defined, empirically informed treatment theories that address the multiple determinants of the problems of target populations;
2. Clear definition of target populations;
3. Provision of training and ongoing supervision in the model being tested to the workers providing the service;
4. Close monitoring of treatment implementation.

By the same token, the modus operandi of child and adolescent psychotherapy research may need to change in order to yield treatment approaches that are (a) effective with serious clinical problems and (b) adopted by community-based practitioners (Kazdin, 1994; Weisz et al., 1995). Treatment studies should be conducted in community-based settings, or, at least, in settings that more closely approximate the conditions faced by community-based practitioners and children and families seeking services from them (e.g., higher caseloads, more serious clinical populations). The focus of treatments being tested should be expanded to accommodate the empirical evidence for the multidetermined nature of serious clinical problems. Thus, for example, variables often conceptualized as mediators of retention or outcome may need to be reconceptualized as indicators of the adequacy of the treatment theory being examined. That is, given consistent evidence that such issues as marital problems, lack of social support, socioeconomic disadvantage, high stress, harsh disciplinary practices, and multiple diagnoses predict drop out or mediate the outcomes of empirically validated treatment approaches prevalent in the child and adolescent psychotherapy literature (Kazdin, 1994; Wierson & Forehand, 1994), it seems reasonable to suggest that these variables should be incorporated into a treatment theory to be tested.

Clearly, psychologists who are committed to the development and dissemination of effective community-based services have much to contribute to the development of effective family-preservation programs for youth with serious clinical problems. Progress in this realm will require that they (a) develop practice models that combine the essential service-delivery features of family preservation with treatment models informed by what is empirically known about the causes and correlates of such problems, (b) broaden the focus of treatment approaches tested in university-based studies to better reflect the multidetermined nature of serious clinical problems, and (c) conduct child and adolescent psychotherapy-outcome research in ways that more closely reflect the "real world" conditions facing families and clinicians in the community-based settings through which family-preservation programs are currently proliferating.

References

Adams, P. (1994). Marketing social change: The case of family preservation. *Children and Youth Services Review, 16*, 417–431.

AuClaire, P., & Schwartz, I. M. (1986). *An evaluation of the effectiveness of intensive home-based services as an alternative to placement for adolescents and their families.* Minneapolis, MN: Hubert H. Humphrey Institute of Public Affairs, University of Minnesota.

Barth, R. P. (1990). Theories guiding home-based intensive family preservation services. In J. K. Whittaker, J. Kinney, E. M. Tracy, & C. Booth (Eds.), *Reaching high risk families: Intensive family preservation in human services* (pp. 89–112). New York: Aldine.

Becker, J. V., Alpert, J. L., BigFoot, D. S., Bonner, L., Geddie, L. F., Henggeler, S. W., Kaufman, K. L., & Walker, C. E. (1995). Empirical research on child abuse treatment. *Journal of Child Clinical Psychology.*

Belsky, J. (1993). Etiology of child maltreatment: A developmental-ecological analysis. *Psychological Bulletin, 114*, 413–434.

Borduin, C. M. (1994). Innovative models of treatment and service delivery in the juvenile justice system. *Journal of Clinical Child Psychology, 23* (Suppl. 2), 19–25.

Borduin, C. M., Henggeler, S. W., Blaske, D. M., & Stein, R. (1990). Multisystemic treatment of adolescent sexual offenders. *International Journal of Offender Therapy and Comparative Criminology, 34*, 105–113.

Borduin, C. M., Mann, B. J., Cone, L. T., Henggeler, S. W., Fucci, B. R., Blaske, D. M., & Williams, R. A. (1995). Multisystemic treatment of serious juvenile offenders: Long-term prevention of criminality and violence. *Journal of Consulting and Clinial Psychology, 63*, 569–578.

Bronfenbrenner, U. (1979). *The ecology of human development: Experiences by nature and design.* Cambridge, MA: Harvard University Press.

Brook, J. S., Nomura, C., & Cohen, P. (1989). A network of influences on adolescent drug involvement: Neighborhood, school, peer, and family. *Genetic, Social, and General Psychology Monographs, 115*, 125–145.

Brunk, M., Henggeler, S. W., & Whelan, J. P. (1987). A comparison of multisystemic therapy and parent training in the brief treatment of child abuse and neglect. *Journal of Consulting and Clinical Psychology, 55*, 311–318.

Burns, B. J., & Friedman, R. M. (1990). Examining the research base for child mental health services and policy. *Journal of Mental Health Administration, 17*, 87–97.

Cicchetti, D., & Carlson, V. (Eds.). (1989). *Child maltreatment: Theory and research on the causes and consequences of child abuse and neglect.* New York: Cambridge University Press.

Cimmarusti, R. A. (1989). *A multi-systems approach to family preservation: A curriculum guide.* Springfield, IL: Child Welfare Training Institute, Department of Children and Family Services.

Cohn, A. H., & Daro, D. (1987). Is treatment too late: What ten years of evaluative research tells us. *Child Abuse and Neglect, 11*, 422–433.

Dishion, T. J., Reid, J. B., & Patterson, G. R. (1988). Empirical guidelines for a family intervention for adolescent drug use. *Journal of Chemical Dependency, 2*, 189–224.

Elliott, D. S., Huizinga, D., & Ageton, S. S. (1985). *Explaining delinquency and drug use.* Beverly Hills, CA: Sage.

Evans, M. E., & Boothroyd, R. A. (1997). Family preservation services for families with children who have mental health problems. In A. B. Santos & S. W. Henggeler (Eds.), *Innovative services for "difficult to treat" populations.* Washington, DC: American Psychiatric Press.

Farrow, F. (1991). Services to families: The view from the states. *Families in Society: The Journal of Contemporary Human Services, May*, 268–275.

Feldman, L. H. (1991). Evaluating the impact of intensive family preservation services in New Jersey. In K. Wells & D. E. Biegel (Eds.), *Family preservation services: Research and evaluation* (33–47). Newbury Park, CA: Sage.

Frankel, H. (1988). Home-based family treatment: A quantitative-qualitative assessment. *The Journal of Applied Social Sciences, 12*, 1–23.

Gordon, D. A., Arbuthnot, J., Gustafson, K. E., & McGreen, P. (1988). Home-based behavioral-systems family therapy with disadvantaged juvenile delinquents. *The American Journal of Family Therapy, 16*, 243–255.

Haapala, D. A. (1996). The HOMEBUILDERS model: An evolving service approach for families. In M. C. Roberts (Ed.), *Model programs in service delivery in child and family mental health* (pp. 295–316). Hillsdale, NJ: Erlbaum.

Haley, J. (1976). *Problem-solving therapy.* San Francisco: Jossey-Bass.

Henggeler, S. W. (1991). Multidimensional causal models of delinquent behavior. In R. Cohen & A. Siegel (Eds.), *Context and development* (pp. 211–231). Hillsdale, NJ: Erlbaum.

Henggeler, S. W. (in press). The development of effective drug abuse services for youth. In J. A. Egertson, D. M. Fox, & A. I. Leshner (Eds.), *Treating drug abusers effectively.* New York: Blackwell-North America.

Henggeler, S. W., & Borduin, C. M. (1990). *Family therapy and beyond: A multisystemic approach to treating the behavior problems of children and adolescents.* Pacific Grove, CA: Brooks/Cole.

Henggeler, S. W., Melton, G. B., & Smith, L. A. (1992). Family preservation using multisystemic therapy: An effective alternative to incarcerating serious juvenile offenders. *Journal of Consulting and Clinical Psychology, 60*, 953–961.

Henggeler, S. W., Melton, G. B., Smith, L. A., Schoenwald, S. K., & Hanley, J. (1993). Family preservation using multisystemic therapy: Long-term follow-up to a clinical trial with serious juvenile offenders. *Journal of Child and Family Studies, 2*, 283–293.

Henggeler, S. W., Pickrel, S. G., & Brondino, M. J. (1995). *Multisystemic treatment of substance abusing/dependent delinquents: Outcomes for drug use, criminality, and out-of-home placement at posttreatment and 6-month follow-up.* Manuscript under review.

Henggeler, S. W., & Rowland, M. D. (in press). Investigating alternatives to hospitalization of youth presenting psychiatric emergencies. *Emergency Psychiatry*.

Henggeler, S. W., Schoenwald, S. K., Borduin, C. M., Rowland, M. D., & Cunningham, P. B. (in press). *Multisystemic treatment for antisocial behavior in youth*. New York: Guilford Press.

Henggeler, S. W., Schoenwald, S. K., & Pickrel, S. G. (1995). Multisystemic therapy: Bridging the gap between university- and community-based treatment. *Journal of Consulting and Clinical Psychology, 63*, 709–717.

Henggeler, S. W., Smith, B. H., & Schoenwald, S. K. (1994). Key theoretical and methodological issues in conducting treatment research in the juvenile justice system. *Journal of Clinical Child Psychology, 23*, 143–150.

Kazdin, A. E. (1994). Psychotherapy for children and adolescents. In A. E. Bergin & S. L. Garfield (Eds.), *Handbook of psychotherapy and behavior change* (pp. 543–594). New York: Wiley.

Kazdin, A. E., Siegel, T. C., & Bass, D. (1990). Drawing upon clinical practice to inform research on child and adolescent psychotherapy: A survey of practitioners. *Professional Psychology: Research and Practice, 21*, 189–198.

Kinney, J., Haapala, D., Booth, C., & Leavitt, S. (1990). The Homebuilders model. In J. K. Whittaker, J. Kinney, E. M. Tracy, & C. Booth (Eds.), *Reaching high risk families: Intensive family preservation in human services* (pp. 31–64). New York: Aldine.

Kinney, J., Madsen, B., Haapala, D., & Fleming, T. (1977). Homebuilders: Keeping families together. *Journal of Counseling and Consulting Psychology, 14*, 209–213.

Knitzer, J. E., & Cole, E. S. (1989). *Family preservation services: The policy challenge to state child welfare and child mental health systems*. New York: Bank Street College of Education.

Lipsey, M. W. (1988). Juvenile delinquency intervention. In H. S. Bloom, D. S. Cordray, & R. J. Light (Eds.), *Lessons from selected program and policy areas: New directions for program evaluation* (pp. 63–84). San Francisco: Jossey-Bass.

Lipsey, M. W. (1992). Juvenile delinquency treatment: A meta-analytic inquiry into the variability of effects. In T. D. Cook, H. Cooper, D. S. Cordray, H. Hartman, L. V. Hedges, R. J. Light, T. A. Louis, & F. Mosteller (Eds.), *Meta-analysis for explanation: A casebook* (pp. 83–127). New York: Russell Sage Foundation.

Lloyd, J. C., & Bryce, M. E. (1984). *Placement prevention and family reunification: A handbook for the family-centered service practitioner*. Iowa City, IA: University of Iowa, National Resource Center for Family Based Services.

Melton, G. B., & Pagliocca, P. W. (1992). Treatment in the juvenile justice system: Directions for policy and practice. In J. J. Cocozza (Ed.), *Responding to the mental health needs of youth in the juvenile justice system* (pp. 107–139). Seattle, WA: National Coalition for the Mentally Ill in the Criminal Justice System.

Minuchin, S. (1974). *Families and family therapy*. Cambridge, MA: Harvard University Press.

Mitchell, C., Tovar, P., & Knitzer, J. (1989). *The Bronx Homebuilders Program: An evaluation of the first 45 families*. New York: Bank Street College of Education.

Nelson, D. (1990). Recognizing and realizing the potential of "family preservation." In J. K. Whittaker, J. Kinney, E. M. Tracy, & C. Booth (Eds.), *Reaching high-risk families; Intensive family preservation in human services* (pp. 13–30). New York: Aldine de Gruyter.

Nelson, K. E. (1990). Family based services for juvenile offenders. *Children and Youth Services Review, XII*(3), 193–212.

Nelson, K. E. (1994a). Innovative delivery models in social services. *Journal of Clinical Child Psychology, 23* (Suppl. 2), 26–31.

Nelson, K. E. (1994b). Family-based services for families and children at risk of out-of-home placement. In R. Barth, J. D. Berrick, & N. Gilbert (Eds.), *Child welfare research review, Vol. 1* (pp. 83–108). New York: Columbia University Press.

Nelson, K. E., & Landsman, M. J. (1992). *Alternative models of family preservation: Family-based services in context*. Springfield, IL: Charles C. Thomas.

Nelson, K. E., Landsman, M. J., & Deutelbaum, W. (1990). Three models of family-centered placement prevention services. *Child Welfare, Vol. LXIX*(1), 3–21.

Oetting, E. R., & Beauvais, F. (1987). Peer cluster theory, socialization characteristics, and adolescent drug use: A path analysis. *Journal of Counseling Psychology, 34*, 205–213.

Pecora, P. J., Fraser, M., & Haapala, D. A. (1992). Intensive home-based family preservation services: An update from the FIT project. *Child Welfare, 71*, 177–188.

Pecora, P. J., Haapala, D. A., & Fraser, M. W. (1990). Comparing intensive family preservation services with other family-based service programs. In E. M. Tracy, D. A. Haapala, J. Kinney, & P. Pecora (Eds.), *Intensive family preservation services: An instructional handbook* (pp. 117–142). Cleveland, OH: Case Western Reserve University.

Quay, H. C. (Ed.). (1987). *Handbook of juvenile delinquency.* New York: Wiley.

Rossi, P. H. (1992). Strategies for evaluation. *Children and Youth Services Review, 14*, 167–191.

Rzepnicki, T. L., Schuerman, J. R., & Littell, J. H. (1991). Issues in evaluating family preservation services. In E. M. Tracy, D. A. Haapala, J. Kinney, & P. Pecora (Eds.), *Intensive family preservation services: An instructional handbook* (pp. 71–93). Cleveland, OH: Case Western Reserve University.

Santos, A. B., Henggeler, S. W., Burns, B. J., Arana, G. W., & Meisler, N. (1995). Research on field-based services: Models for reform in the delivery of mental health care to difficult clinical populations. *The American Journal of Psychiatry, 152*(8), 1111–1123.

Scherer, D. G., Brondino, M. J., Henggeler, S. W., Melton, G. B., & Hanley, J. H. (1994). Multisystemic family preservation with rural and minority families of serious adolescent offenders: Preliminary findings from a controlled clinical trial. *Journal of Emotional and Behavioral Disorders, 2*, 198–206.

Schoenwald, S. K., Scherer, D. G., & Brondino, M. J. (1997). Effective community-based treatments for juvenile delinquents. In S. W. Henggeler & A. B. Santos (Eds.), *Innovative models of treatment for "difficult to treat" clinical populations.* Washington, DC: American Psychiatric Press.

Schuerman, J. R., Rzepnicki, T. L., & Littell, J. H. (1994). *Putting families first: An experiment in family preservation.* New York: Aldine de Gruyter.

Schwartz, I. M., AuClaire, P., & Harris, J. (1991). Family preservation services as an alternative to the out-of-home placement of adolescents: The Hennepin County experience. I. K. Wells & D. E. Biegel (Eds.), *Family preservation services research and evaluation* (pp. 33–47). Newbury Park, CA: Sage.

Stroul, B. A., & Friedman, R. M. (1994). *A system of care for children and youth with severe emotional disturbance.* Washington, DC: Georgetown University Child Development Center.

Stroul, B. A., & Goldman, S. K. (1990). Study of community-based services for children and adolescents who are severely emotionally disturbed. *Journal of Mental Health Administration, 17*, 61–77.

Thomas, C. R. (1994). *Island youth programs.* Galveston, TX: University of Texas Medical Branch.

Tracy, E. M. (1991). Defining the target population for family preservation services. In K. Wells & D. E. Biegel (Eds.), *Family preservation services: Research and evaluation* (pp. 138–158). Newbury Park, CA: Sage.

Weisz, J. R., Donenberg, G. R., Han, S. S., & Weiss B. (1995). Bridging the gap between lab and clinic in child and adolescent psychotherapy. *Journal of Consulting and Clinical Psychology, 63*, 688–701.

Weisz, J. R., & Weiss, B. (1993). *Effects of psychotherapy with children and adolescents.* Newbury Park, CA: Sage.

Wells, K., & Biegel, D. E. (Eds.) (1991). *Family preservation services research and evaluation.* Newbury Park, CA: Sage.

Wierson, M., & Forehand, R. (1994). Parent behavioral training for child noncompliance: Rationale, concepts, and effectiveness. *Current Directions in Psychological Science, 3*, 146–150.

Wood, K. M., Barton, K., & Schroeder, C. (1988). In-home treatment of abusive families: Cost and placement at one year. *Psychotherapy, 25*, 409–414.

7

Educating Children and Youth for Psychological Competence

Joseph E. Zins and Donald I. Wagner

Children and youth today face a number of challenges and demands that their parents either did not experience or that in the past were less intense or prevalent. Issues such as interpersonal violence, AIDS, excessive stress, teen pregnancy, and drug abuse have become important concerns for nearly all young people. A significant segment of our youth experience or are at risk for social, behavioral, and health problems that may interfere with their academic performance, their physical and mental health, and their potential to become productive, contributing family members, citizens, and workers (Dryfoos, 1990). In fact, the manner by which each of us handles our emotional responses can have direct consequences on our sense of well-being and at times can even be the difference between life and death (e.g., anger control and interpersonal violence; Goleman, 1995b). Although we recognize that many aspects of these problems are societal in origin and that academic achievement, proficiency testing, and related educational issues are extremely important, schools nevertheless must deal with the consequences of such issues if they are to educate their students most effectively.

In this chapter we review the current status of children and youth with respect to their behavioral and health competence. The service system now in place for addressing the academic and emotional needs of young people is not working as effectively and efficiently as most would envision, and there is greater interest in alternative approaches. Based on the chapter's title, it should be predictable that we conclude from our review that there is a need for additional specific efforts to address the many social, emotional, and health challenges they face. In the next section, we describe social and emotional learning as one approach to helping young people cope with and inoculate themselves against potentially threatening issues such as illicit drugs, violence, and school failure, and we discuss such endeavors from remedial, prevention, and promotion perspectives. Examples of several promising school-based approaches that have been developed to promote healthy behaviors and minimize problems through social and emotional competence education are provided, and we conclude by suggesting that practice must be reoriented so that prevention and promotion approaches are included routinely.

Need for Facilitating Social and Emotional Learning

At the turn of the century, the leading causes of death for all ages in the United States, in rank order, were pneumonia and influenza, tuberculosis, diarrhea and enteritis, heart disease, and stroke. In contrast, the leading causes of death today are heart disease, cancer, stroke, injuries, and pneumonia (U.S. Preventive Services Task Force, 1989). For youth ages 10–24 years, however, the most recent Youth Behavior Risk Survey data indicated that the leading causes of mortality and morbidity were motor vehicle crashes (37%), homicide (14%), suicide (12%), and other injury (e.g., burns; 12%), HIV infection (1%), and other causes (24%; e.g., congenital heart disease; Kolbe, 1995). For children under 14, motor-vehicle-related injuries also were the major cause of death, but substantial numbers of unintentional injury deaths resulted from drowning, fires or burns, and ingestions (poisons, choking on food; National Safety Council, 1992). Thus, significant numbers of young people's deaths are at least in part the result of violence, risk taking, and other behavioral factors, making them potential targets for prevention efforts.

The shift in leading mortalities is indicative of the increasing contribution that lifestyle has in the causation of disease and death, which is now estimated to be more than 50% (see Table 1). The choices that youth make today about alcohol, seat belt use, nutrition, school, exercise, sleep, stress, relationships, and methods for resolving conflict will have a significant influence on their future health. Clearly, psychosocial forces play a major role in determining health and well-being. Furthermore, social issues will have a significant influence in driving the health care and prevention needs of youth into the next century. Over 20% of American children reside in a family living in poverty, millions are abused and neglected, thousands are born to single teen parents, many others experience the consequences of their parents' divorces, and increasing numbers witness violence each day (Children's Defense Fund, 1995).

In recognition of the changing mortality and morbidity for all age groups in this country, the U.S. Office of Disease Prevention and Health Promotion, in its report, *Healthy People 2000: National Health Promotion and Disease Prevention Objectives* (U.S. Department of Health and Human Services, 1990) and in its 1995 update, identified the need for increased attention to prevention and health promotion activities. (See Exhibits 1 and 2 for examples of health objectives that have been established for youth.) In addition, the American Medical Association provided additional support for an emphasis on youth-based prevention and health-promotion activities in its report, *Healthy Youth 2000* (U.S. Department of Health and Human Services, 1990). The U.S. Department of Education (USDE) also recognized a similar need and established a relevant goal in its American 2000 Plan (i.e., by the year 2000, every school in the United States

Table 1.   High School Youth Risk Behavior Surveillance—United States Data (Percentages)

Behavior	Prevalence
Unintentional and Intentional Injuries Behavior	
Carried a weapon during past month	22%
Carried a handgun during past month	8%
Were in a physical fight during past year	42%
Attempted suicide during past year	9%
Never or rarely wore a safety belt	19%
Rode with a drinking driver during past month	35%
Alcohol and Other Drug Use Behavior	
Ever drank alcohol	81%
Ever used marijuana	33%
Ever used cocaine	5%
Ever used steroids	2%
Ever injected drugs	1%
Sexual Behavior	
Ever had sexual intercourse	53%
Had four or more sexual partners	19%
Did not use condom during last intercourse (among sexually active students)	47%
Used birth control pills at last sexual intercourse (among sexually active students)	18%
Tobacco Use Behavior	
Ever smoked cigarettes	70%
Smoked cigarettes during past month	31%
Used smokeless tobacco during last month	12%
Dietary Behaviors	
Thought they were overweight	34%
Were trying to lose weight	40%
Did not eat at least 5 servings of fruits and vegetables yesterday	85%
Ate more than two servings of foods typically high in fat yesterday	34%
Physical Activity Behavior	
Were not enrolled in physical education class	66%
Did not attend physical education class daily	66%

Note: Among high school students only. From L. J. Kolbe (1995, March 24). *Building the Capacity of Schools to Improve the Health of the Nation: A Call for Assistance from School Psychologists.* Paper presented at the 27th Annual Convention of the National Association of School Psychologists, Chicago.

will be free of drugs, violence, and the unauthorized presence of firearms and alcohol, and will offer a disciplined environment conducive to learning). Parents, teachers, students, and the general public increasingly recognize that the development of socially competent young people is a high priority for our country.

The onset of many of the behaviors associated with these problem areas typically is early in life, and they can establish a trajectory that may

Exhibit 1.   Key Risk Reduction Objectives Targeting Children

---

1.3   Increase to at least 30% the proportion of people aged 6 and older who engage regularly, preferably daily, in light to moderate physical activity for at least 30 minutes per day.

1.4   Increase to at least 20% the proportion of people aged 18 and older and to at least 75% the proportion of children and adolescents aged 6–17 who engage in vigorous physical activity that promotes the development and maintenance of cardiorespiratory fitness 3 or more days per week for 20 minutes or more per occasion.

1.5   Reduce to no more than 15% the proportion of people aged 6 and older who engage in no leisure time physical activity.

1.6   Increase to at least 40% the proportion of the people aged 6 and older who regularly perform physical activities that enhance and maintain muscular strength, muscular endurance, and flexibility.

3.5   Reduce the initiation of cigarette smoking by children and youth so that no more than 15% have become regular smokers by age 20.

3.8   Reduce to no more than 20% the proportion of children aged 6 and younger who are regularly exposed to tobacco at home.

8.3   Achieve for all disadvantaged children and children with disabilities access to high quality and developmentally appropriate preschool programs that help prepare children for school, thereby improving their prospects with regard to school performance, problem behaviors, and mental and physical health.

9.12a Increase the use of occupant protection systems, such as safety belts, inflatable safety restraints, and child safety seats to at least 95% of children aged 4 and younger who are motor vehicle occupants.

17.1   Increase to least 80% the proportion of providers of primary care for children who routinely refer or screen infants and children for impairments of vision, hearing, speech, and language, and assess other developmental milestones as part of well-child care.

Based on *Healthy People 2000: National Health Promotion and Disease Prevention Objectives*, U.S. Department of Health and Human Services, conference edition, 1990.

---

lead to a variety of long-term negative outcomes. Accordingly, it is not surprising that recent evidence suggests that at least half of our children and youth are extremely or moderately vulnerable to the consequences of engaging in multiple high-risk social and health behaviors, such as unprotected sexual intercourse, drunk driving, negative self-talk, tobacco use, a sedentary life style, poor impulse control, and school drop out (e.g., Dryfoos, 1990; Report of the Task Force on Education of Young Adolescents, 1989), but vast numbers do not receive appropriate services (Tuma, 1989).

Schools increasingly are recognizing that they must address these issues. One means by which they are doing so is by promoting the development of health-enhancing behaviors and reducing or preventing negative ones. The goal is to promote the health, learning, development, adaptation, and well-being of young people. Put simply, children must learn to get along with others and to care about themselves (Gresham & Elliott, 1991). Such proactive, intentional, broad-scale activities are re-

Exhibit 2.   Key Risk Reduction Objectives Targeting Adolescents and Young Adults

3.9	Reduce smokeless tobacco use by males aged 12 through 24 to a prevalence of no more than 4%.
4.5	Increase by at least 1 year the average age of first use of cigarettes, alcohol, and marijuana by adolescents aged 12 through 17.
4.6a	Reduce alcohol use during the past month by young people aged 12–17 to a prevalence of no more than 12.6%.
4.6b	Reduce marijuana use during the past month by young people aged 12–17 to a prevalence of no more than 3.2%.
4.6c	Reduce cocaine use during the past month by young people aged 12–17 to a prevalence of no more than .6%.
4.10	Increase the percentage of high school seniors who associate risk of physical or psychological harm with the heavy use of alcohol to 70%.
4.11	Reduce to no more than 3% the proportion of male high school seniors who use anabolic steroids.
5.4	Reduce the proportion of adolescents who have engaged in sexual intercourse to no more than 15% by age 15 and no more than 40% by age 17.
5.5	Increase to at least 40% the proportion of ever-sexually-active adolescents aged 17 and younger who have abstained from sexual activity for the previous 3 months.
5.6	Increase to at least 90% the proportion of sexually active, unmarried people aged 19 and younger who use contraception.
7.9	Reduce by 20% the incidence of physical fighting among adolescents aged 14–17.
7.10	Reduce by 20% the incidence of weapon-carrying by adolescents aged 14 through 17.
8.2	Increase the high school graduation rate to at least 90%, thereby reducing risks for multiple problem behaviors and poor mental and physical health.
18.4a	Increase to at least 60% the proportion of sexually active, unmarried young women aged 15 through 19 who used a condom at last intercourse.
18.4b	Increase to at least 75% the proportion of sexually active, unmarried young men aged 15 through 19 who used a condom at last sexual intercourse.

Based on *Healthy People 2000: National Health Promotion and Disease Prevention Objectives*, U.S. Department of Health and Human Services, conference edition, 1990.

flected in schools' efforts to promote social and emotional learning. The following discussion explains what we mean by this concept.

Social and emotional learning efforts are guided by a number of relevant theories. For example, two intelligences from Gardner's (1983) well-known theory of multiple intelligences are especially relevant: the interpersonal (social understanding) and the intrapersonal (self-knowledge). He posited that artistic, bodily, and personal intelligences are as important as the so-called general intelligence and suggests that schools should cultivate capacities such as helping students take into account the feelings of others (Gardner, 1995). Also related is the concept of emotional intelligence, first developed by Salovey and Mayer (1990) and promoted widely in the popular press by Goleman (1995a). Similar to Gardner's beliefs,

Goleman concluded that our society's traditional view of intelligence is too narrow because it ignores many abilities that are crucial to how we do in life. Emotional intelligence includes self-awareness and impulse control, persistence, zeal and self-motivation, empathy, and social deftness. Goleman also demonstrated that deficits in emotional intelligence can lead to a wide range of negative outcomes, from marital problems to poor physical health. Correspondingly, society's perspective of what constitutes social and emotional learning (or psychological competence) is quite broad, as it refers to efforts that support the establishment, maintenance, and improvement of knowledge, skills, behaviors, beliefs, attitudes, and lifestyles conducive to attainment of emotional health and well-being (Wagner & Zins, 1985; Zins & Wagner, 1987, 1997). Children and youth who are psychologically competent are likely to engage in behaviors that enhance their overall emotional and behavioral health and also avoid those likely to result in negative outcomes (Consortium, 1994). As a result, they may be more effective learners, tend to be viewed positively by others, are less likely to be injured or to become physically ill, and are more apt to become responsible family members and productive citizens. Because of the close relationship between mind and body, these efforts also often result in physical health benefits.

Another perspective that guides many social and emotional learning activities is social learning theory (SLT; Bandura, 1977b). SLT has been widely applied to understanding human behavior within a social context and is based on the notion that an individual's behavior can be understood only by examining interactions among the individual, other persons in the environment, and key aspects of the environment itself. Thus, it is important to consider the person from within an environmental context. This model predicts that new behaviors are learned through a combination of (a) observations of competent models; (b) direct experiences in the performance of the desired behaviors (e.g., obtained through role playing and behavioral rehearsal) with corrective feedback; and (c) positive reinforcement for accurate performance.

Reciprocal determinism is another key concept in SLT, and it suggests that individuals are influenced by their environment, and in turn, have an influence on the environment (Bandura, 1977a, 1982). SLT also recognizes the importance of intrapersonal variables such as thoughts, perceptions, and attributions. Furthermore, individuals' behavioral histories affect their personal views of themselves, which reciprocally mediate how they behave. Thus, behavior results from interactive cycles of intrapersonal factors, behavioral actions, and reactions from others.

A final guiding framework is the health belief model (HBM), which provides a framework for explaining why people do and do not practice health-related behaviors (Becker, 1974, 1979; Becker & Maiman, 1975). It suggests that people will take action when their behavior leads to an outcome that is valued and when they have an expectancy that the outcome can be achieved.

The HBM is based on the assumption that health behaviors are more or less rationally determined by an individual's assessment of a potential health threat. From this viewpoint, a person's readiness to engage in a health action primarily is related to perceptions of susceptibility and evaluations of severity or seriousness of the illness or injury. The likelihood of taking health actions is also determined by the individual's beliefs in the efficacy of his or her behavior. In other words, people proceed through a cost–benefit analysis associated with the action. Finally, Bandura's concept of self-efficacy (Bandura, 1977a, 1982), that is, an individual's belief that he or she can successfully accomplish the action required to achieve the goal, recently has been proposed as an additional contributor to decisions concerning health behaviors (Rosenstock, Strecher, & Becker, 1988).

Activities designed to promote social and emotional learning can help educators and society realize several important goals: (a) promoting the development of children and youth; (b) reducing the need for diagnostic and therapeutic services; and (c) decreasing demand for rehabilitative and remedial programs (Simeonsson, 1994). In the next section we outline some general approaches to achieving these goals.

Remedial, Prevention, and Promotion Approaches

Efforts that can be undertaken to address the educational, physical, and social problems experienced by children and youth can be viewed from several perspectives. Gordon (1983) and Simeonsson (1994) proposed that the scope of these services ranges from universal efforts intended to benefit everyone (e.g., a community-wide program to prevent youth alcohol and drug use), to those aimed at selected youth who are at increased risk because of membership in a certain category (e.g., a transition program for middle school students moving to high school), to those directed to a more limited indicated subgroup at greater risk because of individual characteristics (e.g., a behavioral self-management program for students diagnosed with attention-deficit/hyperactivity disorder).

A similar but more often used method of conceptualizing social and emotional learning is according to whether such efforts (a) remediate existing problems, (b) prevent the onset of new disorders, or (c) promote the development of or strengthen competencies to enable children to better handle life stressors. Elaboration on these points follows.

Treating Existing Problems

Schools, and our society in general, have adopted a rehabilitative, reactive focus for most treatment efforts, and thus significant resources are directed toward resolution of existing problems and maladaptive behaviors (e.g., school detection and suspensions, special education services, Chapter 1 reading programs). Indeed, "curative care is what the U.S. does best" (Miller, 1990, p. 1126). Vast numbers of students with existing academic, social, and emotional problems are served in schools and by related organizations, and many more are in need of such assistance. However, there remains a question as to whether the educational and other systems can address all of these needs adequately using current resources and service-delivery systems. As Dryfoos (1994) found, in some schools virtually all of the students have social, emotional, behavioral, or health disabilities that almost preclude academic and social success. Education in particular has not been proactive in its approach to addressing the multitude of problems that many children experience, and psychologists in schools continue to focus on traditional treatment and diagnostic activities.

Prevention Through Risk Reduction

Risk factors are correlated with an increased likelihood of susceptibility to a problem. Social and emotional learning can be directed toward the reduction, elimination, or mitigation of behavioral factors that put children at risk by intervening before the problem occurs, thereby reducing the incidence of the problem behavior. For example, in a recent study of 47,000 youth in grades 7 through 12, Benson (1993) identified 20 at-risk indicators associated with negative health outcomes (see Table 2). What is particularly noteworthy is that each of these risk factors is modifiable and can serve as the focus of social and emotional learning efforts.

Other examples of risk reduction include decreasing the availability of alcohol in the community or the number of violent episodes portrayed in the media. Or, risk factors known or suspected to be associated with youth interpersonal violence, such as academic failure, externalizing problem behaviors, interactions with antisocial peers, alienation from family and community, substance abuse, life transitions, poor parent child-rearing, and exposure to violence can be targeted (e.g., Commission on Violence and Youth, 1993; Hawkins & Catalano, 1992). Furthermore, environments in which children live also can be changed, such as by prohibiting cigarette smoking in public places, removing lead-based paints from homes and apartments, or structuring classrooms to promote interaction rather than isolation.

Enhancing Protective Factors and Increasing Resiliency

Children vary in their vulnerability and thus their risk for development of problem behaviors (Lorion, 1991). Because we are still learning how to identify those most at risk and those who are more resilient, it remains desirable to focus on increasing students' skills and competencies so they learn positive, health-enhancing behaviors. The goal is to promote health, learning, development, adaptation, and well-being. Interventions can also focus on improving children's environment so that it serves to buffer or mitigate the effects of various risk factors and reduces the need for remedial programs. With respect to the example of preventing interpersonal violence presented earlier, the presence of skills in social interaction, conflict resolution, social problem solving, stress management, and assertive-

Table 2.   Risk Indicators

Risk Indicator	Percentage of Youth With
Used alcohol six or more times in the last 30 days	11%
Had five or more drinks in a row during last 2 weeks	23%
Smokes one or more cigarettes per day	12%
Has chewed tobacco 20 or more times in last 12 months	5%
Has used an illicit drug six or more times in the last 12 months	8%
Has had sexual intercourse two or more times	30%
Is sexually active and self or partner does not always use contraceptives	47%
Is sad or depressed "most of the time" or "all of the time"	15%
Has attempted suicide once or more	13%
Destroyed property "just for fun" two or more times in last 12 months	10%
Took part in a fight between two groups or gangs two or more times in last 12 months	13%
Got into trouble with the police two or more times in the last 12 months	7%
Stole something from a store two or more times in the last 12 months	10%
Used a knife, gun, or other weapon to get something from a person two or more times in last 12 months	2%
Skipped school two or more times in last month	10%
Wants to quit school before completing high school	1%
Has driven after drinking two or more times in last year	11%
Has ridden with a driver who has been drinking two or more times in last year	33%
Does not use seat belts "all" or "most" of the time	50%
Vomits on purpose after eating once a week or more	2%

Data from P. Benson (1993). *The Troubled Journey: A Portrait of 6th–12th Grade Youth.* Minneapolis, MN: Search Institute.

ness, as well as parental involvement, are associated with lower levels of interpersonal violence (e.g., Dryfoos, 1990; Hawkins & Catalano, 1992; Jessor, 1993).

In the next section some issues to consider related to program design and implementation are presented.

Enhancing Psychological Competence Through School-Based Programs

Children and youth who can be considered psychologically competent tend to engage in a variety of behaviors that help them to avoid high-risk activities and that encourage the development and maintenance of behaviors likely to lead to short- and long-term positive outcomes. A variety of efforts can be directed toward enhancing student competence, but the most effective ones in the aggregate address multiple risk and protective factors, and include training in general life skills as well as skills specific to the topical area (Dryfoos, 1990). They also focus on factors amenable to change rather than on those that are difficult to alter, such as poverty; (Leitenberg, 1987). Although psychological competency may be judged to be a desirable outcome by most people, the question of how to achieve it remains somewhat elusive. Some of the major issues related to this goal are considered in this section.

Schools as Centers for Social and Emotional Learning

Responsibility for promoting psychological competence belongs to the family and the community, as well as to the school. Unless families and the community support the school's efforts and schools do likewise for them, the overall success of any individual's or any group's effectiveness will be diminished substantially.

Several characteristics of schools make them excellent, and perhaps preferred, settings for promotion and prevention programs.[1] First, the public in general mandates that they educate the whole child, that is, that they address social, emotional, and physical, as well as academic needs (although not necessarily in that order!). Students who are dealing with concerns about safety, interpersonal conflicts, depression, and so forth are not ready to be effective learners, so these issues cannot be ignored. On the other hand, students who are involved in extracurricular activities may have fewer risk factors. Second, schools provide access to virtually all children and youth because of mandatory attendance laws, thereby making it feasible to implement universal primary prevention programs. Third, the professional education staff has the skills to deliver these programs, or at least the background that would make learning the techniques a realistic and attainable goal. Fourth, schools are a central, highly influential environment for children (Consortium, 1994; Waxman, Walker deFelix, Anderson, & Baptiste, 1992). Furthermore, as Dryfoos (1994) has argued convincingly, schools also may be excellent settings through which health and mental health services are coordinated and administered. Finally, schools already are mandated legally to address many issues related to psychological competence.

Need for Coordinated, Integrated, and Comprehensive Services

As detailed throughout this volume and therefore not discussed in depth here, the current system for addressing the academic and emotional needs of students is not working as well as desired. Services often are provided without sufficient coordination among school personnel, and the problem becomes even more complex when health, social service, religious, and

---

[1] For an in depth discussion of integrated services in a school setting, see chapter 2, this volume.

community organizations are considered. Those in need of services frequently are not served even though assistance is available, and individuals receive duplicative services from multiple agencies. Consequently, children and families are frequently confused by inconsistent, redundant, or conflicting advice (Dryfoos, 1994). As evidenced by the focus of this book, interest in methods by which services can be better integrated and coordinated is growing rapidly. For instance, social and emotional learning should involve the joint efforts of many professionals, including the counseling and social services team and health education, health services, physical education, and even nutrition services (Kolbe, Collins, & Cortese, in press), and their work should be supported by the involvement of parents and the community at large. Only then can an organizational climate be created that fosters bonding, caring, and trust—characteristics essential to promoting effective social and emotional learning.

Characteristics of Effective Prevention Efforts in Schools

There is increasing agreement among researchers regarding the characteristics of effective prevention and promotion programs. They should be comprehensive (i.e., incorporate cognitive, affective, and behavioral skills and beliefs), multiyear (i.e., conducted from kindergarten through grade 12), be coordinated across grade levels, and involve the support and involvement of all individuals and institutions who affect children's lives. Students' active participation is required, and programs should include activities such as role playing, behavioral rehearsal, and performance feedback. The instruction should be developmentally appropriate and culturally sensitive. Specific topics such as AIDS, conflict resolution, and assertiveness should be covered, while at the same time students should learn generic problem-solving and decision-making skills (Consortium, 1994; Hawkins & Catalano, 1992; W. T. Grant Consortium, 1992). These efforts also are interdisciplinary in nature, have strong family and community orientations, ensure that services are convenient and accessible, and minimize bureaucratic boundaries (Schorr, 1991). Elias (1997) presents an excellent summary of social problem solving skills to be taught at various ages.

Many schools elect to use a specific curriculum to teach social and emotional skills, and they supplement the curriculum through extracurricular activities, small teacher-led advisory groups, and relevant policies. With all of these efforts, there are significant advantages to developing agreement among everyone involved in social and emotional learning regarding a cohesive framework or theory that underlies and unifies these activities. If such agreement is not reached, there is risk that fragmented messages will be given and that generalization and maintenance of learning will be hampered.

Systems and Ecological Perspectives

Psychologists and educators can no longer afford to focus solely on individuals but must also examine the organizational climate of the school and the influence that factors within and outside this institution have on children. From this perspective, problems occur as a function of the interactions of individuals and the systems of which they are a part. A problem does not reside only within a child, nor solely within the child's environment. Rather, consideration must be given to the reciprocal interactions and influences among students, schools, families, and communities if effective social and emotional learning is to occur.

Throughout this chapter, the importance of having families and the community as partners has been emphasized. Ecological and systems theories are the basis for this stance, as linkages among the various aspects of the child's world are essential to success (Apter, 1982). Schools and parents must understand one another's concerns and provide reinforcement and support for their respective efforts. School policies and philosophies should support and explicitly express the value placed on development of psychological competence. Furthermore, as noted earlier, having an organizational climate in the schools in which children feel safe to bond, care, interact, trust, and share is essential. Such a climate should exist in individual classrooms as well as within the school and the district.

Expertise of School Staff

Many school staff have the expertise to contribute to social and emotional learning activities, and effective, comprehensive prevention and programs should take advantage of the contributions that can be made by disciplines such as health education, nursing, physical education, nutrition, counseling, social work, and psychology. Traditionally, however, classroom teachers in science, social studies, or health have had virtually total responsibility and other staff have had only minimal involvement.

When considering the following examples of roles that various specialists in the school can assume, it should be remembered that in the most effective programs these professionals coordinate their efforts so that a unified program is provided. Moreover, social and emotional learning should be the primary domain of the general education classroom teacher, although it is also planned and developed through the collaborative efforts of other staff, as described subsequently. In addition, it is critical that everyone involved be appropriately trained to deliver them and to develop an environment supportive of the safe use of these skills.

Psychologists have tremendous potential to play a major role in helping healthy students stay well. On one end of the continuum, possible activities include those requiring the direct involvement of the psychologist (e.g., conducting social-skills or stress-management groups for students, teaching parents communication and behavior-management techniques). At the other end is acting in a consultative capacity and helping enact system-wide change (e.g., assisting the district in implementing so-cial problem solving and decision making in the curriculum, developing a policy requiring the use of bicycle helmets for children who ride to school). Another major contribution psychologists in the schools can make is in designing and conducting evaluations of prevention and promotion programs—an activity that is often neglected (Cohen & Wilson-Brewer, 1991).

Other professionals also have important contributions to make. The health educator can help students learn life skills that increase their re-silience and lead to positive educational, social, and health outcomes. These goals can be accomplished through the health curriculum, through creation of an emotionally supportive school climate, and through consul-tation with general education teachers. School nurses can coordinate stu-dent and family health fairs, conduct immunization reviews and updates, and assist with appropriate health screening and appraisal tests. They might also be involved in developing school policies that promote student health. Likewise, the physical educator can develop students' appreciation for exercise, physical fitness, and cardiovascular health through involve-ment in lifetime sports and activities. They can also help children value the benefits of teamwork. Dieticians can assure the nutritional content of the school food service, thereby increasing the daily consumption of fruits, vegetables, and whole grain foods while reducing the amount of saturated fat. Also, dieticians can assist with the nutrition-education program and programs aimed at the prevention of eating disorders. Small group and class-wide social-skills programs can be facilitated by the school counselor and might also help students prevent the development of hypertension or avoid tobacco and alcohol. In addition, all of these professionals can con-sult with general education teachers and parents and provide relevant in-service training to enable the staff to recognize risk factors and danger signals.

Coordination With Community Agencies and Professionals

Social and emotional learning efforts will be most effective if the activities of the school and families are supported by the larger community. Many of the problems students face are societal in nature, and consequently multiple constituencies have a responsibility to address them. Religious groups and recreation centers are examples of resources that may not routinely be considered but that have the capacity to support and supple-ment school efforts. Spirituality increasingly is being seen as an important element of social and emotional learning and intelligence (Gardner, 1995). Boys and Girls Clubs and similar organizations may even provide pro-grams that directly target psychological competence, such as the Talking With TJ program, which introduces kids to differences in culture, race, and abilities; resolving conflicts; and playing cooperatively (Hallmark Cor-porate Foundation, 1994).

Examples of Psychological Competence Education

We have selected several examples of activities to illustrate the range of social and emotional learning efforts undertaken in schools. In presenting these examples we have attempted to include programs that represent a variety of age groups and that range from classroom-based curricula, to those that can be implemented school-wide, to those targeting the community. Most of them have some empirical data supporting their effectiveness. Although these examples tend to be of more structured programs, schools can facilitate social and emotional learning in many ways, as noted earlier. In addition to using a specific curriculum, they include teacher facilitated advisory groups, selecting students-of-the-month on the basis of caring and other appropriate behaviors, having all-inclusive interscholastic sports and clubs, and publishing monthly newsletters for parents/community members that focus on accomplishments of all children. The net result is a message of caring and support. Additional examples of specific programs are available from several sources (e.g., Dryfoos, 1994).

Social skills training. There is mounting evidence that children who lack a variety of prosocial skills are at risk for peer rejection, school underachievement, and crime (e.g., Asher & Coie, 1990), and a youthful history of untreated antisocial behavior has been found to be associated with significant adjustment problems in adulthood (Massachusetts Medical Society, 1992). Consequently, the promotion of prosocial, caring behaviors among children and youth, and the associated prevention of antisocial behavior, have been the focus of a variety of programs.

The Structured Learning curriculum, as outlined in *Skillstreaming the Elementary School Child: A Guide for Teaching Prosocial Skills* (McGinnis & Goldstein, 1984; also available in preschool and high school versions), uses a behavioral-skills approach including modeling, role playing, performance feedback, and transfer of training (generalization). In this widely adopted program, the skills taught are first broken down into their constituent steps, and then students are provided with examples of them. Next, students practice these skills and receive feedback from their teacher and peers. Finally, specific procedures are undertaken to increase the likelihood that students will generalize the skills. The program has 60 prosocial skills arranged into five groups: friendship making, dealing with feelings, alternatives to aggression, dealing with stress, and classroom survival skills.

Program skills are based primarily on Bandura's (1977b) social learning theory and on investigations of social competence (Spivack & Shure, 1974), peer acceptance (Mesibov & LaGreca, 1981), and positive teacher attention and academic success (Cartledge & Milburn, 1980), and also includes practice with skills likely to promote effective performance in the student's natural environment (Goldstein, Sprafkin, Gershaw, & Klein, 1980). Studies have found positive outcomes for the acquisition of targeted skills, although generalization and maintenance have been less consistent (Goldstein & Pentz, 1984).

Helping transfer students. School transfers have been described as one of the most stressful life events for young people because they require adaptation to new peers, teachers, academic standards, school rules, curricula, and so forth. As a result of these demands, these transitions are a time of particular vulnerability for engaging in a variety of maladaptive behaviors, although they may be mitigated by whether the transfer was planned (e.g., entering high school from junior high) or unscheduled (e.g., a student moving in the middle of the school year). Going from middle school to high school, for instance, has been found to increase the risk for health-compromising behaviors such as violence, academic failure, and social and emotional difficulty (Felner & Adan, 1988; Jason and Associates, 1992). School transfers also are a frequently occurring life event, and perhaps for that reason do not appear to receive the attention from educational personnel that they warrant.

A number of programs have been developed for students involved in school transitions. For example, Felner and Adan (1988) modified the ecology of the school setting in their program. Middle and high school students are assigned to take their core academic subjects (e.g., English, math) together so that they do not have to continually shift peer groups. In addition, participants' classrooms are in close proximity to one another to help them feel comfortable in the school. Home room teachers engage in many tasks typically performed by guidance personnel, such as helping with class assignments, follow-up on student absenteeism, and assisting with personal problems. Among the outcomes have been a reduction in absenteeism and school drop out, and enhanced bonding to school as a result of increasing the interaction occurring among participating students and between teachers and students.

Car safety seats. Childhood injury is the leading cause of death among children above the age of 1, and many people are surprised to learn that more children die from injuries than from infectious diseases (Baker & Walker, 1989). In addition, hundreds of thousands of additional children are hospitalized, acquire permanent disabilities, and experience considerable physical and emotional stress as a result of injuries. By far the major mechanisms of injury deaths are motor-vehicle-related, and many are associated with failure to use safety seats or safety belts properly (National Safety Council, 1992).

Targets for prevention can be selected on the basis of the frequency of the injury, the severity of the injury, and the effectiveness of available interventions (Grossman & Rivara, 1992). Zins, Garcia, Tuchfarber, Clark, and Laurence (1994) applied these guidelines in a program that focused on child safety seat use. They found that in the preceding year, the child had not been restrained in 78% of the motor-vehicle-occupant deaths that had occurred locally. Observations conducted in the community found that only 53% of the children under the age of 4 were safely restrained, even though such protection was mandated by law. However, data from the Centers for Disease Control and Prevention (1991) indicated that use of safety seats and safety belts substantially reduces the risk of death and injury. Therefore, a multidimensional, community-wide injury-prevention program was undertaken, with the early childhood center being a setting that was specifically targeted.

Because there were no satisfactory car safety seat programs available for this population, a curriculum and a variety of educational media were developed through the efforts of preschool faculty and administrators, pediatric health-care professionals, and university faculty. The goal was to teach parents and children the importance of proper restraint use. Demonstrations of appropriate use of this equipment were provided, and the children had access to child-sized play cars in which they could use safety seats. In addition, a monthly newsletter that addressed specific occupant safety issues was sent home. Other community-wide efforts were also undertaken, such as using television public service announcements and billboards to promote the use of safety seats and seat belts. At the end of the school year, it was found that 82.3% of the children in intervention schools were properly restrained, compared with 72% observed in control schools (Zins et al., 1994).

Violence prevention. Students are engaging in interpersonal violence and causing a variety of intentional injuries at an alarming rate. Groups such as the U.S. Department of Health and Human Services (1990), the National Association of State Directors of Special Education (LaRue, 1994), and many other medical, social, and political leaders have identified information on how to cope with this public health problem (Zins, Travis, Brown, & Knighton, 1994). Among the most widely used programs developed to address this issue is *Second Step: A Violence Prevention Curriculum* (Committee on Youth, 1995).

Four versions of Second Step are available, including editions that target students from preschool through junior high. The intent is to reduce aggressive and impulsive behavior and increase social competence. A variety of prosocial skills designed to enhance students' self-efficacy and to change their attitudes and behaviors in a culturally sensitive manner are taught. Units on *empathy* (providing appropriate emotional responses based on feelings of others), *impulse control* (problem solving, communication, social skills), and *anger management* (stress management, controlling angry feelings) are included. The curriculum is supported by several videotapes and activities for parents.

Second Step was developed on the basis of a review of the literature that identified common skill deficits found in persons whose behavior is excessively aggressive and impulsive and leads to peer rejection (Kendall & Braswell, 1993). The skills taught target these specific behavioral deficits. Although only initial pilot data that yielded encouraging results are available, studies in several locations are underway (K. Fry, personal communication, April 22, 1996; Wilson-Brewer, Cohen, O'Donnell, & Goodman, 1991) and the program is recognized as a potentially effective intervention by leaders in the field (Brewer, Hawkins, Catalano, & Neckerman, 1995).

Implications and Concluding Comments

Emerging societal, political, legislative, and professional trends support the concept that service delivery models must be redefined to provide a wider array of services for children and their families. Consequently, there are virtually limitless opportunities for psychologists in schools to become involved in promoting children's psychological competence through social and emotional learning activities. Students who are socially competent are more likely to engage in health enhancing behaviors and avoid behaviors that potentially have negative outcomes and may be better prepared to be effective learners (Consortium, 1994). From a different perspective, the future of specialties like school psychology are dependent to a large extent on how effectively these professionals are able to transform their primary focus from traditional, individual assessment and classification functions to include more population-wide prevention and intervention (Zins, Conyne, & Ponti, 1988; Zins & Wagner, 1997).

Comprehensive school health programs in particular, which are being developed in schools in many states, offer tremendous promise as a means for schools to more effectively organize and provide health services (Allensworth & Kolbe, 1987; Kolbe, 1995; Task Force, 1994). The advantages of comprehensive, coordinated services delivery have been well documented (Dryfoos, 1994), and we agree with Talley and Short (1995) that such approaches will continue to expand in the future. Psychologists, by virtue of their expertise in understanding and changing behavior, have the opportunity to become leaders in these efforts. To do so, however, they must reorient their practices and sell schools on the value of the wide range of individually and organizationally focused prevention and intervention services they can provide. Further, psychological and counseling services cannot continue to be conceptualized as distinct from school health services.

The psychologist's role as consultant also needs continued emphasis as it is the primary means by which psychologists can promote social and emotional learning. Development and maintenance of a supportive, caring school climate is essential to the effectiveness of these efforts, and organizational consultation can be a useful mechanism in this regard. It can also help in establishing a common framework that links the various social and emotional learning activities that occur in most schools. In addition, consultative support to classroom teachers who are providing curriculum-based and other types of social and emotional learning can help to ensure that they are provided effectively and efficiently.

Our goal has been to discuss the many complex issues related to social and emotional learning in schools. We are encouraged that there is increasing recognition of the importance of developing these skills, attitudes, knowledge, and behaviors, as well as of the close link between young people's emotional health and physical health. Nevertheless, tremendous challenges remain. Better coordination and integration of the efforts of school personnel, families, and the community is needed for effective psychological-competence education. These efforts cannot be isolated or "added on" activities, or the domain of a single discipline. Rather, they must be part of the educational mainstream and based on contributions from all who are involved in children's lives. There is a clear opportunity for psychologists to be major contributors to social and emotional learning, but they must decide to actively market themselves and to apply their skills to this growing movement.

References

Allensworth, D. D., & Kolbe, L. J. (1987). The comprehensive school health program: Exploring an expanded concept. *Journal of School Health, 57,* 409–412.

American Medical Association. (1990). *Healthy youth 2000.* Chicago: Author.

Apter, S. J. (1982). *Troubled children/troubled systems.* Elmsford, NY: Pergamon.

Asher, S. R., & Coie, J. D. (Eds.). (1990). *Peer rejection in childhood.* New York: Cambridge University Press.

Baker, S. G., & Walker, A. (1989). *Childhood injury: State-by-state mortality facts.* Washington, DC: National Maternal and Child Clearinghouse.

Bandura, A. (1977a). Self-efficacy: Toward a unifying theory of behavioral change. *Psychological Review, 84,* 191–215.

Bandura, A. (1977b). *Social learning theory.* Englewoods Cliffs, NJ: Prentice-Hall.

Bandura, A. (1982). Self-efficacy mechanism is human agency. *American Psychologist, 37,* 122–147.

Becker, M. H. (Ed.). (1974). *The health belief model and personal health behavior.* Thorofare, NJ: Charles B. Slack.

Becker, M. H. (1979). Understanding patient compliance: The contributions of attitudes and other psychosocial factors. In S. J. Cohen (Ed.), *New directions in patient compliance* (pp. 102–122). Lexington, MA: Heath.

Becker, M. H., & Maiman, L. A. (1975). Sociobehavioral determinants of compliance with health and medical care recommendations. *Medical Care, 13,* 10–24.

Benson, P. (1993). *The troubled journey: A portrait of 6th–12th grade youth.* Minneapolis, MN: Search Institute.

Brewer, D. D., Hawkins, J. D., Catalano, R. D., & Neckerman, H. J. (1995). Preventing serious, violent, and chronic juvenile offending: A review of evaluations of selected strategies in childhood, adolescence, and the community. In J. C. Howell, B. Krisberg, J. D. Hawkins, & J. J. Wilson, (Eds.), *A sourcebook: Serious violent and chronic juvenile offenders* (pp. 61–144). Thousand Oaks, CA: Sage.

Cartledge, G., & Milburn, J. F. (1980). *Teaching social skills to children.* Elmsford, NY: Pergamon.

Centers for Disease Control and Prevention. (1991). Child passenger restraint use and motor-vehicle-related fatalities among children—United States, 1982–1990. *Morbidity and Mortality Weekly Report, 40,* 600–602.

Children's Defense Fund. (1995). *The state of America's children.* Washington, DC: Author.

Cohen, S., & Wilson-Brewer, R. (1991). *Violence prevention for young adolescents: The state of the art of program evaluation.* Washington, DC: Carnegie Council on Adolescent Development.

Coie, J. D., Dodge, K. A., & Kupersmidt, J. B. (1990). Peer group behavior and social status. In S. Asher & J. D. Coie (Eds.), *Peer rejection in childhood.* New York: Cambridge Press.

Commission on Violence and Youth. (1993). *Violence and youth: Psychology's response.* Washington, DC: American Psychological Association.

Committee on Youth. (1995). *Second Step: A violence prevention curriculum.* Seattle: Author.

Consortium on the School-Based Promotion of Social Competence. [Elias, M. J., Weissberg, R. P., Hawkins, J. D., Perry, C. L., Zins, J. E., Dodge, K. A., Kendall, P. C., Gottfredson, D., Rotheram-Borus, M. J., Jason, L. A., & Wilson-Brewer, R. J.]. (1994). The school-based promotion of social competence: Theory, research, practice, and policy. In R. J. Haggerty, L. R. Sherrod, N. Garmezy, & M. Rutter (Eds.), *Stress, risk, and resilience in children and adolescents: Processes, mechanisms, and interaction* (pp. 268–316). New York: Cambridge University Press.

Dryfoos, J. G. (1990). *Adolescents at risk: Prevalence and prevention.* New York: Oxford University Press.

Dryfoos, J. G. (1994). *Full-service schools: A revolution in health and social services for children, youth, and adolescents.* San Francisco: Jossey-Bass.

Elias, M. J. (1997). Social problem solving skills: Competencies for social and academic success and emotional intelligence. In G. G. Bear, K. M. Minke, & A. Thomas (Eds.), *Children's needs II: Development, problems, and alternatives* (pp. 27–38). Washington, DC: National Association of School Psychologists.

Felner, R., & Adan, A. M. (1988). The school transitional environment project: An ecological intervention and evaluation. In R. H. Price, E. L. Cowen, R. P. Lorion, & J. Ramos-McKay (Eds.), *14 ounces of prevention* (pp. 111–122). Washington, DC: American Psychological Association.

Gardner, H. (1983). *Frames of mind: The theory of multiple intelligences.* New York: Basic Books.

Gardner, H. (1995). Reflections on multiple intelligences: Myths and messages. *Phi Delta Kappan, 76,* 200–209.

Goldstein, A. P., & Pentz, M. A. (1984). Psychological skill training and the aggressive adolescent. *School Psychology Review, 13,* 311–323.

Goldstein, A. P., Sprafkin, R., Gershaw, N., & Klein, P. (1980). *Skillstreaming the adolescent.* Champagne, IL: Research Press.

Goleman, D. (1995a). *Emotional intelligence.* New York: Bantam.

Goleman, D. (1995b). *Emotional literacy: A field report.* Kalamazoo, MI: Fetzer Institute.

Gordon, R. S., Jr. (1983). An operational classification of disease prevention. *Public Health Reports, 98,* 107–109.

Gresham, F. M., & Elliott, S. N. (1991). *Social Skills Rating System.* Circle Pines, MN: American Guidance Service.

Grossman, D. C., & Rivara, F. P. (1992). Injury control in childhood. *Pediatric Clinics of North America, 39,* 471–485.

Hallmark Corporate Foundation. (1994). *Talking with TJ.* Kansas City, MO: Author.

Hawkins, J. D., Catalano, R. F., & Associates. (1992). *Communities that care: Action for drug abuse prevention.* San Francisco: Jossey-Bass.

Jason, L. A., and Associates. (1992). *Helping transfer students.* San Francisco: Jossey-Bass.

Jessor, R. (1993). Successful adolescent development among youth in high-risk settings. *American Psychologist, 48,* 117–126.

Kendall, P. C., & Braswell, L. (1993). *Cognitive-behavioral therapy with impulsive children* (2nd ed.). New York: Guilford.

Kolbe, L. J. (1995, April). *Building the capacity of schools to improve the health of the nation: A call for assistance from school psychologists.* Paper presented at the annual meeting of the National Association of School Psychologists, Chicago.

Kolbe, L. J., Collins, J., & Cortese, P. (in press). Building the capacity of schools to improve the health of the nation: A call for assistance from psychologists. *American Psychologist.*

LaRue, S. (1994). No. 1 information need: Appropriate services for violent, aggressive behavior. *Counterpoint, 14*(3), 1, 24.

Leitenberg, H. (1987). Primary prevention of delinquency. In J. D. Burchard & S. N. Burchard (Eds.), *Prevention of delinquent behavior* (pp. 312–331). Newbury Park, CA: Sage.

Lorion, R. P. (1991). Targeting preventive interventions: Enhancing risk estimates through theory. *American Journal of Community Psychology, 19*(6), 859–865.

Massachusetts Medical Society. (1992). Public health assessment: Physical fighting among high school students. *Mortality and Morbidity Weekly Review, 41*(6), 90–94.

McGinnis, E., & Goldstein, A. P. (1984). *Skillstreaming the elementary school child: A guide for teaching prosocial skills.* Champaign, IL: Research Press.

Mesibov, C. B., & LaGreca, A. M. (1981). A social skills instructional module. *The Directive Teacher, 3,* 6–7.

Miller, C. A. (1990). Summation and commentary. *Pediatrics, 86*(6), (Suppl.), 1124–1126.

National Safety Council. (1992). *Accident facts, 1992 edition.* Itasca, IL: Author.

Report of the Task Force on Education of Young Adolescents. (1989). *Turning points: Preparing American youth for the 21st century.* Washington, DC: Carnegie Council on Adolescent Development.

Rosenstock, I. M., Strecher, V. J., & Becker, M. H. (1988). Social learning theory and the health belief model. *Health Education Quarterly, 15,* 173–183.

Salovey, P., & Mayer, J. D. (1990). Emotional intelligence. *Imagination, Cognition, and Personality, 9,* 185–211.

Schorr, L. B. (1991). Children, families, and the cycle of disadvantage. *Canadian Journal of Psychiatry, 36*(6), 437–441.

Simeonsson, R. J. (1994). Promoting children's health, education, and well-being. In R. J. Simeonsson (Ed.), *Risk, resilience, and prevention: Promoting the well-being of all children* (pp. 3–31). Baltimore: Brookes.

Spivack, G., & Shure, M. B. (1974). *Social adjustment of young children.* San Francisco: Jossey-Bass.

Talley, R. C., & Short, R. J. (1995). Schools as health service delivery sites: Current status and future directions. *Special Services in the Schools, 10,* 37–56.

Task Force on Comprehensive and Coordinated Psychological Services for Children: Ages 0–10. (1994). *Comprehensive and coordinated psychological services for children: A call for service integration.* Washington, DC: American Psychological Association.

Tuma, J. (1989). Mental health services for children: The state of the art. *American Psychologist, 44,* 188–199.

U.S. Department of Health and Human Services. (1990). *Healthy people 2000: National health promotion and disease prevention objectives.* Washington, DC: U.S. Government Printing Office.

U.S. Department of Health and Human Services. (1995). *Healthy people 2000: Midcourse review and 1995 revisions.* Washington, DC: U.S. Government Printing Office.

U.S. Preventive Services Task Force. (1989). *Guide to clinical preventive services: An assessment of the effectiveness of 169 interventions.* Baltimore: Williams and Wilkins.

Wagner, D. I., & Zins, J. E. (1985). Health promotion in the schools: Opportunities and challenges for special services providers. *Special Services in the Schools, 1*(3), 5–7.

Waxman, H. C., Walker deFelix, J., Anderson, J. E., & Baptiste, H. P., Jr. (Eds.). (1992). *Students at risk in at risk schools.* Newbury Park, CA: Corwin.

Wilson-Brewer, R., Cohen, S., O'Donnell, L., & Goodman, I. (1991). *Violence prevention for adolescents: A survey of the state of the art.* Washington: Carnegie Council on Adolescent Development.

W. T. Grant Foundation Consortium on the School-Based Promotion of Social Competence. [Elias, M. J., Weissberg, R. P., Dodge, K. A., Hawkins, J. D., Jason, L. A., Kendall, P. C., Perry, C. L., Rotheram-Borus, M. J., & Zins, J. E.]. (1992). Drug and alcohol prevention curricula. In J. D. Hawkins & R. F. Catalano, *Communities that care: Action for drug abuse prevention* (pp. 129–148). San Francisco: Jossey-Bass.

Zins, J. E., Conyne, R. K., & Ponti, C. R. (1988). Primary prevention: Expanding the impact of psychological services in schools. *School Psychology Review, 17*(4), 540–547.

Zins, J. E., Garcia, V. F., Tuchfarber, B. S., Clark, K. M., & Laurence, S. C. (1994). Preventing injuries in children and youth. In R. J. Simeonsson (Ed.), *Risk, resilience, and prevention: Promoting the well-being of all children* (pp. 183–202). Baltimore, MD: Brookes.

Zins, J. E., Travis, L. F., III, Brown, M., & Knighton, A. (1994). Schools and the prevention of interpersonal violence: Mobilizing and coordinating community resources. *Special Services in the Schools, 8*(2), 1–20.

Zins, J. E., & Wagner, D. I. (1987). Children and health promotion. In A. Thomas & J. Grimes (Eds.), *Children's needs II: Psychological perspectives* (pp. 258–267). Washington, DC: National Association of School Psychologists.

Zins, J. E., & Wagner, D. I. (1997). Health promotion. In G. G. Bear, K. M. Minke, & A. Thomas (Eds.), *Children's needs: Development, problems, and alternatives* (pp. 945–954). Washington, DC: National Association of School Psychologists.

8

Integrating Services for Children With Severe Emotional Disabilities Through Coordination

T. Kerby Neill

A large number of children require extensive services because they are damaged by "deteriorating family life—divorce, drug addiction, violence, and a crescendo of child abuse" (Rothman, 1994, p. 4). Service coordination is a means of ensuring that children and families receive the services they need. Children with serious emotional disabilities (SED) require mental health services, remedial and special education, and family support because of stressed caretaking environments. They are frequently served by the child welfare and legal systems as a function of child protection issues, poverty, and conflicts with societal norms. These are systems that are "central to the care of some of the most severely affected children with mental disorders" (Institute of Medicine, 1989). In a classic monograph, Stroul and Friedman (1986) proposed an ideal system of care for these children. They asserted that service coordination is the "glue that holds the system together" (p. 109). In this regard, service coordination for children with SED involves a coherent philosophy, special skills, and knowledge of emerging strategies.

This chapter explores the place of service coordination in the practice of psychology, considers its historical roots, and surveys its evolving forms for children with SED. This survey will include (a) the current state of service coordination, (b) the goals and functions of service coordination, (c) program examples and models of service coordination, (d) implementation problems, and (e) the status of research. I have joined others (Illback & Neill, 1995; Poertner & Friesen, 1995) who prefer the term *service coordination* to the dominant term in the literature—*case management*. Not only is "case" management not a client-friendly term (Hobbs, 1979, p. 30), but "service coordination" clearly presumes a multiservice environment and emphasizes the integrative function of the service. Friesen and Poertner (1995) emphasized that service coordination can occur at the client level (to match client need with service) or system level (to effect system change). The terms *service coordination* and *case management* are used in this chapter with emphasis on the former.

Service Coordination—The Systemization of "Conventional Wisdom"

Service coordination has always been part of good mental health intervention—psychologists talked to teachers; hospital staff formed interdisciplinary teams to collaborate; clinicians were advocates for families. It is not surprising that early efforts at systematic approaches to case management were met with skepticism:

> It's sort of the things you've always done
> But a new name is always a lot of fun
> We can make it more complex indeed
> Than just doing the things your clients need.
> (Eisenstadt, 1983, p. 175)

It is also true that common-sense service coordination is frequently absent. Most clinicians have seen the consequences of failed coordination. Several years ago I evaluated a boy described as a "placement problem," because of frequently running away. Old records revealed a long pattern of isolated services. When he was in elementary school, his mother was dying of cancer. A child welfare agency failed to intervene until the mother became so ill that the boy would need a foster home. The home health agency caring for his mother arranged his after-school care with a nearby family where, unknown to any agency, he was sexually abused by a visiting teenager. The school, unaware of the mother's illness, documented declining performance, "lack of family involvement," and parental failure to respond to letters sent via the child. The school resorted to corporal punishment for assignments missed after repeated warnings. This was only the prologue to years of disjointed services for this young man.

Service coordination has deep roots in social service. Weil and Karls (1985) traced its roots to the earliest days of social work, Jane Addams's Hull House and the mid-nineteenth-century Charity Organization Societies. They also cited a 1901 outline of case coordination by Mary Richmond that looks highly contemporary. Although service coordination may have much in common with "good old fashioned social work," it has new forms and is a shared responsibility of all disciplines in a complex system that includes mental health services. Psychologists, whether they provide direct service or clinical supervision, train, or serve as program administrators, need to understand this dimension of care.

Many principles of good service coordination are explicit or implicit in the *Ethical Principles of Psychologists and Code of Conduct* and the *Specialty Guidelines for the Delivery of Services* (American Psychological Association, 1981, 1992).[1] Although these principles constitute a professional mandate for service coordination, the implementation of solid service coordination in a multiservice environment is not easy. It is a rare psychologist who completes his or her training with a working grasp of multi-

---

[1] General principles A, D, E, and particularly C apply, as do Guidelines 2.2.5, 2.2.6, and 2.3.2 of both the clinical and counseling specialty guidelines.

service systems or contemporary service coordination. Often clinicians who seek to foster local teamwork on behalf of a client are frustrated by the same bureaucratic rules and turf boundaries that thwart clients. The temptation is to rein in the scope of their efforts. When psychologists persist in ensuring that their services are part of a comprehensive and coordinated effort on behalf of a child and family, everyone is better served. Such activity by clinicians can invigorate local standards for service by creating new working relationships and raising both consumer and agency expectancies.

Forces Shaping Contemporary Service Coordination

Growth of Systems Perspectives

In conceptualizing intervention with children, there is growing understanding of the need for a systems perspective. Families are the primary context of children (Minuchin & Minuchin, 1974). The context of a family whose child has problems is shaped by service systems (Hobbs, 1975) and larger ecosystems (Bronfenbrenner, 1979). To address a child's needs, society must also address the needs of the child's family. Families require many supports beyond therapy. Providers must understand the larger systems within which they and the family are functioning. Services organized to meet agency agendas or narrow funding mandates may not be perceived by families as appropriate. As several mothers of children with SED have asserted, services must be offered "with" families rather than "for" families (Donner et al., 1995).

Mental Health Reform

While conceptual frameworks grew, service systems were slower. In the early sixties, the community mental health movement (and advances in psychotropic drugs) succeeded in reducing the census in adult psychiatric hospitals. By 1977, the General Accounting Office had issued a strong critique of community mental health's results for people with serious mental illness. Reforms instituted in the 1980s to assist seriously mentally ill adults included the federal Community Support Program and a range of community networks, all with an emphasis on coordination of services (Breakey, 1990).

Services for families and children were also targeted for innovation. The report of the Joint Commission on the Mental Health of Children (1969), chaired by Reginald Lourie, reflected the influence of Nicholas Hobbs in its strong emphasis on coordinated, community responses to children's needs. Although the commission's report stimulated the inclusion of services to children in federal community mental health legislation, little of the commission's vision was implemented. In 1975, Hobbs would write that the overall picture of services to children was "one of unconscionable disarray" (p. 180). In 1982, Knitzer published her research on services to children with serious emotional disturbance and concluded that they were virtually "unclaimed" by agencies one would expect to serve them. Knitzer's work, and the follow-up study by the Office of missing Technology Assessment (1986), triggered the establishment of the Children and Adolescent Service System Project (CASSP) within the National Institute of Mental Health. Under the leadership of Reginald Lourie's son, Ira Lourie, the creative staff at CASSP fostered a conceptual and technical literature for serving children with SED and leveraged strategic change through demonstration projects and state level policy initiatives (Day & Roberts, 1991).

In the early eighties, a few communities were beginning to address the needs of their most troubled children. The *Willie M. v. Hunt* lawsuit forced North Carolina to provide a continuum of care for disturbed and violent youth (as cited in Knitzer, 1982). With strong local leadership, a county-wide model system of care was initiated in Ventura, California (Goldman, 1992). These movements caught the attention of the Robert Wood Johnson Foundation (Cole & Poe, 1993). The foundation formulated a Mental Health Services Program for Youth (MHSPY) for innovative projects to serve children and adolescents with SED. Twelve projects received planning grants and a year later, 8 sites received implementation grants of $2.4 million each (to match state and local funds over 4 years). The MHSPY projects were able to effect major systems change. Two states, Vermont and Kentucky, produced statewide reforms in response to the MHSPY initiative. Strong systems of service coordination were central to each of these projects. Because of my familiarity with the program, I cite many examples from IMPACT, the Kentucky MHSPY program (see also Illback, Neill, Call, & Andis, 1993; Illback, Nelson, & Sanders, 1997).

In 1992, federal legislation (the Comprehensive Community Mental Health Services Program for Children with Severe Emotional Disturbances) sought to further the MHSPY models. This program has now funded over 20 demonstration projects for children with SED.

Attention to Higher Standards of Care

The Joint Commission on Accreditation of Healthcare Organizations (1995) places emphasis on the coordination and continuity of services in their standards for mental health centers. Greater rigor is expected in treatment and service plans. Service coordination is mandated for families who have young children with disabilities served under the Education of the Handicapped Act Amendments (PL 99-457). According to Public Law 102-321, states are required to provide case management for persons using "substantial amounts of public resources" (Jacobs, 1995, p. 373). State mental health plans submitted to the National Institute of Mental Health must include provisions for case management services to children (PL 99-660).

Managed Care

Service coordination is becoming common in managed mental health care. For youth who tax the provider (and payer) system, service coordination may not only broker community services, but serve as a gatekeeping function to divert clients from more expensive levels of care. Broskowski (1995) makes a strong case for the encouragement and coverage of case management for children with SED in provisions of health insurance. Gatekeeping is characteristic of insurance programs or publicly funded programs that are capitated. In capitation the provider assumes some of the risk of the insurer or other payer and agrees to meet the service needs of a defined population in return for a fixed sum. Usually many regulations guiding service delivery are suspended, allowing the provider freedom to make the most of resources. Service coordination has a significant role to play in systems of managed care as a means of both cost containment and quality enhancement, but there is a danger of emphasizing cost containment over optimum services.

Dominant Philosophies in the Service-Coordination Culture

General Service Values

Service coordination has grown in tandem with new philosophies of care. In their original monograph on the system of care, Stroul and Friedman (1986) cited two core values to guide services—that services be determined by the needs of the child and family and that services be community based. A diversity of local and national efforts to address the needs of families with families and within an ecological perspective has earned the name of the family-support movement. Weissbourd (1994), who described the history of this movement, considers Head Start the first large-scale implementation of a family-support approach. She cited the Children and Adolescent Service System Project as reflecting the values of the movement in child mental health. Community-based programs are committed to the least restrictive form of intervention necessary. Children with SED should remain with, or close to, their family. The use of institutional care is minimized. The National Commission on Children (1991) expressed grave concern over the large numbers of children in state custody. They recognize that the child welfare system is overwhelmed. They express concern that federal funding for family support remained relatively constant while funding for children in placement was an entitlement. This only encouraged placement. The Commission strongly endorsed a family-centered and community-based approach:

> The Commission recommends a framework for a comprehensive, community based, family focused system that will lessen the need to place

vulnerable children in substitute care by ensuring that their families have the necessary supports to raise them. (National Commission on Children, 1991, p. 293)

Two other movements influential in current approaches to service coordination are the strengths model of intervention and the need for culturally competent services. These are discussed in the following sections.

Strengths Model

A *strengths model* assumes that each person has the capacity to change, that people are more readily engaged if their strengths are recognized, and that supporting strengths is more effective in reducing problems than a focus on pathology. At least two groups have articulated strengths models for working with children and families—one at the University of Kansas School of Social Welfare (Ronneau, Rutter, & Donner, 1988) and another in North Carolina (Dunst, Trivette, & Deal, 1988, 1994; see also chapter 4, this volume). *Empowerment* is a key term in the strengths model. In services that are empowering, helper and client are in a partnership, the clients chooses the goals, and clients capitalize on their skills to achieve a sense of mastery in reaching the goal.

Cultural Competence

The differences between the experiences of youth in the cultural mainstream and those in minority cultures are so different as to make comparison between the two "spurious at best and invidious at worst" (Stiffman & Davis, 1990, p. 17). Ethnic issues are so pervasive in America that none of us remains untouched by some form of bias. Efforts to develop professional awareness of cross-cultural issues date from the late 1960s and gained a systematic statement in the work of D. W. Sue and D. Sue (1981). Cross, Bazron, Dennis, and Issacs (1981) defined a culturally competent system as one that reflects a respect for diversity, a capacity for cultural self-assessment, and an awareness of the dynamics of interacting cultures. Culturally competent organizations have institutionalized cultural knowledge in their system and have adapted their services to the cultural realities of their target populations. If there is not the opportunity to match the ethnic backgrounds of family and service coordinator (see Blank, Tetrick, Brinkley, Smith, & Doheny, 1994, for positive effects of ethnic matching on service use), it is crucial that the family's service coordinator be culturally sensitive.

Culturally sensitive practitioners should recognize resources in their client's community. For instance, ministers or members of a family's church can be crucial in the family's natural support system. Religion represents a set of sociocultural values that gets insufficient attention in much of the cultural diversity literature. Exceptions occur when there is a strong tie between ethnic minorities and particular forms of religious expression. The positive role of churches in the Afro-American community is one source of support that is likely to get attention in the literature (Caldwell, Greene, & Billingsley, 1994; chapter 3, this volume). The meaning of a family's religious commitment is an important part of assessment. If it is central for the family, then it must become a parameter of service planning and implementation.

Functions and Goals of Service Coordination

To illustrate the goals and functions of service coordination, it is helpful to consider a sample program. Kentucky IMPACT is a program of formal service coordination delivered by regional community mental health centers. A local resource coordinator supervises a staff of service coordinators and outreach workers. Each child accepted into the program is assigned a coordinator. The service coordinator assembles a team of key players in the child's life. A sample team might include parents, a grandparent or sibling, and the child's therapist, teacher, school counselor, and welfare worker. If the child is sufficiently mature, she or he is included. The team is oriented to the collaborative process and the need to remain together as long as the child requires intensive services. The team agrees on the critical needs of the child and family, then develops a common service plan. The plan is detailed with tasks to be done, persons responsible for the tasks, and timelines. A written copy of the plan is mailed to all team members with a date of the next team meeting. Each team meeting generates an updated plan. The service coordinator constantly monitors progress and keeps team members informed so that adjustments can be made. New services needed by the child and family are provided by team members, IMPACT outreach staff, or the service coordinator. Each child-specific team can recommend a budget for the purchase of materials or services not readily available but considered important to the plan's success. Funds for these budgets come from pooled agency dollars or state general funds allocated to provide individualized services for children and families.

Although IMPACT staff are located within the mental health system, by history and design it is an interagency program. At the heart of the design is the Regional Interagency Council (RIAC). The RIAC's core membership is determined by statute. It includes administrative-level mental health, school, and court personnel and a parent. The council is chaired by a local administrator of the Kentucky Department for Social Services. In larger communities other agencies also participate. The RIAC decides which children receive services, approves child-specific budgets within the funds available, monitors treatment plans, sets policy, and oversees plans to exit families from IMPACT. Interagency difficulties unsolved at the line level are usually solved by the RIAC. In my experience, the dedication of RIAC members to children and families clearly exceeded their concern with turf issues. RIACs have a state-level counterpart, the State Interagency Council (SIAC), composed of administrators from the Kentucky State Departments of Mental Health, Education, Social Services, and Health;

a state parent council; and the Administrative Office of the Courts. Agency or service problems that cannot be resolved at the local level are referred to the SIAC. The SIAC also works with statewide IMPACT staff to provide technical assistance and quality control feedback to the RIACs. Kentucky IMPACT includes many elements common to other programs seeking to provide coordinated services to children with SED.

Like most case managers, IMPACT service coordinators are often "jacks-of-all-trades," especially in areas with few services. This trend has encouraged some writers to produce long lists of functions for service coordination—Kanter (1989) named 13 and Rothman (1994) has listed 15. The listing Stroul (1995) has culled from the literature is probably most representative. Six tasks are assigned to case management: assessment, service planning, service implementation, service coordination, monitoring and evaluation, and advocacy. Analogies for the function of service coordination refer to coordination efforts as "glue" for the system, the "hub of the wheel," or the principle that "meshes the gears." Good service coordination goes well beyond mechanical linkages—it is catalytic. It creates and evokes new possibilities. It is in this spirit that the functions of service coordination are discussed subsequently in the context of desired outcomes.

As a Means of Empowering Families

Parent role. The tendency to blame parents for the difficulties of their children, overly emphasized in a number of psychological theories (Terkelson, 1990), has been a long-standing barrier to the enlistment of families in the treatment process (Kanner, 1941). This does not mean that well researched theories of family influence on the development of child problems (Patterson, Reid, & Dishion, 1992) should not guide treatment strategies, but they should not flavor efforts to engage parents.

Since 1971, *Exceptional Parent* magazine has provided compassionate articles and resource information for and by parents of children with disabilities. Most critically, the magazine's title recognizes that parenting an exceptional child requires an exceptional parent. Articles in *Exceptional Parent* also can sharpen the sensitivity and humility of professional helpers who cannot presume exceptional parenting in all cases, and must provide special support. Lourie (1995) puts this in simple perspective, "case management must be . . . seen as an extension of the child management functions that parents and other guardians perform every day" (p. xiii). This begins with an assessment that recognizes that all the players in the team, especially the family, have their own assessment of the child's needs and difficulties. Advocates of the strengths model suggest assessment and engagement are actually a reeducation of the client, a "role induction" in which clients are encouraged to question the service provider and clarify their own wants and needs (Kisthardt & Rapp, 1992, p. 113). The parent is recognized as an essential member of the service team. For this reason, IMPACT service coordinators typically reschedule service-team meetings if a parent cannot be present.

Parent support networks. A sign of increasingly empowered families is the number of parents of children with serious emotional problems who are organizing for mutual support and advocacy. Stigmatization and tendencies to treat parents as pathogenic may explain why support and advocacy groups for families of the mentally ill are only recent. Fine and Borden (1989) chronicled the development of a support group of parents in southeastern Pennsylvania. They described successful recruitment strategies and the evolution of parents from seeking personal support to providing mutual support and advocacy for children's issues. Clearly many parents receive critical support from such groups. Thus, referrals to a parent support group may be a vital part of the service plan.

The collective responses of parent support groups is manifest nationally in the Children and Adolescent Network of the National Alliance for the Mentally Ill and the more recent Federation of Families for Children's Mental Health. In 1986, a group of professionals, themselves members of the alliance, organized a conference to address the education of professionals regarding the families of the mentally ill (Lefley & Johnson, 1990). The education or reeducation of professionals with respect to families that include a member with a serious emotional disturbance is now high on the agenda of such groups. Recently, Donner asked six parents who were active in advocacy for children with SED in Kansas (Donner et al., 1995) to specifically outline their expectancies of case management. They look for case managers who establish positive relationships, have supportive attitudes, have the "pull" to move service systems, help their children enter more normal and informal child activities, put parents in touch with parents facing similar struggles, and remain responsive and flexible.

Advocacy role. Often parents require advocates to address issues that are critical for their child. They may need information regarding their rights. They may need help writing a letter. A case manager or member of a parent support group may accompany a parent to a meeting where they will have to confront agency staff. Although there will be times when professionals working with the family will have to be direct advocates, extra time and preparation may allow a parent to become his or her own advocate. Such an approach often leaves a client with skill and confidence that rewards the effort.

The collective voice of families is being heard nationally. In 1990, Knitzer and colleagues (Knitzer, Steinberg, & Fleisch, 1990) looked at the failure of schools in serving children with SED. The accumulating data on system failure prompted the National Mental Health Association and the Federation of Families for Children's Mental Health to issue a joint challenge to current systems of care (Koyanagi & Gaines, 1993). This report cited high proportions of school failure and dropouts among youth with SED and called for a wider range of services and better mental health profession–school system collaboration.

As a Means of Maximizing Resources

Pooling expertise. Teams in clinical settings bring together specialties to answer challenging questions. Is the patient confused, retarded, resistant, experiencing a toxic reaction, hard of hearing, or a combination of these? No single team member has a complete answer. The same is often true in the community. Youth may present differently in various settings or with particular individuals. Such information may be crucial to an effective plan of care. However, unless a special initiative is taken, therapist, pediatrician, teacher, parents, speech therapist, coach, and youth are unlikely to meet together. Knowledge of the skills and alliances of the various team members may also determine who on the service team takes certain roles. For instance, a Big Sister mentor may be in a better position to resolve a homework crisis than the parent, therapist, or teacher.

One barrier that may restrict the sharing of the insights and expertise is the issue of confidentiality. Collaborating agencies in service coordination programs have developed agreements on the interagency level and forms on the team level that routinely simplify the sharing of information.

Psychologists often have unique skills to contribute to an interagency service team. They are usually well grounded in intervention techniques. Considerable research on innovations in intervention is in the psychological literature. Psychologists play a major role in research and developing models of intervention for the treatment of conduct problems (Barkley, 1990; Henggeler & Borduin, 1990; Kazdin, 1993; McMahon & Greenberg, 1995; Moffitt, 1993; Patterson, Reid, & Dishion, 1992). Conduct problems are heavily represented in programs serving children with serious emotional disabilities (Illback et al., 1997; Rosenblatt & Attkisson, 1992). The contribution of a psychologist's clinical understanding to the child's service team may greatly enhance the intervention. Working teams allow psychologists to more efficiently extend their input to family, school, and neighborhood.

Accountability for services and funds. For years children in need of service "followed the dollar." If only hospital care was funded, children who could have thrived with intensive outpatient programs were hospitalized. In the absence of local services or an operational sense of community responsibility to a child, many children are still placed unnecessarily in residential centers or other restrictive forms of care. For parents, the price of access to services is often loss of custody, because payment for such services might come from dollars available only to youth in state custody. In such situations, neither payer, child, nor family is well served. For many policy makers, flexible dollars in tandem with service coordination is a compelling option for reducing expensive hospital and residential services. The new principle is for dollars to follow the child.

The Alaska Youth Initiative pioneered this new route for the dollar. Youth in expensive, out-of-state hospitals or residential placements were returned to their communities. The Initiative used some of the funds formerly allocated for out-of-state care to provide aides, family support, foster families, and other "wraparound" services for these youth at significant savings (Katz-Leavy, Lourie, Stroul, & Zeigler-Dendy, 1992).

On a systems level, agencies want outcome data to share with consumers and legislators. The risks and advantages of such results-based accountability have been well stated by Schorr (1994). Accountability can lead to change in services, wider clarity, and ownership regarding goals for children, and reallocation of resources. Legislative concern over the high cost of out-of-state placements or in-state hospitalization has driven a number of system-of-care innovations. I was present at hearings before members of the Kentucky legislature as several parents reported the huge costs in family and governmental dollars to treat their children in private psychiatric hospitals. The parents read incredibly bland and unfocused treatment plans from the hospital record, complained of the serious lack of resources in their communities, and described their children's continuing problems. These hearings were a prelude to the legislation that made Kentucky IMPACT a statewide program.

Facilitating community ownership. The concept of community-based services is hollow unless key agencies and community members truly adopt vulnerable children and families as their local responsibility, not as commodities for export. Most successful community programs began by casting a wide net in their planning process and drawing in all levels of leadership. Without broad-based leadership, such appealing concepts remain at the slogan level.

One rural Kentucky county provides a good example of the synergy possible with flexible dollars and a sense of community ownership. With no summer programs for youth, workers were able to combine IMPACT staff and funds with similar resources from a school, a YMCA, and a migrant-worker project. The result was an 8-week day camp for close to 100 children (within which 8 youth with SED and their siblings participated) for no more expense than if the SED youth had been transported out of the county to a summer program. Swan and Morgan (1993) advocate such moves beyond coordination to serious collaboration. They described a developmental sequence from cooperation to coordination and finally collaboration in which expertise, vision, financial responsibilities, and problems are shared by local agencies. Joint ownership is the working attitude for serious system-level service coordination.

As a Means of Coordination Over Time

Establishing patterns of communication. Although an interagency meeting may be invaluable for bringing expertise together, sometimes it is more critical to share basic information and establish open communication. The previously discussed situation of the boy with a dying mother is a clear example. Child protective service workers may refer families to intensive, coordinated mental health programs when they suspect, but cannot confirm, serious abuse and neglect. These workers may need to demonstrate that maximum reasonable efforts have been made for the family before asking for court removal of children. Mental health staff providing intensive services may find themselves in tension between helping and protecting. This role tension requires extra supervisory support and training. Protective service workers must be clear about their concerns and maintain a strong role in the service team. Hidden agendas are cancerous in the world of service coordination. Work with potentially abusive families requires a service team that communicates well and regularly in an atmosphere of mutual respect.

In formal systems of care for children with SED, trained service coordinators have developed communication channels with key workers; they share home phone numbers and send messages quickly through designated clerical staff or computerized mailing lists to reduce interminable "telephone tag." They know when, and when not, to use answering machines for crucial messages.

Dague (n.d.), in summarizing the outcomes of a series of interagency planning retreats in Stark County, Ohio, emphasized the group statement, "We are unique in that we trust each other" (p. 13). This underpinning seems to have been the basis for fruitful communication, planning, and significant advances (still in progress) in Stark County.

Common plan of intervention. It is easy for agencies to be at cross purposes, particularly when children present unusually challenging problems. Whether the service team is an ad hoc arrangement or the product of a larger effort to improve care, a common service plan is a powerful tool. To develop a common service plan, the central figures in a child's life must first forge a working consensus. The process helps identify gaps in service and encourages the team to address them. A common plan can stimulate that catalytic role of service coordination. Efforts made in tandem can be far more powerful than those made in isolation. The day after efforts are begun by a tutor, for instance, the teacher may be primed to comment on slight gains in the quality of work. This feedback may be provided to the parent, who can compliment both child and tutor.

Continuity. A written, common plan of intervention allows the team to continually reassess its own effort. It provides a basis for documenting both success and blind alleys. When there is turnover among team members, the plan provides a basis for continuity. Hobbs (1975) lamented how rarely either agencies or professionals "assume long-term responsibility" for severely handicapped children (p. 181). Friesen and Briggs (1995) expressed concern about how well services are coordinated depending on the organization structure of the service. They have chosen two prime values from which to assess these structures—continuity and accountability. Events such as foster placement or residential care can create situations for youth with SED that pose special challenges to continuity. Friesen and Briggs pointed out that using the parent as case manager offers the greatest potential continuity, but parents may lack the preparation and may have great difficulty holding other service agencies accountable for service delivery. Some Kentucky IMPACT service coordinators began training parents to assume the service coordination role. This may allow them to carry on when the child leaves the program or may permit earlier exit and create an opening for another child. Further discussion of parents as case-managers is included in the subsection on personnel.

Models of Service Coordination

Systems of service coordination can take many forms. The models presented below are organized in terms of their increasing formality and intensity.

The Ad Hoc Model: An Extension of Traditional Mental Health Services

Service coordination may be a personal, professional, or agency-mandated extension of a worker's established role as a clinician. Many psychologists undertake case-level service coordination with the realization that youth are caught up in systems so uncoordinated that they are damaging rather than helpful. Psychologists may seek to improve relationships with staff of agencies with whom they work regularly. If providing assessments for a school, psychologists may seek to understand how their reports are received by teachers, special education administrators, or other key players in the child's life. They may seek a solid working knowledge of laws, procedures, and the local school system so as to guide and empower parents to more than an understanding of Johnny's need for a reading tutor (Cutler, 1993; Neill & Stevens, 1982). They may visit residential programs to which they refer to ascertain their quality. They may gain a sense of the information valued by agency staff—not just information on the official list (e.g., "All children admitted must have an individually administered intelligence test"), but a grasp of information that enables a program to work effectively for a child and family. The following demonstrates information that provides insight a psychologist may need:

> Mrs. Jones is extremely concerned about her son, Roger. She has indulged him to "compensate" for his handicaps. She is embittered by the failure of her family, her former husband, and many agencies to assist her in meeting Roger's needs. She responds to new "helpers" in a demanding manner. Even routine conversations have an antagonistic edge. When staff have moved beyond this initial distrust and demonstrated understanding of Roger, Mrs. Jones has become a close and loyal program ally.

Follow-up meetings on referrals and joint planning meetings with parents, teachers, or other key players in a child's life should all be standard. Frequently third-party payers do not reimburse for such activities, but this is changing. The staff providing the authorization for payment may be as important a part of the team as any other, and they need to be cultivated as joint players. The absence of payment, however, should not deter basic good practice. When service coordination is clearly needed, there is no reason psychologists cannot assume a formal case-management role, encourage another agency worker to adopt that role, make a formal referral, or guide parents in the assumption of the role. Many of the arrangements described subsequently can be adapted to individually initiated, ad hoc arrangements for service coordination.

The Agency Collaboration Model: A Systematic Way of Interfacing Between Agencies

Coordination is a value that agencies accept easily, but it is often seen as ancillary to their primary mission. Because coordination is not a means of measuring staff performance, many agencies that accept the need for coordination do not sanction or allocate necessary time to their employees. Simply the failure to list interagency collaboration as a value on forms used for staff evaluation can profoundly reduce the incentive for teamwork. Programs that place a value on coordination need to train their staff in efficient means of coordination.

In Kentucky IMPACT, a number of strategies were employed to facilitate the commitment of agency personnel to the time it takes to coordinate. It began when a broad spectrum of agencies were involved in planning the IMPACT program. For families enrolled in IMPACT, agencies agreed on common forms for release of information. Administrators in the Department for Social Services and the courts expected participation of their staff. Therapists were usually reimbursed by third-party payers on a fee-for-service basis that did not cover meetings. Provisions were made for therapists to be reimbursed for meetings either through Medicaid or discretionary funds budgeted into the child's service plan. Furthermore, the majority of service-team meetings are held at schools to facilitate teacher participation. If the child is in special education and is partially mainstreamed or is beyond elementary school, there are probably more staff at the school involved with the child than there are from any other agency.

In many jurisdictions, particularly counties, agencies are coming together to create systems of service coordination for children who are consumers of multiple services. Bolstered by formal interagency agreements and local protocols, child-specific service teams are established for target groups of children. The protocols may specify formats for a common plan of care, guidelines for monitoring the service plan, methods for requesting extra services or funds, and avenues of support when the service team is stuck. One agency may have its workers assume coordination responsibility or several agencies may designate staff for training in service coordination. Such arrangements are usually supported by a standing committee of mid-level agency supervisors who can act in support of interagency teams when special challenges or conflicts arise. Ohio is a state with a strong commitment to service coordination as the proper way to conduct the business of serving children. Stroul's (1992) account of the services in Stark County, Ohio, described a program that is the result of 2 decades of collaboration. This program is characterized by a tradition of interagency collaboration at both the case and county level, pooled funds to meet the needs of more challenging youth, and continuing innovation (Dague, n.d.).

Katz-Leavy, Lourie, Stroul, and Zeigler-Dendy (1992) have described a variety of similar systems in their work in individualized services. Many of these programs can be initiated using existing resources. They do not require a new agency, but they may require additional funds and they definitely require leadership. On the basis of her Florida experience, Zeigler-Dendy (1989) provided a guide for establishing effective child mental health programs. Zeigler-Dendy suggested that the task force, which many areas develop to address problems, follow up by seeking a legislative study, by educating legislators and their staffs, by consolidating goals within co-alitions, and by issuing "report cards" on coalition objectives. Though her focus was on state-level implementation, her design is adaptable to juris-dictions of any size.

The Service-Coordination-Unit Model: A Separately Organized Service

Community-based services for children and adolescents with SED are de-pending more and more on well-defined systems of service coordination with specialists trained and assigned to the service coordination role. The Vermont New Directions program (Lovas & Gardner, 1992) instituted the use of therapeutic case managers after piloting their concepts using two part-time staff members to facilitate the return of two adolescents from out-of-state placements. The positions that have evolved are now part of a state-wide service coordination effort. Their workers have small case-loads, intensive involvement with families, and responsibility for fulfilling most traditional case management roles. There is a strong emphasis on the development of individualized service plans in conjunction with the family, and the case managers have the role of providing education to "parents, providers and the general public regarding community integra-tion of children and adolescents with a severe emotional disturbance" (Lo-vas & Gardner, 1992, p. 36).

In Cleveland, Ohio, a contract agency provides a mental health spe-cialist case manager to individualized service-planning teams (Lovas, Geismer, & Gardner, 1992). The major goal of this specialist is to enable parents of youth with severe emotional disturbances "to become the child's primary problem solver" (p. 33). In the Family Mosaic Project in San Fran-cisco, which serves a remarkably culturally diverse population, case man-agement services are provided by 14 workers called *family advocates* who are contributed to the project by five different participating agencies (Lo-vas & Geismer, 1992). In spite of the potential confusion in such a staffing pattern, the interagency enthusiasm and commitment to the project were sufficient to offset staff role confusion, according to the project director (A. Boles, personal communication, June 21, 1994). This program required multiple cultural and language competencies among the staff. Thus, it may be that the program's ability to integrate multiagency staff and cultures among themselves enhanced their capacity to meet the challenges they would face in the community. The Kentucky IMPACT program also represents a unit model of service coordination.

Friesen and Briggs (1995) have considered the organizational advantages of a number of means of delivering case-management services. They suggested that specifically funded, semiautonomous or autonomous case-management units, supported by interagency agreements, may provide the strong accountability, authority, autonomy, and continuity needed to most effectively facilitate services for children with SED.

Problems

Sustaining Commitment

Interagency collaboration requires continual nurturing. For psychologists who assume a service-coordination role, what happens when therapy is over but coordination functions are still needed? A preoccupation with countertransference issues has encouraged absolute forms of "termination" when therapy is done. Such closure is destructive to many families with severely handicapped children. There is a clear role for a family psychologist who remains involved or at least "stays in touch," more like the family physician than the traditional therapist.

Maintaining organizational commitment is difficult, though. In the Bluegrass region of Kentucky, over 120 parents and agency personnel participated in the planning and development of the IMPACT program. A challenge in the area was the "crazy quilt" of local jurisdictions. There were 23 school districts, three social service districts, three mental health catchment areas (not congruent with the social service districts), and multiple court jurisdictions. In the early years, there was an annual all-day meeting involving several hundred parents, administrators, judges, and providers. At the meeting, progress reports and exercises kept the IMPACT constituency aware of the program and promoted a crucial sense of community ownership. Personnel turnover at service and particularly administrative levels can erode this spirit. A study of the North Carolina MYSPY site suggests that the time and commitment needed to implement system change in larger communities is greater than in small communities (Morrissey, Johnson, & Calloway, 1994).

The Family Council of Stark County, Ohio, continues to raise performance goals for improving interagency performance, better services, and reducing indices of youth and system problems (Dague, n.d.). IMPACT discovered that part of its start-up effort needed to be replicated because true community-based projects need to continually reinvent themselves. After 4 years of implementation, the statewide project undertook a strategic planning initiative (State Interagency Council, 1995). Committees were established drawing on consumers and the spectrum of agencies to review program priorities and design the improved service of the future. The committees addressed the following issues:

1. *Outcomes*—to develop quality measures at state and regional levels and refine measures at the case level.
2. *Standards and successful practices*—to establish state guidelines and committees to review services and recognize achievement.
3. *Regional interagency councils*—to enhance their functioning and their ownership of the program and the children served.
4. *Human-resource development*—to improve working conditions and professional development of the IMPACT staff.
5. *Training*—to ensure that training addresses the needs of staff, recognizes changing training needs over time, and includes training for collaborators in the project.

Training and Cross Training

Weil, Zipper, and Dedmon (1995) cited the strong need for both inservice and preservice training for case managers. Social workers are the most likely to have service coordination training as part of their professional curriculum, but this is still rare. Service coordinators are often in formal or informal consultative roles with other agency staff. They require a working grasp of both the consultative process and community process—areas where psychologists often have formal training and expertise to contribute (Brack, Jones, Smith, White, & Brack, 1993; Kelly, 1971; Kurpius, Fuqua, & Rozecki, 1993). "Given that case management is a new role, it is unlikely that new staff will be experienced at this function" (Friedman & Poertner, 1995, p. 261). Most organizations undertaking service coordination must broker or provide their own training.

Kentucky IMPACT developed a basic training program that was required of service coordinators so they could bill Medicaid. The early focus was on service philosophy, how to form an interagency team, how to develop and record a service plan, and particularly, how to conduct an interagency meeting. Staff role-played efforts to evoke an interagency plan with specific tasks. They practiced facilitating input of family members. They learned to channel talk that was off the task and to pull these tasks together in an hour's time. Caseloads for new service coordinators were smaller and time was available to share difficulties and provide suggestions for more advanced training. Advanced training deals with issues of team building, resource development, and cultural competence. Training of IMPACT service coordinators has been supplemented by training of personnel in the collaborating agencies, administrators, and parents. During quarterly training meetings, key groups—service coordinators and agency administrators, parents and social service staff—are frequently trained together.

Formalized manuals or curricula for service coordination with children and adolescents and their families have been developed in several university settings such as the School of Social Welfare at the University of Kansas (Ronneau et al., 1988) and the University of North Carolina at Chapel Hill (Zipper & Weil, 1994). (See also chapter 4, this volume.)

Personnel

As Hobbs (1975) warned, "children can get lost quite as easily in the community as in the wards of massive hospitals . . . In the final analysis, it is people who make the difference" (p. 204).

Service coordination is a responsibility of all mental health professionals, but service-coordination specialists have a special role. These staff are usually master's- or bachelor's-level workers or, in some cases, paraprofessionals hired because of their life experiences or ethnic background. When hiring specialists for service coordination, who makes a good service coordinator? In choosing youth workers, Hobbs (1975, p. 217) sought to hire "natural workers" whose commitment and ability to work with children was more the product of an entire life history than of training. Often programs seek master's-level staff, considering the background and skills that come with such training essential (Bryant & Heflinger, 1993). Because most critical training will occur after hiring, a particular degree may not be essential. There are remarkable workers who lack advanced degrees. If paraprofessionals are used because the program is in a geographic area where professionals are hard to recruit or because the program is struggling to match staff with a particular cultural group, however, staff may face the classic problems of paraprofessionals in the mental health system (Bayes & Neill, 1978), including minimal recognition and no place to advance. Program developers must be aware that reduced staff turnover is linked to continuity of service, but continuity of service presumes a career ladder for staff. Furthermore, mixing staff with similar responsibilities but sharply divergent professional levels is difficult.

Continuity is also related to the interests of staff. When IMPACT began, there was no pool of experienced service coordinators. Many applicants for service coordinator had a master's degree and professional experience but were primarily interested in being therapists. They left as soon as therapy jobs became available. The Fort Bragg project reports a similar experience (Bryant & Heflinger, 1993). Finding candidates with a strong commitment to the task of service coordination is critical to reducing turnover.

One solution to finding dedicated staff has been to hire and train parents of children with severe emotional problems to be case managers—either for their own child or for other children. Ohio has pioneered a number of such parent–case manager projects (Ignelzi & Dague, 1995), and many projects train parents as case managers as a basic part of their intervention strategy. In an area of rural Florida, parents do the bulk of the service coordination and the professional staff assume a consultation role (Pierce & Freedman, 1988). Some programs offer stipends to parents who are ready to assume service coordination responsibilities for their children (Ignelzi & Dague, 1995).

Dealing With Limited Resources

The nature of work with vulnerable populations is to struggle in an environment in which services are limited in range and depth. Eligibility criteria established by some programs for children mean that a child often has to have a narrowly defined problem to access the needed service. Finding the right service recipe for a well developed individualized service plan, one that begins with the child and family and not with the agency's service definition, can be difficult.

The solution that pervades much of the current service-coordination environment is to loosen central definitions and place more responsibility on local programs to assess needs and determine eligibility. Because there are gaps in categorical programs, both in their organization and especially in their geographic availability, funds are often made available to a service coordination agency or a consortium of local agencies. The idea of flexible funds may produce initial resistance in administrators or agency accountants, but governing bodies and local programs have evolved clear ways to monitor and legitimate the use of flexible funds. With flexible funds, IMPACT service coordinators can ask the family and the rest of the service team to think in terms of needs and goals first and think of the availability of funds later. The RIAC will usually authorize expenditures that are integral to the service plan. One exhausted family's situation was transformed when the service team obtained authorization for a high-fenced play area behind their trailer. Previously their extremely hyperactive preschooler could not play without constant supervision. The expense was far less than providing family aides to relieve the parents.

The Entry Process

Service coordination involves considerable time and cost and must be allocated wisely. Eligibility for intensive service coordination may require a diagnosis, but criteria usually direct attention to the child's service needs—involvement of multiple agencies, problems exceeding the community's normal service capacity, danger of removal from the home, or risk of placement in a more restrictive level of care. The messiness of the situation argues for inclusion rather than exclusion. Entry to more intensive levels of care may be driven by both service and political agendas. Goldman (1992) is clear in her emphasis on carefully defining the target population if cost savings are crucial to the project's outcome and future. It is not clear where the line might be drawn regarding populations for whom formal systems of service coordination may be cost-effective. This issue may vary depending on the expense of the service coordination system employed and the expense and availability of more restrictive services.

Narrowing access to service coordination seems ironic because service coordination has been a partial response to previous barriers erected by restrictive eligibility criteria. According to Lourie (1994),

> Decategorization of children and their problems forces the system of care to perceive children and families as clients of the entire system, rather than of some subcomponent of the system. (p. 8)

Funding realities remain, however. Programs often proceed using some method of triage. Restrictions may be eased if funders are responsive to organized parent advocates. Parents are the strongest ally of effective programs.

Programs may assess the potential for parental cooperation as part of the screening process. Clearly services cannot be provided without parental permission. But many programs are cautious about excluding youth from service on the basis of parental resistance. It may be that programs that have fought to overcome interagency turf battles now have a less pathological view of resistance. Still, there may be populations for whom the chance of success seems low. Harris (1990), for example, is concerned that certain case management approaches can exacerbate problems with character-disordered young adults. On the other hand, a policy of admission for children with SED in terms of need rather than other means of classification is supported by research. Data reported on 1,971 children served in the first 5 years of the Kentucky IMPACT program (Illback, Sanders, & Birkby, 1995) found that demographic, diagnostic, and specific risk variables did not predict gains or successful completion of the program. The raw number of risk variables was slightly predictive of behavioral outcomes, but not of gains in social competence, perceived increases in family support, or successful program completion.

The Exiting Process

The exiting process in intensive case management is as much a part of the service allocation process as the entry decision. In Kentucky IMPACT local regions can establish their own exiting criteria. Exiting criteria can provoke heated debates at quarterly meetings both within and between regions. The decision can have much in common with decisions to terminate therapy. It can involve debate over philosophy, objective criteria, and risks as well as issues of transference and dependency.

In the spirit of community ownership, when children exit Kentucky IMPACT, the child's family and service team usually make a recommendation for exit. When there are questions, a council of local administrators and parents decide on both policy and its individual application. The general experience has been that youth admitted to the program stayed much longer than anticipated. This was something that IMPACT found it shared with other MHSPY projects. Either the problems of children with severe emotional disturbance were subject to significant improvement but were more intractable than predicted in the program planning phase, or there remained large service gaps that made it difficult to transfer youth out of the program, or both. Issues governing length of stay in intensive services will be hotly debated for some time. It was a critical issue in the Fort Bragg project discussed later.

Rothman (1994) has stressed that vulnerable populations often need continuing services:

> Cure or substantial improvement of clients toward normal functioning receives high marks on the professional scoreboard. Providing continuing care that maintains the client stably at a reasonable but impaired level of living, however, does not. This is a professional task without status or glitter. It is appropriate . . . to measure success not only by the distance we raise clients up, but also by the distance we prevent them from falling. (p. 21)

Fortunately the number of young people who require continual intensive service coordination is small, but, even among them, a positive exit experience may be based on factors other than client improvement. Stronger community support may be in place after a period of intensive case management. Increases in the strength of the service team may allow continued care when another service team member or family member assumes the case management function.

Effectiveness

Research on Adult Case Management

Literature on the effectiveness of case management is relatively new. In spite of many ambiguities, system of care approaches lend themselves to evaluation. Psychologists have played a major role in early evaluation efforts. The bulk of the research is on adult case management, particularly adults with chronic mental illness (Chamberlin & Rapp, 1991; Dietzen & Bond, 1993; Hornstra, Bruce-Wolfe, Sagduyu, & Riffle, 1993; Muijen, Cooney, Strathdee, Bell, & Hudson, 1994). The most common criteria selected for effective case management are hospital recidivism, quality of life, and consumer satisfaction. Consumer satisfaction is the most common positive result, but is not uniformly present. The results for rehospitalization are mixed, with some researchers showing that case management leads to a decrease in hospitalization, some showing no effects from case management, and a few showing an increase in hospitalization (either over the control group or over prior rates of hospitalization). McRae, Higgins, Lycan, and Sherman (1990) cited evidence that 5 years of intensive case management broke the rehospitalization cycle for most adults in their

study. It is difficult to compare adult and child service coordination sce-
narios. The adult research is most valuable to the child field for the methodological lessons it provides. The nature of case management must be
well defined, the service array that is coordinated must be clear, and the
intensity of case management needs to be described more adequately than
by time in a case management program or the number of contacts with
case managers. Recent research (Ryan, Sherman, & Judd, 1994) has demonstrated for adults with serious mental illness that significant positive
effects are attributable to individual case managers and possibly the type
of services they offer (habilitation and community support being associated
with faster community adjustment than traditional psychiatric services).
The mixed results of case management may also relate to the value frames
that individual researchers choose for their work. Kirkhart and Ruffolo
(1993) suggested that six value frames govern case management research
with advantages and disadvantages for each. Research may be directed at
determining how well case management activity (a) meets consumer
needs, (b) meets consumer wants, (c) attains established goals and objectives, (d) meets professional standards, (e) conforms to models of practice,
or (f) is judged to have merit by a key reference group. Assessment of
frames "d" and "e" is critical but too often is omitted. Only if a system is
being implemented as designed does it make sense to ask if the system is
effecting client outcomes.

Child and Adolescent Models of Service Coordination

There is little research on mental health case management with children.
Rivera and Kutash (1994) cited two reasons for this: (a) the difficulty of
separating case management from other system effects (case management
cannot be provided in isolation), and (b) the recency of case management
applications to children with SED. Systems of care models have been implemented that include strong case management programs, and these programs have shown much improvement for children as compared with those
same children before entering the program. Attkisson and Rosenblatt
(1993) reported improved school performance in three California counties.
Stroul (1993) summarized gains and cost savings of a number of system
of care projects. Similar results were reported by Evans, Dollard, and
McNulty (1992) and Illback and colleagues (1995). Gains included improved behavior, more parent satisfaction, less restrictive placements, and
greater placement stability.

Some system-of-care programs report a reduction in overall service
cost within a specific jurisdiction (Rosenblatt & Attkisson, 1993; Rosenblatt, Attkisson, & Fernandez, 1992) and have made efforts to capture
possible cost-shifting factors (e.g., lower costs in the mental health and
social service systems but higher cost in juvenile corrections). Strategi-
cally, some programs have made the case for strong service coordination
and individualized services by choosing a small number of youth using the
most expensive services. Then they demonstrated that these youth could

be served at less restrictive levels of care in their home communities at reduced cost. Such strategies characterized the AYI, early work in Vermont (Katz-Leavy et al., 1992), and the first phases of the Ventura program (Goldman, 1992).

Clark et al. (1994) studied foster children with emotional and behavioral disorders who were randomly assigned to regular foster care services or a fostering individualized assistance program (FIAP). The FIAP workers organized a "life-domain planning" team of key adults in the child's life who met monthly to develop, maintain, and implement plans for the child. The worker also provided clinical case management, consisting of direct or brokered clinical services to the children and families and sought linkages to natural and community supports. Eighteen months later both groups of children had improved significantly on caretaker and self-report measures of symptoms, with the FIAP group showing a trend toward lower pathology scores and faring significantly better than controls in adjustment in permanency placements, runaways, serious criminal activity, and days incarcerated. Preliminary data on another study involving random assignment (Evans et al., 1994) suggested that children supported by intensive, family-focused case management may remain with their own families and do as well as children who are removed to a well-supported system of therapeutic foster care.

Burns, Farmer, Angold, Costello, and Behar (1996) compared 148 youth with SED who were randomly assigned to different conditions of case management—the child's psychotherapist assumed case management responsibility or a specialized (bachelor's level) case manager was assigned. Follow-up occurred at 3-month intervals for 12 months. Therapists in both conditions were part of the treatment team, and there was an effort to provide a meaningful service array. Specialized case managers (SCM) spent significantly more time than therapists working with their cases, especially in performing traditional case-management functions. Therapists assigned case-management responsibility did not give more time to their case-management functions than non-case-manager clinicians participating with similar service teams. Youth with SCM were more likely to remain in the project and to receive community-based services rather than hospital or residential care. Youth who began the project in an inpatient setting (more of whom had SCM) were more likely to be receiving community services at the end of 12 months if they had SCM. Parent satisfaction with mental health services was higher for youth with SCM. The entire sample showed significant clinical improvement. Follow-up measures at 12 months did not differentiate the groups with respect to behavioral outcomes or a measure of the family's burden of care.

One study, conducted by a team of researchers at Vanderbilt University, was so extensive that it promises to be a benchmark for much future work. This was an evaluation of mental health services to children within a system of care—the Fort Bragg Evaluation Project (Bickman, Bryant, & Summerfelt, 1993; Bickman et al., 1994, 1995; Heflinger, 1993). The project established a continuum of services modeled on Stroul and Friedman's (1986) systems of care. Distinguished mental health experts participated in the design. The services, costs, and clinical outcomes at Fort Bragg were contrasted with those at two other Army installations without a formally organized service continuum or formal case management. On the basis of system-of-care literature, Bickman et al. (1994) had predicted that the Fort Bragg project should result in

- improved mental health
- lower cost per case
- quicker recovery
- more client satisfaction (p. 5).

Although the Fort Bragg study was not an evaluation of case management per se, the research included a highly detailed description of the case management process and evaluations of case management in at least 4 of the 6 frames suggested by Kirkhardt and Ruffolo (1993). These included client satisfaction, meeting of professional standards, conformity with models of practice, and merit judged by a key reference group. A unique element of the Fort Bragg research was a network study of the three sites (Heflinger, 1993). Before and after the demonstration was in place, Heflinger surveyed child-serving agencies to determine who makes referrals and plans, and who communicates with whom, and how often and with what degree of satisfaction. By the time the second measures were taken, the Rumbaugh Clinic at Fort Bragg was receiving high rankings as a central and active agency in the service network.

Bickman et al. (1993) noted that "Systematic inquiry has long been needed to document both the process and effectiveness of different models of case management" (p. 29). Case management at the Rumbaugh clinic at Fort Bragg was determined to be "exemplary" (Bickman et al., 1995, p. 196) and essentially faithful to its design.[2] In the final ranking of services in the Fort Bragg project (Bickman et al., 1994), case management received the second highest ranking of overall satisfaction by the parents and the highest by adolescents. Most highly ranked by parents was day treatment; this received the lowest ranking by adolescents.

The Fort Bragg study sought not to study the clinical effectiveness of case management, but the cost and effectiveness of the total system of care theory. Case management, however, has strong links to system of care theory. Interpretations of the Fort Bragg project could have important consequences for case management particularly because the caution researchers express about the generalizability of a study may not be shared by funding agencies or policy makers.

The results of the Fort Bragg project were mixed. Bickman et al. (1995) determined that a broad array of services faithful to the system of care model was achieved at the demonstration site. This resulted in many

---

[2]Although data reported in the Fort Bragg study was gathered between October 1, 1990, and September 30, 1993, and all project elements were in place by 1992, the staff of the Rumbaugh Clinic described the project "as 'adolescent' and 'still immature,'" in 1992. They were continually refining services—such as converting an adolescent group home into a crisis unit in early 1993 (Heflinger, 1993, pp. 49–50).

more clients (clinically comparable to the comparison sites) being served, with clients likely to remain in service for a longer time with improved continuity. The demonstration project served children with equal success in less restrictive environments. The demonstration project also received higher rankings of satisfaction on a number of comparisons. Extensive clinical and family measures, which were assessed over 12 dimensions after 1 year, showed improved clinical outcomes in both sites. However, no advantage in clinical outcomes was noted for Fort Bragg. Differences in clinical outcome were as likely to favor the comparison site as Fort Bragg. It is not clear if differences would emerge with more time. A measure one would hope to improve with service coordination was the Burden of Care Questionnaire (BCQ). This seeks to assess the effect of intervention on the objective and subjective burden experienced by the family as the result of having a troubled child. There was not a significant difference between BCQ scores; the most improved scores occurred in the comparison sites. The average cost of care per client was 1.59 times higher at Fort Bragg.

The Fort Bragg study is not a sound basis for judging costs. Because the project wished to test a strongly developed model of a system of care, the grant reimbursed whatever costs were incurred by the Fort Bragg providers. Youth stayed in treatment longer. There were no incentives for providers or consumers to control costs. Bickman et al. (1995) has acknowledged that this feature, more than any other, probably accounted for the high costs at Fort Bragg. Greater length of time in treatment at Fort Bragg contributed significantly to the higher costs. Behar (1995) has also suggested that cost shifting could have occurred in the comparison group that was not captured in the study. It may be that longer care was justified and that follow-up at a longer interval (the study assessment interval was 1 year) may differentiate the groups (see also Freidman & Burns, 1997). The study also raises the possibility that a well-developed system of care may be just as vulnerable to overuse as the hospital programs whose excesses helped garner fiscal support for alternative systems of care.

Strong advocates of community-based service coordination might have problems with case management as practiced at the Rumbaugh Mental Health Clinic. In the Rumbaugh clinic's intake process, child and parents were interviewed separately. After the assessment, the intake clinician met with a supervising clinician and the interdisciplinary team (including the case manager) for development of an initial treatment plan. Bickman et al. (1993) noted that parents were not included in this meeting as a matter of policy, although parental involvement was valued by clinic staff in a measure of philosophy of care (p. 27). Parents were more likely to be told their child's diagnosis at the comparison sites than at Fort Bragg. Parents in the demonstration project were no more satisfied with their involvement in treatment planning than parents at the comparison sites.

A quality review of intake and case management records at Fort Bragg yielded generally high ratings. The lowest ratings were related to the assessment of, and response to, family needs (Bickman et al., 1993). Rankings of case managers on coordination of services and on assistance in dealing with treatment professionals were high. Rankings on assistance in dealing with teachers and school officials and on providing information about community resources were lower. There were no items for rating the identification or use of client strengths.

Average attendance at treatment-team meetings at Fort Bragg was seven. It was not clear what agencies were represented or what percentage of treatment-team meetings were attended by parents. A survey of parents receiving case management revealed that 92% of the parents had attended a treatment team meeting in the previous 60 days (Sonnichsen & Heflinger, 1993). Treatment-team meetings were generally held at the Rumbaugh clinic. It has been the experience of Kentucky IMPACT service coordinators that full participation of community team members is best when meetings are held off site. The school is the most common meeting site. Many meetings are held in the office of the Department for Social Services, and more meetings are held in homes than at the office site of the case managers.

It appears that the case management program at Fort Bragg was strong in facilitating the coordination of the various mental health services received by the families in the demonstration project, but weaker in reaching the child's larger environment. It is not apparent that parents were "first string" players on the treatment team, as they were in the MHSPY projects (Cole & Poe, 1993, p. 67). The Fort Bragg program seems to have functioned with more of a medical model than a strengths model and to have had some weaknesses in family involvement, community outreach, and advocacy. Recent scrutiny of the Fort Bragg study has questioned whether the demonstration: (a) represented a true system of care, (b) targeted the population addressed by Stroul and Friedman's model, or (c) embodied key philosophies of that model (Friedman & Burns, 1997; Pires, 1997). The integrity of the case management model has also been questioned in terms of caseload size (Friedman & Burns, 1997) and the evolution of the case management approach over the life of the project (Lourie, 1997).

Two decades ago, Hobbs (1975) noted that data suggested community programs were less expensive than institutional programs, but acknowledged that routine operation of community programs could be more expensive. The author wrote, "The real and substantial saving promised by well-designed and executed community-based programs should be in their superior performance in preparing children and youth to live lives that are as normal and productive as circumstances will allow" (p. 203).

The Fort Bragg project seems to have produced comparable clinical results at greater expense than conventional programs. Because the Fort Bragg project is a high-profile study that may be subject to misinterpretation, this chapter has devoted particular attention to the project, to the model's variation from a more community-based form of service coordination, and to issues contributing to the project's unrealistic expense. Bickman et al. (1995) clearly acknowledge that "a continuum of care is not necessarily more expensive" (p. 206). With equal outcomes and costs, the differences in restrictiveness of placement and consumer satisfaction would readily support the choice of the Fort Bragg product over the comparison sites.

Summary and Prospects

Service coordination is a crucial element in the array of services required for children with SED. The new emphasis on service coordination grew in reaction to the staggering, extensively documented failure of existing systems to serve children with SED—a population that has been chronically "unclaimed," as their numbers of problems have increased. Current service coordination not only seeks for providers to sing from the same music (the common-service plan), but to increase family and client participation, to create client-focused synergy within service teams, to address service gaps, and to reshape systems of care. Service coordination is usually characterized by a commitment to community-based care, family integrity and empowerment, and culturally competent services.

Psychologists have significant roles to play in this new service culture. On the most basic level of the ad hoc model, psychologists, who realize that a child or family requires multiple services, may convene a child-specific team to prevent problems and enhance the total quality of service delivery. If child and family needs require it, psychologists can continue to facilitate coordination or encourage a team member or agency to assume case-management responsibility. When such quality practice becomes standard, the entire community benefits.

The second model is based in collaborative agency practice. Agencies must share responsibility, roles, and funds. Service coordination roles are shared or designated in local agreements. Leadership is essential to the evolution of this model. Leadership knows no professional boundaries, but people with a background in community psychology should be well prepared to facilitate local efforts. Psychologists with skills in clinical and agency consultation have much to contribute to the development and implementation of strong systems of service coordination and to the training of service coordinators on case and systems levels.

A number of communities have introduced a third model, a specialized unit to effect service coordination for highly vulnerable populations. The third model presumes the community and interagency developments of the second model. In fact it is advantageous for all the models to coexist, with more specialized coordination reserved for the youth whose service demands are greatest. All these practices reflect a new sense of community ownership of children with SED.

A range of creative interagency programs are described in the literature and are functioning across the nation. These interagency efforts are often supported by legislation, executive orders, or formal agreements. Specific guides to advocacy and program implementation for children with SED are available. The literature is addressing the introduction of practices of service coordination into systems of managed care and the plans of insurance carriers. Academic institutions, while central to many of these innovations, seem slowest to move in adapting their training to the world of service coordination. Training in service coordination needs to become commonplace in mental health graduate programs.

The financing of service coordination varies with the value frames of the community as reflected in their fiscal decision makers. In fiscally conservative communities a narrow strategy has been used to garner financial support for intensive, well coordinated, individualized services for children with SED. Services are usually targeted to a small population of children—often in state custody—who use the most restrictive and expensive services. Evidence repeatedly supports the conclusion that most of these youth can be well served at reduced costs outside of institutional settings.

The size of the population for whom intensive coordinated services becomes cost-effective depends on the community values that define effectiveness. There are few studies addressing the effectiveness of service coordination for children with SED. The available research suggests that service coordination in a system of care is associated with reduced use of hospitalization, higher levels of consumer satisfaction, better continuity of placements for children at risk, and, probably, cost savings. If the value is to retain youth in their home community, case management gets high marks, particularly when paired with systems of individualized care. Service coordination has become central to new financing strategies in which the dollar follows the child to create the most appropriate service. Older strategies funded categorical services and then fit the child into the service—requiring the child to follow the dollar.

The Fort Bragg study suggests that affordable, well integrated systems of care may also increase expenses by increasing access for the underserved population of troubled children. Children may receive longer intervention when there is no incentive to end. Gatekeepers for service may have to have one eye on the child's needs and another on budget realities. The potential of quality service coordination for catalyzing and bridging and therefore maximizing local services is critical in the face of limited resources.

System-of-care and service-coordination literature reflect a new understanding of how children with SED may be served. Psychologists are in an excellent position to help integrate research-based service innovations into evolving systems of care. The articulation of systems of care and of service coordination provides inviting opportunities to psychologists for program evaluation and services research. These new programs seem much more conscious of the value of ongoing research than many earlier service models. If the movement for coordinated, community-based services for children with SED can grow, garner supportive research, influence professional training, and make its case in the national fiscal forum, fewer youth are likely to enter adulthood wounded and unproductive because they remained unclaimed as children.

References

American Psychological Association. (1981). Specialty guidelines for the delivery of services. *American Psychologist, 36,* 639–663.

American Psychological Association. (1992). Ethical principles of psychologists and code of conduct. *American Psychologist, 47,* 1597–1611.

Attkisson, C. C., & Rosenblatt, A. (1993). Enhancing school performance of youth with severe emotional disorder: Results from system of care research in three California counties. *School Psychology Quarterly, 8,* 277–290.

Barkley, R. A. (1990). *Attention deficit hyperactivity disorder.* New York: Guilford.

Bayes, M., & Neill, T. K. (1978). Problems for paraprofessionals in mental health services. *Administration in Mental Health, 6,* 133–146.

Behar, L. B. (1995). The Fort Bragg child and adolescent demonstration: The implications of its evaluation results. *The Child Youth and Family Services Quarterly, 18*(3), 6–8.

Bickman, L., Bryant, D., & Summerfelt, W. T. (1993). *Final report of the quality study of the Fort Bragg Evaluation Project.* Nashville, TN: Center for Mental Health Policy, Vanderbilt University.

Bickman, L., Guthrie, P. R., Foster, E. M., Lambert, E. W., Summerfelt, W. T., Breda, C. S., & Heflinger, C. A. (1994). *Final report of the outcome and cost/utilization studies of the Fort Bragg Evaluation Project, Volume I.* Nashville, TN: Center for Mental Health Policy, Vanderbilt University.

Bickman, L., Guthrie, P. R., Foster, M. E., Warren, E. L., Summerfelt, W. T., Breda, C. S., & Heflinger, C. A. (1995). *Evaluating managed mental health services: The Fort Bragg experiment.* New York: Plenum.

Brack, G., Jones, E. S., Smith, R. M., White, J., & Brack, C. J. (1993). A primer on consultation theory: Building a flexible worldview. *Journal of Counseling & Development, 71,* 619–628.

Breakey, W. R. (1990). Networks of services for the seriously mentally ill in the community. In N. L. Cohen (Ed.), *Psychiatry takes to the streets: Outreach and crisis intervention for the mentally ill* (pp. 16–41). New York: Guilford Press.

Bronfenbrenner, U. (1979). *The ecology of human development: Experiments by nature and design.* Cambridge, MA: Harvard University Press.

Broskowski, A. (1995). Financing case management services within the insured sector. In B. J. Friesen & J. Poertner (Eds.), *From case management to service coordination for children with emotional, behavioral, or mental disorders: Building on family strengths* (pp. 133–148). Baltimore: Brookes.

Bryant, D., & Heflinger, C. A. (1993). Implementation of case management at the Rumbaugh Mental Health Clinic. Appendix F to *Final report of the implementation study of the Fort Bragg Evaluation Project.* Nashville, TN: Center for Mental Health Policy, Vanderbilt University.

Burns, B. J., Farmer, E. M. Z., Angold, A., Costello, E. J., & Behar, L. (1996). A randomized trial of case management for youths with serious emotional disturbance. *Journal of Clinical Child Psychology, 4,* 476–486.

Caldwell, C. H., Greene, A. D., & Billingsley, A. (1994). Family support programs in Black churches. In S. L. Kagan & B. Weissbourd (Eds.), *Putting families first: America's family support movement and the challenge of change* (pp. 137–160). San Francisco: Jossey-Bass.

Chamberlin, R., & Rapp, C. A. (1991). A decade of case management: A methodological review of outcome literature. *Community Mental Health, 27*(3), 171–188.

Clark, H. B., Prange, M. E., Lee, B., Boyd, L. A., McDonald, B. A., & Stewart, E. S. (1994). Improving adjustment outcomes for foster children with emotional and behavioral disorders: Early findings from a controlled study on individualized services. *Journal of Emotional and Behavioral Disorders, 2,* 207–218.

Cole, R. F., & Poe, S. L. (1993). *Partnerships for care: Systems of care for children with serious emotional disturbances and their families: Interim report of the Mental Health Services Program for Youth.* Washington, DC: Washington Business Group on Health.

Cutler, B. C. (1993). *You, your child, and "special" education: A guide to making the system work.* Baltimore: Brookes.

Dague, B. (n.d.). *You can get there from here! Moving towards a seamless systems approach to family-driven services.* Canton, OH: Stark County Family Council.

Day, C., & Roberts, M. C. (1991). Activities of the Child and Adolescent Service System Program for improving mental health services for children and families. *Journal of Clinical Child Psychology, 20,* 340–350.

Dietzen, M. S., & Bond, G. H. (1993). Relationship between case manager contact and outcome for frequently hospitalized psychiatric clients. *Hospital and Community Psychiatry, 44,* 839–843.

Donner, R., Huff, B., Gentry, M., McKinney, D., Duncan, J., Thompson, S., & Silver, P. (1995). Expectations of case management for children with emotional problems: A parent perspective. In B. J. Friesen & J. Poertner (Eds.), *From case management to service coordination for children with emotional, behavioral, or mental disorders: Building on family strengths* (pp. 27–36). Baltimore: Brookes.

Dunst, C. J., Trivette, C. M., & Deal, A. G. (1988). *Enabling and empowering families.* Cambridge, MA: Brookline.

Dunst, C. J., Trivette, C. M., & Deal, A. G. (1994). *Supporting and strengthening families, Volume 1: Methods, strategies and practices.* Cambridge, MA: Brookline Books.

Eisenstadt, M. (1983). Case management blues. In C. J. Sanborn (Ed.), *Case management in mental health services* (pp. 175–176). New York: Haworth Press.

Evans, M. E., Armstrong, M. I., Dollard, N., Kuppinger, A. D., Huz, S., & Wood, V. M. (1994). Development and evaluation of treatment foster care and family-centered intensive case management in New York. *Journal of Emotional and Behavioral Disorders, 2,* 228–239.

Evans, M. E., Dollard, N., & McNulty, T. L. (1992). Characteristics of seriously emotionally disturbed youth with and without substance abuse in intensive case management. *Journal of Child and Family Studies, 1,* 305–314.

Exceptional parent: The magazine for families and professionals. Published monthly. Brookline, MA: Psy-Ed Corporation.

Fine, G., & Borden, J. R. (1989). Parents involved support network project: Support and advocacy training for parents. In R. M. Friedman, A. J. Duchnowski, & Henderson, E. L. (Eds.), *Advocacy on behalf of children with serious emotional problems* (pp. 68–77). Springfield, IL: Thomas.

Freidman, R. M., & Burns, B. J. (1997). The evaluation of the Fort Bragg demonstration project: An alternative interpretation of the findings. In S. A. Pires (Ed.), *Lessons learned from the Fort Bragg demonstration* (pp. 113–127). Tampa, FL: Research and Training Center for Children's Mental Health.

Friedman, C. R., & Poertner, J. (1995). Creating and maintaining support for case managers. In B. J. Friesen & J. Poertner (Eds.), *From case management to service coordination for children with emotional, behavioral, or mental disorders: Building on family strengths.* Baltimore: Brookes.

Friesen, B. J., & Briggs, H. E. (1995). The organization and structure of service coordination mechanisms. In B. J. Friesen & J. Poertner (Eds.), *From case management to service coordination for children with emotional, behavioral, or mental disorders: Building on family strengths* (pp. 63–94). Baltimore: Brookes.

Friesen, B. J., & Poertner, J. (1995). Introduction. In B. J. Friesen & J. Poertner (Eds.), *From case management to service coordination for children with emotional, behavioral, or mental disorders.* Baltimore: Brookes.

General Accounting Office. (1977). *Returning the mentally disabled to the community: Government needs to do more.* Washington, DC: U.S. Government Printing Office.

Goldman, S. K. (1992). Ventura County, California. In B. A. Stroul, I. S. Lourie, S. K. Goldman, & J. W. Katz-Leavy (Eds.), *Profiles of local systems of care for children and adolescents with severe emotional disturbances* (pp. 287–338). Washington, DC: Georgetown University, CASSP Technical Assistance Center.

Harris, M. (1990). Redesigning case-management services for work with character-disordered young adult patients. In N. L. Cohen (Ed.), *Psychiatry takes to the streets: Outreach and crisis intervention for the mentally ill* (pp. 156–176). New York: Guilford Press.

Heflinger, C. A. (1993). *Final report of the implementation study of the Fort Bragg Evaluation Project.* Nashville, TN: Center for Mental Health Policy, Vanderbilt University.

Henggeler, S. W., & Borduin, C. M. (1990). *Family therapy and beyond: A multisystemic approach to treating the behavior problems of children and adolescents.* Pacific Grove, CA: Brooks/Cole.

Hobbs, N. (1975). *The futures of children: Categories, labels and their consequences.* San Francisco: Jossey-Bass.

Hobbs, N. (1979). *Helping disturbed children: Psychological and ecological strategies, II: Project Re-ED, 20 years later.* Nashville, TN: Vanderbilt Institute for Public Policy Studies.

Hornstra, R. K., Bruce-Wolfe, V., Sagduyu, K., & Riffle, D. W. (1993). The effect of intensive case management on hospitalization of patients with schizophrenia. *Hospital and Community Psychiatry, 44,* 844–847.

Ignelzi, S., & Dague, B. (1995). Parents as case managers. In B. J. Friesen & J. Poertner (Eds.), *From case management to service coordination for children with emotional, behavioral, or mental disorders: Building on family strengths* (pp. 327–336). Baltimore: Brookes.

Illback, R., & Neill, T. K. (1995). Service coordination in mental health systems for children, youth, and families: Progress, problems, prospects. *Journal of Mental Health Administration, 22*(1), 17–28.

Illback, R. J., Neill, T. K., Call, J., & Andis, P. (1993). Description and formative evaluation of the Kentucky IMPACT program for children with serious emotional disturbance. *Special Services in the Schools, 7*(2), 87–109.

Illback, R. J., Nelson, C. M., & Sanders, D. (1997). Community based services in Kentucky: Description and 5 year evaluation of Kentucky IMPACT. In M. H. Epstein, K. Kutash, & A. J. Duchnowski (Eds.), *Outcomes for children and youth with emotional and behavioral disorders and their families: Programs and evaluation best practices.* Austin, TX: Pro-Ed.

Illback, R. J., Sanders, D., & Birkby, B. (1995). *Evaluation of the Kentucky IMPACT program at year five: Accomplishments, challenges and opportunities.* Louisville, KY: R.E.A.C.H. of Louisville.

Institute of Medicine. (1989). *Research on children and adolescents with mental, behavioral, and developmental disorders.* Washington, DC: National Academy Press.

Jacobs, D. F. (1995). State's policy response to the need for case management. In B. J. Friesen & J. Poertner (Eds.), *From case management to service coordination for children with emotional, behavioral, or mental disorders: Building on family strengths* (pp. 373–385). Baltimore: Brookes.

Joint Commission on Accreditation of Healthcare Organizations. (1995). *Accreditation manual for mental health, chemical dependency, and mental retardation/developmental disability services.* Oakbrook Terrace, IL: Author.

Joint Commission on the Mental Health of Children. (1969). *Crisis in child mental health.* New York: Harper and Row.

Kanner, L. (1941). *In defense of mothers, or how to bring up children in spite of the more zealous psychologists.* Springfield, IL: Thomas.

Kanter, J. (1989). Clinical case management: Definition, principles, components. *Hospital and Community Psychiatry, 40,* 361–368.

Katz-Leavy, J. W., Lourie, I. S., Stroul, B. A., & Zeigler-Dendy, C. (1992). *Individual service in a system of care.* Washington, DC: Georgetown University, CASSP Technical Assistance Center.

Kazdin, A. E. (1993). Treatment of conduct disorder: Progress and directions in psychotherapy research. *Development and Psychopathology, 5,* 27–31.

Kelley, J. G. (1971). Qualities for the community psychologist. *American Psychologist, 26,* 897–903.

Kirkhart, K. E., & Ruffolo, M. C. (1993). Value bases of case management evaluation. *Evaluation and Program Planning, 16,* 55–65.

Kisthardt, W. E., & Rapp, C. A. (1992). Bridging the gap between principles and practice: Implementing a strengths perspective in case management. In S. M. Rose (Ed.), *Case management and social work practice* (pp. 112–125). New York: Longman.

Knitzer, J. (1982). *Unclaimed children: The failure of public responsibility to children and adolescents in need of mental health services.* Washington, DC: Children's Defense Fund.

Knitzer, J., Steinberg, Z., & Fleisch, B. (1990). *At the schoolhouse door.* New York: Bank Street College of Education.

Koyanagi, C., & Gaines, S. (1993). *All systems failure: An examination of the results of neglecting the needs of children with serious emotional disturbance.* Alexandria, VA: National Mental Health Association.

Kurpius, D. J., Fuqua, D. R., & Rozecki, T. (1993). The consulting process: A multidimensional approach. *Journal of Counseling & Development, 71,* 601–606.

Lefley, H. P., & Johnson, D. L. (1990). *Families as allies in treatment of the mentally ill: New directions for mental health professionals.* Washington, DC: American Psychiatric Press.

Lourie, I. S. (1994). *Principles of local system development for children, adolescents, and their families.* Chicago: Kaleidoscope.

Lourie, I. S. (1995). Foreward. In B. J. Friesen & J. Poertner (Eds.), *From case management to service coordination for children with emotional, behavioral, or mental disorders: Building on family strengths* (pp. xii–xiv). Baltimore: Brookes.

Lourie, I. S. (1997). Service delivery lessons from the Fort Bragg project. In S. A. Pires (Ed.), *Lessons learned from the Fort Bragg demonstration* (pp. 23–55). Tampa, FL: Research and Training Center for Children's Mental Health.

Lovas, G. S., & Gardner, J. K. (1992). *Baseline assessment of the State of Vermont mental health services for youth project.* Waltham, MA: Family and Children's Policy Center, Brandeis University.

Lovas, G. S., & Griesmer, M. R. (1992). *Baseline assessment of the State of California mental health services for youth project.* Waltham, MA: Family and Children's Policy Center, Brandeis University.

Lovas, G. S., Geismer, M. R., & Gardner, J. K. (1992). *Baseline assessment of the Cleveland, East Cleveland, Ohio mental health services program for youth demonstration project.* Waltham, MA: Family and Children's Policy Center, Brandeis University.

McMahon, R. J., & Greenberg, M. T. (1995). The FAST track program: A developmentally focused intervention for children with conduct problems. *Clinician's Research Digest, Supplemental Bulletin, 13,* 1–2.

McRae, J., Higgins, M., Lycan, C., & Sherman, W. (1990). What happens to patients after five years of intensive case management stops? *Hospital and Community Psychiatry, 41,* 175–179.

Minuchin, S., & Minuchin, P. (1974). The child in context: A systems approach to growth and treatment. In N. B. Talbot (Ed.), *Raising children in modern America: Problems and prospective solutions* (pp. 119–134). Boston: Little Brown.

Moffitt, T. (1993). Adolescent-limited and life-course-persistent anti-social behavior: A developmental taxonomy. *Psychological Review, 100,* 674–701.

Morrissey, J. P., Johnson, M. C., & Calloway, M. O. (1994). *Evaluating performance and change in mental health systems serving children and youth: An interorganizational network approach.* Paper presented at the meeting of the American Public Health Association, Washington, DC.

Muijen, M., Cooney, M., Strathdee, G., Bell, R., & Hudson, A. (1994). Community psychiatric nurse teams: Intensive support versus generic care. *British Journal of Psychiatry, 165*(2), 211–217.

National Commission on Children. (1991). *Beyond rhetoric: A new American agenda for children and families.* Washington, DC: U. S. Government Printing Office.

Neill, T. K., & Stevens, K. B. (1982). Needs of the educationally handicapped. In J. Henning (Ed.), *The rights of children: Legal and psychological perspectives* (pp. 233–252). Springfield, IL: Charles C Thomas.

Patterson, G. R., Reid, J. B., & Dishion, T. J. (1992). *Antisocial boys.* Eugene, OR: Castalia Press.

Pierce, P. M., & Freedman, S. A. (1988). The REACH Project: Training in case management. In K. Fisher & E. Weisman (Eds.), *Case management: Guiding patients through the health care maze* (pp. 65–70). Chicago: Joint Commission on Accreditation of Healthcare Organizations.

Pires, S. A. (1997). Lessons learned from the Fort Bragg Demonstration: An overview. In S. A. Pores (Ed.), *Lessons learned from the Fort Bragg demonstration* (pp. 1–21). Tampa, FL: Research and Training Center for Children's Mental Health.

Poertner, J., & Friesen, B. J. (1995). Service coordination in children's mental health: A vision for the future. In B. J. Friesen & J. Poertner (Eds.), *From case management to service coordination for children with emotional, behavioral, or mental disorders: Building on family strengths* (pp. 387–400). Baltimore: Brookes.

Rivera, V. R., & Kutash, K. (1994). *Components of a system of care: What does the research say?* (Publication # CFS 04211). Tampa, FL: Florida Mental Health Institute.

Ronneau, J., Rutter, J., & Donner, R. (1988). *Resource training manual for family advocacy case management with adolescents with emotional disabilities.* Lawrence, KS: University of Kansas, School of Social Welfare.

Rosenblatt, A., & Attkisson, C. C. (1992). Integrating systems of care in California for youth with severe emotional disturbance I: A descriptive overview of the California AB377 Evaluation Project. *Journal of Child and Family Studies, 1,* 93–113.

Rosenblatt, A., & Attkisson, C. C. (1993). Integrating systems of care in California for youth with severe emotional disturbance III: Answers that lead to questions about out-of-home placements and the AB377 Evaluation Project. *Journal of Child and Family Studies, 2,* 119–141.

Rosenblatt, A., Attkisson, C. C., & Fernandez, A. J. (1992). Integrating systems of care in California for youth with severe emotional disturbance II: Initial group home expenditure and utilization findings from the California AB377 Evaluation Project. *Journal of Child and Family Studies, 1,* 263–286.

Rothman, J. (1994). *Practice with highly vulnerable clients: Case management and community-based service.* Englewood Cliffs, NJ: Prentice-Hall.

Ryan, C. S., Sherman, P. S., & Judd, C. M. (1994). Accounting for case manager effects in the evaluation of mental health services. *Journal of Clinical and Consulting Psychology, 62,* 965–974.

Schorr, L. B. (1994). *The case for shifting to results based accountability with a start-up list of outcome measures with annotations.* Cambridge, MA: Harvard University Improved Outcomes for Children Project.

Sonnichsen, S., & Heflinger, C. A. (1993). Preliminary assessment of parent involvement. Appendix G. in C. A. Heflinger, *Final report of the implementation study of the Fort Bragg Evaluation Project.* Nashville, TN: Center for Mental Health Policy, Vanderbilt University.

State Interagency Council. (1995). *Kentucky IMPACT strategic work groups present recommendations for the future of IMPACT.* Frankfort, KY: Kentucky Department of Mental Health.

Stiffman, A. R., & Davis, L. E. (1990). *Ethnic issues in adolescent mental health.* Newbury Park, CA: Sage.

Stroul, B. A. (1992). Stark County, Ohio. In B. A. Stroul, I. S. Lourie, S. K. Goldman, & J. W. Katz-Leavy. *Profiles of Local Systems of Care for Children and Adolescents with Severe Emotional Disturbances* (pp. 211–286). Washington, DC: Georgetown University, CASSP Technical Assistance Center.

Stroul, B. A. (1993). *Systems of care for children and adolescents with severe emotional disturbances: What are the results?* Washington, DC: Georgetown University, CASSP Technical Assistance Center.

Stroul, B. A. (1995). Case management in a system of care. In B. J. Friesen & J. Poertner (Eds.), *From case management to service coordination for children with emotional, behavioral, or mental disorders: Building on family strengths* (pp. 3–25). Baltimore: Brookes.

Stroul, B., & Friedman, R. (1986). *A system of care for children and youth with severe emotional disturbances* (rev. ed.). Washington, DC: Georgetown University, CASSP Technical Assistance Center.

Sue, D. W., & Sue, D. (1981). *Counseling the culturally different: Theory and practice.* New York: Wiley.

Sue, S., Fujino, D. C., Hu, L. T., Takeuchi, D. T., & Zane, R. (1991). Community mental health services for ethnic minority groups: A test of the cultural responsiveness hypothesis. *Journal of Consulting and Clinical Psychology, 59,* 533–540.

Swan, W. W., & Morgan, J. (1993). *Collaborating for comprehensive services for young children and their families.* Baltimore: Brookes.

Terkelsen, K. G. (1990). A historical perspective on family-provider relationships. In H. P. Lefley & D. L. Johnson (Eds.), *Families as allies in treatment of the mentally ill: New directions for mental health professionals* (pp. 3–21). Washington, DC: American Psychiatric Press.

Weil, M., Karls, J. M., & Associates (1985). *Case management in human service practice: A systematic approach to mobilizing services for clients*. San Francisco: Jossey-Bass.

Weil, M. O., Zipper, I. N., & Dedmon, S. R. (1995). Issues and principles of training for case management in child mental health. In B. J. Friesen & J. Poertner (Eds.), *From case management to service coordination for children with emotional, behavioral, or mental disorders: Building on family strengths* (pp. 211–238). Baltimore: Brookes.

Weissbourd, B. (1994). The evolution of the family resource movement. In S. L. Kagan & B. Weissbourd (Eds.), *Putting families first: America's family support movement and the challenge of change* (pp. 28–47). San Francisco: Jossey-Bass.

Zeigler-Dendy, C. A. (1989). Florida's advocacy experience: Empower yourself for children. In R. M. Friedman, A. J. Duchnowski, & E. L. Henderson (Eds.), *Advocacy on behalf of children with serious emotional problems* (pp. 91–105). Springfield, IL: Thomas.

Zipper, I. N., & Weil, M. (1994). *Case management for children's mental health: A training curriculum for child-serving agencies*. Unpublished manual. Chapel Hill, NC: School of Social Work, University of North Carolina.

9

Organizing for Effective Integrated Services

George W. Noblit and Carolyn T. Cobb

Interagency collaboration, as important as it is, is only an organizational technology. When collaboration is in place, practitioners assume that we will be able to deliver appropriate services and, ultimately, improve client self-sufficiency. The literature is largely silent on precisely how inter-agency collaboration is to lead to more self-sufficient clients. There are many reasons for this, but in fact, agencies—even when they collaborate—are structured largely to deliver the services they have funds and author-ity to deliver. Collaborating with this orientation only ensures that clients actually receive the services they are eligible to receive (Adkins, Awsumb, Noblit, & Richards, in press). Collaboration in this scenario serves to make the agencies more efficient but does little to change their effectiveness.

The increasingly complex and diverse needs of the poor demand that professionals begin to consider the effectiveness of agency efforts. The APA Task Force on Comprehensive and Coordinated Psychological Services for Children (TFCCPSC, 1994; see also introduction to this volume) argued that numerous social, demographic, and economic factors have weakened the ability of families to provide healthy and developmentally appropriate environments for children. This, in turn, has overwhelmed existing, often single-purpose, programs. Increases in funding are needed to provide min-imally adequate levels of service, but changes in the needs of clients seem to require interagency collaboration to lead to more cohesive, integrated, and responsive services, and ultimately to increase client self-sufficiency. Achieving effective integrated services will require that agencies change the systems that deliver these services. However, agencies and programs are relatively discrete and insular entities—creatures structured by fund-ing and legislated authority. Historically, it has been exceedingly difficult for agencies to collaborate (Weiss, 1981), which testifies to the challenge collaboration represents to the ways service agencies operate. The true challenge is to collaborate to design an effective system even as we use it to provide immediate services.

In this chapter, two case studies of interagency collaboration demon-strate how organizationally effective interagency collaboration affects the delivery of integrated services. Effectiveness is defined as the institution-alization of the system and the smooth functioning of structures and processes. Further, an examination of enhancers and barriers to interagency collaboration are used to develop a set of lessons about how to organize for effective integrated services.

Integrated Services: From Social Movement to Institutionalized System

A systems perspective provides a framework for examining interagency collaboration and efforts to deliver more effective services. A coherent system would have two or more interlocking components and boundaries that are permeable enough to respond to external needs and influences and to interact with other agency systems in a meaningful way. Figure 1 illustrates the basic components of a typical social services system. Each agency can be viewed as a system embedded within a larger suprasystem, and as having its own interagency subsystem. However, the larger interagency context may only approximate a system at present. The client typically enters a social service agency at the service delivery ("throughput") stage, receives the benefits available, and is moved to the next agency, usually by uneven and fragmented transitions. Later in this chapter we use this model to consider the concept of interagency system.

The current system for delivering services to families and children grew in fits and starts over the last century. It is, of course, a misnomer

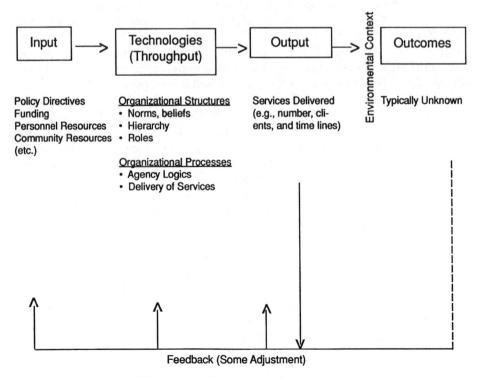

Figure 1. A social service system.

to refer to current services as a *system*. Rather, there is now a patchwork quilt of agencies, each created by separate legislation to meet a perceived need at a particular point in history. These agencies typically function as separate systems that relate to each other with varying degrees of linkage. It is also true that repeated attempts at reform have largely failed to be sustained. In part, this is because interagency collaboration is a woefully undertheorized concept. There is all too little research and thought concerning definitions, the necessary organizational processes, appropriate evaluation strategies, or even the objectives actually being pursued (Adkins, Awsumb, Noblit, & Richards, in press). Nonetheless, policy makers and service providers alike see collaboration as a way to increase both the effectiveness and efficiency of services. In part, this is because the pursuit of collaboration and integrated services is both a social movement and an organizational strategy.

What is now called *interagency collaboration* is a recent manifestation of a social movement that has used a number of terms over the years to define its focus: *agency cooperation, integrated services, interagency services*, and so on. All are defined by the same components: a structure of connections between agencies; processes of exchange and cooperation; and, as the intended results, improved efficiency and effectiveness of services to a given population. The precise nature and relative importance of these structures, processes, and results, however, vary from definition to definition—some emphasizing administrative connections, others links among "front-line" providers; some exchanging through shared information systems, others through face-to-face meetings; some measuring success by the achievement of collaboration itself, others by the greater satisfaction of the clientele. Each change represents tactical moves of a social movement trying to institutionalize itself.

In the late 1980s, the tenor of the literature on interagency collaboration began to change, with renewed optimism about interagency collaboration. Schorr and Schorr (1988) framed the issue as a redefinition of the capacity of public service. They argued that breaking the cycle of disadvantage is "within our reach" and "that we know what needs to be done and how to do it" (p. xix). Their reviews of research lead to a conclusion that has relevance to the research reported here:

> In short, programs that succeed in helping the children and families in the shadows are intensive, comprehensive, and flexible. They also share an extra dimension, more difficult to capture: Their climate is created by skilled committed professionals who establish respectful and trusting relationships and respond to the individual needs of those they serve. The nature of their services, the terms on which they are offered, the relationships with families, the essence of the programs themselves—all take their shape from the needs of those they serve rather than from the precepts, demands, and boundaries set by professionalism and bureaucracies. (p. 259)

Their argument that practitioners know enough to proceed effectively reflected a maturing of the social movement of interagency collaboration. It appears that what is needed now is the political will to change current systems.

A social movement, of course, is usually less concerned about the lack of theoretical clarity or empirical research than with promoting change itself. Proponents are "true believers" (Hoffer, 1951), assured that inter-agency collaboration will be effective if they can just get collaboration es-tablished. True believers enable a social movement to come into being and fuel the movement with belief and commitment.

Interagency collaboration is essentially a revisionary movement that accepts some of the purposes of the existing social order but wishes to modify these in order to better serve families and children (W. Cameron, 1966). *Institutionalization* involves shared, habitualized actions that be-come taken for granted (Berger & Luckmann, 1967). A social movement becomes institutionalized when its beliefs and practices are assumed to be the normal way of doing things. Thus, institutionalization also involves becoming an organization in itself. Benson (1975) maintains that institu-tionalizing collaboration requires achieving (a) *domain consensus*—agree-ment among participants in organizations regarding the appropriate role and scope of an agency; (b) *ideological consensus*—agreement among par-ticipants in organizations regarding the nature of tasks confronted by the organization and the appropriate approaches to those tasks; (c) *positive evaluation*—the judgment by workers in one organization of the value of another organization; and (d) *work coordination*—patterns of service col-laboration and cooperation among organizations. When these conditions are approximated, interagency collaboration is in fact an institutionalized practice. Interagency collaboration has been effectively institutionalized when it exists as a system. Institutionalizing interagency collaboration is a prior condition to determining the effectiveness of the services that are provided.

Defining Effectiveness of Interagency Collaboration

Once institutionalized, the effectiveness of the organizational arrange-ments can then be addressed. However, organizational theorists caution us against simplistic understanding of effectiveness (Katz & Kahn, 1978; Noblit & Dempsey, 1992; Clark, 1995). In fact, there are many possible ways for an organization to be effective.

K. Cameron (1984) discussed seven major models of organizational ef-fectiveness. In the *goal model*, an organization is effective when it accom-plishes its stated goals, and this model is preferred when the goals are clear and measurable. For the *system resource model*, effectiveness involves ac-quiring necessary resources; it is a useful model when there is a clear con-nection between inputs and outputs. Effectiveness in the *internal process model* involves smooth functioning when there is a clear connection between processes and the organization's primary task. The *strategic constituencies model* is useful when an organization must respond to powerful constitu-encies and involves keeping strategic constituencies minimally satisfied.

In the *competing values model*, the organization is unclear about internal priorities or is changing and is effective to the extent that the organization matches the preferences of constituents. Effectiveness in the *legitimacy model* involves organizational survival focusing on legitimate activities when decline or survival are at issue for the organization. Finally, the ineffectiveness model is useful when the criteria of effectiveness are unclear; it defines *effectiveness* as avoiding the characteristics associated with perceptions of ineffectiveness.

Clark (1995) has argued that effectiveness "would include anything (and everything) that satisfies the groups involved" (p. 2) when the groups examine the organizational tactics and processes that in turn produce evidence of outcomes that satisfy various constituencies. Thus effectiveness has a very different face depending on the constituent group.

Assessing the effectiveness of interagency collaboration is then a complex endeavor. Professionals must first assess the degree to which interagency collaboration is institutionalized. Second, we must ask what constituencies and conditions are currently powerful. Interagency collaboration, of course, has a range of constituencies, but also seems to have established a dominant coalition of policy makers, service providers, and clients that perceive integrated services as the system *throughput* (i.e., the delivery mechanism). There has been less consideration of the organizational outputs and outcomes to be achieved. For many professionals and their clients the primary goal is to increase client self-sufficiency. For many policy makers, the primary goal is to reduce costs. Some maintain both are goals, and others see integrated services per se as the goal. Our research (Adkins, Awsumb, Noblit, & Richards, in press) even found that clients may perceive the goal of integrated services to be more closely control their lives. Following K. Cameron's (1984) argument, it makes little sense to define effectiveness in terms of output or outcomes when there is so little agreement on goals. There is simply no agreed-upon goal, nor any agreement on how to evaluate interagency collaboration.

A systems model could reflect several of the effectiveness models, depending on where emphasis is placed. The internal process model reflects a systems approach, with inputs that influence agency's technologies (throughput) creating the services delivered (output) and ultimately client outcomes. Figure 2 illustrates this model. The factors influencing service delivery technologies include funding, human resources, and legislated authority. Service delivery includes the structures (e.g., individual agency organizational structures, policies, roles, and relationships within and among agencies) and processes (e.g., agency decision logics, rules, and delivery of services) that constitute integrated services to clients.

The literature has addressed both structures and processes. There are typologies of structures (Gans & Horton, 1975): *voluntary* (an agency seeks collaboration), *mediated* (a separate body established to develop more collaborative efforts), and *directed* (separate body mandates collaboration). Martin, Chakerian, Imershein, and Frumkin (1983) saw a continuum of structural development: independent, confederated, consolidated, and fully integrated. There is also some research documenting how collabora-

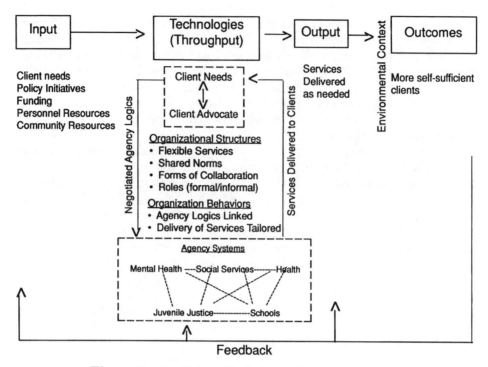

Figure 2.   A collaborative/integrated-services system.

tive projects may produce both structures that inhibit change (McGrath, 1988), and structural obstacles to improved collaboration (Berliner, 1979). As to agency operations, advice on steps toward attaining collaboration and integrated services is abundant: must-do lists, suggestions, calendars, warnings of common pitfalls, and smooth-flow charts (Beatrice, 1982; Daniels & Bosch, 1978; Guthrie & Guthrie, 1991; Hooyman, 1976; Iles & Aulack, 1990; Melaville & Blank, 1991; Nordyke, 1982; Roberts-DeGennero, 1988; Vander-Schie, Wagerfeld, & Wagers, 1987; Wimpfiemer, Bloom, & Kramer, 1990). Even so, it is clear that the "integration of services is not extensive even in projects recommended as being successful projects" (Gans & Horton, 1975, p. 5). It is one thing to collaborate, but to collaborate with sufficient effectiveness as to actually integrate services is another thing entirely.

Services that meet the needs of families and children are the output of a collaborative or integrated system. In turn, the outcome is more self-sufficient individuals and families. Although some evaluations are beginning to tackle this challenge (e.g., Illback, Sanders, & Birkby, 1995), there is little research on client-centered outcomes that is more than assertions of possibilities (Adkins, Awsumb, Noblit, & Richards, in press).

Each phase of this system is linked by feedback mechanisms on how well outcomes and collaborative services are accomplished, representing that the system is constantly learning and adapting. The system model for interagency collaboration currently is concerned primarily with the service delivery, implementing structures and processes to integrate services. The focus on implementation reveals both that interagency collaboration is only relatively institutionalized and that the current goal is to get the structures and processes in place. Only when efforts are effective in both of these ways does it make sense to think about effectiveness in terms of services delivered (output) or self-sufficient clients (outcome).

In the following sections, we present two case studies of service delivery, examining their relative effectiveness defined in terms of institutionalization and smooth-functioning structures and processes. The comparison is telling and suggests the full challenge that must be addressed to effectively collaborate and integrate services.

The North Carolina Studies on Interagency Collaboration

The Divisions of Student Services and Development Services of the North Carolina Department of Public Instruction (NCDPI) initiated three studies in the fall of 1992 to discern what could be done to improve interagency collaboration by looking at current practices, client experiences, and successful collaboratives. The North Carolina studies fall into one of the "promising" kinds of studies referenced by Knapp (1995): investigations of typical and exemplary practice. The NCDPI studies were designed to document (a) current practices of collaboration and service delivery in counties reputed to have some collaborative mechanisms in place, (b) client experiences with agencies, and (c) existing successful collaboratives. Each study used case study methods (Merriam, 1988; Yin, 1984), providing a range of perspectives grounded in agency, client, and organizational experiences.

The goal of the first NCDPI study was simply to document current practices so as to know the "state of the art" of collaboration in North Carolina, in common parlance, "warts and all." Six counties, which varied in income, region, and population density, agreed to participate. In each of these counties, the researchers, doctoral students at the University of North Carolina at Chapel Hill, traced fictional cases or case vignettes from their point of entry in one agency through the full provision of services. Each case vignette was written as a composite of school-age children based on the experience of the educators who helped design the study. Furthermore, each case vignette was written to prompt interagency involvement, and thus the researchers followed the case as it went through agencies and across agencies. There were six case vignettes: one for each point of entry in county agencies of social services, mental health, health, and juvenile services and two case vignettes for the schools. At each step, the researchers interviewed the professionals involved to determine how the case would be treated, why it would be treated in the way suggested, and where it likely would go from there. As a result, the researchers were able to discover when interagency collaboration was and was not taking place, and what seemed to facilitate or hinder it. The researchers spent 10 person-days on site in each county and then developed detailed reports of each county that serve as the database. One of these counties, Pickard County, is used as one of the cases in this chapter. These studies also provide a relatively comprehensive list of inhibiting factors, which can be useful in considering how to become more effective at interagency collaboration.

The second NCDPI study focused on client experiences with services. In this area, the concern was to give voice to those being served in four of the six counties included in the first study. Given concerns about confidentiality, the women were selected and interviewed by local advocates of the North Carolina Child Advocacy Institute. The research team developed the interview guide, provided the training for the interviewers, transcribed the interviews, analyzed the data, and wrote narratives of the clients. By design, the 12 clients varied by whether they were approaching self-sufficiency, maintaining themselves via services, or growing increasingly dependent on services. By chance, clients were all women. These data will not be used directly in this chapter.

The third study examined existing collaboratives. The focus here was on understanding what could be learned from their best efforts. The NCDPI selected five exemplary collaboratives for case studies. The research team developed a data-collection protocol and interview guide, and wrote case studies of each. Phone interviews and document reviews were followed by a one-day on-site visit for each collaborative. The result was a set of case studies that highlight the differences between current practice and state-of-the-art practice. For this chapter, additional interviews were conducted with staff at UPLIFT, Inc., which are used later in the chapter for a comparison of effectiveness. More details on research procedures for the three studies can be found in Noblit et al. (1995).

Our definitions of effectiveness require a focus on the degree to which interagency collaboration is institutionalized and services are integrated. The first (current practices) and the last (best efforts) of the North Carolina studies provide the best databases. We focus our efforts here on a comparative case study design.

A Comparative Analysis of Effectiveness

One case in each of the first and third NCDPI studies addressed urban contexts. The urban county (a pseudonym is used) in the first study had a reputation for being on the vanguard in services, including having interagency councils in place. The urban collaborative from the third study is, by reputation, the most successful collaborative in the state. Comparing these two efforts allows us to focus more on effectiveness via institutionalization and integration of services. If the urban county described in the first NCDPI study is less effective, it is not because of effects of urban context. Rather, institutionalization and organizational processes are less accomplished. Moreover, both of these aspects of effectiveness are alterable by people and thus have direct implications for practice. We present and compare the cases next, and will conclude this chapter by returning to findings across all three of the North Carolina studies.

Our focus here is on how interagency collaboration can be institutionalized and effectively establish an integrated system of services. In the two cases that follow, we examine how a fictitious client would be processed through each organization's system. The narrative of the fictitious client (named Justin) was written to prompt interagency collaboration and, if anything, overestimates the collaboration and integration of services found. We first present Justin's narrative and then describe how he would be treated in each context.

Justin, age 5, entered kindergarten at the beginning of the school year. His mother enrolled him in this school because it was closest to the shelter where she, Justin, and Justin's younger sister Julia, age 2 1/2, are living. Justin's mom, who is a recovering alcoholic, is trying to make a new life for herself and her two children. She left an abusive home situation a few months earlier to enter a shelter for abused women. Both children have witnessed the physical abuse of their mother several times and have been physically abused themselves.

Justin's mother is concerned about his lack of readiness for kindergarten; his speech and language development are very slow, making it difficult for him to follow directions or express his needs. He is functioning below kindergarten level and is unable to follow simple directions, identify or print any letters, or count to 10. The school-based committee referred Justin for speech and language services through the school system. While he waits for the special education assessment, he is given extra assistance to enable him to follow directions and function in a group setting.

Soon after his arrival, the teacher discovered that Justin quickly became frustrated and has difficulty managing his anger. He has been placed on behavior contract and earns extra stars for good behavior. On frequent occasion, Justin needs a safe place to express his emotions; his teacher and counselor often hold him while he cries or expresses his rage. It sometimes takes as long as 45 minutes before Justin is ready to resume activities with the rest of his class. At the school's recommendation, Justin began seeing a counselor at the mental health clinic.

Case #1. Pickard County

Pickard County is an urban retail center with an ethnically diverse population of about 500,000. The county seat has grown rapidly since the construction of an industrial complex nearby, which has confounded efforts at city planning. Traffic is usually heavy, with long delays, and road construction is the norm. Meanwhile, tiny rural communities also exist, thus a broad range of conditions are presented to county agencies. Demands on the county's social service agencies have increased significantly in recent years as the region's economy suffers "growing pains."

Very busy roads and size prevent easy pedestrian access to municipal services. Construction is underway to relocate and centralize the complex of social services to facilitate access. Although this relocation may improve the working conditions of social-service agents and locate them in a setting conducive to cross-agency contact, clients with limited access to private transportation may not find the change as beneficial.

Unlike most of North Carolina, efforts at collaboration in Pickard County are more likely to be stymied by the myriad possibilities for collaboration than by scarcity. There are so many programs, and so many faces and voices attached to those programs, that a client-contact worker seeking information may quickly become overwhelmed (to say nothing of the potential client's dilemma before even choosing a door to enter). In order to function in such a complicated system, most workers develop a few standard referrals that they use for most clients. This in turn creates case "bottlenecks" and paperwork "logjams," as everyone's favorite next steps become flooded while other possible paths remain unexplored; worker burnout, client frustration, and lost opportunities are among the predictable results of this complex urban web. The high caseloads of service providers exacerbate these problems.

Pickard County has the usual array of services organized by separate agencies: social services, health and mental health facilities, schools, and juvenile justice and family courts systems. The county also has a rich array of private services to support each of these, and often contracts with agencies to serve particular clients. Pickard County has an active group of professionals who see interagency collaboration as important and who work to develop cooperative and collaboration relations whenever possible. They have not, however, fully institutionalized collaboration or achieved any significant level of services integration, as the treatment of Justin will reveal.

Justin's services. The case of Justin in the Pickard County milieu would start by assignment to a mental health case manager (who in this case has worked in other local social service agencies). Justin's case is very similar to those Mental Health Services regularly sees, except that at 5 he is a little younger than most clients. The case manager estimates that around 90% of the clients taken by her agency are sexually and/or physically abused children and Justin may have suffered as much. At least half of the children are in the custody of the Department of Social Services, which means that Mental Health Services must regularly work closely with that agency.

Mental Health Services would first arrange for an outreach consultation to evaluate Justin's needs at no cost to the family. This assessment would include an interview with the mother (at which time she may be referred to the local alcohol rehabilitation program or substance abuse center [SAC], as well as SafeHaven, a service that aids abused women). The assessment would also include discussions with the mother's therapist if she has one, meetings with representatives of Justin's school; a meeting with Justin's little sister, Julia, who is also likely to need assistance; and an evaluation of the mother's financial situation. If Justin were found to be in need of mental health services, then he would be referred to private therapy programs if the family could afford them. Otherwise, he would be assigned a mental health intake worker, who would set up a doctor's appointment to assess Justin's need for medicine such as Ritalin. The intake worker would then assign Justin either to a clinic or to a treatment team, which is the more likely outcome.

If Justin were assigned to a team, either a Mental Health Services case manager or therapist would assume primary responsibility for his progress. Team members would include the therapist and representatives from Justin's school, from the Department of Social Services, and from SAC and SafeHaven, should Justin's mother seek such treatment. Mental Health Services would act as the lead agency at periodic meetings of the treatment teams. The team might suggest play therapy. The team would also arrange to work with the mother to ensure that her mental health needs were being met. The team would try to get the family into its own home as a stable environment. If this meant changing schools for Justin, his new teachers and counselors would be invited to work with the team. Finally, the family's basic needs might be met by the Catholic Parish Outreach, a private charity that provides clothing and other necessities; DSS, which can offer emergency rent money or utility bill relief; and school nurses, who can serve as liaisons to Health Department services.

Every agency practices some case management, but one lead agency usually evolves. Large demanding cases usually require the combined effort of several agencies, however, and in Pickard County such cases are coordinated through the Hard-to-Serve Committee. This local committee is composed of representatives of DSS, Mental Health Services, the juvenile court, and others. At meetings, case managers or lead case workers present cases and ask for assistance in planning.

There is also a great deal of informal cooperation among agencies. Case workers and managers regularly call on their contacts at other agencies around the county. It is believed that this system works particularly well in small counties. In large counties such as Pickard, however, the success of a particular case worker or manager depends on his or her ability to establish a strong and broad network of contacts throughout the social service systems.

Statutes are seen as key obstacles to coordination among agencies. Each agency has different regulations by which it must operate to deliver services, some more stringent than others. Confidentiality is obviously one of the greatest concerns. At times these different applicable laws prevent easy coordination among agencies. To make matters even more confusing, many of these statutes serve important functions and cannot be done away with entirely.

Other systemic problems hindered successful interagency collaboration as well. As one interviewee put it, "There have been lots of attempts at interagency collaboration but these have been around individual cases. There needs to be something more ongoing . . . People get wrapped up in an agency identity. It's scary for them to change. Some people are afraid of growth." Some of these people are also afraid of job loss. Increased paperwork can cause backlogs at the administrative level, which can result in underestimates of service delivery. These underestimates translate into workforce reduction and layoffs. Rather than provoke such a chain of events, workers in vulnerable positions may prefer not to enter into formal collaborative ventures.

Mental Health Services has invested substantial effort in working well with other agencies. Although these cooperative relationships have their bounds (the work of therapists, for example, must be private), the case workers and managers have made great strides toward cooperation with other agencies.

Justin's mother would be referred next to Project Enterprise (PE), the Pickard County Schools project designed to offer proactive help for anyone concerned with effective child rearing. PE would establish contact with the teacher who had referred Justin to Mental Health Services. Justin's mother then would be contacted and told about the programs offered by PE, including individual counseling for Justin and his mother. Most services are offered at the PE facility, and PE would try to help the mother coordinate transportation. Should the mother decide to take advantage of services offered by PE, someone may observe Justin in the field. If Justin manages well at school, someone would just check up on him.

In assessing the state of collaboration in Pickard County, one interviewee at PE candidly explained, "It's my sense that in small counties, things are easier to coordinate. In large counties, it's harder to coordinate." The human factor is important. With large turnover, it is difficult for other social service providers to collaborate: "The key is an individual's trustworthiness." Turnover between case workers and clients hurts developing trusting relationships. Work is divided among so many agencies, and everyone gets spread thin: "Committees work best, but then there are time problems." With so many agencies involved for each child and family, an interviewee wondered, "How must it be for the families?" One family had recently received home visits from representatives of five different agencies. The mother, exasperated, asked the last, "OK, where are YOU from?"

With Mental Health Services and Project Enterprise serving as coordinating bodies, Justin's case would be seen by a broad spectrum of public and private social services agencies. This may work both for and against the child. Many agencies working together may assemble a package of services to meet multiple needs of the family, but they also may catch the family in a tangle of regulations and forms from which little service may actually result. When the former is the goal, the latter is a danger, especially in a city in which agencies are struggling to handle enormous caseloads.

Pickard's effectiveness. Justin's treatment is shaped by its urban context. In such a complex system, the challenge is to assemble a sufficient, efficient package of services for the client, without incompatible or redundant services that trap the family in a thicket of regulations and paperwork with little helpful result. Some urban crises demand collaborative attention, because no one agency has been conceived to address them. The scale of services in Pickard leads to some fragmentation of roles. A smaller county may have one office supplying multiple treatments, but in Pickard each individual facet of a child's life may attract a different caseworker, resulting in enormous teams that resist coordination.

Interagency collaboration, the focus of this study, was itself a term with various meanings. It was striking to discover that in Pickard County the meaning of the term varied more by position within agency hierarchy than by individuals or particular agencies. Generally, client contact workers tended to view collaboration as a process, as calling on particular other persons at various agencies for advice, for joint action, or to make referrals. These webs of contacts are unique for every client contact worker and are usually built over a period of years. Almost every such person interviewed indicated the importance of these systems of connections and stressed that the work of new persons is complicated by the necessity of first establishing these networks. *Collaboration* to these people usually meant informal exchange of information or services rather than a formally structured organization or system. In contrast, individuals in administrative positions tended to view collaboration in structural terms. To them, a collaborative process is one in which agency roles are formally designated, case responsibility carefully delineated, and information flow defined and routinized.

Figure 3 depicts the referral and communication processes for Justin in Pickard County. Note the linear, sequential nature of the process with no feedback loops built in. In fact, there is nowhere for feedback to go. In short, Pickard County has a lot of collaboration going on, but little of it is institutionalized. There is not even a shared definition of what collabora-

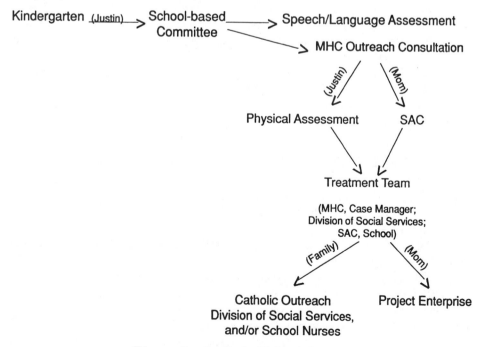

Figure 3.   Justin in Pickard County.

tion is. The institutionalized process, in fact, reifies the separate agencies. Because of the separateness of agencies, informal collaboration guides the process and, when formalized, a lead agency sets up referrals to other agencies. In either scenario, little evidence of interagency collaboration becoming institutionalized is seen.

On the other hand, agency workers, in general, appeared to be committed to client interests, a commitment that persists in spite of enormous job stress and obstacles. This commitment to children's interests, however, often manifested itself in a protective or even controlling approach to cases. Workers use phrases like "I know what's best for this person" and believe in themselves to the point that they may be unwilling to share responsibility for a case. Whenever several agencies worked together on cases, each seemed to prefer assuming the lead on case management rather than playing merely cooperative or secondary roles. This preference for leadership may stem from idiosyncrasies of paperwork requirements or funding regulations. For some agencies, leading the case is the only way to receive full funding reimbursement in a cooperative arrangement. This tendency to "own" cases, at both the caseworker and agency levels, works against collaborative relationships among service providers. Client contact workers did not seem to have the schedule flexibility or time to participate in many formally organized interagency efforts. Finally, the referral system has noticeable glitches. Transportation is not provided, and the client is left unsupported during the referral process itself. In the end, services are never actually integrated, but rather existing services are sequenced.

Pickard County is ineffective in the sense that structures and processes of interagency collaboration did not result in an integration of services. Separate agencies provided their normal services. Informal collaboration ensured that the client is considered for all the normal services for which Justin and his family qualify, but there were no structures or processes to actually integrate the services. In sum, Pickard County has neither institutionalized collaboration nor achieved any significant level of services integration.

Case #2: UPLIFT, Inc.

UPLIFT, Inc., is in an urban manufacturing retail city with an ethnically diverse population of about 200,000. Like many cities in the South, Greensboro has had sufficient immigration from the North and elsewhere to create new affluent neighborhoods, traffic jams, and an intensification of poverty. Social service agencies have also experienced an increase in demands for services. The services themselves are mostly located in the central city where few people live. Service agencies in Greensboro have a history of cooperation, as evidenced by various interagency councils, each focusing on a particular issue. People work together on single issues (e.g., drug abuse) but rarely are able to collaborate across issues to deal with families and children's needs as a whole.

Greensboro-based UPLIFT, Inc., is a private, nonprofit organization that works to improve services to children and their families on a number of levels. Their vision of collaboration includes providing direct services to children and families, community building, and developing policies and interagency agreements that foster more integrated family services. UPLIFT believes that it is able to articulate its vision of integrated services in a more comprehensive way than collaboratives that focus either on direct service or coordination or advocacy; they strive to do it all. UP-LIFT places significant emphasis on empowering families to become less dependent on conventional service systems. They see formal service delivery systems as inadvertently fragmenting and disempowering families through the autonomous imposition of their services and professional expertise. UPLIFT believes that families who learn to negotiate the service-delivery system on their own and to access information increase their ability to control their own lives.

UPLIFT has flourished in part because of the drive of a strong leader with a clear vision. UPLIFT was founded by Robin Britt, former Congressman and current Secretary of the North Carolina Department of Human Resources. During his term in Congress, Britt had several experiences in the area of human services that had a strong impact on him and provided some of the seed ideas that later blossomed into UPLIFT. The Z. Smith Reynolds Foundation awarded Britt a planning grant that enabled him to establish an office, research program, and potential sites while seeking ongoing financial support. Major government grant awards in recent years have had significant impact on UPLIFT, Inc., as an organization, raising questions about how they will retain their activist, community orientation as they expand. The executive director emphasizes that, "There is no way in the world that a bureaucratic and hierarchical organization can meet the needs of families."

Of UPLIFT's three components—service delivery, community building, and policy development—direct service delivery was the initial focus and remains the cornerstone. The first service-delivery project was the Child Development Center for 4-year-olds, which opened in November, 1988, at Ray Warren Homes, one of the city's poorest and most drug-infested housing projects. It provides an enriched early childhood program with strong parental involvement and is designed to prepare at-risk children for kindergarten.

The next step was to supplement the Child Development Center with a Family Resource Center. The current mix of services includes maternal and child health care, community building, "brokering" services, and intensive family development. Bringing these services on site and under the UPLIFT model brings significant differences from the family perspective. For example, with their maternal and child health program, the Family Resource Center simplified and consolidated what had been two separate programs at the Health Department, one for expectant mothers and babies up to 3 months in age and a separate program covering children from 3 months to 3 years. Providing health services under the UPLIFT umbrella enables a more comprehensive approach to the needs of the family.

One of the more nontraditional efforts of the Family Resource Center is the focus on community building. Community building is viewed by UPLIFT as an ongoing effort to work with families to develop community ownership of the programs and to build informal support networks among client families. The goal is to give families the tools and skills to define and manage their own needs, rather than just being "serviced" by agencies. For example, UPLIFT helped the Ray Warren residents to organize a transportation program. Lack of transportation had previously been a major barrier to many residents' participating in programs, receiving services, or just going about the business of everyday life. Robin Britt negotiated with GATE, Greensboro's transportation service, to donate a van. The residents are now responsible for operating the program and planning the schedule to rotate van-driving duties among themselves.

The Family Resource Center also provides child care to Ray Warren residents who are attending Center programs or have appointments at the Maternal and Child Health Clinic. In keeping with the UPLIFT philosophy, a Ray Warren resident is employed as child care coordinator. Because of her involvement with UPLIFT, she has taken child care classes at the local community college and plans to pursue further education as a child care assistant. Additionally, she has brought in other members of the Ray Warren community to assist her. According to the director of the center, when the residents are involved, they feel they have more control and feel good about their community.

Another of the core activities of the Family Resource Center is *brokering* services, defined as linking families with other service providers in the community. As a staff member puts it, "I make contact with the agencies where the services already exist. I serve as liaison; bringing it on site, if available." When asked how she established relationships with the various service agencies, this staff member responded, "It was a learning experience from what families told me they needed." Staff act as advocates for families, identifying barriers and relating success stories to encourage service providers to help.

Family development, another of the Resource Center's tactics, is described as moving beyond traditional services by providing an intensive, long-term commitment to families around general issues rather than specific and limited-term services. The family development specialist (FDS) works with up to 15 families at a time and serves as the liaison between families and other agencies. Because of the paperwork and transportation involved in accessing services, families would often become discouraged. Families unable to complete the required paperwork would be unable to receive financial supplements; some of them were unable to read and did not want anyone to know. The FDS assists with any part of the application process as requested by the families. The FDS meets with the family and other agencies on a monthly basis to discuss needs, barriers, what is working, what is not working, and what goals they need to establish. The meetings are held at the Family Resource Center, where the families feel more comfortable and less intimidated because they are on their own turf.

Justin's treatment at UPLIFT, Inc. Justin's is not an unusual case to UPLIFT, and it would be intercepted at the mother's admission to the shelter. It would also have two other distinctive features. First, Justin's case would be handled as part of an effort to respond to the needs of the family: the mother, sister, and Justin together is the focus. Second, the family would have immediate services from someone who would stay with the family throughout the process and who would advocate for the family.

At the shelter, the mother and family would be met by an FDS who would immediately begin a process of relationship building. The FDS would first start a process of support that included listening to the family members and personal help with the children to give the mother a respite from the effort and to model parenting for the mother. This support would continue as the FDS began to arrange services for the family.

For the mother, the FDS would make a referral to a 12-step program. As there is often a waiting list, UPLIFT staff have developed relationships with the program staff and usually find a request for special attention results in prompt admission to the program. The FDS would also provide transportation and child care if the 12-step program did not have it.

UPLIFT sees a hierarchy of relationships that are important in helping the family. The highest priority is to try to find a family member to involve from intake on, followed by the UPLIFT staff and, third, a volunteer. During intake to the shelter, the FDS would see if there were any other family member the mother wanted involved. If a volunteer were available at the shelter, the FDS would work with the mother to see who would be best to be "matched up." They would also develop a pairing or group of clients from the shelter who share some concerns, interests, or services.

Once the mother was in rehabilitation, the FDS would arrange with Mental Health Services for counseling for the physical abuse. The advocate would seek counseling for the mother and children, together and separately. If there were a waiting list for mental health, the FDS would try to get a private psychologist as a "bridge" until mental health services could start. A referral to the school system would also result in counseling for Justin in school.

The FDS would personally do some assessments of the children and would not delay psychological evaluation of the 2 1/2-year old until she entered school. A referral would be made to a child developmental evaluation center. The FDS can do these assessments before referring the sister and speed intake at the receiving agency because these assessments are required as part of intake itself. The mother would also be encouraged to put the 2 1/2-year old in a half day of day care. The logic here would be that the mother has to deal with her own problems successfully before she can deal effectively with parenting. The FDS would ask the mother if it would help to have a regular respite from parenting and would seek a family member to provide it. If not, the FDS or a volunteer would provide the respite. These would be an ongoing part of the family's routine. The FDS would arrange physicals for everyone in the family with the Health Department.

The mother would probably qualify for public assistance, and there is an interagency person at the shelter to complete the necessary paperwork for the screening process. The mother would only need to go to the DSS office to officially sign up. Again, transportation and child care would be provided. After that it would be managed by the caseworker on site in the shelter. There is also a computer terminal for DSS at UPLIFT enabling easy record keeping and reporting. Permanent housing would be sought. As the mother's recovery proceeded, she would increasingly be encouraged to go on outings with friends from the shelter, family, and the FDS. Enrolling the family with community organizations would proceed. The YMCA offers both scholarships and a wide variety of athletic activities for the children and mother, as well as day care and after-school care for the children.

The FDS would also work with the mother to set realistic goals so that the mother would be less likely to fail. The FDS would begin to work towards having the mother thinking about a career. No agencies provide the necessary services for this, so the FDS would personally work with the mother on computer skills, resume writing, identifying work strengths, visiting job sites, learning to schedule appointments, practicing interviewing, exploring day care options, and working out routine bus lines with the mother. The last point would be again guided by realistic expectations, including discussions of reasonable travel time for work and day care, for example. The FDS also would work with the mother on budgeting skills, both to manage public assistance and to effect a transition to work.

For Justin, the FDS would approach the guidance counselor at his school to help with counseling, as was discussed earlier. He would also get the respites from his mother with consistent child care provided and be reunited with family members who help give support in the shelter and school. The FDS would work with his mother on Justin's appropriate classroom placement and would even recommend changing schools if it would enable the mother to walk him to school from the shelter. The FDS would also see that Justin's mother received training to deal appropriately with Justin, including how to hold him when he needs to safely express his emotions. A Big Brother and Sister would be arranged. He would also benefit from all the services the mother is receiving, including the ongoing support of the FDS. As above, his sister would be evaluated by the Developmental Evaluation Center, would receive many of the nonschool services that Justin receives, and would be in day care.

UPLIFT's effectiveness. Justin's care is handled quite differently by UPLIFT than Pickard County. Figure 4 illustrates that the family is the unit of focus, with services coming to that family as much as possible. An advocate works with the family to get services; and in some cases UPLIFT can do necessary diagnostics, screening, and follow-up, reducing the family's time spent in agencies other than the shelter. The FDS also provides direct, personal support based in a relationship. Relationship building is the key and can link everything together. UPLIFT, however, does even more. It uses a conscious strategy of empowering the family. UPLIFT argues that agencies have such a caseload that they are quick to make a

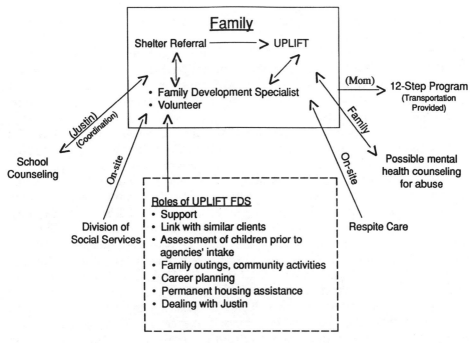

Figure 4. Justin at UPLIFT.

decision, rather than taking the time to consider the full range of decisions possible (as seen in Pickard County). UPLIFT "can relax the press to decide" because the person is getting care and has an advocate. Moreover, the FDS best knows the mother and is in a position to negotiate with agencies.

UPLIFT also sees a family like Justin's as needing a contact person. The FDS would help the mother to schedule the necessary appointments, provide the transportation and child care necessary for the mother to get to the appointments, and monitor the entire process. Moreover, the FDS would call for periodic assessments, in which the advocate, the mother, and all the agencies involved would get together and talk about the family's progress, discuss needed improvements in services, and make plans for such improved services.

The value of UPLIFT's carefully nurtured neutral role in the community is demonstrated by the cool reception the on-site social worker initially received. Because she had previously worked for DSS, when she first started working at UPLIFT, Ray Warren residents would see her car and not come to the Family Resource Center because they associated her with DSS. Although she remains technically employed by DSS, she is referred to as an UPLIFT social worker, which has helped the Ray Warren residents accept and trust her. She mentioned that DSS and UPLIFT are working on overcoming technical barriers; for example, linking their computers so she is able to access DSS files from her computer at UPLIFT.

She feels that an intimate knowledge of both organizational cultures helps her negotiate some of the barriers.

"My job on site here has fewer constraints and works on a more personal level. Of course, DSS has their guidelines and that doesn't change, but I have a good understanding of DSS and how they operate. I haven't had any problems with conflicting rules and regulations because I understand both and know what to do."

UPLIFT, in its effort to focus on developing a relationship with the family, also has minimal paperwork. The FDS, child care, and transportation are the primary expenses, and all are covered by federal grants.

As is evident, UPLIFT has achieved something Pickard County has yet to achieve. Both Pickard County and UPLIFT have existing interagency councils that work on policy issues, but UPLIFT is itself an organization that acts on its own. It has its own charter, policies, procedures, and organizational processes. Further, the clients see themselves as more attached to UPLIFT than to the separate agencies that provide the services that UPLIFT organizes. Institutionalization has also created integrated services for its clients.

There are a number of obstacles to UPLIFT's efforts being even more effective. First, agencies vary in their willingness to allow UPLIFT to integrate its services. Some take expedited referrals, but others have moved on site with staff and computer linkages. UPLIFT is institutionalized to the extent that it operates for a specific community and has established a coherent philosophy, structures consistent with that philosophy, and a system of delivering services. In short, UPLIFT is more effective than Pickard County in terms of both institutionalization and having a smooth functioning process of integrated services. However, it operates core services with private funding and is not assured of ongoing operations without continued fund-raising efforts, a factor noted by Edelman and Radin (1991) for any nongovernmental entity seeking to cut across categorical lines. UPLIFT continuously must search for funding for the collaborative, meaning both that institutionalization is not complete and organizational efforts must be expended on this instead of working with families and children.

Organizing for Effective Interagency Collaboration

In the preceding section, we analyzed how a collaborative that seems to have been effective in integrating services is different from another less effective county. Collaborative initiatives are institutionalized as an organization or system, and the internal organizational processes work to integrate services usually provided by an otherwise fragmented services system. Increasing the effectiveness of interagency collaboration involves many things. It means building on existing cooperative efforts to create collaborative initiatives and then institutionalizing these initiatives in organizational structures and processes designed to integrate, not just deliver services.

The North Carolina Studies on Interagency Collaboration provide some data on creating organizationally effective collaboration. These two cases and the data from all six county case studies of current practice suggest a number of lessons in organizing for more effective services. We obtained information about some of the structures and processes that might be necessary, as well as enhancers and barriers to increased collaboration. The data from existing collaboratives also provide practical suggestions about how to move toward institutionalized, effective collaboration.

Spurs and Reins, Grease and Gravel

Moving to effective collaboration seemingly requires distinguishing between two levels of collaboration. The first level refers to issues surrounding whether to collaborate at all. The second refers to issues that arise once agencies have decided to collaborate and are trying to do so effectively. *Spurs and reins* refer to the issues involved in deciding to collaborate. Thus, spurs (which promote collaboration) and reins (which inhibit collaboration) are most likely to be seen as the inputs in a systems model. *Grease and gravel* refer to things that make collaboration easier (grease) or harder (gravel), respectively, once the decision to collaborate has been made. They are most likely to be part of the throughput (structures and processes) in the system. One final clarification should be kept in mind. Some spurs or grease, while fostering interagency collaboration, are undesirable on other grounds. Insufficient funding for the service needed, for example, can be a spur to collaboration while also working against the best interests of children and families. Furthermore, some spurs to collaborate may be gravel in the actual process of collaboration. Service providers may seek to collaborate in an effort to better use their resources, but find in the process that the effort itself is an intensive drain on already strained budgets, time, and work loads.

Exhibit 1 summarizes the major conditions acting as spurs, reins, grease, and gravel to collaboration in the six counties. A full enumeration of all observed factors would be unwieldy and would obscure the major points. Thus, this composite includes conditions frequently noted across the six sites. This list, therefore, includes major factors that affect formal and informal collaboration among the public agencies studied. There may be, however, different conditions that affect collaboration when private organizations are taken into account. We encourage practitioners and policy makers to consider these lists and adapt them to their own situations. We discuss Pickard County as an example.

Pickard County's large, concentrated, and ethnically diverse population has prompted the creation of several interagency collaborative initiatives from which lessons may be drawn. One effort, which reviews sexual abuse cases, put particular energy into the planning stages of the project: Models were sought and studied, goals specified, rules established, and obstacles anticipated. A group-building step preceded regular meetings,

Exhibit 1. Enhancers and Barriers to Collaboration: Observed Conditions in Field Research

The Decision to Collaborate		The Process of Collaboration	
Spurs (Promote Collaboration)	Reins (Inhibit Collaboration)	Grease (Makes Collaboration Easier)	Gravel (Makes Collaboration Harder)
Geographic proximity of agencies	Geographic distance among agencies	Geographic proximity of agencies	Geographic distance among agencies
Good past experience with others	Personality conflicts	Legal permission to share information	Confidentiality restrictions
Positive image of other agencies	Negative images of other agencies	Appropriate/compatible technologies	Asymmetrical relationships
Access to appropriate technologies	Outmoded, incompatible technology	Common understanding of client needs	Duplicative, contradictory services
"Pay now or pay later" philosophy	No perceived need for other perspectives	Workers familiar with area services	High personnel turnover
Threat of lost funding if no collaboration	Stigma of association with agencies	Concerted effort to streamline client experience	Unrealistic mandates
Will/ability to exceed requirements	Funding competition among agencies	Specific mechanisms in place	Inertia, fear of change
Flexible procedures, job roles	Incompatible schedules	Informal ways to cut red tape	Confusion of jargons, forms
Increased application pool	Cost of following cases across lines	Strong, enthusiastic leadership	Funding complications
Mandates to collaborate	Legal prohibitions	Worker-level teams	Personality conflicts
Invitations to collaborate	Confidentiality restrictions	Established division of labor	Lack of information
Voluntary/pilot programs	Paperwork avoided	Parent motivated to consent by threat of DSS	Rigid agency ideologies
Adequate time	Professional elitism	Cross-agency friendships	Inconsistent rules, procedures
Parent open to collaboration	"Superman" syndrome	Access to current information	Uncooperative parents
Closed files	Parents reluctant to consent	Group-building exercises	
Sense of isolation from capital	Image of others as overburdened	"Service brokers" exist	
Client/community crises	No internal coordination	Parental consent	
Cross-agency friendships	Client unable to pay for services		
Multineeds clients	Bad past experience with other agencies		
Scarce in-house/private resources	Unattractive cases		
Recognized need for other perspectives	Private/in-house referral preferred		
Worker familiar with area services	Inadequate time/personnel		
Models of successful collaboration studied	Inertia, fear of change		
Professional specialization	New workers not part of network		
Help-seeking, proactive personnel	Illusory collaboration		

now directed by a strong team leader. Success has been quantified in a drastic reduction in the average life cycle of cases. A second effort was undertaken "to put a human face on DSS," consistently found to be the most beleaguered of agencies. This initiative, also based on existing models, has been in planning for nearly a decade, and has yet to be fully implemented. Preventive programs, it was explained, are difficult to fund because the effects are long in coming and hard to prove. Neither schools nor Mental Health Services are regularly involved in these two initiatives.

Pickard's spurs include a positive approach, leadership, increased funds and mandates for collaboration, and considerable experience with collaboration both informally and formally. Some of the reins are ironically parallel to the spurs. Mandates have short lives, informal mechanisms are preferred over formal, and beliefs about the difficulties of collaboration come from extensive experience with it. Other reins are more mundane; these include agency stigma, overload, and desires to do all for the clients within single agencies; parent consent; administrative barriers; and organizational problems internal to agencies. Once collaboration is decided on, it is usually greased by a set of formal procedures (group building, objectives, evaluation criteria, leadership, uniform eligibility requirements, record sharing agreements, and models of successful collaboration) and the technology to communicate. The gravel includes services that are less than fully involved (mental health, schools, transportation), bureaucratic and legal constraints, insufficient time and excessive paperwork and workload, outmoded and underused technology, ideological differences between agencies, and logjams in service streams. The large, concentrated, and diverse population also challenges Pickard County's existing social agency structures. Rural counties experience gravel as gaps and shortages in service, but the experience in Pickard is described in terms of logjams and bottlenecks occurring in a complex web of services.

Organizing for More Effective Services

Systemic change often seems impossible, as noted by Seymour Sarason (1991) in his incisive book, *The Predictable Failure of School Reform*. The political agendas, the intransigence of systems to change (homeostasis), protectionism among agencies, and the extensiveness of interlocking components within and across systems all portend almost insurmountable challenges to transforming the way business is done. Typically, interagency collaboration involves a slight adaptation of existing processes or adding on new procedures to link to other agencies—basically tweaking the existing systems. This strategy is often referred to as *first-order change*: the original beliefs, assumptions and structures are still in place. A true redesign of social service systems would be required for second-order change and institutionalization—going back to zero. The need to change the whole system and not just one or two agencies has been noted by others (Carreon & Jameson, 1993; Dunkle, 1994; Gardner, 1991). In fact, Carreon and Jameson found that participants in collaborative efforts in seven California communities believed that state and federal action would be needed for true systemic change. No effort to date has been able to effect this level of change, although the synergy building around this issue and the political climate may lead to second-order changes in the near future.

In the interim, there are lessons learned from the North Carolina studies that also are reflected in other research regarding factors affecting the delivery of more effective services. Both barriers and successes found in the study of six counties' existing services and the promises of the five new collaboratives offer valuable guidance. Some of these suggestions relate to organizational structures and processes, whereas others involve the context of an integrated services system.

Lesson 1: There is no one best way. Studies of the existing collaboratives offer lessons for creating similar endeavors (Awsumb, in press), but there is no one best way (Dunkle, 1994). The five collaborative initiatives in North Carolina that were studied vary in the ways they understand and practice collaboration. Because each developed from the particular needs and resources of a community, each has found its own approach. In fact, the spurs, reins, grease, and gravel for interagency collaboration are not generalizable from one community to another. What improves collaboration in one county might constrain it in another. All collaboratives, however, are united in their commitment to integration as a better model for human services delivery.

Lesson 2: Be community-based and focused. Whatever the particular contours of the models, they all emphasize that successful collaboration requires board ownership and participation in the community. This implies a willingness to take risks in redefining traditional agency boundaries and roles. There are clear benefits to traditional public agencies' working together, and the rewards multiply geometrically when nonprofits, community groups, businesses, and services recipients get in on the action. Broad and diverse participation tends to generate new perspectives on problems and solutions and create a sense of ownership and pride that emerge infrequently from formal bureaucratic structures. They also share a belief in empowering the recipients of services and making them full partners in collaboration, empowering them to name their own problems and take responsibility for solutions. UPLIFT, for example, embodies Gardner's (1991) assertion that neighborhood-based leadership is essential. The more effective partnership efforts may occur when focused on specific communities (Edelman & Radin, 1991).

Lesson 3: The ironic role of mandates. Mandates from "above" played a somewhat ironic role in the development of these collaborations. Although there was unanimous agreement that "collaboration can't be mandated," in fact, mandates in several situations provided the initial push towards collaboration. Necessity is sometimes the mother of invention, and sometimes people only begin to work together in the face of an obvious crisis or a budgetary imperative. However, although a mandate may be what first gets diverse service providers around a table, it is not enough to sustain momentum. For genuine collaboration to occur, ownership and support must be generated from "below," from the people who will have to take the risks and do the everyday work. Often what a mandate does is give people the opportunity to define their common ground. Once this consensus has been reached, collaboration takes on a life of its own, often far exceeding the scope of the original mandate.

Lesson 4: Define and understand differences and similarities up front. All of the collaboratives stressed the importance of early, open, and on-going communication among group members. There is a danger in being overly polite and trying to steer clear of conflict. Gaps in understanding or philosophy that are not explored early come back to haunt the group later. As the group strives to come together, members should be brutally honest about what they have in common and what they do not, establishing clear boundaries for collaboration. One of the areas in which it is most crucial to be explicit is the definition of the "problem" that the group is trying to address. Who is the target population and what are its most pressing needs? Using safe, vague language that encompasses everyone's view is insufficient. When it is time for action, differences will reassert themselves. All of these groups found plenty of common ground from which to work, but they also emphasized that it is important to recognize differences where they exist rather than sweeping them under the rug. Frank conversation is also important as the group tries to nail down the specifics of how collaboration is to be practiced. Will the group focus on direct service delivery, coordination and infrastructure, or policy development? Talking about the right mix early keeps everyone on track.

Lesson 5: Establish neutral turf. All of these groups felt strongly that neutrality was crucial to their success. Although it may sometimes be necessary to formally empower an existing agency for purposes of grant administration or other funding flows, decision-making autonomy is a must. Payzant, a San Diego Schools Superintendent, noted that this factor was critical to the success of New Beginnings (Dunkle, 1994). An autonomous structure creates a safe environment in which agencies may practice innovative strategies without fear of losing in political or turf battles. If the collaborative is perceived to be under the inequitable control of one agency or group, participants will play defensively and collaboration will stall. Autonomy may also make the collaborative more attractive and inviting to the community at large and particularly to service recipients. In fact, non-governmental entities based around the community may be more neutral and better able to lead to institutionalized systems change. Traditional agencies come with a great deal of baggage and may be less able to get things done under their own banners, whatever their good intentions. Neutral turf allows ownership to be established from the ground up. All of these groups felt that freeing funds to flow directly to collaboratives rather than through agency channels was a crucial next step in providing an environment in which collaboration can flourish.

Lesson 6: Ensure both formal and informal collaboration. Interagency collaboration is a two-tiered system, both formal and informal. Formal collaboration is often limited to top administrators who design ways for agencies to better serve clients. Informal collaboration is practiced by front-line service providers. Ironically, it appears that the two tiers often do not communicate with each other and at times seem to work at cross purposes. Formal structures are most likely to be effective when designed with the input of front-line service providers.

Although formal mechanisms are important to restructuring service delivery to be more integrated, the most effective forms of collaborations are informal. Informal networking was easiest when staff had worked in other agencies and understood their logics, limitations, and possibilities. These networks might be protected by cross-agency training and internships, informal cross agency gatherings, better use of technology, designing cross-agency directories, and creating confidentiality and other procedures that facilitate access by personnel from other agencies.

Lesson 7: Put the client at the center of the system. The TFCCPSC (1994) maintains that services are only integrated when viewed as such from the perspective of the clients. As Figure 2 suggests, services should be brought to the client rather than sending the client to services in linear fashion. To the extent feasible, services should be provided where the client is (see lesson 2). Similarly, the best collaborators in our studies were client advocates. These collaborators shared some personal characteristics, such as persistence, resourcefulness, being trustworthy, proactively seeking services, willingness to work with others regardless of status or authority, and getting what the client needed, not what the agency provided. Agencies can help foster this focus by setting time to explore options, providing access to technologies and up-to-date information about services, and providing experience with other agencies. Staff might even be encouraged to live in the communities of concern.

Lesson 8: Address diverse agency logics. This lesson may be imbedded in lesson 4, but it is important to understand how agencies do their work and make decisions. Differences in agency logics affect how they view their roles in collaboration. The knowledge and understanding of how agencies work and why can be crucial in implementing effective system processes and structures.

Lesson 9: Move decision making to the front line. Client contact workers need increased decision-making authority in order to most effectively help children and families in a timely manner. As noted previously, the most effective collaboration was seen in informal networks of front-line providers. Yet, the different agency decision-making logics make it difficult to use these informal networks systematically. The collaboration of front-line providers requires those in authority to delegate more of the decision making.

Lesson 10: Define beliefs, norms, and roles explicitly. Lesson 10 is also related to lesson 4, understanding similarities and differences. However, this recommendation specifically addresses organizational behavior and variables that often are not made explicit. Agencies and staff may have competing assumptions, values, and system norms as well as organizational procedures and structures. Changing procedures without clarifying these underlying assumptions may doom any collaborative effort. Views of clients, goals of services, appropriate roles, and values and perspectives of staff all influence their behavior. The work required to mesh these organizational factors up front will strengthen the collaborative system and relationships. In fact, the two authors of this chapter, although both involved in education, approached this topic from somewhat different perspectives and frameworks—one perhaps best described as drawn from sociology and the other from organizational/system behavior. Even though an outline was developed for the chapter, our perspectives played out in different ways when written. Synthesis took some time, but the result is probably stronger than either approach separately.

Lesson 11: Patience is a virtue. Nearly every participant in every collaborative studied volunteered that patience and perseverance are required to make collaboration work. Collaboration is sometimes sold as the "Holy Grail" of human services delivery and thereby burdened by unrealistic expectations. As exciting as the vision may be, however, it takes trial and error to make it work in practice. The transition from a period of activism and enthusiasm to one of increasing structure can be frustrating, but the collaboratives studied indicate that it is part of the normal organizational growth process. By constantly returning to the roots of their shared beliefs, collaboratives can maintain momentum. One useful strategy is to set achievable early hurdles rather than setting out to save the world. By building collaboration around a specific problem or population, groups can create tangible success stories that will make a solid core for enlarging and expanding their vision.

Concluding Remarks

Collaboration is a vision, not an organization. The evolution of the successful collaboratives brings home the importance of focusing on a core vision and on not getting too attached to the particular structures used to implement it. All of them went through many permutations of membership, organizational structure, and services, evolving in response to issues and opportunities. By holding to a commonly defined problem and a vision of integrated services, they were able to go through these changes without losing focus. It also helps to keep this in mind as the organization grows and the day-to-day realities of doing the work threaten to make people lose sight of why this should be done. As long as people maintain their faith in the "why," the specifics of "how" can evolve without disturbing the core.

Transforming a social movement into an effective, institutionalized organization is a complex endeavor. There are spurs and reins in deciding to collaborate and grease and gravel in actually collaborating. New structures and procedures must be established and old ones diminished. It appears to work best when new interagency structures become relatively independent organizations. These new organizations in turn have to develop processes to integrate services, which in the end are delivered to meet specific client needs. The entire system(s) must be examined to move toward institutionalization.

As we have shown in this chapter, there is much to learn from current attempts. Limited efforts can teach us much about the issues to be addressed and barriers to be overcome. More successful initiatives can reveal both what needs to be put in place and how others have done so. As Schorr and Schorr (1988) have argued, "more Americans must become aware of the high stake that all of us have in what happens to these children, and more Americans must become convinced that we know what needs to be done and how to do it" (p. xix). The North Carolina Studies on Interagency Collaboration demonstrate their latter point. We still need to make more Americans aware of their stake in all children and families.

References

Adkins, A., Awsumb, C., Noblit, G., & Richards, P. (in press). *Working together? Grounded perspectives on interagency collaboration*. Cresskill, NJ: Hampton Press.

Awsumb, C. (in press). Realities of collaboration: Lessons learned from best efforts. In A. Adkins, C. Awsumb, G. Noblit, & P. Richards (Eds.), *Working together? Grounded perspectives on interagency collaboration*. Cresskill, NJ: Hampton Press.

Beatrice, D. F. (1982). Solving problems through cooperation. *Exceptional Children, 48*(5), 400–407.

Benson, J. K. (1975). The interorganizational network as a political economy. *Administrative Science Quarterly, 20*, 229–245.

Berger, P., & Luckmann, T. (1967). *The social construction of reality*. New York: Doubleday.

Berliner, A. K. (1979). Integrating child care services: Overcoming structural obstacles to collaboration of institutional and community agency staffs. *Journal of Sociology and Social Welfare, 6*(3), 400–409.

Cameron, K. (1984). The effectiveness of ineffectiveness. *Research in Organizational Behavior, 6*, 235–285.

Cameron, W. (1966). *Modern social movements*. New York: Random House.

Carreon, V., & Jameson, W. J. (1993, October). *School-linked service integration in action: Lessons drawn from seven California communities*. San Francisco: California Research Institute.

Clark, D. (1995). *Organizational effects*. Unpublished manuscript. Chapel Hill: University of North Carolina.

Daniels, M. S., & Bosch, S. J. (1978). School health planning: A case for interagency collaboration. *Social Work in Health Care, 3*(4), 457–467.

Dunkle, M. (1994). *Linking schools with health and social services: Perspectives from Thomas Payzant on San Diego's New Beginnings (Special Report #4)*. Washington, DC: Institute for Educational Leadership.

Edelman, P. B., & Radin, B. A. (1991). *Serving children and families effectively: How the past can help chart the future*. Washington, DC: Education and Human Services Consortium.

Gans, S. O., & Horton, G. T. (1975). *Integration of human services: The state and municipal levels*. New York: Praeger.

Gardner, S. (1991). A commentary. In P. B. Edelman & B. A. Radin, *Serving children and families effectively: How the past can help chart the future*. Washington, DC: Education and Human Services Consortium.

Guthrie, G. P., & Guthrie, L. F. (1991). Streamlining interagency collaboration for youth at risk. *Educational Leadership, 49*(1), 17–22.

Hoffer, E. (1951). *True believers*. New York: Mentor Press.

Hooyman, N. R. (1976). The practice implications of interorganizational theory for services integration. *Journal of Sociology and Social Welfare, 3*(5), 558–564.

Iles, P., & Auluck, R. (1990). Team building, inter-agency team development and social work practice. *British Journal of Social Work, 20*(2), 151–164.

Illback, R. J., Sanders, D. S., & Birkby, B. (1995). *Evaluation of the Kentucky impact program at year five: Accomplishments, challenges, and opportunities*. Louisville: R.E.A.C.H. of Louisville, Inc.

Katz, D., & Kahn, R. (1978). *The social psychology of organizations*. New York: Wiley.

Knapp, M. S. (1995, May). How shall we study comprehensive, collaborative services for children and families? *Educational Researcher, 24*(4), 16.

Martin, P. Y., Chakerian, R., Imershein, A. W., & Frumkin, M. L. (1983). The concept of "integrated" services reconsidered. *Social Science Quarterly, 64*, 747–763.

McGrath, M. (1988). Inter-agency collaboration in the all-Wales strategy: Initial comments on a vanguard area. *Social Policy and Administration, 22*(1), 53–67.

Melaville, A., & Blank, M. (1991). *What it takes: Structuring interagency partnerships to connect children and families with comprehensive services*. Washington, DC: Education and Human Services Consortium.

Merriam, S. (1988). *Case study research in education*. San Francisco: Jossey-Bass.

Noblit, G., Adkins, A., Awsumb, C., & Richards, P. (1995). *Working together? The report on interagency collaboration for children and their families in North Carolina*. Raleigh: North Carolina Department of Public Instruction.

Noblit, G., & Dempsey, V. (1992). Creating organizationally effective desegregated schools. *Equity and Excellence, 25*(2–4), 113–120.

Nordyke, N. S. (1982). Improving services for young, handicapped children through local, interagency collaboration. *Topics in Early Childhood Special Education, 2*(1), 63–72.

Roberts-DeGennaro, M. (1988). A study of youth services networks from a political-economy perspective. *Journal of Social Service Research, 11*(4), 1–7.

Sarason, S. (1991). *The predictable failure of school reform*. San Francisco: Jossey-Bass.

Schorr, L. B., & Schorr, D. (1988). *Within our reach: Breaking the cycle of disadvantage*. New York: Anchor Books.

Task Force on Comprehensive and Coordinated Psychological Services for Children. (1994). *Comprehensive and coordinated psychological services for children*. Washington, DC: American Psychological Association.

Vander-Schie, A. R., Wagenfeld, M. O., & Worgess, B. L. (1987). Reorganizing human services at the local level: The Kalamazoo County experience. *New England Journal of Human Services, 7*(1), 29–33.

Weiss, J. A. (1981). Substance vs. symbol in administrative reform: The case of human services coordination. *Policy Analysis, 7*, 21–45.

Wimpfheimer, R., Bloom, M., & Kramer, M. (1990). Interagency collaboration: Some working principles. *Administration in Social Work, 14*(4), 89–102.

Yin, R. K. (1984). *Case study research: Design and methods*. Newbury Park, CA: Sage.

10

Conducting an Integrated Practice in a Pediatric Setting

Carolyn S. Schroeder

Pediatricians and child psychologists appear to form a natural collaborative team given their many common interests in the health and development of children. Even before the establishment of the American Academy of Pediatrics in 1930 and the Society of Pediatric Psychology in 1968, there are early reports of these two professions working together. Jean McFarlane, a developmental psychologist, worked in a children's hospital as early as 1917–1918, and Arnold Gesell, an MD interested in pediatrics and a PhD psychologist, wrote in 1919 about the important role for clinical psychology in medical settings working with children (Drotar, 1995; Gesell, 1919; Routh, 1994). It seems that pediatricians were initially more aware of the potential benefits of collaborating with psychologists, or at least wrote more about this team approach, than were psychologists. For example, Wilson (1964), in his presidential address to the American Academy of Pediatrics, stated, "one of the things I would do if I could control the practice of pediatrics would be to encourage groups of pediatricians to employ their own clinical psychologists" (p. 988).

By the late 1960s and early 1970s psychologists seemed to take the idea of collaborating with pediatricians more seriously. Logan Wright (1967) and Lee Salk (1970), for example, described a new breed of psychologists—pediatric psychologists—and their role in nonpsychiatric medical settings. In the years since, pediatric psychology has become a viable specialty with the founding of the Society of Pediatrics (American Psychological Association's [APA] Division 12, Section 5), the publication of the scholarly *Journal of Pediatric Psychology*, and the development of training programs at the graduate, internship, and postdoctoral level. Routh (1970, 1972) noted that the initial members of the Society of Pediatric Psychology worked primarily in large hospitals or in developmental clinics affiliated with university medical schools. Although there has not been a recent survey of work settings, it seems safe to say that the majority of pediatric psychology research, practice, and teaching continues to focus on children who are physically ill and seems to be carried out in large university medical centers versus primary care settings.

The practice of psychology in primary care settings is primarily focused on prevention and early intervention. The need to provide more preventive services for children and youth is clearly illustrated by prevalence studies finding that children can suffer developmental, emotional, and behavioral problems at any time over the course of their development. Clinical dysfunction increases with age: 5.3% of children ages 3 to 5; 12.7% of 6- to 11-year-olds, and 18.5% of 12- to 17-year-olds (Zill & Schoenborn, 1990). The report of the APA Task Force on Comprehensive and Coordinated Psychological Services for Children: Ages 0–10 (APA, 1994) described the primary care setting as the normal point of entry for the prevention, assessment, and treatment of both physical and psychological problems. Indeed, pediatricians are the first professionals most parents are likely to talk to when they have concerns about their children's behavior or development (Clarke-Stewart, 1978; Schroeder & Wool, 1979). An estimated 20% of pediatric primary-care patients have biosocial or developmental problems, which, for the pediatrician seeing 27 patients a day translates into 4 patients per day (American Academy of Pediatrics, 1978). Although the American Academy of Pediatrics (1978) recommended radical changes in pediatric training that would emphasize the biosocial aspects of patient care, the reality is that pediatricians rarely have the time, resources, or skills to meet these needs. Thirty years after Wilson (1964) recognized a role for psychology in primary care, the pediatric office still offers psychology a unique opportunity to provide preventive services and to identify and treat those children and families in need of mental health services.

Although there are some early examples of psychologists working in community pediatric primary care settings (Fischer & Engeln, 1972; Schroeder, 1979; Smith, Rome & Friedheim, 1967) and even a 1983 article in the *American Psychologist* highlighting the value of this work (Routh, Schroeder, & Koocher, 1983), few psychologists have chosen to practice in these settings. Perhaps one reason that this collaborative relationship has not become a standard of care is that both psychologists and pediatricians have found it difficult to know how to go about establishing a formal relationship in nonhospital settings. There simply are not many advertisements for positions available in pediatric offices! This means that in most instances the interested psychologist will have to seek out and set up his or her own collaborative relationship with a pediatrician or group of pediatricians, a seemingly daunting task for even the most seasoned psychologist! Interest in working in pediatric offices, however, is on the rise, and the time seems ripe for psychologists to be as much a part of pediatric practices as nurses or nurse practitioners. Health care reforms are making traditional private practice for psychologists less appealing, and pediatricians have even less time to devote to mental health issues. There is also a greater awareness of the importance of providing comprehensive and coordinated educational, psychological, and medical care for children and families (APA, 1994).

The goals for this chapter are to share the varied and worthwhile work that psychologists can do in community primary care settings and to provide information on how psychologists can prepare themselves for a career in this work. Following a brief description of different models of collaboration with pediatricians, several examples of psychology practices in primary care settings will be outlined. Finally, some of the activities, knowledge, skills, implementation, and professional issues unique to these settings will be discussed.

Models for Pediatric–Psychological Consultation

Pediatric psychologists who collaborate with pediatricians rank this relationship as one of the highest sources of job satisfaction (Drotar, Strum, Eckerle, & White, 1993). Although there have been descriptions of the process involved in consulting with pediatricians (Burns & Cromer, 1978; Roberts & Wright, 1982; Stabler, 1979, 1988), the nature of these collaborative relationships has been seen as idiosyncratic (Hamlett & Stabler, 1995). In a recent book, Drotar (1995) provided a discussion of these relationships, including a description of the ingredients of interdisciplinary consultation and collaboration; how to make these activities more effective and efficient; the salient obstacles to this collaboration; the training necessary to do this work at a quality level; and how we can use this collaborative relationship to enhance the lives of children and families through service programs, research, and advocacy. The reader is referred to Drotar (1995) and a chapter by Hamlett and Stabler (1995) for in-depth information on developing and sustaining an interdisciplinary relationship with physicians. This section gives a brief review of some models of consultation between psychologists and physicians and some of the factors that influence the success of this collaborative effort.

The *independent functions model* (Roberts & Wright, 1982) has also been described as a resource consultation model (Stabler, 1979) and a client-centered model (Burns & Cromer, 1978). This approach to consultation is the one most frequently used by physicians and mental health workers and involves the psychologist and pediatrician independently seeing the patient. The focus is on sharing information to arrive at a diagnosis and possible treatment program for a patient, but it does not require a great deal of interaction between the physician and psychologist. The request often comes to the psychologist in the form of a written note, a telephone conversation, or a request as parties pass in the hall; the feedback is most often in written form with little verbal explanation. Drotar (1995) pointed out that this model is quick, cost effective, and familiar to most pediatricians. It does not, however, allow for much discussion of complex cases. Furthermore, this model can result in the narrow definition of issues from only one professional's perspective, and given the limited contact between professionals, does not allow time to promote a relationship (Drotar, 1995; Hamlett & Stabler, 1995). This method of consulting seems particularly viable for established professional relationships in which the pediatrician and psychologist know each other's strengths and orientation and have mutual respect and trust, and where there are other opportunities to communicate on a regular basis (e.g., at staff meetings).

In the *indirect consultation model* (Roberts & Wright, 1982; Stabler,

1979) the psychologist does not see the patient but rather provides information to the physician, who is solely responsible for the patient. This is an educative or teaching approach to collaboration and, as such, has the potential for informing the physician of the unique contributions and skills of the psychologist. It can be done in case conferences, didactic presentations, or more informally as a "curbside" consultation in the hall (Drotar, 1995). According to Roberts (1986) the focus of this type of consultation is usually on (a) the age appropriateness of a child's behavior and how to handle it, (b) interpreting psychological tests, (c) providing community resources for a particular problem, and (d) whether there is a need to refer for psychological services. Indirect consultation is usually done when one has an ongoing relationship with the pediatrician, and is certainly best done under those circumstances, given the potential for the pediatrician to present incomplete information or to present a narrow view of the situation (Hamlett & Stabler, 1995). It is, however, a valuable way to share one's professional knowledge and to demonstrate the variety of roles the psychologist can play in the pediatric setting. The drawback is that it does take a fair amount of time for both the pediatrician and the psychologist. This can be particularly frustrating or difficult to do at a quality level in the middle of a busy schedule and active clinic (Drotar, 1995).

The *collaborative team model* (Roberts & Wright, 1982; Stabler, 1979) has inherent appeal given that pediatricians and psychologists (and perhaps other disciplines) share joint responsibility and decision making. It allows each discipline to share its expertise in diagnosing or treating a particular problem and thus there is both an increased appreciation for the other discipline and a broader view of the issues important to a child and family. Drotar (1995) pointed out that this approach takes time, careful organization, leadership, and an ability to preserve unique professional and personal contributions as one assimilates knowledge from another profession. In the primary-care setting, this model is most likely to be used only with complex or chronic problems (e.g., intrafamilial sexual abuse or a more benign but often intractable problem, such as a 12-year-old with a long history of encopresis).

What are the factors that increase the likelihood that psychologists and pediatricians will want to collaborate and what factors influence the successful outcome of these collaborative efforts? Drotar (1993) described three broad categories of factors that set the stage for collaboration and influence the collaborative outcomes: the professionals' beliefs and expectations that the collaboration is necessary and will be helpful; the professionals' collaborative skills and knowledge (i.e., skills in being able to identify a problem, to effectively communicate a request for help, and to be able to use the requested information); and the ratio of constraints and incentives in a particular setting (i.e., accessibility, time pressures, multiple responsibilities, funding patterns, reimbursibility patterns and administrative organization). Factors influencing the potential outcomes of the collaboration include the physician's frequency in using psychological services, the frequency of mutual consultation, efficacy and quality issues such as perceived benefits and satisfaction, more efficient patient care, and economic benefits (Drotar, 1993).

Hamlett and Stabler (1995) also described a number of factors that influence the consultation process in medical settings, including time pressures, size of caseload, amount of time allotted to a patient, case formulation, language, organizational issues (e.g., structure, rules, codes, expectations of staff and patients, "unspoken politics," visibility and availability), and communication issues. This work and the work of Drotar (1993, 1995) has pointed out that to successfully share one's expertise one must take into account many interpersonal and setting factors and be aware of the professional culture in which she or he works.

Models for Collaborative Practice

To provide an understanding of how psychologists actually practice in primary care settings this section presents an overview of the practices of four psychologists, including the location of practice, entry into the setting, staff, services, ages served, types and frequency of presenting clinical problems, and financial arrangements (Schroeder, 1994).

Ann R. Ernst, PhD
The Medical Associates Clinic, PC
Dubuque, Iowa

Location: The Pediatric Psychology Unit is in the Department of Pediatrics/Adolescent Medicine of the Medical Associates Clinic. This is a multispecialty medical clinic serving patients from southwestern Wisconsin and northeastern Illinois, a population of approximately 100,000. The entire clinic has 80 physicians covering many different medical specialties.

Entry Into Setting: Seventeen years ago the local pediatricians invited Dr. Ernst to work in their offices 4 hours a week. The referrals initially were from the physicians. Although the majority of referrals in recent years have been self-referrals, the practice has flourished because the pediatricians have continued to support its presence within the Department of Pediatrics/Adolescent Medicine.

Staff: Pediatric Psychology Unit staff include three full-time and one part-time PhD, licensed health-service providers in psychology, one part-time DSW, and one EdS certified school psychologist who has completed a fellowship in pediatric psychology. The Department of Pediatrics/Behavioral Medicine has nine pediatricians, including a pediatrician with a fellowship in adolescent medicine. The Department of Psychiatry/Behavioral Medicine recently added a second psychiatrist with training in child/adolescent psychiatry.

Services: Services include education and training; crisis and emergency intervention; consultation; evaluation; standardized psychological testing; and individual, group, and family intervention. These services are offered on both an outpatient and inpatient basis because all staff members have hospital privileges at local hospitals. The Health Service Providers have admitting privileges.

Ages Served: Birth through 18 years or high-school completion.

Types of Problems: Adolescent adjustment problems; attention-deficit/hyperactivity disorder (ADHD); behavioral or conduct concerns; developmental anxiety, depression, fears, phobias, and grief; family difficulties such as adjustment to a new move, a new baby, remarriage, sibling rivalry, and communication breakdown; learning difficulties; psychological problems associated with physical conditions such as asthma, abdominal pain, arthritis, cancer, convulsive disorder, diabetes, and headaches; reaction to trauma, including abuse; school avoidance; and sleep disturbance. The most frequent problems are depression, frequently with suicidal ideation; ADHD; and adjustment disturbances and oppositional behaviors. The staff also provides consultation on a contractual basis as follows:

1. Facilitates groups in two local high schools for youngsters returning from inpatient treatment.
2. Provides weekly consultation to an outpatient and inpatient program for adolescent substance abuse.
3. Provides monthly consultation to a branch clinic of the University of Iowa.

Financial Arrangements: Staff are salaried. Licensees have a $1,200 education fund. Medical and dental insurance and a pension plan are among the benefits offered.

Professional Background: Dr. Ernst earned her PhD in school psychology from the University of Iowa in 1982. She had supervised training at a community mental health center. She worked for 7 years at the Gannon Center for Community Mental Health and 5 years at Hillcrest Services to Children and Youth.

Mary Evers-Szostak, PhD
Durham Pediatrics
Durham, NC

Location: The Pediatric Psychology services are housed in the offices of Durham Pediatrics, which is a private practice that has been operating since 1930. It is located in a city with a diverse population of 300,000, including poor, working class, middle class, professional, and upper class families. The surrounding area has three major universities, including two university hospitals, and is near the Research Triangle Park. The practice serves approximately 20,000 patients.

Entry Into Practice: Dr. Ever-Szostak approached several groups of pediatricians in 1988 and began working part-time out of two practices. In 1990 she began full-time in Durham Pediatrics.

Staff: There are six full time pediatricians, one nurse clinician, three nurses, a lab technician, 7 office staff, and one PhD licensed psychologist.

Services Offered: Telephone consultation, parent groups, developmental screening, parent training, school consultation, standardized psychological testing, child psychotherapy, behavior management, and curbside consultation for pediatricians.

Ages Served: Birth to college age.

Types of Problems: Negative behavior (24%), ADHD (20%), anxiety (14%), learning disabilities/school problems (13%), divorce/separation (8%), depression (8%), developmental delays (6%), physical complaints (4%), chronic illness (2%). Referrals average about 13 per month. Referrals were initially primarily from the pediatricians but now are primarily self-referred.

Financial Arrangements: Dr. Evers-Szostak is an independent contractor who pays the pediatricians for overhead at the rate of 25% of collections.

Professional Background: Dr. Evers-Szostak received her PhD in clinical psychology from the University of North Carolina at Chapel Hill in 1986. She worked in an interdisciplinary developmental disabilities clinic and in a university hospital prior to her work in the primary care setting.

Linda Hurley, PhD
Fort Worth Pediatric Clinic, PA
Ft. Worth, Texas

Location: Dr. Hurley practices in the Fort Worth Pediatric Clinic, which is a private pediatric practice located in the hospital district of a city with a population of 375,000. The practice has approximately 20,000 patients who are primarily of middle- to upper-class income level.

Entry Into Practice: Dr. Hurley initiated contact with the practice and over a 6-month period negotiated an agreement to join the practice. The pediatricians called Dr. Evers-Szostak's group to discuss the positive aspects of such an arrangement. She began her work with them in 1991.

Staff: There are 4 full-time pediatricians, 7 full-time nurses, 6 part-time nurses, 10 office staff, and 1 PhD licensed psychologist/health-service provider. The group recently merged with two other groups, increasing the number of pediatricians to 13.

Services Offered: Parent education groups, parent training, standardized psychological testing, evaluations, individual child therapy, parent training, school consultation, and hospital consultation. She also has a contract with a hospital for inpatient consultation.

Ages Served: Birth to 15 years.

Type of Problems: ADD/ADHD (16%); negative behaviors (15%); emotional (including depression and anxiety) problems (15%); school problems (11%); adjustment problems (10%); chronic illness (9%); divorce/separation (6%); developmental delay (4%); eating (3%); and a variety of other child, parent, and family problems such as sleep, sex abuse, somatic complaints. The majority of referrals are from HMOs and the physicians, with some self-referrals. In January, 1994, she received 30 referrals.

Financial Arrangement: Dr. Hurley is an independent contractor who pays a flat overhead rate to the pediatric group for space and administrative services.

Professional Background: Dr. Hurley received her PhD in clinical psychology from the American University in 1986. She was on the faculty at a university hospital for 5 years and held a position at an interdisciplinary child study center for a year.

Carolyn S. Schroeder, PhD
Chapel Hill Pediatrics, PA
Chapel Hill, NC

Location: Pediatric Psychology Services are located in a building adjacent to the offices of Chapel Hill Pediatric, PA, a private practice located in a small university town of 60,000, with the university and university hospital the primary employer. The pediatric practice also has a satellite office in Durham, NC, and serves approximately 20,000 patients from both cities and the surrounding rural area.

Entry Into Practice: Dr. Schroeder and colleagues (Schroeder, Goolsby, & Stangler, 1975) began offering prevention and early intervention services in the pediatric office 24 years ago. These services were part of a university-hospital-based training program and were offered free of charge. At the invitation of the pediatricians 15 years ago, Dr. Schroeder joined the practice on a full-time basis.

Staff: There are 6 full-time pediatricians, 1 nurse practitioner, 5 nurses, and 8 office staff. The pediatric psychology group consists of 5 full-time and 2 part-time PhD licensed psychologists, 2 part-time psychiatrists, a full-time MS in child development who is also a family and marriage counselor, a part-time MSW, 3 office staff, and an administrator.

Services Offered: Parent groups; telephone consultation (call-in hour); educational materials; standardized psychological testing; individual, family, and group treatment; a clinic that offers a blind, placebo-controlled medication trial for ADHD; a sex-abuse clinic; consultation to the schools; evaluation of children referred by the Department of Social Services. The staff also provides services on a contractual basis to a private school and, periodically, to the Department of Social Services.

Ages: Birth to adult.

Types of Problems: Negative behavior (18%), anxiety (15%), ADHD (12%), learning disabilities (11%), divorce/separation (9%), peer problems (7%), school problems (6%), depression (6%), child abuse (6%), chronic illness (2%), developmental delays (1%), and fears (1%). Referrals came initially from the pediatricians but there is now approximately a 50–50 split between self-referred and pediatrician-referred. The pediatric psychology group receives on the average 37 referrals a month.

Financial Arrangement: Dr. Schroeder has a separate corporation that employs the mental health professionals, pays rent, and has its own administrative support staff.

Professional Background: Dr. Schroeder received her PhD in clinical psychology from the University of Pittsburgh in 1966. She was on the faculty at a university medical school with a position in an interdisciplinary clinic prior to joining the pediatric practice, and continues to be affiliated with a university.

Each of the four models is unique in its setting and financial relationship with the pediatric practice, but they all focus on some aspect of prevention and early intervention, and provide short-term treatment. The setting or location of the pediatric practices determines, in part, the range of services offered. For example, Dr. Ernst's group is part of a larger medical specialty clinic, has greater access to an inpatient population, and offers more services directed to that group, such as the consultation to the transition group at the high school. Dr. Hurley practices alone with a heavy number of referrals and has limited time to engage in many preventive services directed to the general pediatric population. She does, however, do hospital consultations. Dr. Schroeder's group has a special interest in child abuse and offers an array of services for these children. The larger mental health staff in that practice also permits more prevention services, such as the parent call-in hour.

The diverse financial arrangements (a salaried position, the payment of a percentage of receipts to the pediatric practice, the payment of a mutually determined set overhead regardless of receipts, and a corporation that is independent of the pediatrician's finances) are based on the pediatrician's and psychologist's coming to a mutually agreed-on arrangement. It is not apparent from the above outline of practices that, regardless of the financial arrangement, all of the psychologists devote a great deal of time to nonreimbursable activities, such as preparing parent materials, interacting with a diverse professional staff, and doing quick consults with parents and community agencies. The professional backgrounds of the mental health staff working with the two psychologists who have been in the primary care setting for over 14 years include social workers, marriage and family counselors, and educational specialists. The diverse staff points to the varied problems presented by families and children that can be treated in the primary care setting as well as the range of mental health professionals who can effectively work in this setting. Three of the psychologists heading up the practices have degrees in clinical psychology and one has a degree in school psychology, again indicating that the educational road to this work can vary. However, it is not surprising, given the previous discussion of factors influencing the establishment of successful collaborative relationships, that all four psychologists had previous experience working in interdisciplinary clinics.

It is interesting to note that the targeted clinical problems are similar across settings and geographical locations, with the focus primarily on emotional, behavioral, and learning problems and environmental events impinging on the child (e.g., sex abuse, divorce, death of a parent) versus children suffering from chronic physical illnesses. These are distinctly different practices from those of many psychologists who work in hospital settings and reflect the fact that primary care settings focus on healthy children and acute illness.

The next section explores some of the psychological activities that occur within the primary care setting, including clinical, community, training, and research activities, with my practice used to illustrate this work. The Chapel Hill Pediatric Psychology service delivery model has evolved over a period of 23 years. In addition to developing a variety of prevention programs and clinical services, the staff has been able to coordinate our work with that of other community agencies that serve children and engage in professional training and research. These activities have been described, in part, in other publications (e.g., Hawk, Schroeder, & Martin, 1987; Kanoy & Schroeder, 1985; Mesibov, Schroeder, & Wesson, 1977; Routh et al., 1983; Schroeder, in press, 1979, 1996; Schroeder & Gordon, 1991; Schroeder, Gordon, Kanoy, & Routh, 1983).

Psychological Activities in Pediatric Health Care Settings: Chapel Hill Pediatrics

As was discussed in the previous section, there are a number of ways that psychologists have entered pediatric practices. Currently, the psychologist is the one most likely to initiate the contact, but with psychologists becoming more visible in these settings and pediatric residents being trained by psychologists in these settings (Sharp & Lorch, 1988), more primary care physicians should be asking psychologists to join them. Regardless of how one enters a primary care setting, the activities or services offered will depend on the particular setting, including the needs of the parents and children, the interests of the pediatricians, the interests and skills of the psychologist, time constraints, and the available space.

The work at Chapel Hill Pediatrics grew out of an interest in early intervention and prevention on the part of a public health nurse, a social worker, and psychologist who worked in a University of North Carolina training clinic serving children with developmental disabilities (Schroeder, Goolsby, & Stangler, 1975). At the time, the pediatricians had a morning call hour that was originally set up to handle questions about health issues and to schedule children who were sick. Many of the calls, however, focused on developmental and management issues that both took considerable time to answer and kept the parents with more pressing health issues "on hold." The pediatricians were, therefore, interested in finding a better way to handle these concerns. To further explore this need, as well as to determine how best to meet the need, a randomly selected group of parents from the pediatric office were surveyed by telephone. As a result of that survey, three services were developed: (a) a call-in hour scheduled twice a week, during which parents could ask questions about child development and behavior; (b) weekly evening parent groups, which focused on different ages and stages of development; and (c) a "come-in" time 2 to 4 hours a week, to give parents an opportunity to discuss their child-related concerns in greater depth. These services were offered to the parents and pediatricians free of charge in exchange for allowing graduate students in psychology, medicine, nursing, and social work to participate in these services.

In 1982, as a result of requests from the parents and pediatricians to provide more in-depth assessment and treatment, as well as a desire to demonstrate the viability of a fee-for-service mental health practice in primary care, I left the university for a full-time position in the pediatric practice. Although parents and children receiving psychological services are primarily from the pediatric practice, anyone in the community may use the services, and a referral from a pediatrician is not necessary. The population served is primarily well educated, middle class, and White. Contracts with the Department of Social Services and other community agencies also have given us an opportunity to work with a more diverse cultural, ethnic, and economic population.

Clinical Services

The primary care setting requires a shift in the way mental health services have been traditionally offered: (a) More clients are seen; (b) less time is spent with each client; and (c) clients generally present with less debilitating disorders (Wright & Burns, 1986). Thus, there is a greater focus on prevention and early intervention than on treatment of severe psychopathology. A developmental–behavioral approach that targets specific behaviors or problems and takes into account the child and family's development is imperative.

In a review of 714 new referrals over a 2-year period (1989–1990), Schroeder (1992) found 54% were boys and 46% were girls, with an age distribution as follows: birth to 5 years, 22%; 6 to 10 years, 44%; 11 to 15 years, 21%; and 16 years and older, 13%. The most frequent problems were negative behavior (18%), anxiety (15%), ADHD (12%), learning problems and school problems (17%), divorce and separation (9%), peer/self-esteem (7%), depression (6%), child abuse (6%), and developmental or medical problems (3%). These figures represent a decrease of 9% in the developmental or medical problems being referred to the psychology clinic as compared with an earlier 5-year survey by Hawk et al. (1987). It is not clear if the rate at which children with developmental or medical problems are referred has actually decreased or if the primary referral question for these children is now behavioral or emotional problems versus chronic illness or disability (Schroeder, 1996). Although we initially expected to see a significant number of children with physically related problems, we learned that not only do most children in outpatient clinics not have major medical or developmental problems, but also that those who have serious physical problems tend to be followed in tertiary settings that have their own psychologists.

A goal of psychologists in primary-care settings should be to enhance the development of children and reduce the number of children with significant emotional and behavioral problems through early identification and intervention. One way to determine if early identification and intervention occurs is to look at how many clients are seen and the length of time they are seen. At the Chapel Hill Pediatric office, an early survey by Hawk et al. (1987) indicated that 681 new referrals were received in a 5-year period. More recently (Schroeder, 1992) it was found that referrals had increased considerably, to 714 within a 2-year period. Currently new referrals average 37 per month or approximately 444 in a year. The length of time children and families are seen has remained fairly stable over time, with 13% seen for only one session and five sessions the mean length of time seen (Schroeder, 1992). Although the staff tries to focus on problems requiring short-term treatment, the reality is that in a population of 20,000 pediatric patients, one can expect that 200 children will have significant emotional or behavioral problems at any point in time. The parents and pediatricians do not want us to refer these cases out of the clinic, arguing for continuity of care and a working relationship with people with whom they have come to trust (Schroeder & Gordon, 1991). The dilemma is how to meet the extensive needs of this population and see the large number of other children with less significant problems. We have handled this by increasing our staff, but that solution also presents the problem of having to coordinate with more people within and across disciplines.

Chapel Hill Pediatrics staff have discovered that certain children are psychologically more vulnerable and benefit from brief intervention at particular stages of their development (e.g., the child with a chronic illness or developmental problem or the child who has been sexually abused) or when environmental stresses increase (e.g., when dealing with a parent with psychopathology or when the child with learning disabilities enters junior high) or when they have emotional or behavioral problems that persist at a subclinical level but are exacerbated by a certain developmental stage. Gordon and Jens (1988) described this as the *moving-risk model*, wherein these vulnerable children appear to need help at different points in their lives, but not necessarily ongoing treatment. Successful treatment does not necessarily mean a cure for these children (Schroeder, 1996). Rather, with periodic help they can be helped to learn to cope with the stresses of life. Thus, psychologists and pediatricians in primary care settings are offered the opportunity to follow children over the course of their development and help make the trajectory of that development more successful. This is perhaps one of the most rewarding aspects of working in a pediatric primary care setting.

Prevention Services

Prevention and early intervention services for children and their families have generally been given a low priority in federal, state, and local funding as well as in the private sector (Schroeder & Gordon, 1991). This is disappointing given the available information on the factors that place children at risk for significant emotional and behavioral problems. The primary care setting follows children over the course of their development and seems the ideal place to do prevention, but financial and time constraints limit the extent of this work. The type of prevention services offered is also guided by the population being served. For example, most community primary care settings serving children and families are private and serve clients who are usually well educated and middle class. Their needs and the services to meet those needs are likely to be very different from those for families who are struggling to provide food and shelter. The prevention services to be described should be read with that consideration in mind.

Parent education groups are a popular way to provide information to parents about developmental and management issues. In my group, the pediatricians offer prenatal parent groups that focus on health, development, and safety issues. There also are ongoing weekly group meetings for parents of newborn to 6-month-olds and of 7- to 24-month-olds. Parents bring their children to these groups, and the staff has found that a great number of them form supportive relationships outside the clinic. These latter groups are free to the parents, with the pediatricians paying the psychology group to run them. Other parent groups include a weekly hour and a half evening group that focuses on different ages and stages in development, and groups that meet over a period of 4 to 6 weeks and focus on a specific topic such as divorce or ADHD. Each month topics for the general parent groups are organized around a particular age. For example, a month of sessions might focus on toddlers with the following topics: ages and stages; toilet training; preventing power struggles; survival tactics: dinner through bedtime. For adolescence the topics might be adolescence: what to expect; balancing their needs: independence and rules; and tips for parenting during the adolescent years. The sessions are limited to 20 parents each and are organized to include a didactic presentation of material and an opportunity for questions and answers. Handouts that focus on the presented materials are provided. These sessions are advertised in the community and in the pediatric examination rooms; parents must register in advance for individual sessions, and there is a modest charge (Schroeder, 1996). There has not been a formal evaluation of the effectiveness of the groups, but consumer satisfaction questionnaires have high ratings, and the fact that classes have been ongoing and well-attended since 1973 indicates that they are meeting a need. Class popularity often results in two separate sessions on the same topic in order to accommodate the number of parents who wish to attend. There was no charge for the first 10 years these groups were offered, but the staff has not found that the current charge has decreased the number of parents attending the groups.

Cunningham (1995), who works in a private pediatric gastroenterology practice with three physicians, described a unique prevention activity that grew out of a support group for parents who had children with inflammatory bowel disease. The parents, as a way of providing information to other parents, organized a 1-day educational workshop that included a psychologist, physicians, and nutritionists from the community. Additional workshops on other topics of interest are being held on a biannual basis.

This group has also developed videotapes to give support and information about other gastroenterology problems and to have a children's library with books related to clinical issues such as digestion and elimination.

Written material is another medium Chapel Hill Pediatrics has used to provide prevention services to parents and children. Parents' first choice of an information source is books or reading material (Clarke-Stewart, 1978), although there is little empirical evidence on the effectiveness of books in preventing problems (Bernal & North, 1978). The staff developed a Parent Library in response to the continual requests of parents for reading material on child-related issues. The Parent Library is located in the receptionist's office, and an annotated list of books (organized by topic) in a three-ring notebook is kept in the waiting area. The books can be checked out for 2 weeks at no charge. Many of the books in the library have been selected from the Books for Parents and Children section of the *Journal of Clinical Child Psychology* (see, e.g., Schroeder, Gordon, & McConnell, 1987). This section was published several times a year from 1984 to 1990 and included reviews of books on divorce, sexuality education, sexual-abuse prevention, learning disabilities, developmental disabilities, general parenting, behavior management, step parenting, single parenting, death, medical problems, and other topics. The library is kept current by a review of publication catalogues on parent materials. These books are widely used by the general pediatric clientele, in addition to being used as adjuncts to treatment. The psychology practice buys and maintains the books and operates the library.

Parent handouts provide quick information or anticipatory guidance and typically are produced by drug companies for use in pediatric offices. Chapel Hill Pediatrics staff developed handouts about common problems to use as follow-up material for parents who use the call-in hour and to be used in conjunction with well-child physical examinations. For example, a toilet training handout was to be included in the 18-month physical examination. We have discovered, however, that unless the nurses remember to include the handout with the chart, the pediatricians do not routinely give these to the parents. It is usually a parent's request for information that results in a handout being given. Although this has been rather disappointing, particularly given this group of pediatricians' interest in and support for anticipatory guidance, it is not an atypical problem (Schroeder & Gordon, 1991). One observational study (Reisinger & Bires, 1980) of 23 pediatricians found that the time spent on anticipatory guidance averaged a high of 97 seconds for children under 5 months and a low of 7 seconds for adolescents. One way to ensure that certain areas are discussed with parents both before and after the birth of a baby is to include forms in the patient's medical chart that include the physical and psychosocial areas to be covered at the well-child visit (Christophersen & Rapoff, 1979). Without such a system, it is not likely that this information will be shared with parents at the proper "anticipatory" time. The staff has found that developing a checklist for the chart on developmental milestones and safety issues is best done as a joint psychologist–pediatrician effort and alerts both professions to areas considered important.

The call-in hour, offered twice a week, is a time when parents can ask questions about child development and behavior management concerns. Parents routinely call pediatricians for information, and the staff has found this to be an excellent way to make contact with parents when they have an initial concern. From the inception of this program in 1973, a log has been kept of the phone calls received, the nature of the parents' concerns, and the advice given to them (Schroeder & Gordon, 1991). Reports on the types and frequency of problems, as well as the effectiveness of the advice given, have been published in a number of sources (Kanoy & Schroeder, 1985; Mesibov et al., 1977; Schroeder et al., 1983). In general, the suggestions given to parents focus on environmental changes, rewarding and encouraging appropriate behavior, and punishing (using time-out by isolation or removing privileges) or ignoring inappropriate behavior. An important part of this program is to share information on appropriate developmental expectations and behaviors, so that the parents can put their children's behavior in perspective.

Telephone follow-up has indicated that the availability of the call-in hour and the specific suggestions given are rated highly by parents (Kanoy & Schroeder, 1985). On a 5-point scale (1 = not helpful and 5 = very helpful), every behavior category received ratings of 3 or above. However, suggestions for socialization problems (e.g., negative behavior, sibling/peer difficulties, personality/emotional problems) were rated as more effective than those for developmental problems (e.g., toileting, sleep, developmental delays). Only about 25% of the suggestions for sleep and toileting difficulties were rated between 4 and 5, whereas about 75% of those for socialization problems were rated between 4 and 5.

Kanoy and Schroeder (1985) found that parents were much more likely to use both the come-in service and the call-in hour when they had concerns about socialization (about 50% used both services) as compared with developmental problems (fewer than 30% used both services). The increased contact with professionals could account for the parents' finding the suggestions for concerns about socialization issues more helpful. In addition, when parents called about a developmental problem, they were usually concerned about a skill or ability their children had failed to acquire by an expected age, such as toilet training or sleeping through the night. Although the child's behavior was often considered within normal limits, staff found that providing only support and developmental information did not decrease parents' concerns. When this information was combined with suggestions for specific actions, the ratings for both developmental information and support increased. The effectiveness of giving specific suggestions also was evident for socialization problems (most often undesirable behaviors that children had acquired). Suggestions such as time-out and rewarding appropriate behaviors with stars gave parents specific strategies to use. It was on the basis of these findings that the parent handouts were developed.

One concern that staff had with the call-in hour was determining when a parent should be referred for more in-depth assessment or treatment. We have used the criteria that if a problem or concern did not remit after two or three contacts, the parents and child should be referred for further follow-up. In addition, referrals are immediately made when any of the following constellation of problems are evident (Schroeder & Gordon, 1991):

1. A parent has serious personal problems (e.g., depression, marital problems).
2. A child has multiple emotional and behavioral problems that occur across settings (e.g., home, school, neighborhood).
3. A family has multiple psychological problems or stress events (e.g., several children with problems).
4. The child exhibits behavior that has caused (or could cause) significant harm to self or others, or serious property damage.
5. There is evidence or suspicion of child abuse. This is reported to appropriate authorities for further investigation.
6. An infant or preschool child shows delayed development that has been targeted through standardized developmental screening tests and has not responded to stimulation recommendations within a 3 to 6 month period.
7. A child's general development or academic achievement is below the child's, parent's, or teacher's expectations.

Over the years, about 17% of the parents using the call-in hour have been referred for further assessment or treatment. Those parents who followed through with the referral rated the suggestion very highly, but one study (Kanoy & Schroeder, 1985) found that 33% of the parents who had been referred did not follow through with the referral suggestion. Now that more clinical services are readily available in the pediatric setting, it is rare that a parent does not follow through with the recommendation for referral.

The psychologists offer the call-in hour at no cost to the parents or pediatricians. It is, however, one of the best ways to demonstrate the importance of psychologists in the pediatric setting and, as such, is great publicity. It is advertised in the general information about the pediatric practice and in newspapers as one of the services offered by the practice. Anyone in the community may use the service.

Developmental screening is often a routine part of a well baby checkup for children up to age 3 years. This, however, was not a routine service in the Chapel Hill Pediatric practice, but as a result of the number of parents who called in with concerns regarding developmental delays the Denver Developmental Screening Test (Frankenburg & Dodds, 1967) was given to all children at their 3-year-old checkup. Calls about developmental delays decreased accordingly. Chapel Hill staff has found a number of children who could have benefited from extra stimulation at an earlier age and recently made a recommendation to change the age to 24 months and to consider a different screening instrument. Although staff has always been involved in the training of the nurses to do the screening, we have discovered that with frequent staff turn-over, it is important to have regular meetings to monitor test results and provide information on stimulation, referral sources in the community, and information on when to refer to a psychologist for a more extensive evaluation.

Assessment is an integral part of every contact, whether it is having a phone consult with a parent about a specific problem, consulting with the pediatrician about a child, helping a nurse deal with a fearful child, determining the need for treatment, or doing an evaluation that involves gathering and integrating information from multiple sources and with multiple methods to answer specific questions about a child or family. Both the parents and the pediatricians present a wide range of questions and problems that often demand concise, rapid, and "on-target" answers (e.g., "How do I tell my child his mother just died?," "What can I do to calm a 14-year-old girl who is having a panic attack in the exam room?," "How do I help a 5-year old answer questions about a birth mark on her face?"). There are also the more complex questions that demand a more extensive assessment (e.g., "I think my ex-husband is sexually abusing our daughter," "The teacher thinks this child has a learning disability and is hyperactive," "Should I be concerned that my 6-year old has developed a number of motor and verbal tics?")

Chapel Hill psychologists use a behaviorally oriented system for assessment that is based on Rutter's (1975) work, which we call a Comprehensive Assessment-to-Intervention System (CAIS). The CAIS is described in detail in Schroeder and Gordon (1991). The CAIS was developed initially as a framework to systematically and quickly assess a problem and offer suggestions to parents who used the call-in hour. It allows the clinician to get an understanding of the dimensions of the problem without needing to attach a label or initially categorize the problem with a system such as the *Diagnostic and Statistical Manual of Mental Disorders* (*DSM–IV*; American Psychiatric Association, 1994). This is particularly important in the primary-care setting because many of the referral problems would not be considered clinically significant or pathological although they may significantly impact the child or family's life (Schroeder, 1996). The CAIS system clusters information in six categories:

1. *The referral question.* It is important that you and the person asking the question are talking about the same thing. Reflecting back your understanding of the question is an effective and quick way to do this. For example, "It sounds like you are concerned about your child's toilet training and the different ways you and your husband are handling it."

2. *The social context.* Finding out who is concerned and why they are currently concerned and noting the parent's affect as he or she describes the problem gives a great deal of information about the nature of the problem. For example, a mother calmly states that her 12-year-old just tried to hang himself and she wants to know if she should be concerned.

3. *General areas.* Listening for information or asking questions about

the child's developmental status (physical or motor, cognitive, language, social, personality or emotional, psychosexual); parent and family characteristics (e.g., personality, psychopathology, social supports, marital status, parenting styles and techniques, sibling relationships); environmental characteristics (e.g., recent stressful events, subculture norms and values, socioeconomic status); and the consequences of the behavior (e.g., past and present management strategies; "pay-off" for the child; impact of behavior on child, parents, and environment; prognosis with and without treatment); and medical or health status (e.g., family medical or genetic problems, chronic illnesses, medications, current or past injuries, prenatal and early developmental problems).

4. *Specific areas.* Finding out about the type of problem, its situation specificity, changes in behavior, and the persistence, severity, and frequency of the behavior are important for determining the need for and planning intervention strategies.

5. *The effects of the problem.* Who is suffering, and will the behavior or situation interfere with the child's development?

6. *Areas for intervention.* Intervention can occur in a number of areas including development (e.g., providing stimulation, teaching new skills, changing behavior); parents (e.g., changing expectations, teaching new skills, treating parent problems, changing the emotional atmosphere); environment (e.g., changing environment, increase supports, helping child or parent cope with stress); consequences of the behavior (e.g., changing responses to the behavior or the pay off for the child); and medical or health issues (treating problem or effect of problem).

It is often not necessary to have all of this information to assess and plan intervention for a specific problem, but the format alerts the clinician to important factors to consider in assessing the problem. In our experience with the call-in hour, much of the necessary information is shared in the first 5 to 10 minutes of contact with the parent. Staff has found that the CAIS framework allows us to gather and process information efficiently, resulting in a quick understanding of the problem and how it should be handled, including referral for further evaluation.

Using the CAIS can also involve using standardized psychological testing. Standardized psychological testing requires facility with a range of assessment tools; being knowledgeable on the latest research (and fads); and understanding the federal, state, and local guidelines for various problems or services and developing a close working relationship with the schools. Observing children in the school setting, talking with teachers and discussing test results with not only the parent and child but also the pediatrician and teacher are usual parts of the assessment process.

The CAIS system is also helpful in assessing specific problems such as attention-deficit/hyperactivity disorder. The diagnosis of ADHD and the appropriateness of treating the disorder with stimulant medication are frequent questions in the primary care setting. Although pediatricians are the professionals most often asked to diagnose this disorder or treat the child with stimulant medication, they are not always in the best position to make these decisions. Their contact with the child is often limited, and gathering systematic information from the school and parents is often beyond their area of expertise. Through working with the psychologists, the pediatricians in the Chapel Hill practice have come to appreciate the complexity of diagnosing and treating ADHD and now refuse to prescribe medication without some formal assessment of the problem. Thus, if a child is suspected of having ADHD, we work not only with the child but also with the child's pediatrician, the school, and the parents to assess the behavior through formal psychometric testing, direct behavioral observations, parent and teacher questionnaires, and daily observational data (Schroeder, in press; Schroeder, 1996). If the child is diagnosed to have ADHD or attention problems, a trial of medication is often recommended along with recommendations for behavior management in the school and home. A trial of medication in our clinic involves a double-blind, placebo-controlled multimethod assessment of the effects of high and low doses of medication carried out over a 3-week period, and includes teacher and parent questionnaires, laboratory measures of attention, and academic analog tasks. This practice-based clinical protocol is based on a research protocol developed by Barkley (1990). This approach has not only proven to be clinically effective in determining the child's response to medication, but also has been positively received by the children and parents who feel it has given them a better understanding of the effects of the medication. It also presents the opportunity for long-term follow-up on the cognitive functioning of children on stimulant medication. The Chapel Hill staff is now considering the use of similar protocols for assessing the feasibility of other medications and the effect of medications used for conditions such as seizure disorders.

The CAIS has been particularly helpful in assessing child abuse and neglect, another frequent concern in primary care settings. These cases involve close collaboration between the medical, social services, mental health, and legal systems. The primary-care setting is an optimal place for the coordination of assessment for this difficult and complex problem. For example, as part of the state-funded Child Medical Evaluation program, the pediatricians provide physical examinations for abused children and the psychologists assist the Department of Social Services in the investigation process. Dr. Charles Sheaffer, a retired pediatrician in the Chapel Hill Pediatric practice, was responsible for developing many of the services for physically and sexually abused children in North Carolina. Through his efforts, the community and state's awareness of these problems has been raised. Furthermore, through weekly meetings with professionals from the Department of Social Service, the police department, and the mental health system, he encouraged learning about and coordinating this work in the best interest of the child. For example, in the 1970s, the number of times a child was interviewed was decreased by having the initial interview observed by the other involved professionals. Tape recording the session became an established procedure. Dr. Sheaffer

was also instrumental in getting the state to fund psychological evaluations for children for whom abuse or neglect is suspected or has been
substantiated. Chapel Hill Pediatric is now part of the statewide Child
Mental Health Evaluation Program, which involves answering a wide
range of referral questions, including "Has the child been abused?" "What
are the effects of the abuse?" "Is the mother or father capable of protecting
the child?" "Does the child need treatment?" "How will the child be affected
by going to court?" The coordination of this difficult but rewarding work
with other community agencies improves the chances for a successful outcome for both the child and the family.

Most psychologists use the word *treatment*, but psychologists in primary care are most often consultants to parents or teachers who carry out
the necessary program for change. Chapel Hill staff has found itself involved in a number of roles in the process of providing intervention services to children and families (Schroeder & Gordon, 1991) including,

1. *Educator*: Sharing information (verbal or written material), developing written material, offering parent groups, or helping parents or teachers to understand children's needs.
2. *Advocate*: Alerting the community to children's needs, speaking
   for the child in court, helping the parents negotiate the educational system, or advocating for the child's needs within the family
   system.
3. *Treatment provider*: Giving direct treatment to the child or family, or providing indirect treatment (e.g., intervention in the environment).
4. *Case manager*: Accessing and networking services to meet the
   needs of the child and family.

The role of case manager is particularly pertinent to the primary-care
setting. This involves networking the often fragmented and specialized
services of the community in order to meet the individual needs of the
child and family. This approach, as described by Hobbs (1975), involves
looking for unique ways to use the available services and for creative ways
to develop services that are needed but unavailable. It requires the clinician to be very familiar with the resources in the community and to become skilled in negotiating cooperation between agencies (Schroeder,
1996). It takes time to learn about a community and to develop these
relationships with people in day care settings, schools, recreational facilities, social services, and the legal system (i.e., police, lawyers, judges).
These relationships usually begin around a particular child, but they can
also be developed by presenting or sharing material, attending meetings,
and being active in the community.

The Chapel Hill Pediatric practice offers individual treatment for children and parents, as well as couple and family therapy. Although each
child and family is unique, the time spent dealing with recurrent questions
or problems can be cut significantly if materials and resources are easily
accessible and if there is a general plan of action. Protocols for treating

common childhood problems such as enuresis, encopresis, sleep, negative behavior, bad habits, and anxiety, and for stressful events such as death, divorce, and sexual abuse have been published in a book by Schroeder and Gordon (1991), *Assessment and Treatment of Childhood Problems: A Clinician's Guide.* Handouts for parents on these problems have also been developed and are available through the pediatric practice.

The empirical literature indicates that practitioners should be able to meet the needs of parents and children in a more cost-effective and efficient manner through groups; this appears to be particularly true in the primary-care setting. Although the Chapel Hill staff has offered group treatment for both parents and children that has focused on specific problem areas or life events, such as ADHD, divorce, social skills, sexual abuse, and stepparenting, it has actually been very difficult to provide a variety of treatment groups on an ongoing basis. We have had difficulties with scheduling and finding the right mix and number of children or parents at the right time—a problem that is probably not unique to the primary-care setting. Perhaps the availability of the preventive services and the easy access to short-term treatment decreases the need or desire for groups on specific problems. One treatment group that has been very successful, however, is for parents of children with ADHD. This is probably due to the significant number of children who are evaluated in the Chapel Hill practice for this chronic problem. The parents in the ADHD group meet for four consecutive sessions and then may attend a once-a-month support group. The staff also is very involved in the local parent groups focusing on children with ADHD and therefore is readily visible in the community.

The primary-care setting is also a good place to develop treatment programs in coordination with other agencies. In our community, for example, children who were sexually abused and their parents were not always able to access services or the available services were limited (Schroeder & Gordon, 1991). The Chapel Hill staff joined with the local Department of Social Services to get funding to provide group treatment for these children and their parents. The Department of Social Services provided a facility for the treatment and transportation for the families. The goal was to help the children and families deal with the complex emotional sequelae of the abuse and to find ways to cope effectively with the aftermath of the abuse in a timely manner. The ongoing children's groups were divided into preschool, elementary school, and adolescent ages, and met for 10 weekly sessions focusing on the issues of traumatic sexualization, stigmatization, betrayal of trust, and powerlessness (Finkelhor & Browne, 1986; Walker, Bonner, & Kaufman, 1988). The parents met separately and focused on the effects of abuse, the role of the legal system in abuse cases, problem solving for ways to meet their individual needs, and learning about ways to prevent the abuse from recurring. At the end of these sessions a determination was made for each child and family regarding the need for further treatment. Although the pre- and post-data plus the consumer satisfaction questionnaires indicated that the program was effective in treating these children and their families, the funding for the program was discontinued. In general, finding funding for prevention, assessment, and treatment programs is a constant problem for professionals in primary-care settings. In addition, with the advent of managed care, financial resources have further decreased, which makes it even less feasible to provide pro bono services to those families and children who are often in the greatest need. Nonetheless, the Chapel Hill staff continues to explore ways to collaborate with other agencies to provide needed services.

Community Consultation

Being in a primary-care setting gives the professional a great deal of visibility in the community, and also a great deal of responsibility to advocate for children. We have discovered that when the newspaper wants information about a particular issue (e.g., Is it morally right to tell children there is a Santa Claus?) or the court system wants information on a particular problem, they are just as likely to call the pediatric office as parents are to ask the pediatrician for advice on a whole array of issues. The staff has thus increasingly found itself in the position of having to interface with the community on a number of levels.

As noted previously, in the late 1960s and early 1970s, a pediatrician in the practice became the coordinator for all the community agencies involved with children who were physically or sexually abused. Regular meetings were held with representatives from the pediatric office, the police department, the schools, and the Department of Social Services, together with mental health professionals from the community. The focus of the meetings was initially educational, but it quickly moved to case-management issues. Problems of roles and responsibilities were worked out (sometimes hammered out!), and the result has been an ongoing coordinated community effort on behalf of these children (Schroeder & Gordon, 1991). At times the system falters, especially when new people are added to one of the agencies or new regulations change the nature of the services. However, the short- and long-term benefits of this work cannot be underestimated, as is demonstrated by the statewide Child Mental Health Evaluation Program and the contract with the local Department of Social Services to provide group treatment for children in the county who have been sexually abused.

Another example of community involvement grew out of the concern that children were not receiving sex education or sex-abuse-prevention training during their school years. After a number of meetings, the local school system agreed to start providing this information, but no earlier than in the 5th grade, and asked us to consult with them on materials and training. This initial effort was well received by the parents and children. Then, the unfortunate deaths of two 7-year-old girls who were sexually abused brought the reality of this danger to the forefront. Parents and teachers not only wanted sex education and sex-abuse prevention taught at the kindergarten level in the schools, they demanded it, and Chapel Hill staff helped them accomplish it.

The primary-care setting is often viewed in the community as "the" resource for children and parents, and if one is willing to give time and effort, it is not difficult to coordinate and share information. For example, both pediatricians and psychologists from the practice have been asked to provide training for the North Carolina Guardian Ad Litem program (a state program in which a person is appointed to look after a childs best interest), district judges, district attorneys, the Department of Social Services, the rape crisis center, the YMCA, day care centers, and many other community groups that are involved in the lives of children. Recently, after a 9-year-old committed suicide, we were asked to talk with the child's parents and siblings, consult with parents and teachers at the child's school, give information on suicide prevention to the child's minister for use in the funeral service, and field questions from other professionals in the community. All of this work was made possible by the community interaction concerning a particular child or family, which identifies problems and solutions that can then be applied to the benefit of other children in the community.

Training

Training professionals in a busy private clinic takes patience, time, and effort, which in part can be recouped by the trainees' work in the community or with families who cannot afford the full fee for service. The ultimate benefit is having more mental health professionals trained to work in primary-care settings, as well as pediatricians who are more aware of mental health issues and the desirability of having psychologists practice with them (Schroeder, 1996). In reality, however, not many physicians or psychologists working in primary-care settings are in a position to provide professional training. The mental health services at Chapel Hill Pediatrics began, in part, because of a training need and the willingness of a university to support training in that setting. A description of what kind of training can take place in primary care is worthwhile in the hopes that more university training programs will find ways to support this work.

As previously stated, from 1973 to 1982 graduate students, interns, and postdoctoral fellows in psychology; graduate students in social work; and medical students and residents participated in all aspects of the mental health services offered in Chapel Hill Pediatrics. The practice also participated in a training program developed by the Division of Community Pediatrics at the University of North Carolina at Chapel Hill Medical School (Sharp & Lorch, 1988). In 1982, all first-year pediatric residents (and fourth-year medical students who were taking an ambulatory pediatrics elective) began training with the goal of increasing their knowledge of the factors affecting a child's development by having them placed in community agencies serving children. This was a unique approach to training pediatricians in the biopsychosocial aspects of development, and in 1984 the program won the prestigious American Academy of Ambulatory Pediatrics Excellence in Teaching Award. The pediatric psychology practice was one of 25 community agencies involved in this training. Residents and medical students each spent one day a week for a month with a psychologist in the primary-care setting; they learned about the types of developmental and behavioral problems parents bring to the pediatric office, were trained to interview parents and to develop intervention strategies for common problems, and learned what a psychologist has to offer in a primary health care setting and when children should be referred for mental health services. The effort was to alert these residents at an early stage in their careers to the value of psychologists. Although I plan to survey the over 160 graduates of this program to determine how they now interface with psychologists, I already know that a number of them (3 in our area alone) have psychologists in their practices. This program was unique in a number of ways, including paying the psychologist to train the pediatrician. As is often the case, in 1992 the funds for this training program were cut, and opportunities to train residents have been limited since that time.

Other training has occurred over the years, including a 2-year postdoctoral fellow in psychology, who was jointly sponsored by our practice and the University of North Carolina (UNC) Medical School Department of Pediatrics; psychology interns spending 2 days a week for a year in the practice; and clinical psychology graduate students participating in the call-in hour and providing treatment one afternoon a week. Currently, psychology interns from the UNC Psychiatry Department spend a day a week for a 3-month rotation in the ADHD clinic. The majority of this training is done out of interest, with no monetary compensation, and thus interest in doing the training fluctuates over time.

Research

The primary health care setting is a fertile ground for psychological research (Wright & Burns, 1986). The sheer number of children who are developing along a normal continuum and are seen through their early developmental years offers opportunities for interesting developmental research. Moreover, the smaller number of children who have chronic physical and behavioral or emotional disorders encourages research on treatment effectiveness and longitudinal research on these problems (Schroeder & Gordon, 1991). The primary health care setting also offers the opportunity to evaluate the effectiveness of primary and secondary prevention programs. However, all of the previously mentioned problems in doing training (i.e., time, funding, resources) are true for research in primary care settings. In addition, the parents and pediatricians have to be convinced that the research will benefit them in some way. Major research studies, or even most minor ones, must have some type of outside support, given the financial and time constraints of the practicing psychologist. However, program evaluation can and should be an ongoing part of any psychology practice and can be done in the primary-care setting. Indeed, if psychologists want to practice in primary-care settings they will have to demonstrate the need for and the effectiveness of their services. Pediatricians will expect this, and reimbursement by insurance companies will require it.

Being close to several universities and medical schools has afforded numerous opportunities for both the pediatricians and the psychologists in the Chapel Hill practice to be part of research studies. For the most part, research has evolved out of clinical questions, and participation in the research has focused on helping to formulate questions to develop a credible and viable treatment or research protocol to be used in primary-care settings, providing space, and supporting parents and children to participate in the research. For example, our work with children who were sexually abused raised questions from the legal system for which we had no answers: "Can we believe what young children tell us about what has happened to them? Can children remember and report events as completely and as accurately as adults, especially when events may have been traumatic? Are children particularly vulnerable to suggestive and leading questions? What are the effects of repeated questioning on children's abilities to remember particular events?" (Schroeder & Gordon, 1991). To answer these questions we have collaborated with developmental and clinical psychologists from the university in a series of unfunded and funded studies.

An example of the research done in the Chapel Hill practice is a study of children's knowledge of sexuality. A common belief among professionals who testify in court on behalf of preschoolers who have been abused is that young children's knowledge of sexuality is limited, and therefore these children cannot describe sexual acts unless they have actually experienced them. To provide empirical evidence for this belief, we studied 192 nonabused children (ages 2 to 7) to determine their knowledge of gender identity, body parts and functioning, pregnancy and birth, adult sexual behavior, "private parts," and personal safety skills (Gordon, Schroeder, & Abrams, 1990a). There were significant age differences in children's knowledge of all areas of sexuality, but under the age of 6 or 7 years, children had little knowledge of adult sexual behavior. The children's sexual knowledge was directly related to their parents' attitudes about sexuality: Parents with more restrictive attitudes had children who knew less about sexuality than parents who had more liberal attitudes. A second study examined sexual knowledge of children for whom sexual abuse had been substantiated and an age-matched control group of nonabused children (Gordon, Schroeder, & Abrams, 1990b). This study indicated that sexually abused children do not necessarily have greater knowledge of sexuality than nonabused children of the same age. The children who were sexually abused, however, gave qualitatively unusual responses to the stimulus materials. For example, a 3-year-old withdrew in fright when presented with a picture of a child being put to bed by an adult. Carrying out this work in the primary-care setting tested our credibility with parents and children alike. Introducing the studies to parents actually gave us an opportunity to inform them about sexuality, sexual abuse, the importance of educating children, and the importance of learning more about children's development in this area. Very few parents refused to participate, and most were eager to receive the results of the studies.

A second line of research carried out in our practice is more basic and focuses on factors that influence the accuracy of children's testimony. This research initially was supported by a National Institute of Mental Health grant and examines children's memory for a personally experienced event, a physical examination (an analog to sexual abuse). The purpose of this research is to establish baseline data for children's memory over varying periods of time and to examine factors that influence children's memory (e.g., repeated interviews, use of props in interviews, reinstatement, prior knowledge of visits to the doctor, painful procedures, and traumatic injuries). This research has been presented and published extensively (e.g., Baker-Ward, Gordon, Ornstein, & Clubb, 1993; Baker-Ward, Hess, & Flanagan, 1990; Gordon et al., 1993; Ornstein, Gordon, & Larus, 1992). The clinical implications of this work are important, and guidelines for interviewing young children and evaluating their responses have been developed (Gordon & Schroeder, 1995; Gordon, Schroeder, Ornstein, & Baker-Ward, 1995). This basic research, born out of our clinical work and carried out by necessity in the primary-care setting, is an excellent example of the type of research that can be done in natural settings (Schroeder & Gordon, 1991). However, it could not have been done without the existing collaborative relationship we had with the pediatricians and staff and with university-based researchers.

Other research has looked at treatment effectiveness. For example, Martin (1988), as a doctoral dissertation in the University of North Carolina School of Public Health Department of Epidemiology, compared a group of 2- to 7-year-old children who had received treatment for noncompliance with a control group matched for age and level of noncompliance. In view of the number of children identified with this potentially persistent problem, and the desire to provide early intervention to change the course of the behavior, the research questions were whether the treatment would be effective and (given the age of the children) whether the behavior of the untreated control group would improve without intervention. The parent training program for the negative behavior was based on the work by Eyberg and Boggs (1989) and Forehand and associates (Forehand & McMahon, 1981). Martin found that at a 3-month follow-up, the 31 children in the treatment group showed clinically and statistically significant decreases in both the number and frequency of behavior problems. The behavior of the 22 untreated control children did not improve over the same time period. Although a longer follow-up period is desirable and usually possible in a primary-care setting, this information gave support for our continuing to provide this treatment. Other research on the effectiveness of the call-in hour (Kanoy & Schroeder, 1985; Mesibov et al., 1977) has already been described and gave credibility to continuing this unique way of helping parents and children. Data have also been used to improve a particular service. The clinical data of over a 100 children receiving the protocol for stimulant medication were analyzed with a focus on its effectiveness and ways to streamline the protocol to make it more cost effective (Riddle, 1993).

Doing any type of research in the primary setting presents obstacles: lack of sufficient time on the part of the doctors, nurses, and patients to collect extensive data; getting representative subject samples, which usually requires gathering data from several offices in several communities; lack of instruments that focus on the kinds of concerns reflected in a primary-care setting; developing collaborative relationships with the physicians, which takes time; and the lack of time and money on the psychologist's part to carry out the work. The importance of doing this work, however, is reflected in NIMH's and the Agency for Health Care Prevention and Research's funding of research on mental health services in primary health care settings. With the increased interest in providing mental health services for children and parents in this arena, data-driven approaches should be forthcoming. The work by the American Academy of Pediatrics Task Force on the Coding of Mental Health in children that has created the *Diagnostic and Statistical Manual—Primary Care (DSM–PC)* should help to identify emotional and behavioral problems in primary-care settings that are distinct from the psychiatric disorders (e.g. *DSM–IV*; American Psychiatric Association, 1994). These types of activities will generate further training, clinical services, and research in the primary-care setting (Schroeder, 1996, in press).

Knowledge and Skills to Work in Primary-Care Settings

At minimum, the training necessary for psychologists to work in primary-care settings includes a strong background in clinical child psychology with a life-span developmental perspective and the opportunity to work with preschoolers, children, and youth (and their parents) who are developing along a normal continuum; an internship or postdoctoral fellowship in a multidisciplinary clinic or hospital setting; and a strong background in behavioral approaches to treatment (Schroeder, in press). Given the range of problems and issues, the quick pace, and the number of contacts the psychologist confronts on a daily basis, experience in an ambulatory pediatric setting also is helpful, if not imperative, before launching a solo psychology practice with pediatricians. Psychologists are generally trained to assess and treat pathology, and the shift to prevention and health promotion in primary care requires a very different approach. For example, the length of time a patient is seen, their follow-up, and the coordination of services with other community agencies is very different for psychologists and the pediatricians. Psychologists working in primary care must be flexible and change the way they approach a case. For example, extensive interviews or diagnostic tests may not be needed, so one has to be prepared to gather information pertinent to the presenting problem(s) and formulate an intervention plan quickly. The plan then must be communicated to the parent and the pediatrician in a clear, concise, and timely manner. This involves a strong action-oriented approach and an ability to translate psychological information into a "usable form" (Drotar, 1995). Drotar stated, "A successful consultant needs consistently to deliver an extraordinary product: a practical intervention plan that also addresses the complexity of a clinical problem" (p. 223). Training for this work is most likely to take place in outpatient clinics connected with teaching hospitals (Drotar, 1995; Rosenthal, 1995). If a person lacks this experience, then he or she must be prepared to spend some time in training and have supervision readily accessible.

It should be apparent that considerable knowledge and a broad repertoire of skills are required for the effective practice of psychology in a primary-care setting. Among these skills, the ability to collaborate with professionals from other disciplines is central. Interdisciplinary collaboration requires both an appreciation of one's own discipline and a knowledge of the unique information, services, and perspectives of other disciplines. Each profession brings expertise to a collaborative relationship, and mutual trust is developed through the recognition and appreciation of each other's expertise. Drotar (1995) gave a thoughtful discussion of the necessary ingredients for psychologists to collaborate with pediatricians; the chapters by Hurley (1995) and Cunningham (1995) are particularly helpful in describing the process of this collaboration in community health care settings. In addition to knowing what unique skills can be brought to the pediatric setting, it involves learning to communicate information in ways that are understandable and useful to the pediatrician. Thus, one has to have some knowledge of the medical "culture" (e.g., language, expectations, administrative constraints, etc.) if one's professional expertise is to fit into that culture (Hamlett & Stabler, 1995). This usually requires educating and being educated and being flexible while continuing to have a strong professional identity. Hurley's (1995) description of the process of negotiating with and joining a group of pediatricians in private practice clearly demonstrates the necessity for these skills. Even when one has an established relationship with a pediatrician or group of pediatricians, ongoing communication is necessary. Being committed to communicating and finding ways to communicate with each other is a necessary ingredient to this work and will vary with the uniqueness of the individual setting. Another aspect of collaboration is networking with professionals in community service agencies.

There is no way a psychologist can provide all of the services needed by children and their parents, and collaboration with other agencies can provide needed services and help develop new ones. Networking takes time and is most often accomplished through collaborating around a particular child. It can also be done through giving presentations to groups and being involved in the community (e.g., attending meetings for groups focused on learning disabilities and developmental disabilities). The section on community consultation in this chapter gives a number of examples of how this can be done. These relationships are built up over years and need to be nurtured if one is to effectively build a liaison with another agency for services.

Learning how to keep careful records of contacts is particularly important in the primary-care setting. A patient is usually "shared," so information should be readily available. Psychologists in primary-care settings most often keep their own chart on a patient, but sharing that information in a brief note that could be put in the pediatric chart is important. This requires learning to provide factual information that does not breach confidentiality or include sensitive material. Each practice is unique, and it will take some skill to determine the most appropriate way to share this information. For example, at Chapel Hill, we developed a form for written referrals from (or to) the pediatrician with a section to give immediate feedback on the status of the case. This pressure-sensitive form provides a copy of this communication for both charts. We also use a similar form that allows feedback on patients who are being seen over time; this information is routinely shared once a month on those patients.

Having some knowledge of acute and chronic health conditions that affect children is important and allows one to communicate more easily with both the pediatricians and the nursing staff. It should be remembered, however, that even a psychologist who has had extensive experience in health care settings will not have an understanding of the full range of illnesses. Specific medical conditions such as asthma or cranial facial abnormalities will require familiarity with the psychological literature in each area to determine the best plan of action for a particular patient. Sharing information is a two-way street, and pediatric colleagues can provide important information on the diagnosis and treatment of a medical problem. It is through this sharing of information that the parents and children are most able to benefit from the pediatrics–psychology relationship.

In summary, some of the skills and knowledge needed for a psychologist to work in a pediatric primary-care setting include a developmental framework with a focus on normal physical, emotional, and social development; factors effecting the resiliency and vulnerability of children and their families; a health versus pathology perspective; a working knowledge of acute and chronic health conditions; an action-oriented approach to assessment and intervention of psychological problems; consultation skills; interdisciplinary skills; and communication and interpersonal skills. It should be obvious that this work takes a great deal of personal and professional commitment and requires flexibility as well as competence and confidence.

Implementation Issues

Establishing a psychology practice within a pediatric setting involves a respect for the each profession and a belief that a collaborative relationship will be mutually beneficial (Drotar, 1995). If the pediatrician has not had a previous relationship with the psychologist (e.g. Cunningham, 1995), it will take time, careful communication, and data to convince him or her that psychology has something to offer to the primary-care setting. Hurley's (1995) step by step description of this process is a wonderfully clear account of how this can be done; the reader is referred to that work for more information on the "entry process."

Once it is agreed that the psychologist would be a valuable colleague, then the exact nature of that relationship must be negotiated. Setting up a pediatric psychology practice in a primary health care setting is not dissimilar to establishing a private practice, but the options available to the psychologist in a primary health care setting will depend on the particular setting and the relationship the psychologist wants with the other professionals in that setting. It is usually not possible for a psychologist to be a partner in another professional group (e.g., pediatrics); thus, other options for association must be considered. As previously described, a psychologist may be employed by a pediatric practice, with a fixed salary or a salary based on a percentage of the collected receipts, or pay a fixed percentage of collected receipts to the pediatric practice. Another option is for the psychologist to establish an independent practice within the health care setting, with overhead paid by the psychologist. The administrative functions may be contracted to the pediatric practice or handled independently by the psychologist. Establishing an independent practice within the health care setting gives the psychologist the options of sole proprietorship, a partnership (if more than one psychologist is involved), or a corporation (Schroeder & Mann, 1991).

There are advantages and disadvantages to being an independent contractor or corporation versus being salaried. While the salaried position offers income stability and benefits, it does not allow the degree of autonomy wanted by many professionals in private clinical practice. Because of the amount of time spent on non-income-generating activities (e.g., curbside consultation, preventive services, follow-up conferences, time and effort to collaborate with a different profession, filling out endless managed care forms), a set income has some real appeal. However, it is important to note that this "down time" work must be done in any event and salaries in private practice are usually based on production, so it really comes down to a person's individual preference and the agreement one is able to work out with the pediatric practice.

The Chapel Hill pediatric psychology practice described in this chapter was established as an independent corporation and for the first 2 years paid the pediatric practice for overhead costs. As the pediatric psychology staff grew, we hired a secretary, obtained separate phone numbers, did our own billing, paid a fixed rent, and so forth, while still being physically located within the pediatric setting. Over a period of 14 years the number of psychologists and other mental health staff has increased to meet the ever-increasing demands for services. Staff have been added to meet specific patient needs. For example, the child development specialist was added for her skill in parent education, and the psychiatrist was added in response to the increased number of children and parents presenting with severe psychopathology and the need for a physician knowledgeable in psychotropic medication.

We have discovered that even when one is fortunate enough to find a seasoned and flexible colleague who is acceptable to both the psychology and medical staffs, it takes some time and additional adjustment for them to work in the primary-care setting. In our practice, the addition of new mental health professionals and the addition of new pediatricians and a nurse practitioner has demanded increased opportunities for the new staff to develop working relationships with each other. We are now planning to have joint educational/communication meetings once a month. The psychologists will rotate attending the monthly meeting of the pediatricians. We are also considering a jointly published newsletter for the parents. This need to foster the pediatrics–psychology relationship also has been reported as an ongoing issue in other practices (Cunningham, 1995; Hurley, 1995). Time is the issue, but ultimately it is agreed by those working in primary care that the benefits to the patients and both professions are worth it.

Another important implementation issue is negotiation for space. The space available in the primary health care setting is geared to medical rather than psychological needs; it is therefore important to negotiate for space that will permit privacy, in addition to flexibility to serve small children and families for diagnosis and treatment. It has been our experience that private pediatric offices are under renovation every 5 to 8 years; so although the clinician may have to start with less than optimal space, a goal to improve the space options as the value of the practice is demonstrated is usually realistic (Schroeder, in press). Due to the space constraints in the Chapel Hill Pediatrics practice, the mental health part of that practice recently moved to a building directly behind the pediatricians, keeping one office in the pediatrician's space. This decision was a difficult one for all involved, but we felt that our long-term collaborative relationship would survive the short physical distance separating us. It is uncertain how or if this arrangement will change our relationship; only time will tell. We have agreed, however, that if we all survive managed care, we will eventually move to another building that will once again house both the pediatricians and the mental health professionals. It is interesting to note, however, that the parents have actually appreciated the physical separation; they state that it provides them greater privacy and that the atmosphere is more conducive to mental health work.

Finally, it is important to have support staff to help coordinate and carry out the services in the primary-care setting. Pediatricians have long been aware that not only the nurses but the other office staff make it possible for them to carry out their work in the most efficient and effective manner. If you are sharing staff with the pediatrician, then it is important to train designated people to handle referrals, score screening questionnaires, route the myriad of calls (and emergencies) to the proper staff person or community agency, manage prevention services such as a parent library or parent hand-outs, schedule group meetings, and so on, as well as coordinate the variety of managed care requirements for mental health providers. It goes without saying that the office staff have to be friendly, composed, and efficient. Until recently the pediatricians and psychologists in our practice have shared a group administrator who managed the businesses and office staffs of both practices and negotiated the managed care contracts. However, the issues in managed care are different for psychologists than pediatricians, and this can present major problems for patients. Prevention and mental health services for children have never been well funded; and, with managed care, mental health providers are being asked to provide a full range of services at the lowest cost (Drotar, 1995). In our experience, it is not always feasible to deal with certain managed care systems that have contracts with the pediatricians. This means a patient must be referred out or pay the full fee. In our practice, the pediatricians are encouraging these patients to use our services and pay the full fee, but the effects of this decision will have to be monitored. This is likely to be an increasing problem and makes it imperative to demonstrate the value of psychology in the primary-care setting.

Time pressures are a constant issue in primary-care settings. The demands to see patients, collaborate with the pediatricians, consult with the community, provide prevention services, and keep up with professional reading and education plus either manage or help to manage the business aspects of this work can be overwhelming. In general, primary-care settings are very busy places, but the atmosphere is supportive, which makes the work less stressful. It is assumed that in a primary-care setting this is just the way one has to work (Schroeder, 1994). It is important to find ways to reduce the stress; and, if you are the only psychologist in the group, regular meetings with other psychologists in the community are essential. Drotar (1995) suggested that varying one's activities (e.g., teaching or doing research), can help to reduce the stress of this work. It is also important to realize that you will never meet all of the needs presented in primary-care settings and to limit the expectations of others and yourself. Despite the pressure, a common comment of those of us who work in this setting is "It is hard to imagine working in any other place!"

References

American Academy of Pediatrics, Task Force on Pediatric Education. (1978). *The future of pediatric education*. Evanston, IL: American Academy of Pediatrics.

American Psychiatric Association. (1994). *Diagnostic and statistical manual of mental disorders* (4th ed.). Washington, DC: Author.

American Psychological Association, Task Force on Comprehensive and Coordinated Psychological Services for Children: Ages 0–10. (1994). *Comprehensive & coordinated psychological services for children: A call for service integration*. Washington, DC: American Psychological Association.

Baker-Ward, L. E., Gordon, B. N., Ornstein, P. A., & Clubb, P. A. (1993). Young children's long-term retention of a pediatric examination. *Child Development, 64,* 1519–1533.

Baker-Ward, L. E., Hess, T. M., & Flanagan, D. A. (1990). The effects of children's involvement on children's memory for events. *Cognitive Development, 4,* 393–407.

Barkley, R. A. (1990). *Attention deficit hyperactivity disorder: A handbook for diagnosis and treatment*. New York: Guilford Press.

Bernal, M. E., & North, J. A. (1978). A survey of parent training manuals. *Journal of Applied Behavior Analysis, 11,* 533–544.

Burns, B. J., & Cromer, W. W. (1978). The evolving role of the psychologist in primary health care practitioner training for mental health services. *Journal of Clinical Child Psychology, 7,* 8–12.

Christophersen, E. R., & Rapoff, M. A. (1979). Behavioral pediatrics. In O. F. Pomerleau & J. P. Brady (Eds.), *Behavioral medicine: Theory and practice* (pp. 99–123). Baltimore: Williams & Wilkins.

Clarke-Stewart, K. A. (1978). Popular primers for parents. *American Psychologist, 33,* 359–369.

Cunningham, C. (1995). Developing a collaborative pediatric psychology practice in a pediatric primary care setting. In D. Drotar (Ed.), *Consulting with pediatricians: Psychological perspectives.* New York: Plenum Press.

Drotar, D. (1993). Influences on collaborative activities among psychologists and pediatricians: Implications for practice, training, and research. *Journal of Pediatric Psychology, 18,* 159–172.

Drotar, D. (1995). *Consulting with pediatricians: Psychological perspectives.* New York: Plenum Press.

Drotar, D., Strum, L., Eckerle, D., & White, S. (1993). Pediatric psychologists' perceptions of their work settings. *Journal of Pediatric Psychology, 18,* 237–248.

Eyberg, S. M., & Boggs, S. R. (1989). Parent training for oppositional-defiant preschoolers. In C. E. Schaefer & J. M. Briesmeister (Eds.), *Handbook of parent training: Parents as co-therapists for children's behavior problems* (pp. 105–132). New York: Wiley.

Finkelhor, D., & Browne, A. (1986). Initial and long-term effects: A conceptual framework. In D. Finkelhor & Associates (Eds.), *A sourcebook on child sexual abuse* (pp. 180–198). Beverly Hills, CA: Sage.

Fischer, H. D., & Engeln, R. G. (1972). How goes the marriage? *Professional Psychology, 3,* 73–79.

Forehand, R. L., & McMahon, R. J. (1981). *Helping the noncompliant child: A clinician's guide to parent training.* New York: Guilford.

Frankenburg, W. K., & Dodds, J. B. (1967). The Denver Developmental Screening Test. *Journal of Pediatrics, 71,* 181–191.

Gesell, A. (1919). The field of clinical psychology as an applied science: A symposium. *Journal of Applied Psychology, 3,* 81–84.

Gordon, B. N., & Jens, K. G. (1988). A conceptual model for tracking high-risk infants and making services decisions. *Developmental and Behavioral Pediatrics, 9,* 279–286.

Gordon, B. N., Ornstein, P. A., Nida, R. E., Follmer, A., Crenshaw, M. C., & Albert, G. (1993). Does the use of dolls facilitate children's memory of visits to the doctor? *Applied Cognitive Psychology, 7,* 1–16.

Gordon, B. N., & Schroeder, C. S. (1995). *Sexuality: A developmental approach to problems.* New York: Plenum Press.

Gordon, B. N., Schroeder, C. S., & Abrams, J. M. (1990a). Children's knowledge of sexuality: Age and social class differences. *Journal of Clinical Child Psychology, 19,* 33–43.

Gordon, B. N., Schroeder, C. S., & Abrams, J. M. (1990b). Children's knowledge of sexuality: A comparison of sexually abused and nonabused children. *American Journal of Orthopsychiatry, 60,* 250–257.

Gordon, B. N., Schroeder, C. S., Ornstein, P. A., & Baker-Ward, L. E. (1995). Clinical implications of research in memory development. In T. Ney (Ed.), *Child sexual abuse cases: Allegations, assessment and management.* New York: Brunner/Mazel.

Hamlett, K. W., & Stabler, B. (1995). The developmental progress of pediatric psychology consultation. In M. C. Roberts (Ed.), *Handbook of pediatric psychology, 2nd edition* (pp. 39–54). New York: Guilford Press.

Hawk, B. A., Schroeder, C. A., & Martin, S. (1987). Pediatric psychology in a primary care setting. *Newsletter of the Society of Pediatric Psychology, 11,* 13–18.

Hobbs, N. (1975). *The futures of children.* San Francisco: Jossey-Bass.

Hurley, L. K. (1995). Developing a collaborative pediatric psychology practice in a primary care setting. In D. Drotar (Ed.), *Consulting with pediatricians: Psychological perspectives* (pp. 159–171). New York: Plenum Press.

Kanoy, K., & Schroeder, C. S. (1985). Suggestions to parents about common behavior problems in a pediatric primary care office: Five years of follow-up. *Journal of Pediatric Psychology, 10,* 15–30.

Martin, S. L. (1988). *The effectiveness of a multidisciplinary primary health care model in the prevention of children's mental health problems.* Unpublished doctoral dissertation, University of North Carolina-Chapel Hill.

Mesibov, G. B., Schroeder, C. S., & Wesson, L. (1977). Parental concerns about their children. *Journal of Pediatric Psychology, 2,* 13–17.

Ornstein, P. A., Gordon, B. N., & Larus, D. M. (1992). Children's memory for a personally experienced event: Implications for testimony. *Applied Cognitive Psychology, 6,* 49–60.

Reisinger, K. S., & Bires, J. A. (1980). Anticipatory guidance in pediatric practice. *Pediatrics, 66,* 889–892.

Riddle, D. B. (1993, August). *Double blind protocol research within a pediatric practice.* Paper presented at the meeting of the 101st Annual Convention of the American Psychological Association, Toronto, Ontario, Canada.

Roberts, M. C. (1986). *Pediatric psychology: Psychological interventions and strategies for pediatric problems.* New York: Pergamon Press.

Roberts, M. C., & Wright, L. (1982). The role of the pediatric psychologist as consultant to pediatricians. In J. Tuma (Ed.), *Handbook for the practice of pediatric psychology* (pp. 251–289). New York: Wiley.

Rosenthal, S. L. (1995). Collaborative psychological practice in pediatric gastroenterology: Clinical issues and professional opportunities. In D. Drotar (Ed.), *Consulting with pediatricians: Psychological perspectives* (pp. 185–194). New York: Plenum Press.

Routh, D. K. (1970). Psychological training in medical school departments of pediatrics: A survey. *Professional Psychology, 1,* 469–472.

Routh, D. K. (1972). Graduate training in medical school departments of pediatrics: A second look. *American Psychologist, 27,* 587–589.

Routh, D. K. (1994). *Clinical psychology since 1917: Science, practice and organization.* New York: Plenum Press.

Routh, D. K., Schroeder, C. S., & Koocher, G. P. (1983). Psychology and primary health care for children. *American Psychologist, 38,* 95–98.

Rutter, M. (1975). *Helping troubled children.* New York: Plenum Press.

Salk, L. (1970). Psychologist in a pediatric setting. *Professional Psychology, 1,* 395–396.

Schroeder, C. S. (1979). Psychologist in a private pediatric office. *Journal of Pediatric Psychology, 1,* 5–18.

Schroeder, C. S. (1992, August). *Psychologists working with pediatricians.* Paper presented at the 100th Annual Convention of the American Psychological Association, Washington, DC.

Schroeder, C. S. (1994). Models of practice. *Progress Notes, 18,* 4–7.

Schroeder, C. S. (1996). Mental health services in pediatric primary care. In M. C. Roberts (Ed.), *Model programs in service delivery in child and family mental health* (pp. 265–284). Hillsdale, NJ: Erlbaum.

Schroeder, C. S. (in press). Collaborative practice: Psychologists and pediatricians. In R. J. Resnick & R. H. Rozensky (Eds.), *Health psychology through the life span: Practice and research opportunities.* Washington, DC: American Psychological Association.

Schroeder, C. S., Goolsby, E., & Stangler, S. (1975). Preventive services in a private pediatric practice. *Journal of Clinical Child Psychology, 4,* 32–33.

Schroeder, C. S., & Gordon, B. N. (1991). *Assessment and treatment of childhood problems: A clinician's guide.* New York: Guilford Press.

Schroeder, C. S., Gordon, B. N., Kanoy, K., & Routh, D. K. (1983). Managing children's behavior problems in pediatric practice. In M. Wolraich & D. K. Routh (Eds.), *Advances in developmental and behavioral pediatrics* (Vol. 4, pp. 25–86). Greenwich, CT: JAI Press.

Schroeder, C. S., Gordon, B. N., & McConnell, P. (1987). Books for parents and children on behavior management. *Journal of Clinical Child Psychology, 16,* 89–94.

Schroeder, C. S., & Mann, J. (1991). A model for clinical child practice. In C. S. Schroeder & B. N. Gordon (Eds.), *Assessment and treatment of childhood problems: A clinician's guide* (pp. 375–398). New York: Guilford Press.

Schroeder, C. S., & Wool, R. (1979, March). *Parental concerns for children one month to 10 years and the informational sources desired to answer these concerns.* Paper presented at the meeting of the Southeastern Psychological Association, New Orleans, LA.

Sharp, M. C., & Lorch, S. C. (1988). A community outreach training program for pediatrics residents and medical students. *Journal of Medical Education, 63,* 316–322.

Smith, E. E., Rome, L. P., & Freidheim, D. K. (1967). The clinical psychologist in the pediatric office. *Journal of Pediatrics, 21,* 48–51.

Stabler, B. (1979). Emerging models of psychologist-pediatrician liaison. *Journal of Pediatric Psychology, 4,* 307–313.

Stabler, B. (1988). Pediatric consultation-liaison. In D. K. Routh (Ed.), *Handbook of pediatric psychology* (pp. 538–566). New York: Guilford Press.

Walker, C. E., Bonner, B. L., & Kaufman, K. L. (1988). *The physically and sexually abused child: Evaluation and treatment.* Elmsford, NY: Pergamon Press.

Wilson, J. L. (1964). Growth and development in pediatrics. *Journal of Pediatrics, 65,* 984–991.

Wright, L. (1967). The pediatric psychologist: A role model. *American Psychologist, 22,* 323–325.

Wright, L., & Burns, B. J. (1986). Primary mental health care: A "find" for psychology. *Professional Psychology: Research and Practice, 17,* 560–564.

Zill, N., & Schoenborn, C. A. (1990, November). *Developmental learning and emotional problems: Health of our nation's children,* United States 1988. Advance Data: National Center for Health Statistics, Number 190.

Part III

Implications for
Professional Psychology

11

Emerging Perspectives in Child Mental Health Services

Vera S. Paster

Child Mental Health Services: A Troubled Nonsystem

Mental health care for seriously emotionally disturbed children (SED) has long been cited as woefully inadequate in relation to any standard of equity. A most effective early challenge to this state of affairs was delivered by the Joint Commission on the Mental Health of Children (1969). The commission's report became the foundation for an energized advocacy for change that continues to date. The Joint Commission's study was followed by the President's Commission on Mental Health reports, in particular the reports of the subtask panels on Infants, Children and Adolescents, and on Primary Prevention (1978). The report from the Select Committee on Children, Youth, and Families (1990) was another authoritative focus on the nation's neglect of its emotionally distressed children. Thirteen years after the Joint Commission's report, the Children's Defense Fund sponsored another study of the states' patterns of care of emotionally disturbed children, *Unclaimed Children* by Jane Knitzer (1982; see chapter 1 of this volume for further discussion by Knitzer). This study found that approximately 8% of all children who had "serious" emotional and mental disorders and an additional 10–12% who had "significant" problems were not included among those for whom a particular agency had mandated responsibility for service. The study further documented that of the 3 million children with serious emotional disorders, two thirds were not receiving the care they needed, and many others were inadequately provided for (Knitzer, 1982; Stroul & Friedman, 1986).

Despite improvement in particular modalities of treatment and continuing effort to improve the scope of child mental health, progress has been limited. The state of affairs described by Knitzer has remained essentially the same. Recent cutbacks in human services, including mental health care, combined with the overall failure of many states to keep the promise to transfer funds from closing state hospitals to community-based

I wish to acknowledge with thanks the help of the following persons: Lenore Behar, Mary Campbell, Joan Dodge, Joy Dryfoos, Chris Koyanagi, Judith Meyers, Vestena Robbins Rivera, Yvette Rountree, Brian Smedley, Ruby Takanishi, and Brian Wilcox.

mental health services, has resulted in a net decrease of funds for children's mental health. According to the U.S. Department of Health and Human Services, between 1975 and 1986 the number of admissions of youth under 18 years of age to state and county mental hospitals dropped from 25,252 to 17,048. During the same period, psychiatric admissions to general hospitals, which are always short term and are in the community, were generally stable. Admissions to private psychiatric hospitals, however, almost tripled. There were 15,426 in 1975 and 42,703 by 1986. The phase out of public hospitalization left a void to be filled by private, for-profit psychiatric hospitals. Aided by their advertisements, they tapped into the belief that hospitals make sick people well.

There are a number of apparent discontinuities in the current system of care. Troubled children manifest their problems in many spheres. They are symptomatic at home and often exhibit behavior and learning problems in school. In addition, they often have health problems and accidents; get into trouble with the law; are abused, abandoned, neglected, and orphaned; and are socially isolated. They usually remain in the system to which they are initially thrust by the accident of the timing of a particular symptom. The emotional needs of some of these children may be unrecognized or unaddressed as a result. Other biases sometimes exert major influences on the kinds of services received. For example, Lewis, Balla, and Shanok (1979) studied a year's admissions to the public system of Connecticut. They found that children matched for emotional disturbance, behavior disorder, intelligence, age, and other factors were routed into the mental health system or the juvenile justice system on the basis of race. White children were classified emotionally disturbed, African American were classified as delinquent.

Likewise, there is a two-tier system based on income. The poor and those who have exhausted insurance benefits and private resources tend to be relegated to overburdened public systems, while greater choice and, usually, more adequate care is available in the private and voluntary fee charging systems. If the family's tolerance is limited and the child's symptoms are considered intractable or offensive, the child is more likely to be placed in a residential setting, often a hospital (a state hospital if the child is poor), and, increasingly, a for-profit hospital if the family is insured. Until very recently there were few alternatives. There are gaps within the mental health system, sometimes impenetrable barriers between systems, and often the barrier of competition instead of cooperation. According to Friedman (1984), the current situation lacks provisions for consistent integration of multiple services from agencies that in combination and sequentially could address the needs of this population.

Another problem that has hindered progress is a traditional belief that relief from the negative forces in the family will help children, because parents are and have been responsible for the child's pathology. Accordingly, it has been thought that children with serious disturbance are better served if removed from the home temporarily, until they are strong enough, or permanently for their long-term protection. Thus, the residential treatment center or hospital, with the often unfulfilled promise of intensive, milieu treatment of the child, becomes the treatment of choice. This type of treatment continues despite the fact that residential care, especially hospital placement, (a) is disruptive to the family and to the child's lifestyle; (b) can be pathologizing, resulting in a negative self-concept; (c) is often interrupted by exhausted funds through insurance limits; (d) may be absent in follow-up care, and (e) is often expensive. State officials and child advocates alike have long opposed overreliance on hospitalization by default.

In sum, the problems of our current response to emotionally disturbed children and their families include issues of principle, proprietorship, and availability. Agencies and services are not typically organized around the recognition that children are one unit of a complex system that includes immediate and extended family members, school, health, and social welfare agencies, religious organizations, and perhaps community forces. Moreover, mental health service providers are not organized to include families or to collaborate with other agencies. Instead, agencies and practitioners tend to function as independent entities, protective of their authority and autonomy, and reluctant to collaborate with other agencies or disciplines or even with members of their own discipline, except as the leader in charge of the patient. Likewise, family members tend to be treated as clients or patients rather than as fellow problem solvers. Most problematic is the lack of mental health care proportionate to the need and a lack of choices other than psychotherapy once or twice a week or inpatient care. Many of the services that are available have formidable barriers for access. Besides capacity there are financial, diagnostic, geographic, linguistic, and cultural barriers that screen out many emotionally disturbed children who require the help that an agency could offer. Another aspect of the availability problem is the separation of systems. The tendency is to seek remedy for the child's problems within the system in which the child is manifesting the disorders. If the child and family are involved in two or more agencies, such as a school and the juvenile justice system, there is a good chance that the resources of the mental health system will not be integrated into the planning and delivery of the child's psychological treatment.

The Emerging System of Care

When the Select Committee on Children, Youth, and Families of the United States House of Representatives found that child mental health services were failing families and children and required redirection and redesign, the federal Child and Adolescent Service System Program (CASSP) was created in 1983. (It is now the Center for Mental Health Services of the Substance Abuse Mental Health Services Administration, U.S. Department of Health and Human Services.) CASSP was established to assist states and communities to develop systems of care for severely emotionally impaired children and youth. All 50 states and some territories have been allotted funds for these purposes, and the Child Mental

Health Services Initiative provides grants to states and communities to develop community based services. The 1994 budget allocation for this program was $35 million. In addition, technical assistance projects were launched by the Child, Adolescent and Family Branch, including the CASSP Technical Assistance Center at Georgetown University, the Research and Training Center for Children's Mental Health at the University of South Florida, and the Research and Training Center on Family Support and Children's Mental Health at Portland State University. Furthermore, Public Law 102–321 mandates comprehensive mental health planning for children as part of the mental health block grant funding process.

According to Stroul and Friedman (1986), there are a number of central values and guiding principles within CASSP. The values are that (a) programs should be child centered and family focused, with the needs of the child and family determining the type and mix of services provided; (b) services should be community based; and (c) the system and services should be culturally competent for racially and ethnically diverse populations. Core principles include the following:

1. Emotionally disturbed children should have access to a comprehensive array of services that address the child's physical, emotional, social, and educational needs.
2. They should receive individualized services according to their individual needs.
3. Services should be the least restrictive that are appropriate.
4. Families should participate in the planning and delivering of services.
5. Services should be linked, coordinated, and mutually planned.
6. Case managers should facilitate coordination and integration of the multiple services needed by the child.
7. There should be early identification and intervention for children with emotional disturbance.
8. There should be a smooth transition from one service system to another, especially when age limits for eligibility are reached.
9. The rights of children with emotional disturbance should be protected and promoted.
10. Children with emotional disturbance should receive needed services that are responsive to their special needs and their cultures, and are provided on an equal basis notwithstanding race, religion, national origin, sex, physical disability, or other characteristics.

CASSP Components

States and communities are expected to establish a set of essential child mental health services that can be expanded to include more choice. These services are function-specific rather than agency-specific in their operation. Health care, for example, can be provided by a recreational program, and education can be provided by a hospital. These core services are intended to be integrated by a case manager, who seeks to ensure that they are planned and delivered as an integrated whole. This maximizes access to appropriate care, optimizes collaboration among systems, and allows for flexibility in funding services.

The CASSP conceptualization of the child mental health service system is comprehensive (Koyanagi, 1995; Rivera & Kutash, 1994; Stroul & Friedman, 1986). In essence, it provides an ideology to guide system review and development for improved child mental health care. More specifically, the CASSP model delineates eight dimensions, or broad categories, of service that are to be addressed at the local level:

1. Mental health services,
2. Social services,
3. Educational services,
4. Health services,
5. Substance abuse services,
6. Vocational services,
7. Recreational services, and
8. Operational services.

Operational services consist of case management, juvenile justice services, family support and self-help groups, advocacy, transportation, legal services, and volunteer programs. Operational services are considered critical in determining whether the system of care will be effective. Flowing from this conceptual framework are numerous types of services that children and families may need (see Koyanagi, 1995; Koyanagi & Brodie, 1994; Stroul, 1993; Stroul & Friedman, 1986, for more comprehensive descriptions).

Primary prevention. The mental health dimension rests on the foundation of primary prevention as a conceptual base and program guide, recognizing the need to focus on mental health rather than committing all system resources to the unrelenting group of children who become severely involved (Albee, 1986; Presidents Commission on Mental Health, 1978). The primary prevention component has two foci: (a) it seeks to combat noxious social forces that traumatize people in communities, undermining their sense of well-being, and (b) it promotes healthy skills, behaviors, and attitudes through programs offered to "normal" children, families, agency personnel, community members, and those who are in especially vulnerable circumstances. Examples are social-skill building experiences for timid children, conflict resolution for the aggressive, and self-esteem and confidence-building exercises for youth in transition.

Consultation and education. The mental health consultant is available to review programs; provide professional support and information to parents, service providers, and others concerning supportive problem solving; and add mental health perspectives when useful. Education activities include presentations, educational campaigns on relevant mental health issues, teaching, case finding, and promoting psychological understanding for children, families, and caretakers. Except for the most committed programs, prevention, consultation, and education services have to be neglected by the community mental health organizations because they do not readily yield fees for service. CASSP recognizes the importance of this and aspires to reestablish and sustain these components.

Early identification and intervention. Early identification and intervention programs are secondary prevention services that direct the system to intervene as early as possible in the life of the young disturbed child, or at the earliest time in the sequence of a progressive emotional dysfunction. Collaboration with other agencies, such as baby health clinics, pediatricians, and preschool centers; school screening for learning (Silver, Hagin, & Beecher, 1981) and emotional problems (Cowen et al., 1975); and other outreach programs provides opportunities to discover, prevent, reduce and, at the very least, plan for services that will be needed by that child and family. The caveat in implementing this aspect of comprehensive care is to carefully avoid negative labeling of identified children, especially because it is likely that for the most part poor children who receive care in the public sector will be subject to such screening and labeling.

Assessment. To achieve a diagnostic understanding of the individual's problems, a comprehensive evaluation of the child, family, and social context—including strengths and weaknesses—is necessary. This evaluation results in an objective basis for developing a treatment plan specific to the needs of the particular child and family. Formal psychological, neurological, and educational tests have a place in this assessment, as do other specialized examinations, as indicated. The latter is available through ongoing collaboration among the relevant agencies.

Outpatient treatment. Outpatient mental health services represent the traditional and basic approach to children's mental health problems. They are historically based on the child-guidance-center model of regularly scheduled treatment appointments with the child patient for individual, group, or family therapy. One or both parents are almost always involved, and psychotropic medication may accompany the treatment (Casey & Berman, 1985; Sowder, 1979). Indeed, 87% of children and youth receiving mental health care have been shown to rely on outpatient treatment (Sunshine, Witkin, Atay, & Manderscheid, 1991).

CASSP evaluates outpatient care according to timeliness, intensity, and accessibility. These crisis-intervention programs seek to provide the earliest possible response (sometimes on a walk-in basis) when families need immediate care (timeliness). Intensity refers to the amount of service available to the family. In this regard, CASSP promotes an individualized, need-based approach. *Accessibility* refers to the availability of the program to potential recipients of service. Is it geographically reachable within reasonable travel times, and is transportation available and affordable? Are the hours for service practical for a working parent, or for one with many children? Are offices psychologically accessible, culturally inviting, and nonstigmatizing? Whether it is in the office of the independent practitioner, a child-centered clinic, or part of a hospital, or offered by a free-standing mental health center, CASSP recognizes the outpatient service as the basic component of a comprehensive mental health system.

Home-based services. This is a more recently developed component recommended as a preventive alternative to out-of-home placements. Children and families in need of this service tend to be crisis prone and highly troubled. Home-based services provide up to 24-hour coverage for a family in its home in an effort to support, treat, and educate family members, empowering them towards stabilization and family preservation.

This program is controversial. Some object to the expense because a full-time worker or even a team can work with a family on a 24-hour basis over time. Furthermore, child protection advocates believe that child removal is often in the better interest of the child, relegating parental rights and family preservation to secondary consideration in these circumstances. Counterarguments reinforce the belief that the child's family is the best milieu for the child's emotional growth, except if dangerous, and that children removed from their homes become double victims as essentially homeless wards of the state. In addition, when home-based service enables successful treatment of the child, there are important long-term financial gains (Hinckley, 1984; Hutchinson & Nelson, 1985).

Day treatment. Day treatment provides education, counseling, and family interventions for at least 5 hours a day to children and youth. Centers are located in various settings, including free-standing facilities, hospitals, schools, and mental health centers. They are considered the most intensive of available outpatient mental health interventions. It has been estimated that approximately 65–70% of children treated in this manner are eventually reintegrated into regular school systems (Stroul & Friedman, 1986), which is a preferred alternative to placement in more restrictive and expensive residential programs.

Emergency services. Crisis hotlines, mobile outreach teams, walk-in crisis centers, shelters, crisis group homes, hospital emergency rooms, and short-term inpatient beds make up the emergency services component. Education programs directed to children's management of crises and training teachers, police, parents, and other community caretakers to recognize and respond to children in crisis may also be included. Crisis programs are small, staff is flexible, and service is available 24 hours a day, 7 days a week. Client assessment and follow-up planning are integral aspects of the service. Not only do crisis services prevent long-term out-of-home placements, they reduce such tragedies as loss of life by reckless self-endangerment or suicide.

Therapeutic foster care. Therapeutic foster care is a relatively new component of care that is still being defined. There is agreement that it seeks to provide a therapeutic surrounding for troubled children in a nurturant family setting. Therapeutic foster parents work closely with professional staff and the biological parents to support the child's treatment. These programs actively collaborate with the schools and other agencies, as appropriate. Short-term therapeutic foster care can be especially effective as a transition from discharge from residential treatment programs to home or independent living.

Therapeutic group care. Group homes that include 5 to 10 children may be located in regular houses in the community and led either by a set of staff "parents" on a 24-hour basis or by shift staff. A variety of therapeutic interventions are provided to children placed because of emotional difficulties (rather than a need for a nonabusive home situation).

Therapeutic camp services. Wilderness camp experiences offer intensive peer group support and cooperation and opportunities to develop self-reliance and a sense of competency. The challenge is to link intensive wilderness experiences with the home settings of the youth and with their families, because by definition and design these camps are far removed from the youths' familiar psychosocial and geographical setting.

Independent living services. These are living arrangements that prepare youth, especially those who "age out" of special education programs, for employment and independent living. The programs may be in therapeutic group care, residential treatment centers, day treatment, or other program settings. The content emphasizes vocational training and work experience, as well as the rudiments of living independently. The youth are given instruction and practice in managing money, paying bills, traveling, handling their social and recreation needs, and the like. Supervised apartment living in group or roommate situations may be arranged prior to launching the young person to complete independence.

Residential treatment services. Residential treatment services are controversial for many advocates of community-based services. Contention arises because "being put away" may be seen as punishing and pathologizing for children whose disturbance does not warrant the extreme of residential treatment but who are placed for such reasons as lack of family tolerance of the child's problems, lack of alternative, less restrictive programs, or lack of access to appropriate programs.

Residential treatment centers (RTC) may include psychiatric hospitals, long-established residential centers, and campus programs with smaller cottages. Two prominent treatment paradigms are that of milieu therapy and the Re-Ed model (Hobbs, 1979). RTCs tend to be long-term placements (6 months or longer).

Crisis residential services. These are community-located residential or shelter placements (nonhospital) that provide short-term, intensive treatment to avert hospitalization at a time of acute crisis. They include crisis homes in which trained couples serve as foster parents or crisis-stabilization units in free-standing facilities. The youngsters require secure residential placement for several days to 4 weeks. During that time, the child's family is closely involved and follow-up services are arranged.

Inpatient hospitalization. CASSP recommends use of hospitalization for two functions, as a back-up to less restrictive programs for up to several weeks during a child's period of severe breakdown or crisis and as a place for comprehensive 24-hour diagnostic observation and evaluation for a limited period of time (usually 30 days). First of all, less restrictive programs are often more willing to accept severely disturbed children if they are able to hospitalize the child for brief periods when their program cannot cope with occasions of the child's acute distress. This works best when there is a collaborative arrangement of shared responsibility for the treatment of the child by the less restrictive program and the hospital, until the child and program no longer have need of this safety net. Second, a more comprehensive diagnostic understanding of the child's problems and therapeutic needs, accomplished by a multidisciplinary professional team during 30 days of 24-hour testing and observation, can inform planning of particular components selected for individualized work with the child and family.

Summary. The foregoing is the present formulation of a comprehensive system of care to be available to children with serious emotional disturbance. The range is from the least restrictive service, primary prevention, to the most restrictive, indeterminate lengths of time in a psychiatric hospital. All of the program components listed have important contributions to make when made available in accordance with an individualized, comprehensive plan.

Research efforts are underway to determine whether these expectations are being met. Definitive answers as to the efficacy of large-scale, CAASP interventions are not yet available, but emerging research is promising (Kutash & Rivera, 1996). There are numerous evaluative efforts underway across the nation, many of which report positive quantitative and qualitative findings (see Illback, chapter 12, this volume). However, only a handful are controlled studies. In general, it appears that systems of care initiatives involving intensive case management, home-based services, and therapeutic foster care are associated with positive service-level outcomes such as reduced residential placement, placement stability, and less intensive and restrictive treatment modalities. Evidence of differential treatment outcomes for children served in these systems has not yet been found. (Bickman et al., 1995; Friedman & Burns, 1996; Kutash & Rivera, 1996). At the same time, there is considerable evidence for the effectiveness of many of the specific program components (e.g., case management, therapeutic foster care, day treatment) associated with this approach. (See Kutash & Rivera, 1996, and chapters 8 and 12 of this volume for more comprehensive discussions of system of care research.)

System of Care Funding and Support

Government Support

The CASSP program was launched in 1983 with $1.5 million awarded to 10 states for planning, coordinating, and providing technical assistance to community-based services (Koyanagi & Brodie, 1994). Subsequently, 40 other states were added to the 10, so that by 1995 CASSP had allocated $12.1 million to the programs. It also funds 29 states for infrastructure development. As has been noted, CASSP has funded a technical assistance unit at Georgetown University's Child Development Center and two research and training centers. One is at the Florida Research and Training Center for Children's Mental Health at the University of South Florida in Tampa, and the other is at the Research and Training Center on Family Support and Children's Mental Health at Portland State University. The Center for Mental Health Services of the U.S. Department of Health and Human Services has added support to the CASSP concept of community-based, integrated, family-centered systems of care for emotionally disturbed children by funding the Washington Business Group on Health to sponsor the National Resource Network for Child and Family Mental Health Services. NRN provides training and technical assistance to urban centers, small cities and counties, and rural communities organized into "hubs." Hub directors and staff develop expertise, resources, planning for financing, and administrative structures to help these communities succeed in implementing desired service systems (National Resource Network, 1996).

CASSP has also provided grants to eight research demonstrations to determine the effectiveness of innovative models of service and 28 grants for state-wide family networks to improve service systems. The Child Mental Health Services Initiative, or Comprehensive Community Mental Health Services for Children Program, was established by Congress in 1992 under the Alcohol, Drug Abuse, and Mental Health Administration Reorganization Act, PL 102-321. From $5 million in 1992 to $60 million in fiscal year 1995, 22 sites in 17 states were funded for approximately $1 million each to fill in gaps and to expand the system of care model. The Washington Business Group on Health was funded to establish a National Resource Network for Child and Family Mental Health Services, providing a network of experts to offer technical assistance, training, and support to these projects.

Foundation Support

Foundations have played an essential role in redesigning systems of care. The Robert Wood Johnson Foundation has awarded $20.4 million in 5-year grants to eight state and community partnerships to demonstrate integrated systems of care. These Mental Health Services Projects for Youth are located in California (Family Mosaic), Kentucky (Bluegrass IMPACT), North Carolina (Children's Initiative), Ohio (Connections), Oregon

(The Partners Project), Vermont (New Directions), and Wisconsin (Project FIND). The Annie E. Casey Foundation has funded the Urban Child Mental Health Initiative. These programs implement CASSP networks in high-poverty, inner-city, urban centers. Each site is expected to develop neighborhood governance boards that will establish close ties with local and state governments. In 1992, 12 states were awarded planning grants for this program, and in 1993, 4 states were awarded 4-year service-development grants in urban neighborhoods in Massachusetts, Florida, Texas, and Virginia. The Federation for Families for Child Mental Health is also funded by the Casey Foundation to provide technical assistance to these demonstration sites.

Demonstration Projects

According to Cole and Poe (1993) and others, the programs in Ventura County, California; Fort Bragg, North Carolina; and San Francisco are especially successful models, as are the state-level initiatives in Kentucky, Pennsylvania, Virginia, and Vermont. These programs are CASSP, foundation, or state funded. They all have expanded community-based services, use an individually planned package of treatment services developed for each child, have flexible funding and administrative mechanisms to facilitate dealing with each case as a special case, and use multidisciplinary and interagency teams that include family representatives and the child to plan services. These programs all use case managers. Two examples, The Ventura and North Carolina CHAMPUS plans, illustrate the favored systems for emotionally disturbed children.

The Ventura model was formally initiated in 1985, so it is one of the oldest community-based systems of care. It is directed to emotionally disturbed children who are at risk of out-of-home placements. It uses funds formerly allocated for institutional care for these coordinated, community-based alternatives. Agencies collaborate, developing agreements and protocols for individual children and their families. This system has been so successful in achieving its objectives that it has been funded in three additional California counties and is to be extended throughout the state (Family Impact Seminar, 1994; Koyanagi & Brodie, 1994).

The Fort Bragg Child and Adolescent Mental Health Demonstration Project is an iteration of CHAMPUS for eligible children under age 18. This is a program for military dependents. The project was developed and is operated by the North Carolina Department of Human Resources under contract with the Department of the Army, and thus is a federal–state partnership. The services expand those provided under CHAMPUS, with no out-of-pocket expenses or deductibles for the families. It has provided the first opportunity to implement a comprehensive, fully integrated, community-based continuum of care for children on a large-scale basis with a single point of entry, a system for case monitoring and management, and a single-payer source. Clinical services are subcontracted to a child mental health clinic arrangement that either provides the treatment or manages and coordinates it. The effectiveness of this project has been concurrently evaluated by Vanderbilt University, using two control CHAMPUS sites (Behar et al., 1995).

It was found that the Demonstration Project reduced use of inpatient psychiatric hospital and residential treatment-center care, key goals of the program. Access to care was improved, partly by making a range of mental health services available in many community settings, and waiting time for service was reduced from 5 months to 3 weeks. Approximately three times as many children were served at the demonstration site as at the comparison sites. Demonstration-site care was of high quality, and parents and youth were more satisfied. Interestingly enough, however, clinical outcomes were uniformly positive, with no significant differences between the Demonstration site recipients of care and those treated at the control sites. Furthermore, costs per client were "substantially higher" at the demonstration site (Behar et al., 1996, p. 369). These findings raise many questions. The National Institute of Mental Health has funded a 3-year followup of the participants that will help to understand the true costs and gains involved.

Medicaid

Medicaid was enacted in 1965 as Title XIX of the Social Security Act. It is a federal–state program that pays medical bills for certain low-income people who cannot afford to do so themselves. The federal government prescribes certain requirements and options, and each state and territory has its own set of rules and restrictions. Federal funding is by formula according to the state's per-capita income, ranging from 50–78% of costs. States must agree to provide certain mandated services to eligible low-income people on public assistance, Supplemental Security Income, and Aid to Families with Dependent Children. In 1989, legislation was passed that broadened Medicaid reimbursement for children to entitlement to any Medicaid-mandated or optional service needed. The mechanisms were options; waivers; early and periodic screening, diagnosis, and treatment (EPSDT) service; rehabilitation; and targeted case management.

Most community-based mental health services can be reimbursed under this plan. States have been encouraged to avail themselves of these federal funds for more comprehensive treatment services as outlined by CASSP through the enactment of the EPSDT and the Rehabilitation options of Medicaid provisions. EPSDT entitles the Medicaid-eligible child to any federally defined mandatory or optional service that might be needed, and even to any medically necessary service, whether or not the state includes that service in its Medicaid plan. In this context the gap is not in program models but between these legal rules and their implementation. Even though these standards for the care of seriously emotionally disturbed children were set in 1989, they have not yet been clearly or consistently defined by the states, nor necessarily put into practice (Koyanagi & Brodie, 1994).

EPSDT. The law requires states to provide EPSDT services as part of the Medicaid coverage of all who are under the age of 22. The screening is through periodic examinations to identify physical and psychological problems. Treatment must be provided to correct the conditions that have been identified and, since the 1989 legislation, that treatment must include any federally authorized Medicaid service regardless of whether that service is part of the state plan.

Screens. Periodic screening, called *screens*, are to be regularly scheduled and comprehensive, conducted by a "qualified professional." A diagnosis and a plan of care must be formulated for follow-up care. Most states have assigned these screens to pediatricians, who tend to overlook or minimize psychosocial problems (Koyanagi & Brodie, 1994). There are provisions for interperiodic screens, however. These may be partial insofar as they may focus on one area only, such as the child's mental or emotional state. Even informal encounters by any mental health provider or school official are acceptable for schools to become Medicaid-authorized providers of services, but if there is to be follow-up care through Medicaid, the "qualified" Medicaid screen must provide the diagnosis and plan of care. To deal with the problem of underidentification of seriously emotionally disturbed children, some states are using specialized screening tools to identify children in need of mental health care, and many other states call the attention of the screener to the child's mental health as part of the overall assessment. School nurses may be appointed "qualified professionals." It is likely that psychologists and other mental health professionals also could perform a more objective screening of children for emotional, mental, or behavioral disorder. They might well be appointed as a qualified professional by some states, if the case were made.

Waivers. There are several provisions for flexible Medicaid funds that support services for emotionally disturbed and other impaired children. Waivers that adjust the usual operating rules can be sought by the states from the federal government. Waivers can expand the range of services available to a particular group of children rather than providing the service to all who are Medicaid eligible. This is an economy measure. The Home and Community-Based Services Waiver permits states to offer an array of community services to children who otherwise would be institutionalized. The per capita cost must not exceed the average cost of institutional care. The Katie Beckett provision enables funding for the home-based care of Medicaid-eligible, impaired children that is commensurate with state funding they would receive for their care if they were living in institutions instead of with their families. The child must require the level of care provided in an institution and be appropriately cared for outside the facility, and the costs at home must not exceed those for institutional care. Several states specify this waiver for seriously emotionally disturbed children. The freedom of choice waiver removes the family's freedom to choose a provider so that the state may seek cost savings by requiring Medicaid recipients to join managed care or other prepaid health plans.

Rehabilitation option and targeted case management. The panoply of federal encouragements of care for children with serious emotional disturbance includes provisions for many of the intensive community mental health services and the case management they require. The rehabilitation option and the targeted case management service are directed to that purpose. According to the Bazelon Center's survey, 35 states have adopted the rehabilitation option, and 25 of these have combined it with targeted case management (Koyanagi & Brodie, 1994).

The broadly inclusive federal definition of rehabilitation for this option includes any remedial or medical service recommended by any licensed practitioner. These services may be delivered in any setting and need not be supervised by a physician. States can and do use this option to fund community services and social and educational programs that are not covered by Medicaid. Psychotherapy and medication are also provided along with an array of other program components. In fact, the Bazelon Center found that the rehabilitation option is more broadly used than EPSDT to cover intensive community services, and it is also used along with EPSDT for expanded responses to needs. Targeted case management is another option that enhances the effectiveness of Medicaid and the other options. Targeted means that a particular group may be selected to receive the service. Ordinarily, a Medicaid service must be available to all the state's Medicaid recipients. When targeted case management is combined with the rehabilitation option, children with emotional disturbance and their families are assured of receiving all of the services that they require. Programs include the CASSP array, therapeutic nursery schools, any service in the Individualized Education Program, nontreatment contacts with parents or guardians, and any service that promotes the maximum functioning of the child within a family in the community. These services are provided by multidisciplinary teams, children are encouraged to participate in the planning of their care, and a few states specify the need for the services to be culturally appropriate.

Like many of the improvements in response capacity for emotionally disturbed children, those provided by the various options and waivers for Medicaid do not necessarily result in children receiving the services they require. Even when they seek and obtain the options, states may limit or restrict services to the target group or may obfuscate availability to control or justify costs. At the very least, however, they recognize the unique and important needs of this population, assert their entitlement to have their needs met, and set forth the kind of program response required by them.

In fact, intentions represented by the EPSDT legislation, especially as amended, have not yet become the reality for most poor children. In many states the provisions are little known by potential recipients of care and by providers and advocates because of a lack of information or clarity. Some states indicate that services not covered under listed Medicaid offerings may be negotiated on a case-by-case basis. The not-otherwise-covered programs, however, do not have guidelines as to appropriate procedures or, often, even official authorization. Some states have made efforts to correct these problems. Some have listed the services that are specifically available to children and clearly state that limits on amount and duration of certain mental health services do not apply to children, in accordance with the federal mandate. A recent Bazelon Center survey (Koyanagi & Brodie, 1994) found that 28 states list the mental health services that are available to children, but not all mention clearly that limits do not apply. The survey found, however, that five states had greatly expanded their Medicaid mental health services for children: Florida, Georgia, Maryland, Pennsylvania, and Rhode Island. In some instances, the expanded services go well beyond the CASSP range to include, for example, assistance to parents in household management related to the care of the child (Florida); focus on infants and toddlers, and on family-living, social, daily-living, and interpersonal skills (Georgia); and therapeutic nursery services (Maryland, Pennsylvania). Pennsylvania seems to have developed the most comprehensive and detailed EPSDT plans. And four states so far have gone beyond Medicaid–EPSDT offerings to develop entire programs that focus on keeping children healthy and treating problems and conditions as they arise. The programs cover physical and mental health care; emphasize prevention as well as remedial care, clinical treatment, and rehabilitation services, including family-preservation services; and provide case management. The Kansas Kan-Be-Healthy program, North Carolina's Healthy Children and Teens, Oklahoma's Sooner-Start, and Wisconsin's HealthCheck have this child-specific, mental-health-specific focus.

Koyanagi (1995) has described how a coalition of child advocates, led by the National Mental Health Association, the Child Welfare League, and the Children's Defense Fund, helped bring to the attention of Congress the long-standing underfunding of children's mental health systems by the states and the fact that many states had agencies for traditional weekly outpatient treatment sessions and hospitalization for children with more serious problems but no prevention programs or continuum-of-care services between the extremes. The advances in the field of child mental health care, and even in federal mandates, were largely ignored in operation. Advocates won the struggle to convince Congress to enact the legislation that provides federal financial assistance to states to build systems of care for emotionally disturbed children, in accordance with CASSP principles.

The Children's and Communities' Mental Health Systems Improvement Act, passed as Section 104 of the ADAMHA Reorganization Act, requires states to plan for a statewide system of care, identify unmet needs, and involve parents in the planning and implementation of the programs. It requires a partnership between federal and state governments, and partnerships between the various human service agencies that are concerned about emotionally disturbed children. It also promotes a partnership between professionals and the parents of the children. The requirement of these partnerships is the special contribution of this legislation. Funds are distributed to the states, which guarantee the availability of matching funds. Applicants, however, could be any state agency, not only the state mental health agency. It also could be any political subdivision, as long as the services are delivered on the local level by two or more community agencies working cooperatively. Five-year grants are awarded competitively (Koyanagi, 1995). It is not clear whether this is another felicitous legislative encouragement that is honored more in the breech than in enactments. But it does represent a renewed resolve and organizational sophistication by the advocacy communities when, as diverse groups, they come together on behalf of their common interest in securing more adequate services for children who have serious emotional problems.

Managed Care

The analogies of *avalanche* and *tidal wave* have been used to describe the impact of managed care on the nation's health care system. Those who are directly involved and those who are interested observers have their own experience from which to generalize, but almost all agree that it is not yet known what will result. There is agreement that the service system, whether stabilized or changing, will be shaped by influences from funders, public organizations, the provider community, users, interest groups, and the public at large. Political forces in Washington and in state capitols are also of major influence. Advocates, including state mental health officials and professionals who are committed to equitable, appropriate care for children with emotional disabilities are working hard to shape managed care provisions.

One such occasion was the May 1995 State Managed Care Meeting, sponsored by the National Technical Assistance Center for Children's Mental Health Center for Child Health and Mental Health Policy, Georgetown University Child Development Center. This conference was funded by the Child, Adolescent and Family Branch of the Center for Mental Health Services of the Substance Abuse and Mental Health Services Administration (see Stroul, 1996, for proceedings). Participants were officials from child-serving federal and state agencies, representatives of community organizations, managed care officials, private managed-care managers, parents, and the interested public. The purpose of the meeting was to problem-solve managed-care issues among the states as they pertain to children with emotional problems and to develop recommendations for national policy.

Twenty-four states have converted their Medicaid programs into systems of managed care or other kinds of gateway-restricted health care programs. For example, Arizona was the first to conduct Medicaid as a managed-care program. The state added a behavioral health "carve out" that funds behavioral health care separately from general health care procedures. In 1990, Utah and Massachusetts instituted Medicaid-managed mental health care systems, Washington and Tennessee have begun state-sponsored, managed care programs, and more recently (1995) Colorado, Iowa, and Nebraska are doing so. At the same time, every state has a competitive array of private and insurance-sponsored managed care programs, including HMOs. The effort is to enroll as many as possible of the insured into such plans for management of all of their physical and behavioral health needs. It is not yet apparent whether or how the need for health care will be met by the increasing numbers of families who are not eligible for Medicaid, but cannot afford private plans or are not accepted by the plans for various reasons. But Medicaid-eligible children with emotional disabilities have been put into a special category for care intended to improve their chances of receiving what they need.

In general, states have turned to managed care because the steady increase in Medicaid costs were seen as exceeding their budget capacity. For example, the annual growth rate in Tennessee's Medicaid costs was reported to be 20–22%, whereas the state's income was growing at only 4.5% annually, according to the Tennessee Department of Finance and Administration. Mandatory Medicaid costs were using 25% of the state's budget and steadily increasing this percentage. The state neither chose to cut the services it offered nor opted to eliminate groups of children from eligibility for those services. The state would not raise taxes either. Instead it chose to convert its system to managed care as a cost-savings and cost-control measure. It is likely that pending Congressional reductions in Medicaid funding and the relatively unfettered block grant provisions that seem to be forthcoming add weight to the choice to switch, not only in Tennessee but within many other states that have combined Medicaid with managed care delivery systems.

Still using Tennessee as an example, the state found that services for children, especially including those with a mental health, mental retardation, or substance abuse problem, were increasing in costs at about 10% a year. Of that budget, 61% was spent on residential placements, much of it in out-of-state facilities. And yet state officials believed the children were ill served. To control this situation, the state developed its Children's Plan, designed to maximize federal reimbursements by using all supports for emotionally disturbed children. This brought in $100 million in additional funding but did not reduce the rate of growth of demand. Tennessee continues to reorganize its service system in search of finding the right balance between needs and affordability. Plans have used various arrangements among the state's Department of Mental Health, Department of Children's Services, Tenn Care for basic mental health service through Medicaid, Tenn Care Partners for managed care behavioral health agencies, and a Special Services program for residential care management. Tennessee's efforts to extend its resources for emotionally disturbed children are enhanced by the advocacy of Tennessee Voices for Children, a statewide citizens organization, founded by Tipper Gore, that is committed to improving and expanding services that promote the emotional, behavioral, and social well-being of children.

Proponents of the use of managed care for children with emotional disabilities seem to have a vision of a CASSP system of comprehensive services designed in accordance with the specific needs of each child and family, implemented collaboratively and cooperatively among program units, at nonescalating, moderate cost. This hopeful perspective assumes that managed care is in its third stage of development. The first had an effect on health care costs by limiting access, except to the young and healthy. Within the second stage, during the early 1980s, cost containment was sought by limiting services by, for example, setting lifetime limits on mental health care. The third and current stage is described as "managing a full array of individualized services for desired outcomes and cost containment" (Stroul, 1993, p. 11).

Capitation is a funding term that indicates that a set amount of funding has been allocated to provide services for a group of eligible persons, some of whom will require services and some will not. *Wrap-around* services permit the child's need to determine the care to be received regardless of where that care is delivered. *Carve-outs* handle children with emotional disabilities as a special category, not subject to the rules and procedures that pertain to other recipients of managed care. All of these provisions can be used to enhance the flexibility of response to the needs of disturbed children or of any group to which they are applied. Presumably, managed-care companies understand and agree with the need to provide the continuum of care according to CASSP principles, in addition to the cost-containment technologies that are their hallmark. Underlying the desire to manage services to this population are the assumptions that (a) accurate estimates of need for various service components can be made to set reasonable capitation rates, (b) an appropriate provider network can be developed and maintained, (c) use can be controlled through prior authorization procedures, and (d) data collection systems can be established to provide current information about program use, unit cost per patient, patient satisfaction indices, and other business-world efficiencies.

These expectations of managed care may be somewhat optimistic. For example, use predictions based on past rates of use may not be warranted. Tennessee found that costs increased as the state provided increased service options because more children could obtain the care they needed. Similarly, when North Carolina instituted its managed care program of children's mental health, the number of children served increased from 61,000 to 85,000. This substantial increase was attributed to greater access and availability of services (Stroul, 1993). Behar (personal communication, 1996) reminds the public sector of issues to consider when implementing managed care: (a) if amount of dollars used for capitation will be based on underestimated need, the result will be unserved children; (b) there should be design and planning input by those with expertise in children's services; (c) whereas managed care companies may employ concepts like treatment in the least restrictive setting, community-based services, and cultural competence, they should also be helped to recognize the role of parents, the need to bring families into the planning process, the role of other agencies such as education, child protective services, and the like, and the need to coordinate with them; and (d) there is a need for the public sector as well as the managed care community to focus on outcome.

There is a chance that the combination of Medicaid and managed care, the partnership of the public and the private domains, will result in better care of eligible emotionally disturbed children than either could do alone.

If so, a standard could be set for services for similarly troubled children who are not Medicaid eligible.

Implications

Psychologists cannot afford to hold fast to their usual ways of operating when all around them is changing. Psychologists who work with children with emotional disabilities face special challenges. No longer can the professional remain aloof from the politics that determine policy. What priority should be given to the care of these children? What about poor and working-class children who are not eligible for Medicaid? How do psychologists ensure that the understandings of psychology influence the planning and oversight of any system of response to the children's needs? Why should psychologists not be certified as qualified professionals for the purposes of EPSDT? These are only some of the issues that require personal and group activism.

Some psychologists hold a view of the child as the mentally ill patient and the mother as the collateral. The CASSP principles require a shift in that point of view toward seeing the family as part of an interactive ecological system that is to be involved in all aspects of the understanding of the child's problem, including the planning and services to ameliorate them. Psychologists need to learn to work with families, with other systems, and with other disciplines as a member of the team, rather than as the authoritative expert. The cultural competence aspect of the CASSP core values extends beyond knowledge of others' customs and language to basic acceptance and respect for differences. Mental health care professionals can only guess about the changes in the every day practice of psychology that will eventuate from this period of transition. Professional training programs should also reflect psychology's readiness to actively shape the changes to come.

Seriously emotionally disturbed children have been overlooked and underserved for generations. At the same time, advocates have continued to struggle to achieve a fair distribution of mental health resources to these children and support services that recognize the children's special needs. More recently there has been considerable progress in both areas, with emerging research evidence documenting these (at least partial) successes. Unfortunately the gains have been jeopardized by the confluence of economic, political, and demographic forces that have led to cost-cutting, profit-making goals for a reconfigured health care delivery system. The result, so far, is a destabilized, problem-ridden, overregulated service system of competing but essentially similar plans that are noninclusive of subscribers, or some providers, choice. This is a period of transition. It is also a period of crisis, but the mental health community understands that opportunity for salutary change is enhanced at times of crisis. Advocates for children' mental health care have had much success in setting standards. Perhaps the time is ripe to see to the implementation of those goals as the future is shaped. Perhaps also these are fortunate times for the contributions of psychology, if vigorously represented, to be meaningfully included in all aspects of response to the needs of children.

References

Albee, G. W. (1986). Advocates and adversaries of prevention. In M. Kessler & W. E. Goldston (Eds.), *A decade of progress in primary prevention* (309–332). Hanover, NH: University Press of New England.

Behar, L. B., Bickman, L., Lane, T., Keeton, W. P., Schwartz, M., & Brannock, J. E. (1996). Fort Bragg child and adolescent mental health demonstration project. In M. Roberts (Ed.), *Model programs in service delivery in child and family mental health* (pp. 351–372). Hillsdale, NJ: Erlbaum.

Bickman, L., Guthrie, P. R., Foster, E. M., Lambert, E. W., Summerfelt, W. T., Breda, C. S., & Heflinger, C. A. (1995). *Evaluating managed mental health services: The Fort Bragg experiment.* New York: Plenum.

Casey, R., & Berman, J. (1985). The outcome of psychotherapy with children. *Psychological Bulletin, 98,* 388–400.

Cole, R., & Poe, S. (1993). *Partnerships for care-systems for children with serious emotional disturbances and their families.* Washington, DC: Washington Business Group on Health, Mental Health Services Program for Youth.

Cowen, E. L., Trost, M. A., Lorion, R. P., Dorr, D., Izzo, L. D., & Isaacson, R. V. (1975). *New ways in school mental health: Early detection and prevention of school maladaptation.* New York: Human Science Press.

Family Impact Seminar. (1994). *Children's mental health services: Policy implications of the new paradigm.* Washington, DC: American Association for Marriage and Family Therapy Research and Education Foundation.

Friedman, R. M. (1984). *Seriously emotionally disturbed children: An underserved and ineffectively served population.* Unpublished manuscript, Florida Mental Health Institute, Tampa.

Friedman, R. M., & Burns, B. J. (1996). The evaluation of the Fort Bragg Demonstration Project: An alternative interpretation of the findings. *Journal of Mental Health Administration, 23*(1), 128–136.

Hinckley, E. (1984). Homebuilders: The Maine experience. *Children Today, 13*(5), 14–17.

Hobbs, N. (1979). *Helping disturbed children: Psychological and ecological strategies, II: Project Re-Ed, twenty years later.* Nashville, TN: Center for the Study of Families and Children, Vanderbilt University.

Hutchinson, J., & Nelson, K. (1985). How public agencies can provide family-centered services. *Social Casework, 66*(6), 367–371.

Joint Commission on Mental Health of Children. (1969). *Crisis in child mental health.* New York: Harper & Row.

Kansas Department of Mental Health. (1986). *Home-first training program.* Topeka, KS: Kansas Department of Mental Health.

Kirigin, K. A., Braukmann, C. J., Atwater, J. D., & Wolfe, M. M. (1982). An evaluation of the Teaching-Family (Achievement Place) group homes for juvenile offenders. *Journal of Applied Behavior Analysis, 15,* 1–16.

Knitzer, J. (1982). *Unclaimed children.* Washington, DC: Children's Defense Fund.

Koyanagi, C. (1995). Systems change: Moving beyond reports. In L. Bickman & D. Rog (Eds.), *Children's mental health research policy and evaluation.* Newbury Park, CA: Sage.

Koyanagi, C., & Brodie, J. (1994). *Making Medicaid work.* Washington, DC: Bazelon Center for Mental Health Law.

Kutash, K., & Rivera, V. R. (1996). *What works in children's mental health services? Uncovering answers to critical questions.* Baltimore: Brookes.

Lewis, D. O., Balla, D., & Shanok, S. (1979). Some evidence of race bias in the diagnosis and treatment of the juvenile offender. *The American Journal of Orthopsychiatry, 49,* 53–61.

Moore, J. M. (1991). Children's Mobile Outreach: An alternative approach to the treatment of emotionally disturbed children and youth. In A. Algarin & R. Friedman (Eds.), *Third annual research conference proceedings for a system of care for children's mental health: Building a research base* (pp. 301–313). Tampa, FL: University of South Florida, Florida Mental Health Institute, Research and Training Center for Children's Mental Health.

National Resource Network for Child and Family Mental Health Services, Washington Business Group on Health. (1996). *Solving the children's puzzle: Year one.* Washington, DC, Author.

Pastore, C. A., Thomas, J. V., & Newman, I. (1991). Therapeutic in-home emergency services. In A. Algarin & R. Friedman (Eds.), *Third annual research conference proceedings for a system of care for children's mental health: Building a research base* (pp. 293–299). Tampa, FL: University of South Florida, Florida Mental Health Institute, Research and Training Center for Children's Mental Health.

Phillips, E. L., Phillips, E. A., Fixen, D. L., & Wolf, M. M. (1974). *The teaching-family handbook.* Lawrence, KS: University of Kansas Printing Service.

President's Commission on Mental Health. (1978). *Report of the sub-task panel on infants, children and adolescents.* Washington, DC: U.S. Government Printing Office.

Rivera, V. R., & Kutash, K., (1994). *Components of a system of care: What does the research say?* Tampa, FL: University of South Florida, Florida Mental Health Institute, Research and Training Center for Children's Mental Health.

Rosenblatt, A., Attkisson, C. C., & Fernandez, A. J. (1992). Integrating systems of care in California for youth with severe emotional disturbance II: Initial group home expenditure and utilization findings from the California AB377 Evaluation Project. *Journal of Child and Family Studies, 1*(3), 263–286.

Rugs, D., Warner-Levock, V., Johnston, A., & Freedman, G. (1994). *Adding system supports to children's service delivery: The impact on foster care on children in rural West Virginia.* Unpublished manuscript.

Select Committee on Children, Youth, and Families, U.S. House of Representatives (1990). No place to call home: Discarded children in America (House Report 101–395). Washington, DC: U.S. Government Printing Office.

Silver, A. A., Hagin, R. A., & Beecher, R. (1981). A program for secondary prevention of learning disabilities: Results in academic achievement and in emotional adjustment. *Journal of Preventive Psychiatry, 1,* 77–87.

Sowder, B. (1979). *Issues related to psychiatric services for children and youth: A review of selected literature from 1970–1979.* Bethesda, MD: Burt Associates.

Stroul, B. (1985). *Child & Adolescent Service System Program: Technical assistance needs assessment.* Washington, DC: CASSP Technical Assistance Center at Georgetown University.

Stroul, B. (1993). *Systems of care for children and adolescents with severe emotional disturbances: What are the results?* Washington, DC: Georgetown University Child Development Center, CASSP Technical Assistance Center.

Stroul, B., & Friedman, R. (1986). *A system of care for children and youth with severe emotional disturbances* (Revised edition). Washington, DC: Georgetown University Child Development Center, CASSP Technical Assistance Center.

Stroul, B., Lourie, I., Goldman, S., & Katz-Leavy, J. (1992). *Profiles of local systems of care for children and adolescents with severe emotional disturbances* (Revised edition). Washington, DC: Georgetown University Child Development Center, CASSP Technical Assistance Center.

Sunshine, J. H., Witkin, M. J., Atay, J. E., & Manderscheid, R. W. (1991). *Residential treatment centers and other organized mental health care for children and youth: United States, 1988* (Mental Health Statistical Note No. 198). Rockville, MD: National Institute of Mental Health Statistical Research Branch.

12

Creating Responsive Systems of Care: Professional and Organizational Challenges

Robert J. Illback

In the era of managed care, psychology is having an identity crisis. As documented by Peterson (1996), the field experienced dramatic growth (along with a number of other mental health professions, e.g., social work, family counseling) in association with the growth of health care financing. More recently, however, private insurers are eliminating or severely restricting mental health benefits, Medicaid and Medicare benefits are becoming limited, and there is the prospect of wholesale governmental abandonment of health and mental health care entitlements. Suddenly, psychologists (particularly those in solo practice) are faced with the prospect of a reduced client base and reduced reimbursement schedules, leading many to consider joining group practices, public mental health organizations, or community agencies. Some have considered leaving the profession. Still others are seeking to diversify their practice, specialize, or identify new and innovative practice approaches. In the child mental health marketplace that is emerging, many psychological practitioners are likely to survive; this chapter seeks to address the question, What will it take to thrive?

Psychological practice within the child mental health service system will undoubtedly "look" and "feel" different in the future marketplace (Duchnowski & Friedman, 1990). Shrinking financial resources, the adversarial "culture" of managed care, recognition that the needs of children are complex and overwhelming, and an emerging sense that the present system has failed, all contribute to an impetus for change and transformation (Day & Roberts, 1991). (See chapter 11, this volume, for a thorough discussion of these issues.) To the extent that child psychologists are aware of and participate in this change process, they will be likely to preserve and expand a role for their particular areas of expertise. The purpose of this chapter is to examine some of the features of the emerging child mental health market and consider needs and issues that suggest new and innovative roles for psychological practitioners. It is argued that the marketplace of the future is more likely to be integrated, consumer driven, cost conscious, and outcome oriented.

In point of fact, the integrated services concept already pervades the area of child mental health services, especially regarding the need to transform the "system of care" for children and youth whose problems are moderate to severe. Various terms and labels have been used to describe this population, including *emotionally and behaviorally disordered* (EBD) and *severe emotional disturbance* (SED). The integrated services concept also has use for children whose needs are considered mild and are likely to be served through traditional mechanisms such as outpatient therapy within a community mental health center or independent practice setting (see chapter 13, this volume). The present chapter, however, focuses on lessons learned from system of care (integrated services) initiatives targeted toward more moderately and severely involved children, as there is a more well-developed literature in this area (Stroul, Goldman, Lourie, Katz-Leavy, & Zeigler-Dendy, 1992). These perspectives can have significant implications for how psychologists think about and organize for practice.

Experiences gleaned from the implementation of a statewide system of care within the Commonwealth of Kentucky are initially presented, including evaluative findings. As a means to focus discussion on the potential roles of psychologists within emerging integrated systems, six emerging challenges that confront such systems are then delineated. These challenges are in the areas of the range of client needs, service arrays, maintaining and expanding outcomes, encouraging innovation, and family support and community building.

Kentucky IMPACT: A Maturing Integrated Service System

In 1990, the Kentucky Department for Mental Health and Mental Retardation Services estimated that there were about 50,000 children with severe emotional problems in Kentucky, or approximately 8% of the 1990 school population. However, at that time only about 3,000 students, or 0.51% of the students enrolled in Kentucky's schools, were identified and served in programs for pupils with emotional and behavioral disabilities. Similarly, only a small proportion of those eligible were being served within the other child-service systems.

In the late 1980s Kentucky experienced a financial crisis because of the overuse of psychiatric hospitalization for children. Kentucky Medicaid expenditures on hospitalization for children increased from $2.8 million to $36 million (or 1200%) in a period of 9 years. Parents complained in legislative hearings that their children were institutionalized far from their home communities, were returning to their families little improved, and were at home with no local resources to help them.

Concurrently, in 1990, Kentucky received a $2.4 million 4-year implementation grant from the Robert Wood Johnson Foundation to develop comprehensive, coordinated services for children and youth with SED in central Kentucky. This project, Bluegrass Interagency Mobilization for Progress in Adolescent and Children's Treatment (Bluegrass IMPACT), involved close cooperation among all affected state departments, local education agencies, and community mental health and mental retardation programs in a 17-county region.

In planning for the Foundation initiative, an examination of Kentucky's system of care for children with severe emotional and behavioral problems was requested by a legislative committee. The study revealed a range of interrelated problems: (a) there were insufficient services, (b) available services were fragmented and uncoordinated, (c) Kentucky was overly dependent on psychiatric hospitalization of children, and (d) less restrictive, community- and family-based services were underdeveloped and underfunded. When members of the Interim Joint Health and Welfare Committee of the General Assembly asked for a new approach, several agencies in the Kentucky Cabinet for Human Resources developed the IMPACT model.

The Cabinet for Human Resources *Plan to Serve Children With Severe Emotional Problems* was enacted by the Kentucky legislature in 1990. The plan stipulated that state and federal funds be accessed to provide more appropriate community-based services for this population. Emphasis was placed on interagency coordination, more comprehensive service delivery, and limitations on the use of psychiatric hospitalization. The resultant program, now named Kentucky IMPACT, sought to refocus services, using available funding sources and providing additional state funds allocated through the Departments of Mental Health and Mental Retardation Services, Social Services, and Medicaid Services.

Kentucky IMPACT has a number of program components jointly administered by the three major departments within the Cabinet for Human Resources, the Administrative Office of the Courts, and the Department of Education, which are coordinated by the State Interagency Council (SIAC). At the regional level, services are developed, coordinated, and administered through regional interagency councils (RIACs). Core services in each region include interagency service planning teams, targeted case management services, and individual family-based support services (also called *wraparound funds*) used at the discretion of the RIAC when children's needs cannot be met with existing resources but require that creative, individualized services be "wrapped-around" the child. Additional service components that are gradually being developed around the state but that are not yet available in every region include (a) family-preservation programs, (b) intensive in-home services, (c) services to multiproblem children in private child care, (d) therapeutic foster care, and (e) small community-based psychiatric residential treatment facilities (PRTFs).

Target Population and Program Eligibility

Children served by Kentucky IMPACT are considered to have severe emotional disabilities. They are prone to a wide range of problems in home, school, and community settings that interfere with their ability to adjust, learn, and live successfully with their family.

Eligibility for Kentucky IMPACT services is determined by the following operational definition from House Bill 838:

> "Severely emotionally disturbed child" means a child with a clinically significant disorder of thought, mood, perception, orientation, memory or behavior that is listed in the current edition of the American Psychiatric Association's *Diagnostic and Statistical Manual of Mental Disorders (DSM-IIIR)* and that:
>
> (a) Presents substantial limitations that have persisted for at least one (1) year or are judged by a mental health professional to be at high risk of continuing for one (1) year without professional intervention in at least two (2) of the following five (5) areas:
>   (i) "Self-care," defined as the ability to provide, sustain, and protect his or herself at a level appropriate to his or her age;
>   (ii) "Interpersonal relationships," defined as the ability to build and maintain satisfactory relationships with peers and adults;
>   (iii) "Family life," defined as the capacity to live in a family or family type environment;
>   (iv) "Self-direction," defined as the child's ability to control his or her behavior and to make decisions in a manner appropriate to his or her age; and
>   (v) "Education," defined as the ability to learn social and intellectual skills from teachers in available educational settings; or
> (b) Is a Kentucky resident and is receiving residential treatment for emotional disturbance through the interstate compact; or
> (c) The Department for Social Services has removed the child from the child's home and has been unable to maintain the child in a stable setting due to behavioral or emotional disturbance; or
> (d) Is a person under twenty-one (21) years of age meeting the criteria of paragraph (a) of this subsection and who was receiving services prior to age eighteen (18) that must be continued for therapeutic benefit.

Program Goals and Validity Assumptions

A number of systems-level goals are implicit in the development of the Kentucky IMPACT program. Some are stated clearly in the legislative intent, including (a) increasing and improving available services, (b) coordinating services more effectively (interagency involvement and collaboration), (c) reducing dependency on psychiatric hospitalization, and (d) increasing the use of less restrictive community-based services. For the most part, these reflect goals for the development and improvement of the service delivery system for children with severe emotional problems.

At the level of children and families, a range of specific program goals include the following:

1. Children and youth will demonstrate improvement in social competence and concomitant decreases in behavioral and emotional difficulties, in home, school, and community settings.

2. Families will perceive increased social and professional support in their efforts to meet the needs of these challenging children and adolescents, and will perceive this support to be timely and responsive.
3. Children and youth will be placed in less restrictive treatment environments, and their placements will become more stable over time.
4. Professionals, parents, and the children themselves will perceive that they have made meaningful gains as a consequence of their involvement in the program.

Program Implementation: 1990–1995

Since its initiation in 1990, Kentucky IMPACT has undergone a number of changes and transformations in the service of program improvement.

Family involvement. In 1992, changes were sought in the original legislation to ensure a higher level of family involvement in the program. Parent representation became mandated on regional and state decision-making councils. A state advisory group made up of parent representatives and alternates was also formed, and this group has had an extensive role in policy formulation. Concurrently, more active family involvement was developed through a parent advocacy and self-help group aligned with the Kentucky Disabilities Coalition. A concerted effort has been made to develop and support family involvement through a dedicated staff position within the Department of Mental Health. Finally, for the past 3 years, the Department has administered a CASSP service grant to promote family involvement. Regional models of innovative family involvement have been pilot tested and evaluated, including parent advocacy training, parent-designed resource development and allocation, parent networking through a computer-based bulletin board, and cultural competence training.

Organizational development. Another initiative, highlighting organizational development at the regional level, emanated from discussions about evaluation findings. On the premise that organizational barriers or lack of capacity could impede the full use of the IMPACT program, regions were encouraged to apply for "grants" from the Department of Mental Health through a request for proposals. In this context, proposals could solicit technical assistance on developmental issues or specific problems. A range of interventions were funded, including such diverse areas as developing treatment-oriented foster care, coordinating community responses to attention-deficit/hyperactivity disorder programming, "spinning off" a closely held nonprofit corporation for fund-raising and community support, and various training initiatives. Each of these projects was locally designed but approved by a statewide screening committee. Most made use of technical assistance provided by state- or national-level experts.

RIAC review. As it became clear that the evaluation system could provide useful information for ongoing program planning, especially in conjunction with other program data gathered by regions and DMH, it also was noted that the data were underused at the local level. Therefore, efforts began to promote periodic program analysis and review through regional interagency council (RIAC) reviews. RIACs are asked to examine a report comparing certain data elements for their region to statewide data from the evaluation system and other sources. Then, a site-visit team reviews their report, examines relevant data, reviews client records, observes some regional activities, and surveys families. This process resulted in a review document that provides comprehensive feedback and recommendations to the region. The focus of the document is continuous quality improvement, although areas in which the program is not in compliance with standards and regulations are noted for correction. A statewide work group is developing a format and process to assure that such efforts in quality improvement continue.

PRTF. When the project began, one of the primary components envisioned was PRTFs, small community-based programs designed as alternatives to large facilities and hospitals for longer term care of children and youth with SED. These have been slow in developing (there are presently only six in place) due to legislative requirements for Certificates of Need, zoning problems in some communities, and related financial and economic realities. There remains a significant press for such placements, in light of drastically reduced hospitalization and the overabundance of troubled adolescents in the program.

Strategic planning. For approximately a 2-year period extending through spring 1995, an extensive strategic planning process has been carried out involving literally hundreds of IMPACT constituent group members. Early discussions of a strategic planning group identified five major domains in need of development. Strategic planning work groups were formed across the state using a participatory planning process. Each focused on one of the areas identified, as follows: (a) outcomes, (b) standards and best practices, (c) RIAC/ownership (interagency involvement), (d) human resources development, (e) training, and (f) financing (still to be completed). Extensive recommendations were made to the State Interagency Council and adopted in April 1995, establishing the program agenda for the foreseeable future. In the area of outcome evaluation, the work group made recommendations for the development of a more outcome-oriented system with additional and more precise measures of system, child, and family variables.

Evaluation Summary: 1990–1995

Demographic data on program participants indicate that the program primarily serves males with externalizing (i.e., acting-out) problems, early-to mid-adolescents, and individuals and families with multiple risks and problems. Service coordination is the most frequent service; about 80% of participants also receive counseling, 40% receive medication, and only about 10% receive in-home clinical services. Extensive use is made of support services (e.g., respite and wraparound aides) and crisis-response services, but only about half of the participants receive special education. It is not clear to what extent those served in general education may require special education services and are unidentified, versus receiving appropriate education services in a mainstream setting (Illback, Sanders, & Birkby, 1995).

There is ample evidence of program success, with substantial gains in reduction of behavior problems, reduced use of psychiatric hospitals, increased placement stability, and increased family social support associated with the program. More modest gains are seen in social competence. Exiting patterns indicate that more than one third of program participants actually exit having successfully completed the intervention, a notable figure given the nature of the population. However, there is also evidence that, over time, families become more socially isolated in their communities, raising questions about their potential dependence on the program and whether sufficient attention is paid to transition issues. Additionally, reductions in hospitalizations are accompanied by increases in residential treatment. Parents, teachers, service coordinators, and children all endorse general statements about positive change, but there are some differences between the groups as to the extent of change (teachers see less overall progress) and some agreement that school functioning is not evidencing the same degree of progress as family, behavioral, and relationship areas.

Demographics, needs, and presenting risks at intake are functionally unrelated to change scores, a finding that contradicts conventional wisdom. This finding has implications for those who would argue for intentional efforts to select younger children, serve particular categories or "types" of children, or formulate weighted selection criteria. The fact that outcomes are uncorrelated with one another supports the use of multiple outcome measures, but presents a larger challenge. Judging who has been "successful" is more complicated when multiple patterns of outcomes can accrue, because positive outcomes in one area may not necessarily be accompanied by changes in another. Success is relative; it is in the "eye of the beholder."

Four risk-factor subgroups are derived from cluster analysis, with each evidencing certain prominent themes and issues, as follows: (a) antisocial behavior group, (b) distressed families group, (c) family violence and psychopathology group, and (d) depressive and self-injurious group. Four clusters are also delineated for service delivery variables, labeled as (a) *high resource intensive group*, (b) *family-oriented service coordination group*, (c) *school-oriented service coordination group*, and (d) *low-intensity, ongoing service group* (Illback, Sanders, & Birkby, 1995). Although a small portion of participants receive a disproportionate amount of services, there are not different outcomes associated with membership in particular risk-factor or service-delivery subgroups. This implies that variables other than needs and amount of services account for change.

Cluster analysis of agency involvement reveals several underlying dimensions. These include the overall level of agency involvement (high/low), level of wraparound involvement (flexible support services), and social services or court involvement (probably a "proxy" for more coercive and less "family engaged" service programs and patterns). In contrast with need and service variables, group membership in relation to these dimensions is related to four of the five major outcome variables. Further analysis of these data show that high wraparound involvement is positively associated with successful completion of the program, family support, and social competence gains. These findings are especially heartening given the role of these services within the program model. It is hypothesized that qualitative process variables such as teamwork and collaboration, family engagement, and service coordinator style may have promise as predictors of success.

An examination of estimated costs of all services provided in the year prior to IMPACT enrollment, compared with the average cost for the first year of IMPACT involvement, reveals an approximate 36% reduction in average cost. Based on estimations of cost associated with various placements, it appears that the average cost of services per client in the year prior to enrollment is $13,898. In contrast, the average cost of services for the first year of enrollment is $8,886, yielding an average savings of $5,012. Extrapolating to the total group of 1,971 children, this yields a total savings of as much as $10 million. Savings generated by the IMPACT program (most of which are associated with reduction in hospitalization) are spread across all of the child-serving systems and reduce the stress that this population places on overall service capacity, thus allowing more children to be served more effectively.

Overall, Kentucky IMPACT appears to be fulfilling its promise as a system of care that works. Although it is still an evolving program committed to ongoing development and improvement, it can demonstrate that it provides effective and cost-efficient services to the most challenging children. Substantial evidence is now available to show the efficacy of the program model (Illback, Sanders, & Birkby, 1995). In fact, present findings suggest that it is not the severity of needs or types of problems one comes to the program with that make a difference in a client's success, but rather what happens within the program. Future research will focus on discovering and measuring process variables that are associated with outcomes more precisely and path analysis to better understand complex relationships between and among process and outcome variables (Illback, 1995).

Challenges and Opportunities in Emerging Systems of Care

The preceding description of the Kentucky IMPACT program serves as a backdrop for discussion of the challenges and opportunities that psychologists face in the marketplace of the future. This type of program is certainly not the only venue for psychological practice with children and families, but it is hypothesized that many child-serving systems will take on similar characteristics. Although it seems likely that there will always be some market for the practice of child psychology in traditional settings such as outpatient therapy in a mental health center or private practice, the growth opportunities of the future seem more likely to reside in areas of program development, consultation, supervision, administration, and evaluation.

As psychologists consider the marketplace of the future, a fundamental issue will be the extent to which consumers of services are listened to. For the purposes of this discussion, *consumers* are defined both as the immediate clients (e.g., individuals who receive treatment) and the various constituencies with whom they interface, including programs, organizations, third-party payers, and society as a whole. As a field, psychology has been somewhat isolated in its views; services are offered more in regard to what is perceived as "best" for the consumer (e.g., a practice standard or regulatory requirement) than what consumers say they want.

When people involved with developing and implementing systems of care (including recipients of these services) are seen as customers, psychologists need to attend closely to what these individuals and systems say they desire. The primary questions, then, do not involve helping these people to understand and appreciate what psychology has to offer, but rather, Who is the customer? What is the requirement? How can we deliver what our customers will value? Stated alternatively, how can we make psychology indispensable? (Peterson, 1996)

Many of the concerns and issues that have arisen within child mental health systems development mirror other areas of service to children and families. These themes, as mentioned previously, include that (a) the diversity and complexity of needs experienced by children and families present unique challenges and opportunities; (b) service arrays, while broadened by the development of systems of care, require further delineation and integration; (c) maintaining, broadening, and sustaining outcomes requires thoughtful and targeted effort; (d) there is a need to strengthen organizational capacity for innovation within traditionally conservative child-serving organizations; and (e) family support and community-building are vastly underdeveloped aspects of integrated service programs. Each of these represents unique opportunities for the application of systematic psychological knowledge and expertise.

Population Diversity and Program Complexity

A central finding of system of care research in a variety of settings has been that children have multiple and complex problems that do not lend themselves to easy categorization or simple "treatments." Whereas the *SED* label has served an umbrella function to describe a large group of youngsters whose needs are significant and who challenge child-serving systems, it has no particular clinical use. More specific psychiatric nomenclature has also been found limited as a means for conceptualizing and organizing comprehensive and coordinated interventions. Certain labels may have some use for psychotherapy treatment (and even this proposition is questionable), but it seems clear that such formulations become irrelevant when an ecosystemic perspective is taken.

For example, children who have been diagnosed as exhibiting attention-deficit/hyperactivity disorder may have certain features in common (e.g., inability to sustain attention, activity level), but they vary extensively in most respects, including variables such as learning style, resilience, personality characteristics, family relationships and circumstances, extended support networks, and neighborhood and community features. These ecological dimensions undoubtedly play a major role in determining intervention effectiveness. Systems of care are designed to consider these features in problem analysis and intervention planning.

As the marketplace moves to more integrated systems, ecologically sensitive interventions seem likely to become more common rather than the exception. There is an emerging literature on its effectiveness with high-risk populations (see, for example, chapter 6, this volume), and it seems likely that as the child mental health marketplace contracts, high-risk populations will receive a higher proportion of the limited resources. The challenge for psychologists is to contribute and lead in this area. This raises the question, What do psychologists have to offer?

In the emerging marketplace, a central need that has become clear is that of *problem conceptualization*. As program staff wrestle with complex and diverse populations and problems, there is a tendency to lose focus. A common problem faced by service coordinators in Kentucky IMPACT, for example, is, Which of the multiple problems should be dealt with first? A coordinated and thoughtful response to a child who is at risk in his or her home due to prior maltreatment, who has severe learning and peer relationship difficulties at school, whose behavior is extreme, whose family is isolated and lacking in parenting skills, whose extended family network is complicated by problems of substance abuse and poverty, and who lives in a resource-poor region is perplexing to even the most sophisticated and experienced practitioner. As noted by Illback and Neill (1995), it is common for such decisions to be placed in the hands of individuals with limited training and experience, such as case managers, child protective workers, and master's-level counselors.

From their comprehensive training in child development, psychopathology, family functioning, programmatic intervention, and clinical science, psychologists bring a unique perspective to the process. To the extent that they can move away from jargonistic, "diagnosis-driven" formulations dominated by professionalized concepts and toward more descriptive, needs-based, and integrated conceptualizations, psychologists can help direct service providers' focus and coordinate their interventions on behalf of multiproblem children and families.

A related contribution that psychologists can make is in creativity of program design. Even within the systems of care movement, with its emphasis on innovation and family support, a certain categorical thinking about programs and interventions has been detected. For example, in Kentucky extensive use has been made of wraparound aides, who essentially serve as a combination respite provider, mentor, "big brother or sister," and model for the child and family. This approach has been successful in many instances, and it has sometimes been offered as the program model and treatment of choice rather than a targeted intervention based on a specific formulation about how it will address needs in a given situation. Occasionally, this approach seems to be "prescribed" on the basis of staff availability, funding, and program comfort and convenience.

In this same regard, several other questions have arisen. Does everyone need office-based psychotherapy for an extended period, or is it prescribed as a matter of course because it is available, fundable, and preferred by host community mental health organizations? How should intervention programs with adolescents be different from the kinds of work done with younger children, particular with regard to the role of the family system? Are all youngsters with the *SED* label likely to respond to community-based programs and services, or are there subgroups for whom an alternative set of approaches needs to be designed (e.g., mid- to late-adolescents with multiple placements and hospitalizations in their backgrounds who are unlikely to return to a family setting)? Should children with internalizing problems (e.g., major depression, anxiety) receive interventions that are similar to "acter-outers"? How should intervention for adolescent girls, who enter the system at much higher rates than girls at earlier periods of development, be organized? How should transition to adulthood be addressed, given the high potential for this population to experience life-long difficulties of adjustment?

Psychologists at all levels, including direct service providers, program managers, and organization leaders, can play a substantial role in addressing these and similar questions, but they must be willing to think systemically, become involved with broader questions and issues, and be willing to work as part of a team of people who are grappling with these concerns.

Broadening the Service Array

In reaction to earlier reliance on inpatient hospitalization and out-of-state placement for children with severe emotional disabilities, many states and localities began to develop alternative, community-based programs. There is much evidence that hospitalization rates have been reduced, but considerable effort is still required to design and implement a fully functioning, integrated service system. It is insufficient to assume that merely reducing hospitalization will result in better, more family-focused interventions. In fact, it appears that designing and sustaining community-based intervention programs is a far more complex and fragile task than creating facilities, and it may be at least as costly. In this context, psychologists can make a substantive contribution.

Strengthening the breadth and efficacy of community-based offerings so that they are more family-centered, needs-driven, seamless, and accessible requires, first and foremost, commitment to a service delivery model that has these features (see chapter 1, this volume, for a more comprehensive discussion of integrated service perspectives). Many psychologists have been trained in institutional settings (such as hospitals and clinics) and may not be fully aware of (or in support of) the challenges of community-based work.

In addition to commitment to a set of principles, for psychologists to engage in work in this arena they must be able to practice within an ecosystemic perspective. This implies a willingness to (a) conceptualize problems in a multidimensional fashion; (b) engage productively with various social and organizational systems (e.g., family, school, church, neighborhood) within which the focus person is embedded; and (c) recognize that system strengthening must occur on many levels if success is to be sustained.

At the heart of successful community-based interventions are the interactions between helpers and families. Such transactions can be facilitative, empowering, enabling, and supportive, or they can be unfocused, prescriptive, authoritarian, one-directional, and ultimately disabling (see chapter 4, this volume). Working in community settings with complex problems requires an ability to join (consult) with various systems in a healthy and facilitative manner, such that they become strengthened and better integrated. Often, the issue is not whether there are sufficient resources to be successful, but whether resources can be brought to bear in a manner that is effective and sustained.

Thus, psychologists can contribute to strengthening the service array by using their clinical and consulting skills to help families, teachers, friends, neighbors, therapists, social workers, and others to work together toward meaningful objectives. At a simple level, this can involve training for specific competencies such as child management skills. It may also imply the need to teach and model teamwork, recognize and resolve conflict, and help conceptualize the process of strategic intervention.

From the research to date on the Kentucky IMPACT program, it has become clear that a crucial variable to the success or failure of a particular intervention program is the extent to which the family is *engaged*. Stated alternately, it appears that a major challenge for community-based intervention is the need to provide services "in collaboration with" families, rather than provide services "to" families. When families feel coerced into treatment, or when services are provided in a manner that minimizes the role of the family, the likelihood of sustained change is greatly diminished. When families feel they are respected, that they control resources, and that their efforts are valued and supported, their investment and involvement increases (Trivette, Dunst, Boyd, & Hamby, 1995). Here again, a possible role for the psychologist is implied, bridging psychological boundaries and helping to build trust and teamwork between formal and informal systems involved in interventions.

In addition to playing a role in strengthening the service system as currently construed, many opportunities for practice lie in the development of innovative programs. A number of vital community-based forms of programming remain severely underdeveloped across the nation. For example, in many areas it is difficult to find practitioners who are willing to go into people's homes to provide clinical services. Although there are some financial and logistical constraints on such work at present, psychologists in individual or group practices could offer rates specific for such work and achieve efficiencies based on volume and coordination. As many communities move toward capitated forms of care, this market may become more lucrative because the incentives will be on the side of keeping children in their homes and avoiding more costly placements. When service funding in capitated systems is not billed by the hour, disincentives for innovative service delivery are likely to disappear.

There are other areas of potential growth and opportunity within community-based services for psychologists. For example, listening to consumers (i.e., families) leads to the inevitable conclusion that much of what they value (and seek) is not professionalized services (e.g., psychotherapy), but rather family-support services in the form of respite, coordination, social and recreational programs, and the like. Psychologists interested in program development within their organizations, or within independent practice entities, may profit from designing and implementing such programs. An area that seems especially ripe for development is therapeutic foster care, principally because it is a cost-efficient alternative to residential treatment. Psychologists can be usefully involved in identifying, training, supporting, and possibly contracting with specially trained families in this capacity. Most of the organizational obstacles to development of such programmatic alternatives seem likely to diminish as the effects of managed care move systems toward cost-efficiencies and greater flexibility.

Maintaining and Sustaining Outcomes

For systems of care in child mental health, as for other forms and systems of intervention (e.g., individual psychotherapy), the programmatic challenge is not "merely" to change behavior, but rather to maintain, generalize, and sustain the changes that occur. There is widespread recognition of the difficulties of maintenance and generalization in psychological intervention, and many approaches have developed strategies to address these issues, such as booster sessions, long-term follow-up, and cross-system and cross-setting intervention designs. Psychologists can play a role in conceptualizing, systematizing, and implementing programs and strategies that address this need.

For example, it appears that there are different subgroups of youngsters who participate in child mental health programs, ranging from children with attentional and oppositional behavior problems to more severe disorders of conduct and personality. It seems likely that the challenges of sustaining change will vary across problem areas, but also in relation to the density and use of formal and informal support systems. For younger children, where the essential intervention often involves training parents and providers about child-management strategies and service co-ordination, follow-up needs may focus on periodic consultation to ensure that these strategies continue to be employed consistently and in a coordinated fashion. Youth with disorders of conduct, on the other hand, may require a more extensive and longer term involvement, which may include coordination of periodic hospitalization, residential treatment, aftercare planning, and transition to adult services. Such determinations must be made on an individual level (requiring specific clinical expertise), but there is also a programmatic component to considerations of who is in need, to what extent, and how services can be organized and paid for.

Given a commitment to individualized services, psychologists can play an especially useful role in helping treatment teams to consider factors that may facilitate durability of intervention. Within the Kentucky IMPACT program, front-line staff and service coordinators are urged to use family empowerment and community-building approaches as a means to ease program exiting. There is great concern that the program cannot, and should not, be seen as a life-long entitlement. There is related concern that children and families not become dependent on the program, but rather learn to be more self-sufficient and to navigate the service system. Furthermore, there is an intent that informal sources of support within the community, such as friends, neighbors, and relatives of the family, be more fully used because these are more sustainable sources of support.

The notion that social competence, family empowerment, and community-building strategies should be expanded to enhance sustainability seems logical based on research and experience. However, technology and support for implementing such recommendations is limited and often unavailable to front-line staff. Translating these ideas into programmatic intervention requires a conceptual understanding of their relation to successful intervention, specific and sophisticated process and consultation skills, and the ability to negotiate boundaries between various systems. Many practitioners are trained to strengthen the capacity of smaller systems, such as families, but few have had experience with building an informal team of supportive persons around the needs of a child with behavioral challenges. Psychologists with the requisite skills who adopt a multisystemic approach can play a substantial role within this framework, to include consultation with treatment teams, training of service coordinators, program design, and outcome evaluation.

Strengthening Organization Capacity

Human service organizations are, by their very nature, conservative. Integrated service programs are, in contrast, innovative and divergent. A continuing challenge experienced by emerging systems of care programs relates to implementing change in the context of an organizational "culture" that is not always open to flexible approaches. Within Kentucky IMPACT, for example, substantial resistance has been encountered within the host-community mental health organizations to many of the fiscal and programmatic innovations that are essential to the program. For example, some of the expenses associated with wraparound funds do not conform to billing categories that the system has determined to be legitimate. For organizations that undergo continuous scrutiny in the form of Medicaid audits, "creative financing" is not necessarily a valued activity. Unless these kinds of difficulties surface and are resolved, the ability of the new system of care to accomplish its mission is compromised.

Certainly, the contrast between an innovative change program and the conservative culture of mental health organizations is not unique to Kentucky. A further examination of the cultures that underlie the two types of programs reveals that systems of care are driven by concepts such as responsiveness, change, innovation, and outcome. Their larger host organizations, on the other hand, are often driven by concern for risk management in service provision. In some mental health organizations, the dominant paradigm is based on fear—fear of doing something wrong, fear of change, fear of being blamed, fear of failure, fear of scrutiny, fear of bad press, fear of liability, and fear of losing money. As Sophocles observed, "To him who lives in fear, everything rustles."

These organizational fears tend to be paralyzing and immobilizing. Instead of focusing on doing "whatever it takes to make things work for this child and family," in conservative organizations the focus can be all the things that can go wrong, all the regulations that may be violated, and all the "professional" reasons why an innovative intervention will not work. Perhaps the biggest challenge facing those who seek an integrated service system for children and families is to create a service culture wherein people feel free to innovate and empower one another without fear of adverse consequences. People can and will make mistakes in their attempts to respond to complex and challenging needs; such mistakes can be valued and learned from when they are in the service of responsiveness.

In this context, psychologists as leaders can play a role in protecting *paradigm pioneers*, those front-line staff (e.g., service coordinators) who are in a highly vulnerable position by virtue of their commitment to change and innovation. Paradoxically, these individuals often have the least amount of positional power and credibility within their respective organizations, but the expectation for them to work effectively with the most challenging situations is high. To achieve their mission, staff need continuous guidance and supervision regarding their activities, and they must perceive that they will be supported. Although *empowerment* is an overused term that has lost its meaning, suffice it to say that no person can empower another unless they themselves are empowered. The challenge is to create an organizational culture that is trusting enough to allow its members to have latitude to do their jobs. Within this view, the job of the administrator or leader is not to ensure that staff comply with all policies and protocols, but rather to ensure that staff have the resources and supports they need in order to be successful. Only individuals with perspective and positional power can enable this change in organizational culture to occur.

Another method for strengthening organizational capacity relates to the theoretical and conceptual basis for integrated service interventions. The traditional service system bases its practices on a set of beliefs about the efficacy of individual and small-group psychotherapeutic interventions, and their attendant language systems. There are some other program models (e.g., partial hospitalization, crisis intervention), but most outpatient services are delivered within this paradigm. Most individuals within the system have been trained in this view, and the administrative and financial system of the organization reinforces the perspective.

Although the language of health care pervades the current marketplace, it appears that the field's reliance on this funding source will diminish because of managed care. There is a vast literature that is highly relevant to integrated services, in areas such as community psychology and psychiatry, ecological views of child development, ecosystemic therapy, and crisis prevention and intervention. Many of these ideas are part of the training of psychologists but have been lost in the glare of health care conceptualizations (e.g., diagnosis and treatment of mental disorders). Psychologists can play a role in resurrecting and systematizing these concepts and researching their efficacy.

At an individual level, the essence of integrated service systems resides in case conceptualization. Having a more responsive language system that is commonly understood can enable front-line staff to conduct their work. Many paradigm pioneers struggle to integrate the various approaches and perspectives they encounter in the marketplace. For example, many child-serving organizations are dominated by a child-protective view, wherein the primary function of the organization is to safeguard the child from physical or psychological injury. Obviously, this is a crucial function, but it can lead to adversarial and coercive interactions with families in which those who are not "compliant" with treatment activities (e.g., not going to therapy) are seen as "resistant" or worse. Having a clearer, ecologically based conceptualization can help with this.

Similarly, the language and methods of office-based psychotherapy and psychotropic medications can be troublesome for staff to integrate with alternative methods, leading to an implicit "pecking order" in which so-called professional clinical activities take precedence and other activities are relegated to an ancillary role. Staff can benefit from leadership designed to elevate and integrate their roles and responsibilities by helping them frame the words and concepts of their message.

People engaged in systems change within child mental health organizations must also confront the implicit belief system that governs how things work. Underlying much of how organizations work is a shared set of values and ideas about people and about interventions. In promoting an alternative, more integrated formulation, some of the most cherished ideas of the established order will need to be examined. Table 1 presents a partial set of statements that traditional mental health organizations may hold and contrasts these with more integrative alternatives.

A final point in regard to systems building and organizational change is the need to focus more attention on leadership development. Leaders can emerge at all levels and can include family members, program staff,

Table 1.   Traditional Versus Integrated Beliefs in Child Mental Health System

Traditional View	Integrated View
About children	
Children engage in problem behaviors because they are "mentally ill."	Child problem behavior serves a function in the complex systems within which it is embedded.
If the child is having problems, there must be an underlying, undiscovered pathological state.	Problems can only be understood by examining interactions among complex systems.
If the child does not respond to interventions, alternate diagnoses need to be considered.	Lack of response to intervention is due either to inadequate conceptualization or insufficient implementation.
Elaborate and sophisticated case conceptualizations based on high levels of professional expertise are desirable.	Simple, straightforward, and realistic conceptualizations that lead to intervention that is practical and understood by all are desired.
Crises are disastrous and are to be avoided.	Crises can teach about how systems are working (or not working) and lead to creative solutions.
Insight and understanding into the historical sources and developmental bases of problems are necessary and sufficient conditions to create change.	What matters most is what can be done in the "here and now" to change behavior, improve interaction patterns, and achieve more functional systemic balance.
Maladaptive behavior will disappear if its function and communicative intent can be understood.	It is important to understand what function problem behavior serves, but even more important to intervene to change it in a tangible, practical manner.
Rapid and durable change is/is not possible and can be predicted by a diagnostic formulation.	It is impossible to predict with any certainty how individuals will respond to specific interventions; interventions should be seen as evolving experiments to be learned from.
About families	
Things should not be the way they are (e.g., families should not be "dysfunctional").	Things are the way they are. No one sets out to create problems for themselves. Interventions must begin where clients are and not blame them for their difficulties.
If families would only do their part, the client would get better.	Families need support to enhance competence and ameliorate stress, resulting in improved child outcomes.
Interventions fail because clients/families are resistant.	Interventions fail because the service system has difficulty determining how to be helpful in a given circumstance.
There is not much professionals can do, because there is too much "craziness" elsewhere in the person's life that cannot be controlled for.	It is a given that family situations are complex and difficult. The challenge to the system is to determine how to intervene rationally, strategically, and effectively.

Table 1. (*Continued*)

Traditional View	Integrated View
Dysfunctional families cannot be trusted to identify their needs and to make decisions.	Families can articulate what they need if professionals listen carefully. A primary challenge of intervention is to enable families to display new competencies and make better decisions.
Families must participate in all aspects of the intervention in order for any resources to be dedicated.	The perspective of the family in terms of their needs and desires is primary; help is not conditioned on "compliance."
About Programs and Interventions	
There is one right and perfect technique or strategy that, once discovered, will make the problem disappear.	There is no "magic bullet." Complex problems require complex solutions.
If we can find the right placement or people to work with the child, "intense treatment" will occur.	There are no demonstrable levels of "intensity" of treatment, based on placement, professional credential, or technique. Treatment efficacy is based on appropriateness, fidelity, and sustainability.
Treatment is what happens in hospitals, specialized facilities, and professional programs.	Treatment is what happens in "real-life" situations in the context of the person's interactions with the social systems that surround him or her.
If we send the person away for "treatment" they will be more ready for community-based interventions.	It is not always helpful to go to another location (e.g., hospital) to get ready for living in the community; the real challenge is to strengthen community systems to address needs.
Having a plan is the same as implementing a plan.	Instead of investing so much effort in developing written products to satisfy regulatory requirements, team development should focus on ongoing planning.
Once it is demonstrated that the child can change behavior, services can be gradually withdrawn.	Many individuals need ongoing supports in order to sustain the gains they make. Families may need ongoing help in "navigating" the service system.
Intergency collaboration is the same as teamwork.	Merely writing an interorganizational agreement and holding periodic meetings is insufficient; teamwork requires shared values, ongoing development, conflict management, and shared routines.
If everyone would just agree on goals and work together, problems would disappear.	Conflict can be a useful element of intervention planning. Just because consesus is reached about problems and goals, efficacious solutions will not always emerge.

Table 1. (*Continued*)

Traditional View	Integrated View
The more services we can bring to bear, the more change will occur.	More is not always better; the issue is to ensure that resources are allocated in an integrated, targeted manner.
The more advanced the provider's degree, the more helpful will be their involvement.	Persons with advanced training can perform valuable functions, but front-line providers and family members play the most crucial role with respect to sustainable change. All must work together in an atmosphere of trust, equality, and commitment.

administrators, and others. In addition to their presumptive roles as leaders within their organizations and settings, psychologists can help to facilitate the identification and empowerment of leaders in child mental health. Leadership development relates to four essential functions that leaders perform: (a) leaders establish a clear vision of what needs to happen and infuse the intervention with this vision; (b) leaders exemplify commitment; (c) leaders create the conditions under which intervention can be successful, to include focus and collaboration; and (d) leaders discover and unleash talent and resources.

Family Support and Community-Building

One of the most underdeveloped components of integrated systems of care is family support. This strategy is grounded in recognition that children's needs can only be understood in the context of the systems within which they are embedded. This implies, for example, that child-rearing effectiveness is in part a function of the stressors that the family experiences (e.g., poverty), tempered by sources of informal and formal support (e.g., friends, child care) in the environment. Family support interventions are those that seek to respond to family-perceived needs for support, as opposed to addressing only dysfunction, incompetence, and psychopathology. A major challenge for professionals, including psychologists, is to listen carefully to what families say they need, and design interventions around these perceived needs.

Many children and families served by child mental health programs have long and involved histories, some of which involve their interactions with the service system itself. Suffice it to say that not all of this is positive. Professionals come to the process with their own perspectives and biases about how children and families should behave. Given this, it is not surprising that a pervasive problem within the system is learning to trust families, no matter what difficulties they are experiencing.

Despite the fact that much that has transpired in some family backgrounds is likely to have been destructive and perhaps even violent, family systems remain the most powerful elements in children's lives. Family involvement and response to intervention seems likely to account for the most variance in terms of success or failure. Stated alternatively, research and clinical experience suggest that youngsters who do not have an involved family are at the greatest risk for poor outcomes. Parenthetically, no such evidence has emerged to the effect that unavailability of psychologists, social workers, or other program professionals is a risk factor for life adjustment.

Unfortunately, program professionals often find themselves in adversarial relationships with parents, rather than finding ways to align with the family and provide support that is empowering. Even in the most dysfunctional family (a categorization that is often pejorative), there are strengths that can be worked with, resources that can be used, and needs that can be supported. Psychologists can help to create conditions within which families are seen in this more positive manner.

When families are not engaged positively in intervention programs and those programs are unsuccessful, there is a tendency to characterize these families as "resistant" or "unmotivated." In reality, there are only two reasons for intervention failure—the intervention was poorly conceived or the intervention was not implemented effectively. Lack of family involvement can thus be seen as insufficient attention to perceived family needs and trust building, necessary ingredients of case conceptualization. Or, if parents do not learn to manage their children more effectively, perhaps the most efficacious training model was not implemented. This logic argues for the establishment of a blame-free environment in which no one is to be faulted and responsibility for change is shared collectively. Not blaming others is central to psychological theories about healthy family systems. Why should it not also apply to the child mental health system?

Finally, there is the common problem of sources of family support being unavailable or inaccessible in a given community. *Community-building* is a broad term that encompasses intervention activities of resource development. These may be as simple as helping the family identify a church, linking them with concerned parishioners, and ensuring that they can find transportation to church activities. More often it involves working with others, such as service coordinators, to develop needed programs and services. Such services may be of a specialized nature, but in resource-poor communities the problem may be lack of leadership or sufficient need to justify the development of group programs (e.g., child care, after-school activities program, summer recreation). Assisting in the development of such generic programs helps in focusing on the child and family, but helps others with similar needs. Community building can also serve as a preventive, system-strengthening activity.

In a larger sense, community-building is nothing more or less than trying to create for each individual what Sarason (1974) called the *psychological sense of community* that everyone needs. This is the perception of belonging and organic connection to others. Many of the problems experienced by children with emotional disorders and their families are rooted in this dynamic.

Summary

The present chapter has argued that psychological practitioners within the child mental health system are in crisis. In order to survive and thrive, the profession must anticipate and respond to the challenges of the emerging marketplace. This will require attention to a broader range of variables and the ability to function in new roles such as administrator, consultant, educator, planner, and evaluator. The well-established integrated-service movement within child mental health offers instructive lessons for how the marketplace of the future will look and feel, and has implications for how psychologists think about and organize for practice. Through an openness to new ideas, informed by careful listening to consumers, psychologists can make their services indispensable and, at the same time, contribute to a more integrated, responsive service system.

References

Day, C., & Roberts, M. C. (1991). Activities of the Child and Adolescent Service System Program for improving mental health services for children and families. *Journal of Clinical Child Psychology, 20,* 340–350.

Duchnowski, A. J., & Friedman, R. M. (1990). Children's mental health: Challenges for the nineties. *Journal of Mental Health Administration, 17,* 3–12.

Illback, R. J. (1995). *Evaluation of the Kentucky IMPACT program at year five: Accomplishments, challenges, and opportunities.* Frankfort, KY: Kentucky Department of Mental Health.

Illback, R. J., & Neill, T. K. (1995). Service coordination in mental health systems for children, youth, and families: Progress, problems, prospects. *Journal of Mental Health Administration, 22,* 17–28.

Illback, R. J., Sanders, D., & Birkby, B. (1995). *Evaluation of the Kentucky IMPACT program at year five: Accomplishments, challenges, and opportunities.* Frankfort, KY: Kentucky Department of Mental Health.

Peterson, D. R. (1996). Making psychology indispensable. *Applied and Preventive Psychology, 5,* 1–8.

Sarason, S. (1974). *The psychological sense of community: Prospects for a community psychology.* San Francisco: Jossey-Bass.

Stroul, B., Goldman, S., Lourie, I., Katz-Leavy, J., & Zeigler-Dendy, C. (1992). *Profiles of local systems of care for children and adolescents with severe emotional disturbances.* Washington, DC: Georgetown University Child Development Center, CASSP Technical Assistance Center.

Trivette, C. M., Dunst, C. J., Boyd, K., & Humby, D. W. (1995). Family-oriented program models: Helpgiving practices and parental control appraisals. *Exceptional Children, 62,* 237–248.

13

Systems-Oriented Independent Psychological Practice

W. David Driscoll

As professional psychology evolves in the context of late-twentieth-century American culture, new challenges stimulate the field. Psychology professionals are accustomed to rapid change and exciting developments because psychology is an adolescent profession searching for adult roles that permit continued growth while stabilizing and securing its marketplace position. This chapter examines an area of great potential for the independent practice of psychology: serving children and families through an integrated model of care. New models of mental health care are briefly considered. The evolution of professional psychology is reviewed for its potential contribution to this new model of care, with particular reference to relevant competencies of professional psychologists, conceptual bases for its use in independent psychological practice, potential delivery structures, and barriers to implementation. Finally, the appendix to this chapter presents a case example illustrating potential roles for independent psychological practitioners within an integrated-care model.

The need for alternative approaches to mental health service for children and families is well documented (Illback, 1994; National Commission on Children, 1991). With shrinking resources and increased social demands ubiquitous to postmodern society, the era of mental health interventions based on individual belief systems and preferences is past. As our field matures within the evolving culture, interventions must "pass muster" theoretically, empirically, clinically, and economically. Although these demands increase pressure on mental health organizations and professionals, they also present opportunities for professional psychologists to demonstrate the strengths of our interventions.

New Models of Mental Health Care

As illustrated in the first two sections of this book, integrated-services models that redefine basic principles about relationships among care providers, organizations, and consumers have emerged. Parallel developments have occurred in the field of mental health intervention, with effective and integrated approaches to care emerging within family psychology. Many of the distinctive features of integrated care developed independently as separate threads in the field of family therapy. These threads are now beginning to be woven together in integrated models of family systems intervention. Accessibility to services, early identification, family competence and strength orientations, needs-based focus, cultural compatibility, and outcome evaluation have all been cornerstones in the development of family systems intervention (Broderick & Schraeder, 1991). Mikesell, Lusterman, and McDaniel (1995) presented a comprehensive overview of the current state of family psychology, with model systems-oriented approaches to family intervention representing the latest thinking in the field.

While there are many discrete orientations to family intervention (Gurman & Kniskern, 1981, 1991), practitioners are practical and eclectic, drawing techniques as needed from a variety of sources. One integrative approach of particular note is the evolving Rochester model, often referred to as *transitional family therapy* (Seaburn, Landau-Stanton, & Horwitz, 1995). This model conceptualizes, organizes, plans, delivers, and evaluates integrative family interventions. The model is unique in its integration of family therapy theories and techniques. It promotes prescriptive application of systemic interventions, drawing techniques selectively from a variety of theoretical and conceptual models of family systems intervention. Practitioners applying this model may select or combine techniques from broad categories of family intervention: here and now (de Shazer, 1982; Haley, 1976; Minuchin, 1974); transgenerational (Ackerman, 1966; Boszormenyi-Nagy & Spark, 1973; Bowen, 1978; Carter & McGoldrick, 1980, 1988); and ecosystemic (Imber-Coppersmith, 1985; Speck & Attneave, 1973). The exciting aspect of the Rochester Model is its implicit recognition of the maturing family systems psychology field. Competition among theoretical models is irrelevant when seeking effective interventions for clients and families. Conceptually, this parallels integrative developments in individual clinical psychology that emerged as the field matured (see Lazarus, 1989) and represents the direction of the maturing family psychology field.

Beyond integrated-systems intervention at the client or family level, family systems psychology has been applied to intervention with larger systems. Speck and Attneave (1973) pioneered the networking of systems beyond the immediate family as a legitimate focus for intervention. Similarly, Imber-Coppersmith (1985) suggested the involvement of members of social systems beyond the family as potential resources for intervention, on the assumption that these extended systems could be significant naturalistic resources to families coping with problems.

These developments within family systems psychology parallel and complement the developments in integrated care. These similarities are only logical when one considers the compatibility of their charges: to bring about practical, positive, and sustainable change for individuals and families in crisis. The convergence of these two important professional areas suggests possibilities for professional psychology in general and for systems-oriented practitioners specifically.

Macroorganizational systems evolve to accommodate the needs of populations being served (Greiner, 1972; Stanton, 1992). Examining extant organizational systems and structures merely gives one a snapshot in time of the evolution of those systems. As this evolution proceeds unimpeded by artificial regulatory control and is permitted to respond to market forces, the most efficient systems will evolve. Logically, this process can be even more efficient and responsive when informed and guided by current and effective professional knowledge and skills. In the case of evolving integrated mental health services for children and families, professional systems-oriented psychology is in a unique position to inform and lead this change process.

Psychology's Potential in the New Model

At this stage of development, the competencies necessary for psychologists participating in integrated mental health care models are still emerging. Nonetheless, practitioners can consider what competencies psychologists have that might lead the change in practice to an integrated family-systems-oriented approach. Psychologists have a long tradition of clinical innovation and empirical evaluation, which positions them uniquely to lead the human services community toward more effective models of care. Ideas that have revolutionized mental health care in the past often have been developed, applied, and validated by psychologists. Client-centered psychotherapy, Gestalt and experiential techniques, behavioral interventions, cognitive–behavioral therapies, and family systems approaches represent some major examples of psychology's leadership in the evolution of mental health care (Ellis, 1962; Rogers, 1951; Skinner, 1953; Wynne, 1961). Psychologists have also led the way in examining and evaluating the effectiveness of mental health intervention (Garfield, 1991; Seligman, 1995; Smith, Glass, & Miller, 1980; Whiston & Sexton, 1993). Beyond approaches to individual and family mental health care, psychologists have shared in leadership roles developing and validating innovative organizational approaches to mental health care (Cowen, 1996; Cummings & Follette, 1968; Sarason & Doris, 1979).

Psychologists are uniquely trained to play an important role in the evolution of integrated care. The breadth, depth, and intensity of training for professional psychologists in mental health domains is unsurpassed by other professions. Educational standards for psychologists trained at the doctoral level include basic courses in scientific methods of investigation; measurement; psychological theory; ethics; psychological assessment; consultation; individual, group, family, and systems intervention; physiology; and psychopharmacology (Peterson, 1995; Peterson et al., 1991). In addition, predoctoral internship training is required and postdoctoral specialty training is commonly expected for advanced professional psychologists, suggesting a further maturing of the profession. Beyond extensive generic training in psychology, many professional psychologists ultimately focus on an area of intervention or practice on the basis of their own experiences and preferences. This trend is evident by the proliferation of postdoctoral training experiences, external credentialing organizations, and American Psychological Association (APA) professional practice divisions.

In addition to the qualifications and experiences of independent professional psychologists, the marketplace penetration of professional psychologists across the United States is increasing at a steady rate, with independent practitioners currently accessible to most communities. Primary and specialist physicians understand the unique perspective and skill offered by psychologists. Mental health and human services colleagues often refer for assessment, consultation, and intervention services. Health care insurers make wide and effective use of direct patient services by psychologists. Consumers are also becoming more informed about psychologists' skills as they seek services in the health care marketplace.

Another asset of psychologists' participation in integrated care models is familiarity with emerging demand for effective and efficient interventions. For independent psychologists, the marketplace is a source of ongoing feedback on professional effectiveness. Referral sources expect results. Patients want to get better and stay better. Payors expect efficiency and effectiveness. Practicing within the evolving managed care health insurance environment forces psychologists to deliver cost-effective interventions that help patients get better and stay better. Inefficiency and limited effectiveness are forced out of independent psychologists' practices much more quickly than would occur in an organizational environment insulated from market forces, as occurs in many mental health centers and hospitals. These are potentially healthy characteristics that contribute to the foundation of increased effectiveness and relevance demanded by integrated care models (Peterson, 1996).

Not all psychologist practitioners will find integrated care approaches compatible with their professional approaches, practice patterns, or office infrastructures. It would be naive and misleading to suggest that integrated care models could effectively incorporate all current psychological approaches to intervention. While superficially appearing atheoretical and potentially incorporating competing treatment models under a new umbrella, integrated care will not be compatible with all treatment approaches. Integrated care involves more than increasing connections among care givers while delivering the same old product. It represents a true reconceptualization of service delivery. Professional psychology is unique in its potential to participate in this transition, creating new and exciting practice opportunities, and practitioners need to identify relevant professional assets that can inform integrated care approaches.

Systems-Oriented Independent Psychological Practice

In this section, a framework for conceptualizing an integrated-care model of systems-oriented independent practice will be presented. The framework is presented in summary form, followed by an expanded consideration of its application, including practical aspects of practicing within this model. Finally, barriers to systems-oriented independent practice are discussed, including infrastructure issues (e.g., office space and locations, support staff, equipment) and professional and organizational traditions (e.g. patient relationships, interprofessional communications, reimbursement structures).

A Framework for Practice

The revolutionary idea of independent providers participating in integrated care systems may be less intimidating as psychologists begin to conceptualize and shape their roles within those systems. There are many activities in which independent psychologists are currently engaged that reflect dimensions of integrated care. And there are a variety of ways to conceptualize these activities: in a temporal sense or in regard to the stage of professional involvement; in terms of structure, addressing indicated client levels of intervention; in terms of provider distance or whether professional involvement is direct or consultative; and finally, according to the integrated care component being considered. Although each of these concepts has heuristic value for analyzing professional practice and some overlap exists among them, two have been selected for the framework presented here: temporal stage of intervention and component of integrated care. It is intended that this framework will assist independent professional psychologists to assess the compatibility of their current practices with principles of integrated care. Furthermore, this framework can provide a structure for developing systems-oriented psychology practices consistent with integrated care.

Figure 1 presents this two-dimensional framework. The temporal stage dimension considers the point in time of the professional activity, from initial identification through outcome evaluation. The integrated care dimension includes five major components of integrated care models gleaned from those reviewed previously (Illback, 1994; Weissbourd & Kagan, 1989).

The temporal stage of intervention. The temporal stage is a dimension of analysis commonly applied to psychological interventions, useful to clarify the process and check to ensure that professional involvement has proceeded in a sequential and comprehensive fashion. *Identification* (the first stage) considers the source of the problem such as whether a family seeks assistance directly from a hospital emergency room or following a few months of family discussion about whether to seek professional help. *Assessment and planning* (the second stage) includes thorough review and analysis of a problem situation, leading to more in-depth understanding and planned intervention. This stage can be brief or extended. The critical elements are that interventions are selected on the basis of a reasonable understanding of the problem situation and agreement about desired outcomes. Examples of activities at this point include collecting records of previous community involvements, contacting significant collateral sup-

TEMPORAL STAGE OF INTERVENTION

INTEGRATED CARE COMPONENT		Identification	Assessment & Planning	Intervention	Evaluation
	Accessibility	– Location – Availability – Open access	– Provider flexibility – Communication alternatives	– Convenience of consumers (e.g. location, schedule)	– Planning follow-up – Maintaining contact – Permission for access
	Prevention & Early Identification	– Community awareness – Knowledge of risk factors	– Definition of community need – Primary vs Secondary prevention	– Access to risk groups – Packaging interventions – Funding strategies	– Community norms – Comparative occurrence rate – Reduced severity
	Strength Oriented	– Positive framing – Balance of assets & problems	– Expansion on assets – Taxonomy of strengths – Develop strength-based solutions	– Apply strength-based solutions – Retain & expand client strengths	– Compile positive outcomes – Connection to client strengths
	Need Based	– Concrete problem presentation – Need based problem statements	– Taxonomy of client needs – Delineation & results of past interventions	– Prescriptive interventions – Technically eclectic strategies	– Convenient evaluation framework (e.g. met vs unmet needs) – Basis for future planning
	Community & Culturally Compatible	– Awareness of community & cultural norms	– Non-judgmental approach – Agreement on compatible goals & strategies	– Culturally sensitive delivery of interventions (e.g. respect nontraditional family structures)	– Gauging outcomes through community standards

Figure 1. Key issues in systems-oriented psychology practice.

port persons in the community, and doing individual psychological testing. *Intervention* (the third stage) involves applying selected activities to help bring about desired changes. Although often requiring the most time of any of the temporal stages, intervention can also be the point where the professional's thinking is most restricted. Professionals may tend to do what they know in ways they have done before and unwittingly narrow intervention options for those in their care. *Evaluation* (the final stage) is often neglected. This stage involves reviewing the results of interventions to determine effectiveness. This step can be informal or systematic, leading to some objective conclusions about what professionals have done for clients in their care.

The familiarity of the temporal dimensions of service delivery and logical problem-solving processes (Haley, 1976) should reinforce the idea that the professional directions proposed in this framework do not presuppose a total departure from past skills and practices. Combining these logical frameworks with the powerful and revolutionary assumptions of integrated care should enhance professional psychologists' ability to help their clients in a changing society and health care marketplace.

The integrated care component. The integrated care dimension of this model presents relevant components of integrated care. Through a heuristic consideration of these components, professionals can guide their activities consistent with this model and gauge their compliance with the principles of this model. Condensed from the earlier review, the salient dimensions of integrated care include five core components. The *accessibility* component considers the degree to which services are readily available to consumers with no barriers to care. *Prevention and early identification* considers the degree to which services are introduced early in the progressive development of problems and difficulties. The *strength-oriented* component is focused on an orientation to care that emphasizes positive attributes of the client as the starting point for intervention. This component is especially critical in that it confronts assumptions of a disease-oriented medical model of care, that there is something wrong with the client that needs to be fixed. *Need-based* considerations assume that interventions will be developed and targeted to difficulties and problems identified by the consumer. For professional relevance, effectiveness, and durability, consumers need to experience interventions as helpful for problems they are experiencing. *Community and cultural compatibility* covers a wide range of features dealing with contextual parameters potentially affecting the efficacy of interventions. These features include, for example, ethnicity, race, gender, age, and cultural norms. Compatibility on these dimensions can affect significantly the degree of effectiveness of interventions.

Integrating Framework Components

To explain the style of independent psychological practice proposed here, each of the components of Figure 1 is considered. Examples have been selected that highlight the concepts presented, while application of this model to one's own practice will generate unique examples. The two additional factors mentioned earlier, client level and provider distance, will be considered where relevant.

Accessibility. As noted earlier, client accessibility to services is a core component of integrated care. Manifestations of accessibility in independent practice include such features as geographic, physical, electronic, and emergency access. At both the identification and assessment and planning stages, where clients first come to the attention of service providers, this component can be critical. Geographic proximity and ease of traveling to a provider's location often can facilitate communication among colleagues. Ideally, these colleagues would have easy access throughout the process. Being able to drop in or call about a potential client's need or consulting on the spot in an urgent situation can aid the process immeasurably and set a positive foundation for future work. Accessibility is a factor at the intervention stage as well. If a client has to travel a long distance or go to a culturally foreign community for services, the likelihood of reliably continuing with services is reduced. Similarly, for the independent psychologists to participate in treatment planning and follow-up conferences on clients, they need to be accessible. Electronic access systems have streamlined this process, and simple features like flexible office hours can significantly impact effectiveness. Monday-through-Friday 9-to-5 hours, while personally convenient, often prevent real access to professional involvement. In our postmodern 24-hour society, traditional office hours and locations limit access. Evaluation often takes place informally through ongoing interprovider and follow-up client contact, further emphasizing the need for accessibility.

Accessibility is also a frame of mind and a set of beliefs about where one fits into the intervention process for a client. Traditional conceptualizations about psychologists' relationships with clients and referral sources might suggest that privacy and limited external communication might be best for the intervention process. Seeing oneself as one part of a team brings with it clear expectations for open access. Certainly this is not just an issue with the psychologist. Sometimes, community providers or collateral professionals are interested in only limited communication with psychologists, viewing our involvement as a discrete and specialized activity. Attempts at communicating with these individuals can help the psychologist to understand the professional context within which the client is operating and identify opportunities for education of colleagues about alternative perspectives on psychological care.

Prevention and early intervention. The second component of integrated care, prevention and early intervention, addresses treatment issues related to the appropriate point of intervention. Involvement of independent psychologists in this dimension of care presents challenges and opportunities. Identification of situations for interventions takes on new meaning: How do we become involved in intervention for difficulties that have yet to become manifest? Similarly, how do we assess, plan, and intervene with people and systems who have yet to show difficulties or are at the earliest stages of struggling with stressors? Finally, how do we evaluate successful prevention activities? This component of intervention has traditionally been left to community-based organizational programs (Cowen, 1996) and community psychologists. Rarely would these professionals be operating as independent professionals given the traditions of independent psychology practice. Nonetheless, opportunities can exist. Ongoing relationships among community-based care systems can open opportunities for involvement in this dimension of care. Certainly knowledge in the field of psychology is at a stage where external stressors can be anticipated and individual factors that put children and families at risk for adjustment difficulties can be identified (National Advisory Mental Health Council, 1996). From an independent practice platform, much can be done to respond in helpful ways. Community-service presentations, support groups, and reference-material development are examples of proactively helpful activities. Reference lists of self-help materials could be beneficial for colleagues and clients. Educationally oriented programs for children and families, reviewing healthy responses to predictable stressors, could be helpful in primary prevention. Identification of groups and individuals at high risk for dysfunction is a legitimate secondary prevention activity for psychologists also. At the individual level, consulting with colleagues about incipient difficulties with individuals or groups of clients could be valuable.

Again, issues of professional orientation assert themselves. Competencies in preventive and psychoeducational approaches can be developed if considered important for one's practice. Beyond a functional marketing strategy to develop a traditional outpatient practice, prevention and early intervention holds value for communities and can be part of integrated-care initiatives. Nonetheless, the establishment of prevention and early intervention presents unique challenges. Professionals and consumers are accustomed to intervening when problems reach a threshold where some functional impairment is evident. Third-party payors generally require mental health symptoms to reach what they call a crisis before interventions will be reimbursed. Ongoing education of colleagues, clients, and payors about the value of early intervention, both through direct discussion and demonstration with individual cases, could be ongoing activity for psychologists. Developing financing for these initiatives requires creativity and could include community-based service grants, public support from state and federal block grants, and even reimbursement from third-party payors where longer term financial savings on mental health expenditures could be demonstrated at the local level. Ultimately, psychologists may need to contribute pro bono professional time to the development of prevention and early intervention activities.

Strength orientation. The strength orientation component is central to integrated care and may represent the greatest challenge to traditionally trained psychologists practicing independently within this model. Traditional training models and contemporary practice exigencies orient the mental health field toward pathology. Psychologists are generally asked to diagnose and treat problems. Institutions and payors are often interested in labeling disorders so that responsibilities and expectations can be clarified. Strength-oriented interventions represent a way of conceptualizing people and problems that focuses on strengths concurrently with presented problems. At identification and assessment and planning stages, although there is implicit recognition of difficulties, strength-oriented approaches can be used to clarify problems by delineating a client's assets. Presumably these assets form a basis for organizing effective interventions for the client, but also orient the professional relationship positively and give hope to clients who may be discouraged with their circumstances. This approach can be questioned and criticized as superficial and as potentially missing important information about a client's pathology. The intent in this process is not to minimize the client's distress but to balance interactions in ways that will increase the likelihood of producing positive outcomes. Similarly, at the intervention stage, professional activities are oriented to focus on what is occurring already that is positive for the direction of change desired by the client. From behavior theory, reinforcing incremental positive change is a fundamental principle. Within a systems-oriented framework, interventions are generally developed to begin the change process by capitalizing on strengths within families, with the goal of establishing more enduring and resilient patterns of functioning. Evaluation follows logically as the next step, with positive indicators of change already developed for reference in previous steps. Expressing reduction in symptoms as increased positive behaviors may be simply reorienting one's thinking about change.

Remaining oriented to client strengths presents increased professional challenges, especially as the degree of client dysfunction becomes more severe. Attending to positives in a balanced way can be crucial to improved outcome when things are most bleak for clients. Consider a case example of a man whose recurrent outbursts of rage in community agencies and programs led to his exclusion from services and multiple referrals to a local mental health providers. The diagnoses of intermittent explosive disorder, oppositional defiant disorder, and bipolar disorder did not help to contain his rage. Prescriptions for psychotropic medications were refused by the client and reinforced his frustration with a service system he viewed as nonresponsive and blameful. Fortunately, he was referred to a psychologist who listened patiently to his decade-long saga of social and economic frustration. While continually highlighting the positive attributes of his persistence in pursuing a better life for himself and his family, the rage was controlled and eventually channeled toward appropriate self-advocacy and volunteer participation a local community action program.

Needs-based intervention. Developing needs-based interventions represents a unique dimension of independent psychological practice based on integrated care concepts. The application of needs-based principles involves determining the focus of professional activity with a client on the basis of delineation of needs. This process is atheoretical, helping clients formulate their objectives concretely so that relevant help can be delivered and outcomes accurately measured. It is appropriate to assist clients with this process, but the product should ultimately represent a clear compilation of client needs. This process could result in the psychologist playing a minor role in the client's care when needs are outside the scope of professional domains or competencies. Alternatively, the psychologist could play a major role in direct or indirect service delivery. Conceptual challenges for psychologists in this component of integrated care involve expanding thinking about domains and dimensions of needs beyond the individual client level. Integrated delivery systems assume that client needs are embedded in social and community structures. Helping clients may involve pursuing change at these broader organizational levels. Adequate child care, recreational opportunities, transportation needs, and basic academic skill development may be important needs that require psychologists to reach beyond their traditional roles to help a client function more effectively.

Identification and assessment and planning stages in this component are focused on stating client problems clearly and positively, in terms that can be translated into concrete action plans. A depressed adolescent's needs might be to increase the frequency of social contacts, attend school regularly, and reduce illicit drug use. A family member experiencing increasingly violent and dangerous parental behavior might need his or her safety to be secured. Interventions follow logically from needs-based identification, assessment, and planning. Once needs are stated clearly and concisely, interventions can be developed and delivered to address those needs. Evaluation becomes a simple process of gauging whether those needs have been met.

Community and cultural compatibility. Finally, within the community and cultural compatibility components are broader contextual considerations for functioning effectively as a professional psychologist within integrated care service structures. This challenge of practicing compatibly with clients' social and cultural systems transcends intervention stages— from determining the significance and meaning of certain behaviors during identification; to designing and delivering acceptable and effective interventions during assessment, planning, and intervention; to evaluating effectiveness by including the degree to which these factors have been integrated as a component of outcome measurement.

This component is easy to understand and challenging to implement. The professional literature is replete with references to cultural sensitivity in the areas of race, gender, ethnicity, age, and culture (Giordano & Carini-Giordano, 1995; Hare-Mustin & Marecek, 1988; McGoldrick, Pierce, & Giordano, 1982; Philpot & Brooks, 1995). Professional psychologists certainly should be familiar with these ideas on a cognitive level. Translating these laudable concepts into workable professional practice regularities is another matter. Logically, this requires an ongoing process of awareness and renewal whereby cultural sensitivity is constantly scrutinized in the context of professional practice. Beyond just accepting modified cultural norms for child and family behavior, and their relationship to larger societal systems, beyond being an active member of the culture in question for maximum credibility and effectiveness, psychologists hoping to integrate their professional services need to operate with growing awareness and respect for cultural exigencies without compromising professional effectiveness. For example, it is not necessary to accept violence when working in a violent culture. Nonetheless, the interpretation of the violence needs to be done with an awareness of cultural and contextual norms.

Barriers to Professional Psychologist Participation in Integrated Care

Alongside arguments for professional psychologist participation in integrated care exist numerous factors that complicate and potentially limit full involvement in this model. Although heretofore we focused on advantages, it is important to highlight the compromises and sacrifices that come with systems-oriented practice. Many of these are simply modifications to be considered when shifting practice orientation. Some represent major changes in practice regularities. Others involve examination of fundamental assumptions that may prevent a move toward systemic practice.

Infrastructure Issues

All professional practice requires supportive infrastructure (e.g., office space, equipment, support personnel), with the nature and degree of infrastructure often reflecting the practice style of the psychologist. Psychologists practicing alone within an individual model of care may require the least degree of infrastructure for successful practice, such as a home office, telephone answering system, office entry and reception, and appointments. At the other end of the spectrum is the systems-oriented psychologist, who needs to maintain expanded overhead in direct correlation to the degree of integration with other provider and patient systems. Some of these infrastructure demands have evolved for all practicing psychologists, with increased expectations for professional access and communication with payors, but the systemic practitioner bears a special weight in this area. Examples of this infrastructure include adequate sophisticated electronic communication equipment (e.g., fax machines, pagers, cellular phones), office space large enough to accommodate group meetings, multiple locations to assure services are readily accessible to consumers, and office support staffing sufficient to manage increased demands. Time, the professional psychologist's most valuable asset, is under increased demand in systems-oriented practice. Communication with persons other than the client takes time both within planned sessions and in response to other requests for communication. This increased demand can raise costs and reduce income for systems-oriented psychologists unless anticipated and managed effectively.

Organizational Traditions

There are other factors that fall loosely under the heading of organizational traditions that impact the practice of systems-oriented psychology in integrated care. Confidentiality, a historic cornerstone of psychological practice, takes on new significance when practice assumptions call for increased communication among providers and consumers. Rules governing this communication must be established and clarified in the context of helping external systems take on a greater role with a client or family in need. Private practice can become less private in the service of the health and well being of the client. Judgments about confidentiality need constant scrutiny and regular review.

Reimbursement structure is another tradition in transition throughout systems-oriented care. Traditional self-pay and indemnity-based insurance plans in the private sector and Medicare and Medicaid in the public sector are all giving way to managed care delivery and reimbursement models. Whereas these changes will directly affect structural aspects of independent psychology practice like confidentiality, the demands of managed care can significantly affect practice in other ways. Superficially, managed care and integrated care seem compatible with both pursuing more limited direct care in the interest of greater efficiency and reliance on natural helping systems. Unfortunately, the systems are not always compatible. Often, in the interest of managing care, insurance companies limit psychologists' flexibility. For example, some managed care companies require documentation that is based in linear, medical, and pathology-oriented language. Alternative approaches often do not fit these requirements, although both are pursuing the same goal. Other companies' standards of care are more flexible, but still fall short of recognizing alternative models of care. Most companies deny reimbursement for any meeting that takes place out of the psychologist's office and are cautious about supporting meetings without the identified patient present. Psychologists often are proscribed from working with members of the same family. The evolution of alternative reimbursement structures (e.g., capitation, risk sharing, prospective payment) will be most effective if accompanied by increased acceptance of creative intervention practices.

A more insidious threat is the evolving practice of restricted provider panels. In many communities only the more senior psychologists are members of provider panels because they were practicing when the panels were established. Younger and more recently trained psychologists with fresh ideas and approaches are prevented from contributing to the evolving texture of mainstream mental health care in a community.

The current reality today is that systems-oriented psychologists need to prepare themselves for requests to provide care where reimbursement arrangements are not completely secure. Patients and families often fall between the cracks of health care reimbursement systems, and practicing in this environment may mean some risk of lost revenue. Although we would not long survive without regular reimbursement for our services, psychologists may take a lesson in this regard from many community-based family physicians, who understand their commitment to the health of the total community and have been selectively providing noncompensated care to patients and families for years.

Alternatively, systems-oriented psychology practice could mean a higher annual volume of patients, seen for shorter duration, with greater involvement of collateral caregivers. These factors directly impact the total market for psychological services in a community. In short, a psychologist may need a higher volume of referrals, received more consistently over a long period of time in order to sustain a systems-oriented practice. Natural economic factors could threaten a commitment to this model. With lower referral volume and hours to fill, professional psychologists might be tempted to increase activity that could be managed by others in the natural system. This could compromise the effectiveness of the model. More consistent with this author's experience, practicing within this model increases the volume of referrals over time. Professionals are more willing to refer patients with whom they will continue to be involved, and patients are more willing to participate in care when they know their involvement will be convenient and focused, and will maintain the involvement of others on whom they have come to rely and trust.

One final caution is in order about a problem that can negatively affect systems-oriented practice. Whereas many problems, especially those involving children and families, are ideal for integrated systems-oriented approaches, there clearly are some that are best addressed with private, discrete, and individual interventions. Systems-oriented psychologists need to avoid professional reactivity in assuming that narrow application of a new model is the best solution to all problems. A hallmark of systems-oriented care is flexibility and creativity focused on achieving outcomes. If the most efficacious approach to positive change in a system is 25 sessions of insight-oriented psychotherapy for one individual, systems-oriented psychologists need the flexibility to recognize and recommend that approach.

Summary

In my view, systems-oriented professional psychologists will have value as service providers across the temporal spectrum of integrated care. As primary and secondary prevention specialists, psychologists can have impact on the occurrence and development of mental health problems through awareness, education, and modeling. As crisis responders, psychologists can determine who enters care, what the expected outcomes will be, which intervention processes to implement, and how to evaluate progress. Diagnostically, they can continue to contribute in traditional ways while adding perspectives of evolving relational diagnostic systems. Direct intervention with individuals, families, groups, and organizations will continue to be needed. And evaluating treatment outcomes and follow-up care will be more crucial than ever.

Systems-oriented psychologists also will have value in delivering their services at various levels of professional involvement. Individuals, dyads, groups, families, multifamilies, treatment systems, multiple treatment systems, community, and regional levels of involvement all can be encompassed within an integrated care model. Conceptualizing intervention at multiple and simultaneous levels is compatible with the theoretical underpinnings of integrated care, involving of a wide range of individuals and systems in order to bring about sustainable changes for an individual or family in crisis. Intervening at systemic levels beyond the individual directly addresses problem development and problem resolution as isomorphic across relevant systems. Meaningful individual change can thus occur from an organizational or societal intervention; communities can change from individually focused therapeutic processes.

Overall, the main predictor of effective involvement in integrated delivery models will be how care is conceptualized, delivered, and evaluated. Pathology-driven diagnoses and linear modes of treatment are antithetical to integrated care models. They often contribute to isolation, discouragement, and negative self-efficacy, while ignoring important family and cultural assets. Focusing on positives, building on existing strengths, involving families and community care givers, targeting concrete outcomes, and knowing when to pull back artificial professional support will be markers of the independent psychologists' successful participation in integrated mental health care for children and families. The skill involved for independent psychologists will be to negotiate these dimensions of intervention to find a range of functioning that meaningfully and directly contributes to positive outcomes for clients.

In the appendix that follows, an extensive case example is presented. This fictional case represents the application of systems-oriented psychological practice to typical adolescent and family problems.

APPENDIX

Case Example

Damon, an African American teenager, was 15 at the time of the consultation with Dr. B. By all reports, he had stumped and frustrated his care givers. Due to attendence problems he had been involved with special services and programs through school. These included regular meetings with the school counselor, evaluation by the school psychologist, and numerous disciplinary referrals to the school principal. Damon was compliant during these interventions, promising to improve. His record showed that nothing was changing. As a last resort, Damon was placed on a long-term suspension and was assigned a home tutor.

Damon also had been seeing a therapist at the local community counseling center weekly for about 18 months. At first the therapist was quite pleased with her relationship with Damon, who was open and cooperative. Damon had also given permission for the therapist to speak with his parents, who were always supportive of the therapy. The therapist's initial diagnosis had been adjustment reaction, but she became concerned when Damon's behavior in the community did not change after 6 months of treatment. Following psychiatric consultation at the local mental health center, Damon's diagnosis was changed to attention-deficit/hyperactivity disorder, and he was tried on Ritalin for several months. There was considerable discrepancy in reports of the effectiveness of the medication, and it was stopped after a particularly positive week for Damon, when he admitted that he had not been taking it. After a follow-up psychiatric consultation, he was tried on Clonidine, with no apparent effect. Later, his diagnosis was changed to major depression, and a trial of Prozac seemed to be of some help, so he continued on that medication. The therapist moved and Damon was transferred to another therapist specializing in conduct disorders.

Damon's probation officer was especially frustrated, having given him several "second chances." Damon had been involved with probation since he was 12, having been referred to a preventive program after he and a friend stole beer from the loading dock of a local convenience store. Following several years of increasing frequency of minor infractions, most involving curfew violations and vandalism, Damon was remanded to family court. The probation officer was granted his request that Damon's case be transferred to another officer. The judge had been angry about Damon's continued problems in the community. He ordered him into two consecutive community-service programs and finally a 2-week residential program to give him a taste of incarceration. He also ordered a substance evaluation. When this evaluation was positive for marijuana and alcohol abuse, Damon was ordered into treatment through a local youth agency. During the next 6 months of negative reports from counselors (and positive urine screens) in three progressively more intensive substance abuse programs, Damon was dropped from outpatient treatment with a recommendation to the court for inpatient substance treatment. The counselors noted their frustration with the sporadic involvement of Damon's parents, who seemed in denial about their son's drug and alcohol problems. Damon's parents were confused and frustrated. Damon's biological father had abandoned Damon's mother while she was pregnant, and Damon's dad had been involved with him shortly after he was born, adopting him at age 6. There had always been a good relationship between Damon and his parents, and he was especially close to his mother. Damon had three younger half-brothers who looked up to him, and until a few years ago, he had helped care for them at home. Over the years, some of the counselors had seemed like they were blaming Damon's parents for all of the problems, so they became wary of getting too involved. They knew Damon needed something, but they were not sure what it was. When Damon told a friend he was thinking about killing himself, everyone agreed it was time for a change.

Dr. B was a psychologist in the area who had formerly worked several years at the local mental health clinic. He enjoyed a good reputation with most of the human services professionals in the community, although some felt that he minimized problems and terminated treatment prematurely. Several years ago, he had opened a private office where he specialized in short-term treatment. Several days a week, he consulted at various programs in the community. Dr. B was often called on by local agencies to help out with refractory, difficult, or expensive cases. He enjoyed a positive reputation in this context, even though he was not successful with every case. Family court had consented to pay for a few appointments with Dr. B since nothing else seemed to be working. Damon had been an expensive case for the county, in professional time and outright dollar expenditures. When Damon's parents called, Dr. B agreed to a few consultation visits.

Dr. B had Damon's parents sign releases for all the professionals and agencies who had been involved in his care. He also suggested that the first appointment be held at the community center in Damon's neighborhood, including all these professionals, Damon's parents, and Damon. Dr. B was sure that there had been lots of sincere effort put into Damon's case, and he knew from the history that there were many strengths in the family. All of this was confirmed at the first meeting, as particular care was taken to allow each professional to point out Damon's most positive qualities. Dr. B facilitated the group to develop a list of outcome criterion behaviors for Damon, specifying behavioral expectations. At the conclusion of this meeting, Dr. B suggested that Damon's parents be in charge of all treatment decisions. Dr. B was concerned that with so many professionals involved and so many competing diagnoses, Damon's parents had been disempowered. He knew they were caring and concerned people, and suspected that with some encouragement and direction, they could help Damon. Damon himself had demonstrated behavioral competence and personal integrity many times over the years.

One month later, Dr. B met with Damon and his parents at their home for the second consultation meeting. They agreed that while not perfect, Damon had begun to improve. Damon's parents had recommended stopping all medication, put the counseling on hold, and continued with the outpatient substance treatment. Damon had told them he thought he had a problem controlling his drug use. Dr. B collected more extensive family background at that time, which had not been included in previous materials. He discovered that Damon had been named after his biological father. Damon's mother acknowledged increasing fear that he was turning out like his father, who was known to abuse drugs and had a criminal record. She had begun distancing herself from Damon prior to Dr. B's involvement. Surprising to all, Damon revealed that someone on the street had told him his biological father was in town and wanted to see him. He had not told his parents for fear of upsetting them. Dr. B recommended that Damon's parents begin telling him everything they knew about his biological father.

At a meeting at Dr. B's office with Damon and his parents 6 weeks later, things continued improving. They had agreed to locate Damon's biological father and had started with a letter to Damon's biological paternal grandparents. The relationship between Damon and his parents had improved substantially. Damon was still on probation and was attending the substance-treatment program. School grades had begun to improve, and the tutor was suggesting that Damon try some regular classes at the neighborhood high school. The principal agreed with some reluctance after receiving a call from Dr. B about the situation. After encouraging the family to call if things started getting out of control again and helping them to clarify what that would mean, Dr. B scheduled no further meetings. A planned follow-up phone call with the family 3 months later revealed continued improvement, and no further contact was scheduled.

This case example is representative of the application of systems-oriented psychological practice to a case, using principles of integrated care. Throughout the intervention, Dr. B made accessibility easy for the client, family, and professional community by meeting out of the office several times. Dr. B was not available for early identification of Damon's difficulties, but during assessment, he focused on Damon's positive pre-problem behavior as a basis for identifying strengths and establishing realistic expectations. Dr. B was not dissuaded in his approach by previous psychiatric diagnoses. In addition to Damon's strengths, he highlighted the parents' strengths by allowing them to determine their son's treatments. This was done within the structure of consensually established behavioral criteria, targeting Damon's needs. The total intervention was conducted with respect for the cultural context by designing a positive and respectful approach to a common collection of common problems that had discouraged other professionals. The intervention also respected the professional community that had been struggling to help Damon by continuing to use them as the primary intervention professionals. Dr. B remained involved in the treatment system just long enough to catalyze a process of positive change. There is no implication that all cases treated within this model would be amenable to such rapid and positive change. The example does demonstrate how intervening differently can be powerful and effective.

References

Ackerman, N. (1966). *Treating the troubled family*. New York: Basic Books.

Boszormenyi-Nagy, I., & Spark, (1973) *Invisible loyalties: Reciprocity in intergenerational family therapy*. New York: Harper & Row.

Bowen, M. (1978). *Family therapy in clinical practice*. New York: Jason Aaronson.

Broderick, C. B., & Schraeder, S. S. (1991). The history of professional marriage and family therapy. In A. S. Gurman, & D. P. Kniskern (Eds.), *Handbook of family therapy: Volume II*. New York: Brunner-Mazel.

Carter, E., & McGoldrick, M. (Eds.). (1980). *The family life cycle: A framework for family therapy*. New York: Gardner.

Carter, E., & McGoldrick, M. (Eds.). (1988). *The changing family life cycle: A framework for family therapy* (2nd ed.). New York: Gardner.

Cowen, E. (1996). *School-based prevention for children at risk: The primary mental health project*. Washington, DC: American Psychological Association.

Cowen, E. L., Trost, M. A., Izzo, L. D., Lorion, R. D., Dorr, D., & Isaacson, R. V. (1975). *New ways in school mental health: Early detection and prevention of school maladaptation*. New York: Human Sciences Press.

Cummings, N. A., & Follette, W. T. (1968). Psychiatric services and medical utilization in a prepaid health plan setting, Part II. *Medical Care, 6*, 31–41.

de Shazer, S. (1982) *Patterns of brief family therapy: An ecosystemic approach*. New York: Guilford Press.

Ellis, A. (1962). *Reason and emotion in psychotherapy*. New York: Stuart.

Garfield, S. L. (1991). Psychotherapy models and outcome research. *American Psychologist, 46*(12), 1350–1361.

Giordano, J., & Carini-Giordano, M. A. (1995). Ethnic dimensions in family treatment. In R. H. Mikesell, D. D. Lusterman, & S. H. McDaniel. *Integrating family therapy: Handbook of family psychology and systems theory*. Washington, DC: American Psychological Association.

Greiner, L. (1972, July/August). Evolution and revolution as organizations grow. *Harvard Business Review, 50*, 46–53.

Gurman, A. S., & Kniskern, D. P. (Eds.). (1981). *Handbook of family therapy*. New York: Brunner/Mazel.

Gurman, A. S., & Kniskern, D. P. (Eds.). (1991). *Handbook of family therapy* (Vol. II). New York: Brunner/Mazel.

Haley, J. (1976). *Problem-solving therapy*. San Francisco: Jossey-Bass.

Hare-Mustin, R., & Marecek, J. (1988). The meaning of difference: Gender theory, post-modernism, and psychology. *American Psychologist, 43*(6), 455–464.

Illback, R. J. (1994). Poverty and the crisis in children's services: The need for services integration. *Journal of Clinical Child Psychology, 23*, 413–424.

Imber-Coppersmith, E. (1985). Families and multiple helpers: A systemic perspective. In D. Campbell and R. Draper (Eds.), *Applications of systemic family therapy*. New York: Grune & Stratton.

Lazarus, A. A. (1989). *The practice of multimodal therapy*. Baltimore: Johns Hopkins University Press.

McGoldrick, M., Pierce, J. K., & Giordano, J. (Eds.). (1982). *Ethnicity and family therapy*. New York: Guilford Press.

Mikesell, R. H., Lusterman, D-D., & McDaniel, S. H. (1995). *Integrating family therapy: Handbook of family psychology and systems theory*. Washington, DC: American Psychological Association.

Minuchin, S. (1974). *Families and family therapy*. Cambridge, MA: Harvard University Press.

National Advisory Mental Health Council. (1996). Basic behavioral research for mental health. *American Psychologist, 51*, 22–28.

National Commission on Children. (1991). *Beyond rhetoric: A new American agenda for children and families (final report)*. Washington, DC: U.S. Government Printing Office.

Peterson, D. R. (1995). The reflective educator. *American Psychologist, 50*, 975–983.

Peterson, D. R. (1996). Making psychology indispensable. *Applied and Preventive Psychology, 5,* 1–8.

Peterson, D. R., McHolland, J. D., Bent, R. J., Davis-Russell, E., Edwall, G., Polite, K., Singer, D. L., & Stricker, G. (Eds.). (1991). *The core curriculum in professional psychology.* Washington, DC: American Psychological Association.

Philpot, C. L., & Brooks, G. (1995). Intergender communication and gender-sensitive family therapy. In R. H. Mikesell, D. D. Lusterman, & S. H. McDaniel (Eds.), *Integrating family therapy: Handbook of family psychology and systems theory.* Washington, DC: American Psychological Association.

Rogers, C. R. (1951). *Client-centered therapy: Its current practice, implications, and theory.* Boston: Houghton Mifflin.

Sarason, S. B., & Doris, J. (1979). *Educational handicap, public policy, and social history: A broadened perspective on mental retardation.* New York: Free Press.

Seaburn, D., Landau-Stanton, J., & Horwitz, S. (1995). Core techniques in family therapy. In R. H. Mikesell, D. D. Lusterman, & S. H. McDaniel (Eds.), *Integrating family therapy: Handbook of family psychology and systems theory.* Washington, DC: American Psychological Association.

Seligman, M. E. P. (1995). The effectiveness of psychotherapy: The consumer reports study. *American Psychologist, 50,* 965–974.

Skinner, B. F. (1953). *Science and human behavior.* New York: Macmillan.

Smith, M., Glass, G., & Miller, T. (1980). *The benefits of psychotherapy.* Baltimore: Johns Hopkins University Press.

Speck, R. V., & Attneave, C. (1973). *Family networks: Retribalizing and healing.* New York: Pantheon.

Stanton, M. D. (1992). The timeline and the "why now?" question: A technique and rationale for therapy, training, organizational consultation, and research. *Journal of Marital & Family Therapy, 18,* 331–343.

Weissbourd, B., & Kagan, S. L. (1989). Family support programs: Catalysts for change. *American Journal of Orthopsychiatry, 59,* 20–31.

Whiston, S. C., & Sexton, T. L. (1993). A review of psychotherapy outcome research: Implications for practice. *Professional Psychology: Research and Practice, 24*(1), 43–51.

Wynne, L. C. (1961). The study of intrafamilial alignments and splits in exploratory family therapy. In N. W. Ackerman, F. L. Beatman, & S. N. Sherman. (Eds.). *Exploring the base for family therapy.* New York: Family Services Association.

14

Evaluating Integrated Service Programs

Robert J. Illback, John Kalafat, and Daniel Sanders

Psychologists are often involved in leadership roles for the planning, management, and evaluation of human services, including health, mental health, education, and social welfare. In these roles, they are required to make decisions about the nature of services provided, assume responsibility for the implementation of these services, and demonstrate program efficacy. The field of program planning and evaluation provides methods and strategies that can enable psychologists with program management responsibilities to become more effective in their managerial roles and document important child and family outcomes. Also, consultation with other program managers and staff in areas of program planning and evaluation may provide expanded psychological practice opportunities in an otherwise contracting marketplace.

The premise of this chapter is that building systematic evaluation into programs at every stage, from planning through implementation, will enhance their efficiency, efficacy, and generalizability. However, integrated service programs present special challenges for program evaluators. The chapter (a) briefly summarizes essential concepts and strategies in the area of program planning and evaluation; (b) delineates the major conceptual and methodological problems that face evaluators of integrated service programs; and (c) provides a case study to demonstrate a creative response to the need for management-oriented evaluation research.

Program Planning and Evaluation: Principles and Procedures

Program planning and evaluation emerged as a specialty area within psychology, education, and social welfare for a variety of reasons, including requirements for accountability in publicly funded programs, interest among scientists in social relevance, scarcity of resources, and expansion of methods appropriate for applied evaluative research (Flaherty & Morell,

The evaluation research program described in this article was made possible, in part, through the generous support of the Annie B. Casey Foundation.

1978). Especially in the 1960s, large-scale federal projects were initiated for preventive health and health care, family planning, rural and urban renewal, delinquency, education, social services, and mental health. Concern for evaluating program effects gave rise to the technology of evaluation, including survey research, multivariate statistical analysis, and related methodologies.

Currently, program planning and evaluation can be seen as a complex, multidisciplinary field. In contrast with traditional research paradigms that focus on controlled experimentation designed to yield universal concepts, emphasis is placed on helping program managers reach informed judgments about program effort, effectiveness, efficiency, and adequacy (Attkisson & Broskowski, 1978). These judgments are made through the application of methods of systematic inquiry into program processes and outcomes.

In this section, an overview of essential principles and procedures of program planning and evaluation is provided as a primer for those who may have limited familiarity with the field (for a more comprehensive treatment, see list of suggested readings). The domains of major evaluation activities discussed are estimating needs and designing evaluable programs, determining the extent of program implementation, and assessing program-related outcomes. Planning and evaluation activities are integral to management and decision-making processes in organizations. Information from such activities is useful to the extent that it informs decision makers and thereby contributes to the ongoing development and improvement of intervention programs.

Needs Estimation and Program Design

Often, psychologists are asked to become involved in the initial stages of design for new programs (or redesign of programs that are seen as ineffective). Various evaluative strategies are available to assist in the development of responsive, evaluable, feasible, and cost-efficient programs. These strategies center on three evaluative questions: What are the needs of the children and families toward whom intervention will be directed? How will the intervention program be structured? and How will the intervention program be implemented and evaluated?

Needs assessment. All well-designed programs begin by ascertaining the priority needs of the people who will be served by the program. For example, a newly established family resource center, before advertising its program offerings to the public, might be expected to gather information about the perceived needs of families in the service area. Similarly, an independent psychological practitioner, in organizing a practice, might conduct market research to determine what community issues are of concern. A variety of methods are available to enable such information gathering.

The key informant approach is a qualitative method that involves identifying individuals who have knowledge about child, family, and community needs and who may be able to provide perspectives that can inform program development. These individuals (e.g., educators, community leaders, family members) are then interviewed to obtain estimates of the scope of the problem, suggestions for effective methods of intervention, and reliable methods of assessing outcomes. Using key informants has the advantage of obtaining first-hand, qualitative information about the problems and needs of the focus group but may not provide a representative or accurate picture of the constellation of needs.

Another approach consists of a review of available data about demands for service (analysis of demands) and available resources (analysis of service resources). For example, an estimate of need can be gleaned from how many individuals request a particular service offering, or how many people are on waiting lists in community agencies.

Surveys represent a direct (and usually more accurate and representative) approach to needs estimation. There is a well-developed science to survey construction and administration (see, for example, Kosecoff & Fink, 1982). Survey questionnaires ask people who are targeted for intervention to estimate their needs along some dimension and typically use scaling methods (e.g., Likert scales) to rate such dimensions as intensity, duration, and severity of the variable(s) of concern.

Other less structured methods that can prove useful are group format approaches. These include the nominal group approach, in which a broad-based sample of persons is invited to generate their ideas about problems, needs, and possible solutions within a workshop format (Delbecq & Van de Ven, 1971). Service recipients, external resource people, key managers, and staff work together in a multistage process to explore problems and set priorities. The Delphi technique focuses more on using experts to forecast needs through a systematic questionnaire process. Such structured discussions allow for more "freewheeling" discussions among persons with direct experience of the phenomena. Through content analysis, data generated by these qualitative approaches can be quantified (e.g., ranking responses).

Thus, qualitative approaches permit evaluators to organize their inquiries without predetermined categories of analysis and to conduct open-ended, detailed explorations (Marshall & Rossman, 1989). Qualitative approaches are complemented by quantitative methods such as surveys to permit the assessment of responses from a larger, more representative sample. Properly implemented needs assessments, combining qualitative and quantitative methodology, yield succinct, summarized, and generalizable statements about client system needs. A needs description specifies the client or service system that is experiencing problems, distinguishing between the current state of affairs and some desired state.

Program specification. A crucial first step to program design and analysis is to define the parameters of the program (the unit of analysis for the evaluative effort). A clear definition of what the program is (and is not) is essential to understanding and evaluating it. For example, a psychologist manager of family services must first define the nature and scope of the program. Program specification delineates essential features of the program to be evaluated, to include the target population, primary outcome goals, sequential activities designed to foster goal attainment, and resources required (e.g., human resources, facilities, equipment).

When programs are described in this fashion, they are said to be "evaluable" (Rutman, 1980). In fact, many program evaluators begin their program analysis by conducting an evaluability assessment, allowing for (a) an examination of a program's logic, including whether causal links have been established between program goals and activities; (b) an analysis of program operations, including the plausibility and measurability of expected events (activities); and (c) identification of program design options, such as new activities, and possible use of program performance information. The operational design of a program can be assessed in relation to five criteria suggested by Provus (1972). *Clarity* refers to the extent to which the design is understandable and measurable. *Comprehensiveness* is related to whether there is a full statement of the program's purpose, implementation, plan, and expected outcomes. The components of the program design can be examined to ensure that they are logically related (*internal consistency*). *Compatibility* with established needs and circumstances is another evaluative aspect. Finally, the evaluator may concentrate on the general *theoretical soundness* of the program, relative to the available literature.

Program design. Once the overall intent and structure of the program has been determined, the plan for program operation can be delineated. This can be seen as an evaluative activity to the extent that systematic program development procedures are used. Examples of evaluative activities may include (a) writing a policy and procedure manual; (b) conducting a task analysis that specifies the activities of key program personnel; (c) conducting in-service training; (d) delineating data to be collected, such as type of intervention, documentation of response, and outcome data; (e) conducting pilot tests and simulations of the prospective program; (f) developing and acquiring materials and supplies; and (g) designing an automated information system for administrative, programmatic, and financial data.

When evaluative activities are built into the program routine prior to the implementation of the program, there is a greater likelihood that relevant and timely information will be available about salient program processes and outcomes. A vital task in this context is to develop the evaluation framework that will guide information gathering and decision making about program worth. Fundamental to this process is the development of evaluation questions.

There is a tendency among managers and evaluators to focus on methods and strategies for data collection, without being clear regarding the questions that are to be addressed by the data. Human service organizations often have available vast amounts of data about service delivery events, but have difficulty transforming these data into meaningful information that can aid decision making. When the information process is ill conceived due to lack of clear questions, the program manager is left confused about the meaning of the data. This often occurs when evaluators and program personnel do not work collaboratively on the evaluation strategy, resulting in findings that managers do not find relevant or sensitive to the effort.

Implementation Evaluation

The primary purpose of implementation evaluation is to determine the extent to which the program is operating as planned. This information can be used to document that there is compliance with important legal, ethical, and professional mandates and practice codes. Additionally, implementation evaluation facilitates program development and improvement by identifying problem areas that may require adaptation of program standards or operations, and by highlighting program elements that are being effectively implemented (e.g., the "active ingredients" of a program). Finally, implementation evaluation increases confidence in the eventual assessment of program outcomes by ensuring that measured program effects (changes in outcome variables) are attributable to identified interventions that have been implemented as planned. Too often, in the absence of implementation data, oversimplified conclusions that programs do not work are made when in fact they have not been implemented with fidelity.

A sample of evaluation questions for psychologists concerned with implementation evaluation include, How are staff engaged in intervention activities and to what extent? In what ways are program participants (e.g., children and their families) involved in the intervention program? Are appropriate methods and materials being used in the intervention program by staff? What intended and unintended side effects do providers, children, their families, and others perceive? Is there a discrepancy between what was planned and what was actually delivered?

Evaluative methods in implementation evaluation can be categorized into two areas: retrospective monitoring and naturalistic monitoring. *Retrospective monitoring* involves obtaining self-report information from program participants and staff about the extent to which the program has been implemented. The evaluator may conduct a series of individual or small-group interviews or use paper-and-pencil measures to gather perceptual information about process variables, such as frequency of intervention episodes relative to the number planned, range of methods and materials employed by staff during service delivery episodes, and side effects or problems noted. Record reviews or examination of other permanent products may also be used.

In naturalistic monitoring, the evaluator observes the intervention process directly. In addition to observation methods, checklists and rating scales may be used to obtain information on the nature and scope of intervention activities and to compare that information with the program design. For the most part, such instrumentation is developed locally, as opposed to using standardized measures, because of the unavailability of appropriate, program-specific measures in most areas.

Outcome Evaluation

To assess outcomes, there are at least five relevant evaluation domains (Illback, Zins, Maher, & Greenburg, 1990). The first asks, To what extent have service delivery and patient goal attainment occurred? This question is driven by goals that have been established for the program. Presumably some goals have been fully attained, some have been partially attained, some have not been attained at all, and some have been dropped in favor of others. The task of the evaluator is to describe the pattern of goal attainment and seek to draw conclusions about implications for ongoing program development and improvement. If the program has been well-specified and an information system established, extent of goal attainment can be reasonably assessed by reviewing ongoing data, supplemented by more active data-gathering strategies such as interviewing a sample of participants, obtaining perceptual data from staff, and reviewing records in more detail.

Another evaluation question asks, What are program-participant reactions to the program? Normally, this is framed as a consumer satisfaction question. Participant reactions (which may include those of children, staff, family members, and others involved with the intervention) represent crucial information for program managers. It is important to determine whether goals have been attained, but it is also important to know whether the people involved with the program perceive it as a helpful and worthy program. For purposes of program improvement and continuation funding, consumer reactions are often highly persuasive. Such data are normally gathered in survey form when a person exits the program or at some future date. The methods discussed here, such as interviews and direct observation, can also be used.

An additional theoretical reason for including these data in an evaluation design is concern for the social validity of the intervention. Intervention programs can create statistically significant changes, without those changes being considered as meaningful by consumers of services (or those in their immediate environment).

Program managers are also concerned when implementing an intervention program about unanticipated events, and may ask, What related program effects occur within this program? An exclusive examination of information related to goal attainment may obscure relevant data regarding other events within the program, including unanticipated child and service delivery outcomes.

A fourth type of evaluation is focused by the question, Is the program cost-efficient? Program managers (including psychologists), in addition to managing the human resources involved in operating a program, must be responsible stewards of fiscal resources. Indeed, the survival of the program within an increasingly competitive marketplace requires not only that the program be solvent, but also that the manager be able to demonstrate that it efficiently uses the fiscal resources available to it in order to facilitate goal attainment. The logic of cost-efficiency is comparative: What costs are associated with the present program, in comparison to some other contrast condition (e.g., no program, an alternative intervention approach)? This necessitates establishing some baseline or comparative condition that can allow judgments to be made about relative efficiency.

Finally, the psychologist whose program represents a service innovation may be concerned with generating information that demonstrates a cause–effect relationship between the intervention program and the outcomes achieved. Such information contributes to scholarly knowledge and informs prospective adopting sites through the process of knowledge dissemination (e.g., presentation at professional meetings, publications in professional journals). It is important to recognize that not all evaluation questions can be answered within a reasonable evaluation design, necessitating a process of placing the evaluative concerns in priority order. Questions attendant to each of the above evaluative concerns vary in complexity and information requirements. For example, the "rules of evidence" that govern an experiment designed for publication in a journal are more rigorous than what the typical program manager is willing (or able) to support. Most managers do not have the luxury of randomly assigning patients to treatment and control groups.

This inability to exert a high degree of control on the evaluation design should not render the program to the category of "nonevaluable." Rather, it is the task of the evaluator to clarify the questions at hand and then impose the maximum available structure on the evaluation that circumstances will allow. In the "real world," evaluators must continually reach creative compromises with the systems within which they operate in order to generate viable evaluation plans.

Evaluating Integrated Service Programs

Integrated service programs pose particular challenges to evaluators, due to their complex, idiosyncratic, and innovative nature. The following sections discuss problems inherent in formulating responsive integrated service evaluation systems and recommendations for their design.

Problems in Integrated Service Evaluation

As discussed previously, it is not possible to evaluate a program that is in a nonevaluable form. Integrated service programs, due to their emphasis on innovation and linkage of resources across settings, often represent an aggregation of approaches and strategies that are not well-specified or easily operationalized. For example, staff within a program with a mission to empower families may have some vague notion of what this means, but often have little knowledge of how specified methods and strategies (day-to-day operations) support this concept. Many programs are driven more by the personality of the designer than clear concepts about intervention and change. Targeted questioning by the evaluator in the early stages of evaluation planning may uncover that staff cannot clearly state goals for the program, nor can they specify the presumed link between program activities and program intent.

This state of affairs implies concerted effort to help staff articulate what they are doing and why. Often, such effort involves program design and restructuring as people become more clear about their assumptions and the implications of these for program development. In effect, the evaluator helps to facilitate the specification of the program's underlying logic model (the presumed theoretical and conceptual relationships between program activities and child and family outcomes). This activity can be especially problematic when the program design is based on vague and unverified (and sometimes unsupportable) beliefs about intervention and change. Rather than remaining impartial observers, evaluators have an obligation to become engaged to facilitate the development of a program that is sound and verifiable.

In addition to program design problems, evaluators are faced with thorny methodological issues that complicate one's ability to answer essential questions about program efficacy. In a traditional positivist research paradigm (the logic system in which most psychologists are trained), people who receive the experimental condition (the treatment or program) are compared on relevant outcome measures to determine if their functioning differs from those who did not receive the treatment. Within innovative integrated service programs, the rhetoric of the program is such that each individual and group-level intervention is designed on the basis of the needs of the consumer and is therefore idiosyncratic. In this context, it is frequently infeasible to derive a viable contrast condition (e.g., control or comparison group), because aggregation of individual "cases" may serve to obscure real but subtle change. Moreover, designs that make use of withholding of treatment (e.g., waiting list control) or assignment of persons in need to experimental and control groups are fraught with ethical and practical problems. The evaluator is left to use designs that permit more limited causal inference, such as within-subjects repeated measures, ex post facto, and single-subject approaches.

Developing instrumentation that is sensitive to the complex, multisystemic changes sought by integrated service programs is also challenging. Many of the available measures are clinical in nature, and may be more sensitive to diminishing psychopathology than enhancing competence. Also, complex constructs such as family empowerment do not lend themselves to reliable measurement. The limited number of measures that are available in domains that are deemed relevant to the program often suffer in technical inadequacy; that is, there are insufficient measurement devices with demonstrated psychometric characteristics (e.g., reliability and validity) for variables that integrated service programs target. Often, this causes the evaluator to develop local measures, and when this is not done systematically, greater potential for error variance is introduced into the design.

A related methodological problem is that of data standardization. Program evaluators, given their task, often wish to impose structure on data gathering and analysis, seeking replicable program processes and clear, specified outcomes. Program managers, on the other hand, may be more fluid in their orientation to data, particularly in the early stages of program development. There is a natural tension between these impulses, in that the strength of integrated service programs derives from their responsiveness to changing environmental conditions, whereas the ability to derive generalizable findings implies the need to standardize. Variables of concern and targets for change will evolve over time, and it is therefore incumbent on evaluators to design systems that are flexible, leading to compromises in design that are creative (but also limiting). Rather than labeling the desire by managers to not fully standardize as "resistance to evaluation," psychologist evaluators are challenged to accept the condition of continuous program change as inherent to integrated service programs.

The problem of standardization is most acute when the integrated service program to be evaluated occurs at multiple sites (e.g., multiple agencies, various communities, more than one building within an organization). Within an interagency effort, for example, outcome variables may vary. A collaboration between a school system, mental health program, and social service agency may be entered into with varying expectations about outcomes. In this instance, the school might be most persuaded by evidence of change in child learning and behavior, the mental health center by data supporting improvement in social and psychological functioning, and the social service agency by increased family competence (e.g., child management skills) and diminished risk of maltreatment. The task of the evaluator is to help the parties reach consensus on a group of central intentions (hoped-for outcomes) and to value data generated outside of the service model they represent. Although obviously challenging, evaluative attempts to connect, integrate, and value multisystemic data across the service system can be among the most valuable services provided by an integrated service evaluation.

Data gathering, storage, and retrieval is another perplexity, especially when the program operates on a relatively small budget for evaluation and serves large numbers of clients. Most programs do not have the luxury of hiring staff (or graduate research assistants) to observe, administer scales, and interview subjects. They must therefore build evaluation into the routine of the program by self-administering instruments at regular intervals, and creating an information system that may serve to combine evaluative needs with routine program operations (e.g., tracking client demographic data). Of course, some degree of objectivity and reliability is sacrificed when the persons who are implementing the program are involved so intimately in data collection. Other problems of this approach include the potential for systematic bias, difficulty ensuring that data are gathered in a timely fashion, and the pressure to deliver services rather than reflect on outcomes.

Much training and support is required to sustain a system of evaluation in programs that typically are not oriented toward such reflectivity. Often, human service organizations focus most of their informational capacity on fiscal issues (e.g., billing systems). The era of managed care may cause a convergence between fiscal soundness (i.e., the need to self-sustain through revenue generation) and program efficacy (i.e., the need to demonstrate that services result in cost-efficient, meaningful outcomes). However, most human service organizations lack the informational capacity to address these issues. Therefore, the design of evaluation systems in integrated services should include automated management information system development. This may not be an area that psychologist evaluators have technical competency in; fortunately, the technology of applications development in database management has become so user-friendly that the primary barriers to design of such systems are primarily conceptual, not technological.

A final (and perhaps most crucial) exigency confronting the evaluator of an integrated service program relates to knowledge use. Whereas most human service programs are confined to a specific host organization and use a common system of language, integrated service programs are characterized by "stakeholders" representing a wide range of organizations and perspectives. Also, there are likely to be numerous people and organizations involved, either directly or indirectly, in the implementation of the program. The information needs and agendas of these people and their organizations can vary considerably. If the fundamental premise of evaluation is that it must be perceived as useful to stakeholders, a major task is to determine which persons have what information needs, and when.

There are problems of both substance and form inherent in this task. Evaluators must "package" and communicate evaluative findings such that findings are recognizable and reducible for a range of concerned persons. Written reports of findings are most formidable, in that they are read by various audiences who may apply highly divergent criteria in judging their worth. For example, a program manager may need to understand the intricacies of outcomes as they relate to various program components, without needing to know all of the statistical analyses that led to such conclusions. At the same time, managers may be highly sensitive to findings that are suboptimal, and may have difficulty integrating complex and ambiguous outcomes. On the other hand, legislators responsible for continuation funding may be interested in generalizations about program success that can be captured in "bulleted" fashion in an executive summary. Researchers and evaluators, of course, want to see all of the data and apply a level of scrutiny to the findings that others may not. All of these are valid information needs, but they are not always compatible. In addition to clarifying in detail what kinds of information will be most useful to various audiences, the evaluator must clarify the forms that decision makers must have this information in to make it useful. In this context, the technology of presentation design (to include graphic portrayals) may be of great use (see Suggested Readings).

Guidelines for Evaluation Design

Based on the foregoing discussion, the following guidelines are provided for the design of systems of evaluation in integrated service programs:

1. The evaluation system should be designed through a collaborative approach, involving stakeholders at various levels (e.g., service recipients, program staff, managers, funders) in data gathering, analysis, and interpretation. A preferred approach is to form an evaluation committee early on whose task is to delineate evaluation questions, consider a range of data-gathering strategies, review and help to interpret findings, and facilitate use of evaluation results.
2. The evaluation system should measure multiple aspects of the program, including inputs (e.g., characteristics and needs of clients at entry), program processes (e.g., service delivery), and outcomes (e.g., change on relevant child and family variables).
3. The evaluation system should be designed to gather information about multiple levels of the program, including service recipient needs and responses, design and implementation of program components, and system-level variables (e.g., accessibility, integration).
4. In initial design efforts, considerable time should be spent considering the evaluation questions that are of essential concern to the parties, avoiding discussion of methodology (e.g., instruments, experimental design) until a vital understanding about the needs of evaluation consumers are known. Excessive concern about technical adequacy, especially in formulating the evaluation strategy, can lead to narrow and irrelevant data gathering. The task of the evaluator of an integrated service program is to pay close attention to what people perceive as relevant information and then design a system that gathers such information in a creative but rigorous manner.
5. The evaluation system should be predicated on the belief that all programs, and especially those that are innovative and unique, must be viewed from a developmental perspective. The fluid and evolutionary nature of integrated service programs is central to their strength (i.e., responding flexibly to the changing service environment). The task of the evaluator is more than capturing a "snapshot" of the program; rather, it involves capturing the scope and complexity of the maturational process of the program, assessing the responsiveness of these changes to evolving needs and perspectives. The stance of the evaluator in communicating findings, then, should be formative and should focus on how what has been learned can contribute to the ongoing development and improvement of the program. Summative judgments about the relative worth or usefulness of the program cannot usually

be made until at least 3 to 5 years of programmatic data are available.

6. As a practical matter, evaluation systems for integrated service programs most often require the establishment of an automated information system that involves building evaluation into the routine of the host organization. This implies that evaluators, working in collaboration with an evaluation committee, must delineate the variables of concern, establish forms and formats for data collection, enable the automation of data gathering through development of a computer application or use of a generic database, provide for the routine aggregation and use of relevant information through flexible report generation, and ensure that a system of routine database management is in operation.

7. Especially challenging for evaluators of integrated service systems is the need to measure variables that are ill-defined due to their relative newness. For example, whereas there is a vast and well-developed literature on the measurement of child psychopathology and family dysfunction, there are few validated measures for variables such as family support and empowerment. Even more difficult are measures of systems change, such as density of community resources, perceived accessibility of services, interagency collaboration, and service integration. Some instruments are beginning to emerge, but evaluators most often will develop their own measures and interview formats to gauge change on these dimensions. While the technical adequacy of such instrumentation cannot be known initially, there is a greater probability that they will be sensitive to the kinds of changes anticipated by program developers. To the extent possible, multiple measures should be used to allow for triangulation of findings and a more comprehensive understanding of the change process.

8. The methods used for the evaluation system should be both qualitative and quantitative in nature, as dictated by the varied informational needs of stakeholders. Qualitative evaluative designs are growing in popularity due to their ability to capture rich, clinical detail about program processes. (See Suggested Readings.)

9. The evaluation system should be designed principally for the use of program managers—those who have designed and are carrying out the intervention. Questions asked and answered by the system should be immediately relevant to these individuals and allow for decision making about program operation and efficacy.

10. The evaluation system should not place an unnecessary burden on the host organization, service providers, families, or other service recipients. In this sense, it should be nonintrusive and designed to be a routine part of doing business, and one that is seen as relevant and useful. To the extent that it is not, the eval-

uation can be seen as less than successful. The evaluation should not "drive" the program, but rather should reflect the program.

11. Five general orienting questions may help to focus the evaluator of an integrated service program: Who is being served? What services are being delivered? What outcomes are associated with program participation? Is the program being delivered as planned? and How can the program be improved and sustained? These questions, and the data associated with them, can serve as a useful framework for communicating about the evaluation system and findings.

Case Illustration of Integrated Service Program Evaluation

Kentucky's Family Resource and Youth Service Center program (FRYSC) is a statewide, school-based family support initiative, and an essential component of the Kentucky Education Reform Act (KERA). FRYSCs derive from the belief that many children and adolescents do not profit from educational experience because of family and community problems (Steffy, 1993). Such problems may include (but are not limited to) economic disadvantage, limited health and social services, familial stress and conflict, drug and alcohol usage, and mental illness. To the extent that these factors affect school performance, youngsters are not "ready to learn." KERA therefore established funding for school-based programs for children and adolescents who are "at risk" for school failure (Dryfoos, 1994). Grounded in principles of family support and empowerment (Dunst, Trivette, & Deal, 1988), the primary focus of the program is to strengthen the capacity of families to foster child readiness for learning and to enhance family participation in the educational process (Weissbourd, 1987; Zigler & Weiss, 1985). Consistent with KERA's underpinnings, the FRYSC program subscribes to site-based decision making and control of resources.

Family Resource Centers (FRC) in the elementary schools and Youth Service Centers (YSC) in middle and high schools are expected to provide, develop, or broker a wide range of services in collaboration with schools, local child and family service agencies, and related organizations. FRCs are encouraged by legislation to address core services that include (a) full-time preschool child care for children 2 and 3 years of age, (b) after-school care for children ages 4 through 12 with full-time accessibility during the summer and when school is not in session, (c) a comprehensive Family in Training program for new and expectant parents, (d) a Parent and Child Education program, (e) a mechanism to support and train child day care providers, and (f) health service coordination and referral. YSCs provide referrals to health and social services; employment counseling, training, and placement; summer and part-time job development; drug and alcohol abuse counseling; and family crisis and mental health counseling. At the secondary level, focus is on the needs of youth as they face the problems of adolescence and adulthood.

In addition to core services required by legislation, centers may choose to provide a variety of other complementary services. Examples of optional services for an FRC might include an informational clearinghouse; recreation-program development; child and family needs assessment in areas such as housing, social services, and financial management; and any other child and family needs deemed valid. At YSCs, optional services might include the following: (a) coordinating with the local legal system, (b) consulting with school officials regarding behavioral and disciplinary problems, (c) facilitating re-entry into schools from residential programs, (d) developing volunteer programs, (e) providing after-school recreational programs, and (f) any other needs deemed valid for youth and their families.

During the 1991–1992 school year, 133 centers were funded through a request-for-proposals process. The program has since expanded rapidly, with 222 centers operational in the 1992–1993 school year, 385 in the 1993–1994 school year, 455 in 1994–1995, and 560 in the 1995–1996 school year (serving over 900 school buildings). The rapid expansion of the program is consistent with the legislative mandate to implement the program fully in all eligible school buildings across the state. Applicant school districts are required to conduct community-needs assessments and develop annual workplans to meet identified needs. Initially at least 20% of the children or youth enrolled in the school are required to be eligible for free and reduced-price school meals (a measure of poverty), but in order for the center to be funded, all children, youth, and families in a funded school are eligible to receive services.

FRYSC programs are full-coverage programs that encourage adaptation to varying local characteristics. Each represents a "field experiment" in which coordinators are selected, given broad mission and service guidelines, and "turned loose" to meet identified needs however they can. The result is a set of innovative, complex, and largely untested approaches for which it is difficult to specify the program parameters (Weiss & Jacobs, 1988). Additional problems are presented by the variations among multi-site programs (Bond & Halpern, 1988) and by the lack of viable control and contrast conditions inherent in full-coverage programs (Rossi & Freeman, 1993). Also, the conceptual model underlying the program structure has not been fully explicated, and the program continues to evolve.

Evaluation System Development and Structure

To evaluate this program, a number of evaluation components have been used, including evaluation work group, management information system/quantitative evaluation, qualitative implementation assessment, and training and support functions.

Evaluation work group. From the inception of the project, it was clear that there were numerous stakeholders with multiple agendas, and innumerable evaluation questions and concerns. An ongoing evaluation system-design committee (work group) was formed, which was responsible to an interagency governing task force appointed by the governor. The purpose of the work group, comprised of coordinators, central office staff, and other interested parties, has been to formulate and implement the overall evaluation strategy. Early discussion yielded consensus around certain issues, such as (a) the evaluation should not drive the program; (b) the focus should be on using information to help coordinators do their job; (c) the evaluation should not be about accountability, but rather program improvement; (d) the evaluation should be designed to capture something about the complexity of this multisystemic program, rather than merely assessing outcomes; and (e) as much as possible, the system should be automated and take full advantage of available technology, enabling data gathering, aggregation, and analysis at various levels.

Over time, the evaluation workgroup has become more involved in the operational details of the evaluation. As forms and formats for data collection were designed, variables of concern were established through a review of program material and through extensive discussions with work group members. Periodically, the evaluation design and instruments are revised on the basis of recommendations of the group. The work group also plays a significant role in reviewing and interpreting evaluative findings and making recommendations for program improvement. Finally, as conceptual and technological problems have emerged, the work group has been vital in reasoning about problems and brokering solutions. An essential reason for the success of this approach has been the degree of "ownership" of the evaluation system that has occurred because of the leadership of this group.

Management information system/quantitative evaluation. Given the large scale of the program, it became clear that a management information system (MIS) would be required for gathering data about recipient characteristics, service delivery, and outcomes. The work group assisted in the development of a user-friendly software package installed at each site that allows local center staff to generate, review, and analyze their own program data. In addition to site-"owned," cost-efficient information gathering, the MIS allows for collecting and reporting through periodic telecommunication to a state-level host computer. Troubleshooting, technical support, and consultation services are available to center coordinators through a toll-free number, regular training activities, and site visits.

To date, quantitative data have been generated around program parameters such as, What individuals and families, with what needs, are being served by centers? How do clients (children, adolescents and families) become involved with centers? What local services are being accessed? and What child and family outcomes are associated with program involvement?

The MIS has been one of the most successful (and time-consuming) components of the evaluation system. It has allowed for substantial data analysis at the state level, and local coordinators are now beginning to use their database more effectively. The evaluation team has concentrated effort on building more layers of support for coordinators through the toll-free number, use of a full-time staff person to coordinate support and technology efforts, and systematic training initiatives. Software is now being developed for the fourth version, a Windows-based application in Microsoft Access that seeks to become even more user-friendly and flexible (earlier versions were programmed in Clipper, a dBase language). It is anticipated that the system will be further improved through collaboration with the Kentucky Electronic Technology System to integrate data transfer, electronic mail, and related capabilities.

Each year, orientation and update training on the evaluation system and software is provided for the 500+ coordinators and clerical personnel. As software becomes available for use in a Windows environment, the need for such training will expand, particularly around learning to develop clear management questions and effective use of the local center database to address such queries. Linking information systems to the process of managing is the most challenging (and exciting) aspect of the overall initiative.

The MIS has been further supported through the development of Regional Resource Teams comprised of 24 volunteers from centers (regionally distributed) who agree to serve as local supports for their peers. A committed and exceptional group of program staff were identified and provided 3 days of intensive training, supplemented by ongoing telephonic support. Their role has been to serve as the "first line of defense" for problem identification and resolution. In essence they screen problems that are common and provide ready access to solutions that are known, referring on those that cannot be resolved at this level. This approach has succeeded because participants were trained in computer basics, rudimentary evaluation concepts and strategies, the rationale for data collection, and information use ideas. At present regional resource teams are being expanded. In addition to supporting and retooling people already in the network, given the number of centers, a second cadre of persons from the regions (another 25–30 people) will receive similar training.

Qualitative implementation assessment. For three consecutive years, between 10 and 12 centers were visited by evaluators, who conducted structured interviews with key informants, observed program processes, and reviewed relevant documentation. For example, in the third iteration of the implementation evaluation, 10 centers (six FRC, two YSC, and two FRYSC) were randomly selected and three prior centers (one YSC, two FRC) were revisited. For the purposes of standardized data collection, implementation categories that had evolved out of the first two evaluations were combined with some categories from an innovation configuration map (Hall & Hord, 1987) developed by a committee of coordinators and staff from the FRYSC branch, the Kentucky Institute for Educational Research, and REACH of Louisville, Inc. The resulting instrument (see Exhibit 1) provided summary ratings that permit tracking of a given center's progress, comparisons across centers, and overall ratings of a sample of centers. The degree to which centers have established relationships within the school (*market penetration*) was also assessed by means of a teacher survey.

Within the implementation evaluation, case studies of child, family,

Exhibit 1. Implementation Characteristics of Kentucky Family Resource and Youth Services Centers

Relationships with families

Levels of family empowerment
1. Explicitly addresses empowerment issues in interactions with families.
2. Enhances family functioning/involvement in the school in a way that empowers families.
3. Provides services that enhance functioning but retains client status.
4. Provides services in a way that disempowers families.

Levels of principal attitude toward family involvement
1. Has record and traditions of specific strategies for family involvement.
2. Promotes family involvement.
3. Appreciates outreach to families.
4. Acts as a neutral party.
5. Is not open to it.

Relationships with the school community

Levels of needs assessment
1. Ongoing structured needs assessment.
2. Surveys sent out regularly or obtained from program participants.
3. Occasional surveys, surveys concerning specific programs.
4. Key informants through regular meetings and contacts (e.g., teachers, principals, community providers).
5. Key informants through regular interaction with community and families.
6. Advisory council as informant.
7. No regular needs assessment; responding to ongoing demands.

Effective areas of addressing the mission (school readiness).
- School explicitly connects all activities and objectives to mission.
- School focuses on problems that are seen as related to school readiness.
- School addresses range of social, economic, and health problems that enhance family functioning.
- School responds to widespread gaps in services.

Levels of connectedness with school
1. School works collaboratively with FRYSC on programs, buys into family education/involvement mission.
2. School personnel enthusiastic about FRYSC—see it as much needed added resource/capability of school.
3. School personnel make appropriate request/referrals; starting to be impressed with FRYSC capabilities.
4. Inappropriate request/referrals or no request/referrals.
5. Turf-oriented or hostile.

Levels of principal support
1. Involved, collaborative.
2. Advocate.
3. Supportive/customer.
4. Laissez-faire.
5. Overbearing micromanaging or turf/hostile.

Elements of effective program impact on school readiness
- Direct impact (e.g., tutoring services).
- Student support (e.g., glasses, alarm clock, transportation).
- Family support (e.g., parent involvement, GED, family functioning through parent education services).
- Barrier removal (e.g., those related to health, learning disability, drug and alcohol, pregnancy).

Exhibit 1. *(Continued)*

Relationships with the community

Levels of positive community involvement
  1. Participant (attends programs and meetings).
  2. Informant (provides information about needs and resources).
  3. Helper (provides concrete assistance).
  4. Decision maker (helps to decide what is provided/how it is provided).
Levels of community connections
  1. Respected provider in the community (can advocate, but not yet has influence to mobilize services, obtain involvement).
  2. Well respected member of provider network (can advocate for and mobilize services to meet needs).
  3. Well connected in the community (can call on community and families for all levels of involvement).

and center interaction designed to unlock the "black box" of Family Resource Center (elementary-level) activities were also completed. These provide a more fine-grained description of how the program operates "on the ground." It has become clear from the evaluative data that Family Resource Centers and Youth Services Centers are not one and the same thing, however. Although conceptually linked, they look and behave very differently. Thus, detailed case studies on at least three exemplars of Youth Services Center activities are now underway, in order to illuminate more precisely what occurs within the context of services to adolescents (that is distinct from more family-oriented interventions at the elementary school level).

Training, support, other evaluative functions. The development of a coordinator mentoring program has been an exciting outgrowth of the evaluation system. The need for such a program arose from concern that many new coordinators were unclear about the mission of the program and prone to unnecessary stress due to lack of peer support. A week-long pilot training was conducted at the Kentucky Leadership Center, a secluded retreat in southeastern Kentucky. The program combined didactic and experiential formats. New center coordinators were paired with experienced ones in their regions (mentors) and trained as a team. The themes for the week included linkages to learning, the school environment, involving and empowering students and families, community resource mobilization, and center operation. For the remainder of the year, mentors and new coordinators engaged in regular and focused interaction around these and related issues.

Although still under development, this model for linking evaluation findings to program practices has been highly successful and valued by both coordinators and administrators. Given the increased regionalization of the program and realities about program monitoring and supervision, the mentoring concept holds much promise for the ongoing development of support for the program. It is anticipated that mentoring training will be expanded statewide next year.

A related support approach has been the development of a system of self-evaluation for centers. Similar to the process undergone in preparation for program accreditation, centers are being asked to use the implementation assessment framework to conduct self-evaluations. Given that many coordinators have minimal experience in program administration, implementation of the self-evaluation process is supported through training and pilot studies and will eventually involve regional staff to provide technical assistance. Ultimately, all centers will be asked to conduct a self-evaluation (e.g., triennial), possibly in conjunction with a site visit.

An aspect of the program that has received little attention to date is systems change on the local level. Centers are presumed to play a role in developing and integrating community resources, and there is much anecdotal evidence that community coordination and collaboration has improved. An evaluation project is being planned to document and gain insight into such local change. Through site visits and interviews of key informants (with emphasis on network analysis) in a small sample of communities, the processes through which systems change occurs will be explicated. Facilitators and barriers to such change will be considered, and recommendations for promoting systems development at the local level will be made.

A number of other evaluation activities are essential to the project but have taken on somewhat routine characteristics. These include mid-year data summaries, an end-of-year report, ongoing facilitation of the evaluation work group, workshop and activity participation, ongoing consultation, information-request response, periodic briefings of key officials and legislators, and related committee work.

Summary of Evaluative Findings

Demographics. Data on 35,161 families and 40,958 students in the 1994–1995 school year database were available for analysis (more detailed documentation of the descriptive and inferential analyses that follow are available from the senior author). Demographic information regarding these individuals reveals great diversity in terms of caregiver characteristics (e.g., marital status, parental education), financial resources (e.g., estimated income), race, and language. In general, the population being served reflects program goals, with relatively high levels of undereducated and economically disadvantaged persons. More than half of the participants are referred by school personnel, but a large number are either self-referred or enter through another community organization, demonstrating both school and community linkages. Girls and boys are about equally represented in the population, as are all age and grade levels.

These children and youth exhibit diverse, multiple, and interrelated difficulties, with health, behavior, emotional, and learning problems topping the list. Teacher ratings at intake confirm that students experience substantial educational difficulties in areas such as attendance, classroom performance, achievement, grades, peer relations, retention, and drop-out risk. Family and setting risk factors are also numerous and complex, including social isolation, financial problems, clothing, child care, food, family conflict, family crises, divorce, and unemployment. These multiple needs and stressors can be seen as functionally related to children's school performance and as amenable to broad-based community interventions consistent with the aims of the program.

Service delivery. Family Resource and Youth Service Centers, by legislation, provide core (mandated) or optional services to targeted children, youth, and families. Health services and referral emerge as the most frequently used core service, with parent training (e.g., Families-in-Training, Parent and Child Education), child care (e.g., preschool, after-school care), and counseling services also extensively used. Notably, almost half of the targeted families receive one or more optional services (i.e., a service not listed in the original legislation as a core component), calling into question the usefulness of this early service categorization. Most services to targeted families are provided by Family Resource or Youth Service Centers, as opposed to other community providers, indicating that the program serves to fill service delivery gaps in local communities but also raising concerns about maintaining program focus and avoiding duplication. Despite extensive program efforts, continuing unmet needs for many families include health care services, housing, education, parenting skills, recreational services, respite, and employment services.

Educational outcomes. Preliminary findings regarding educational change must be interpreted in light of the lack of controls. Teachers were asked to rate student status on a range of classroom performance variables at intake and at intervention completion (a repeated measures design). Elementary-level participants (ages 3–11) appear more likely than secondary-level participants (ages 12–20) to experience positive gains in global variables such as achievement, academic proficiency, and risk of dropping out of school. Adolescents confront cumulative problems of learning and behavior, and these may be more difficult to overcome within a time-limited intervention, lending support to the importance of early intervention. Both elementary- and secondary-level students appear to experience strong positive gains in important classroom variables such as completing classwork and homework, following directions, obeying school rules, and remaining on task. Similar positive gains are seen for social and emotional variables such as relating appropriately, having friends, participating in activities, and cooperating with others, again for both elementary and secondary students. Level of program involvement (minimal, moderate, extensive) does not appear to be associated with differential gains. Especially with respect to classroom and social competence variables, children and youth served by Family Resource and Youth Services Centers at all levels appear to improve over time.

Gains are less pronounced, in general, for students who are extensively served by centers, probably reflecting severity of need. FRYSC interventions, when considered alone, are probably insufficient to overcome the complex problems of children and youth with extensive needs; change for this group should be evaluated over a longer period of time and in the context of all of the KERA elements working in concert.

It should be noted that the above findings cannot be directly or exclusively attributed to the FRYSC program. They may also reflect contributions of other KERA elements or developmental events. However, these youngsters are targeted by the program, and change is assessed over a defined interval, lending support to the view that the pattern and level of changes seen here reflect program successes. Positive change is occurring. The essential goal of the program, improving school readiness, appears to receive support from these findings.

Family support outcomes. Changes in parent ratings of the helpfulness of social support, including support from the program, are seen through examination of pre- and postintervention data for targeted families on the Support Helpfulness Scale (a modification of an instrument developed by Dunst, Trivette, & Deal, 1988). The scale is administered at the outset and conclusion of the FRYSC intervention program and asks parents to indicate how helpful each of a number of sources of support is to them. These data relate specifically to persons for whom there is an expectation that activities of the center will directly impact schooling and family support variables (FRYSCs engage in many other group and community activities that are not individually oriented and are more preventive in nature). The average duration for these interventions was found to be 228 days for the group as a whole, with younger children in Family Resource Centers (3–11-year-olds) receiving interventions of 237 days' duration on the average, and youth in Youth Service Centers (12–20-year-olds) being served an average of 212 days.

In general, parents appear to perceive positive changes in social support from a number of sources, but primarily from school-based personnel, especially Family Resource Centers, teachers, counselors, and principals. This appears to be confirmatory evidence that the program is being implemented as planned and supports the view that centers seek to make connections between family support and school readiness.

Informal sources of support such as family members, extended social networks, and church members or the minister do not appear to increase over time. Additionally, more formal sources of human services evidence little change. Given that the program seeks to collaborate with other human service organizations and agencies in support of families, this may be of some concern. This finding should be interpreted in light of service delivery data indicating that FRYSCs deliver the majority of services to families. That is, despite the stated intent of the program to serve many families in the role of broker, in resource-poor communities such a role is not always possible. Subsequent analyses may discover that perceived family support covaries by age level and community resource availability.

A more positive finding is that, within the domain of support from social groups and organizations, families perceive greater support available from parent support and social groups. The strong emphasis within the initiative on parent training programs may correlate with this finding.

There are few systematic differences across various levels of program involvement (i.e., minimal, moderate, extensive); that is, outcomes appear to be reasonably consistent irrespective of which level of service is used. It appears that families served minimally do not perceive significant change in social support, as might be expected given the limited role of the center. Families served moderately or extensively perceive significant positive change from the Family Resource Center, teacher, counselor, and principal. Thus, there seems to be a relationship between program "dosage" and perceived family support from educational personnel.

Given the presumed link between family involvement and support and educational readiness, the finding that families perceive most of the increased support available to them as originating from school personnel is most compelling.

Implementation Evaluation

The overall finding of the implementation assessment to date is that FRYSCs provide cost-efficient, responsive, accessible services to families and schools. Services are provided in a manner that generally empowers families to address their ongoing needs by teaching about available school and community resources (and strategies for accessing them) and by increasing family self-efficacy (with some exceptions). Results further indicate that the majority of centers visited are organized to "bridge barriers" for families. Coordinators are well-connected in their community and, for the most part, serve as brokers who bring community services to schools. They also bring families into schools and enhance their ability to assist in their children's education. They typically establish solid relationships within the schools they serve, in which they are seen, particularly by principals, as providing essential services. The degree to which these services impact psychological, social, and economic barriers to children's readiness to learn needs to be more clearly established through further research.

Some issues that need further management exploration include the following:

- Although nearly all principals were highly supportive of the centers, some still preferred them to provide direct services to students, particularly in YSCs in which, for example, a principal might require that the coordinator see troubled students all day, precluding community- and family-based activity.
- There is an ongoing need for coordinators to remind themselves of the educational mission of their activities and to convey the connection between their activities and school performance to school personnel and other stakeholders. It has been recommended that focus groups of coordinators be formed to identify center programs and activities they believe have the greatest impact on both cognitive and noncognitive components of KERA goals.

- In resource-poor communities, the shift from provider to broker of services may be more difficult, or at least take more time, as co-ordinators attempt to prompt service development in their community. Judgments about appropriateness of resource use should be evaluated in this context. More generally, the need to fill service gaps may reduce the capacity of these centers to fulfill other program objectives.
- Serving multiple schools is a difficult role for centers, given that center resources are stretched in serving one school. A special study has been recommended to explore the issue of multiple school centers.

In sum, the ongoing implementation evaluation and training effort is yielding a consensus around a set of strategic goals and objectives to focus centers on removing barriers to learning while permitting local flexibility and creativity in program design.

Summary

Psychologists are in a unique position to assume leadership roles in planning, managing, and evaluating human service programs. Methods of program planning and evaluation provide a system of inquiry that can enable greater managerial effectiveness and expand on practice opportunities for psychologists. In this context, the present chapter (a) summarized essential concepts and strategies in program planning and evaluation; (b) delineated the major conceptual and methodological problems that face evaluators of integrated service programs and (c) provided a case study to demonstrate a creative response to the need for management-oriented evaluation research.

References

Attkisson, C. C., & Broskowski, A. (1978). Evaluation and the emerging human service concept. In C. C. Attkisson, W. A. Hargreaves, M. J. Horowitz, & J. E. Sorensen (Eds.), *Evaluation of human services programs* (pp. 5–23). New York: Academic Press.

Bond, J. T., & Halpern, R. (1988). The cross-project evaluation of the child survival/fair start initiative: A case study of action research. In H. B. Weiss & F. H. Jacobs (Eds.), *Evaluating family programs* (pp. 347–370). New York: Aldine deGruyter.

Delbecq, A. L., & Van de Ven, A. H. (1971). A group process model for problem identification and program planning. *Journal of Applied Behavioral Science, 7,* 446–492.

Dryfoos, J. G. (1994). *Full-service schools: A revolution in health and social services for children, youth, and families.* San Francisco: Jossey-Bass.

Dunst, C. J., Trivette, C. M., & Deal, A. G. (1988). *Enabling and empowering families: Principles and guidelines for practice.* Cambridge, MA: Brookline Books.

Flaherty, E. W., & Morell, J. A. (1978). Evaluation: Manifestations of a new field. *Evaluation and Program Planning, 1,* 1–10.

Hall, G. E., & Hord, S. M. (1987). *Change in schools: Facilitating the process.* Albany, NY: State University of New York Press.

Illback, R. J., Zins, J. E., Maher, C. A., & Greenburg, R. (1990). An overview of principles and procedures of program planning and evaluation. In T. Gutkin & C. Reynolds (Eds.), *Handbook of school psychology* (2nd ed.; pp. 799–820). New York: Wiley.

Kosecoff, J., & Fink, A. (1982). *Evaluation basics: A practitioner's manual.* Newbury Park, CA: Sage.

Marshall, C., & Rossman, G. B. (1989). *Designing qualitative research.* Newbury Park, CA: Sage.

Provus, M. M. (1972). *Discrepancy evaluation.* Berkeley, CA: McCutchan.

Rossi, P. H., & Freeman, H. E. (1993). *Evaluation: A systematic approach.* Newbury Park, CA: Sage.

Rutman, L. (1980). *Planning useful evaluations: Evaluability assessment.* Beverly Hills, CA: Sage.

Steffy, B. E. (1993). *The Kentucky education reform: Lessons from America.* Lancaster, PA: Technomic.

Weiss, H. B., & Jacobs, F. H. (1988). *Evaluating family programs.* New York: Aldine deGruyter.

Weissbourd, B. (1987). A brief history of family support programs. In S. L. Kagan, D. R. Powell, B. Weissbourd, & E. Zigler (Eds.), *American's family support programs* (pp. 38–56). New Haven, CT: Yale University Press.

Zigler, E., & Weiss, H. B. (1985). Family support systems: An ecological approach to child development. In R. Rapoport (Ed.), *Children, youth, and families: The action-research development.* Cambridge, MA: Cambridge University Press.

Suggested Readings

Bronson, D. E., Pelz, D. C., & Trzcinski. E. (1988). *Computerizing your agency's information system.* Newbury Park, CA: Sage.

Dunst, C. J., Trivette, C. M., Starnes, A. L., Hamby, D. W., & Gordon, N. J. (1993). *Building and evaluating family support initiatives: A national study of programs for persons with developmental disabilities.* Baltimore: Brooks Publishing.

Joint Committee on Standards for Educational Evaluation. (1994). *The program evaluation standards: How to assess evaluations of educational programs* (2nd ed.). Newbury Park, CA: Sage.

Kalafat, J. (1996). Planning and evaluating integrated school-based services. In R. J. Illback & C. M. Nelson (Eds.), *Emerging school-based approaches for children with emotional and behavioral problems: Research and practice in service integration* (pp. 209–224). New York: Haworth Press.

Kosecoff, J., & Fink, A. (1982). *Evaluation basics: A practitioner's manual.* Newbury Park, CA: Sage.

Krueger, R. A. (1988). *Focus groups: A practical guide for applied research.* Newbury Park, CA: Sage.

Marshall, C., & Rossman, G. B. (1989). *Designing qualitative research.* Newbury Park, CA: Sage.

Patton, M. Q. (1987). *Creative evaluation.* Newbury Park, CA: Sage.

Pietrzak, J., Ramler, M., Renner, T., Ford. L., & Gilbert, N. (1990). *Practical program evaluation: Examples from child abuse prevention.* Newbury Park, CA: Sage.

Robb, M. Y. (1993). *The presentation design book.* Chapel Hill, NC: Ventana Press.

Rossi, P. H., & Freeman, H. E. (1993). *Evaluation: A systematic approach.* Newbury Park, CA: Sage.

Scriven, M. (1991). *Evaluation thesaurus* (4th ed.). Newbury Park, CA: Sage.

Shadish, W. R., Jr., Cook, T. D., & Leviton, L. C. (1991). *Foundations of program evaluation: Theories of practice.* Newbury Park, CA: Sage.

Weiss, H. B., & Jacobs, F. H. (Eds.). (1988). *Evaluating family programs.* New York: Aldine deGruyter.

Wells, K., & Biegel, D. E. (Eds.). (1991). *Family preservation services: Research and evaluation.* Newbury Park, CA: Sage.

Wolcott, H. F. (1994). *Transforming qualitative data: Description, analysis, and interpretation.* Newbury Park, CA: Sage.

15

Education and Training for Integrated Practice: Assumptions, Components, and Issues

Rick Jay Short

> [A]ssigning a single professional, trained exclusively as a teacher, social worker, or counselor, to work with a family that needs help from more than one profession, agency, or program is equivalent to *malpractice*, since it provides a service in a way that is known to fail to meet the needs of the family . . . . (Cohen & Ooms, 1993, p. ii)

America appears to be undergoing a revolution in its concept of services to children. Traditional services often have been setting or agency based, with little communication across units. In this formulation of children's services, children and their families were defined as a collection of components and were assigned different identities, depending on the part served by the particular mission and frame of the service agency. For example, schools provided primarily educational services to children (called *students*), hospitals and other health agencies tended to health needs of children (called *patients*), social service agencies addressed the social and economic needs of children (called *cases*), and so on. Often, redundant services have been provided in different settings to some children while critically needed services have not been available to other children. This approach to services seems to be based on an underlying assumption that different facets of children's lives and development are relatively independent of each other. Each facet can be addressed by different systems without affecting other parts of the child, the family, or other systems.

The child-as-parts assumption may be yielding to a more holistic picture of children wherein the child, rather than each service delivery system, is at the center of the services picture. Policy makers are now beginning to see that children are whole units that traverse many systems each day and throughout their development, but that cannot be divided into separate segments for the purpose of fitting into the frame of each system. Rather, service systems must collaboratively and efficiently address the needs of the child as a whole. The child is replacing the mosaic of disparate, often competing, service systems as the center of children's services.

Service providers and policy makers have acknowledged for several years that meeting the needs of many children requires multiple professional perspectives and services. The needs of some children exceed the capabilities and resources of school-based professionals, or of any single agency or discipline. In the absence of effective service coordination and collaboration across agencies, these children frequently have moved back and forth among agencies with no agency or profession accepting responsibility for comprehensive treatment (Friedman, 1986). Services often have been unrelated or redundant. Thus, all too many children have participated in a cycle of uncoordinated assessment and referral from agency to agency that yields frustration to parents and ineffective, inefficient services to their children (Knitzer, 1984). These children include handicapped infants and toddlers (McLinden & Prasse, 1991; Short, Simeonsson, & Huntington, 1990), seriously emotionally disturbed children and youth (Saxe, Cross, & Silverman, 1988), and children at risk of academic and social failure (Short, Meadows, & Moracco, 1992).

The increasingly complex nature of the problems affecting children and their families has highlighted difficulties in providing the comprehensive services that are essential to address the diverse needs of children. More and more often, effective children's services require extensive development, implementation, and coordination of integrated services across agencies from a variety of professions and disciplines. Involved agencies include education, health, welfare, social services, juvenile justice, and others dealing with children. Some of the critical professions and disciplines include child development, criminal justice and law enforcement, education, law, medicine, nursing, psychology, public administration, public health, and social work.

Despite heavy emphasis on integrated services policy and development over the last 2 decades, effective provision of such services remains elusive in the United States. A major factor in the continued lack of comprehensive integrated services is limited availability of expertise to establish and maintain these services (Cohen & Ooms, 1993). Acknowledging the importance of expertise in integrated service delivery raises an important question: What special skills and competencies are needed to provide integrated services? Certainly, expertise within a discipline constitutes an important foundation for both within-profession practice and interprofessional (integrated service) delivery. In addition to traditional professional expertise, several skills and competencies have been proposed as critical components of interprofessional practice. Schorr (1993) suggested that interprofessional expertise includes building relationships based on respect and trust; collaboration with families, agencies, and other discipline; and facility in addressing complex interactions of information and problems. Overall, these skills represent competence in working in an "unbureaucratic, outcome-oriented" manner (Schorr, 1993, p. 100). Gardner (1993) emphasized the importance of maintaining sufficient knowledge of other disciplines to allow problem recognition, appropriate referral, and collaboration. He further noted that interprofessional practitioners need skills in individual assessment and interventions, along with skills in collaborative, family-based assessment, and intervention (Gardner, 1993). Cohen and Ooms (1993) added that each interprofessional team member must be a skilled consumer, provider, and collaborator. They argued for balanced competencies as a specialist and a generalist. Overall, perhaps the most important facet of integrated service delivery is a world view or conceptual framework that focuses on whole-child and family needs, addressing both individual and context.

For many years, universities have recognized the importance of high-quality specialized within-discipline training for children's services professionals. However, few universities have developed programs with a sufficient emphasis on identifying and solving the complex problems of children and their families in comprehensive, coordinated ways. Perhaps due to the traditional department-based structure of higher education, professional training programs have continued to emphasize within-discipline expertise applied in single settings. Although the expertise and identity associated with each profession are important, current societal needs dictate that effective personnel preparation address comprehensive, child-centered, outcome-oriented service provision training.

Assumptions Underlying Interprofessional Preparation

The assumptions for interprofessional education just discussed provide the theoretical basis for programs that teach interprofessional collaboration as an integral part of their professional curriculum. These assumptions define and describe the essential elements of interprofessional education at both the professional and continuing education levels. They suggest a high level of commitment to theories of interprofessional collaboration, its value for professional practice, its importance within the structured curricula of professional education, and its continued influence in the lifelong learning goals of practicing professionals. A number of factors and conditions, however, are necessary to establish and sustain collaborative programs (Casto, 1987).

Casto (1994) has suggested that training programs seeking to provide substantive preparation in interprofessional practice should be guided by established, but flexible, principles to ensure integrity of educational experiences. On the basis of his extensive experience with the National Consortium on Interprofessional Education and Practice, he proposed several assumptions that should serve as foundations of interprofessional education and training (Casto, 1994). A summary of Casto's assumptions is presented subsequently.

Interprofessional programs should focus on issues of concern across professional training programs. A holistic perspective on service delivery mandates examination of multiple facets of client needs and characteristics. Such a perspective also requires acknowledging the interrelated nature of many of these needs. For example, children's educational needs often have health, socioeconomic, and family components that must be addressed to provide adequate services. These diverse components typically are provided by multiple professionals in a variety of settings. Professional training programs must be comprehensive in developing conceptualizations of the problems their trainees address and recognize the necessity of multiple professional perspectives. Where these conceptualizations overlap with other professional training programs, integrated training for coordinated service delivery is a natural and powerful approach.

Interprofessional education should emphasize those client needs and issues that integrated services are most well suited to address. Not all problems of children and families are addressed best by collaborative efforts among agencies and professionals. Solutions to many problems (e.g., treatment of broken bones, reading instruction) may be provided efficiently by a single discipline and should be addressed accordingly. Interprofessional programs should identify and develop training around areas that clearly serve clients and the public. Sometimes these activities will require considerable communication among professional preparation programs, first to increase awareness of the necessity of collaboration to address complex societal needs and problems, and later to plan for training content and experiences.

Education and training for integrated services should enhance both intraprofessional and interprofessional competence. It is important to note that interprofessional practice does not constitute a new discipline, but rather a different way for existing disciplines to interact. The contribution of interprofessional practice lies in the integration of multiple professional skills and perspectives. Integrated-service delivery represents the blending of diverse, specialized perspectives and competencies to deal with complex and difficult problems. It cannot replace or supplant expertise or identity within disciplines. Strong identity and competence within each profession is just as critical to successful service integration as the collaboration across professions to solve such problems. An important part of these assumptions is that effective interprofessional training also must address high quality intraprofessional preparation. That is, interprofessional education must integrate a holistic service delivery orientation with strong identity and skills within each discipline.

Education and training for integrated services is a lifelong endeavor, beginning in preservice training. Interprofessional preparation may be an important influence on the attitudes, values, and identity of preservice students as they become socialized into their professions (Casto, 1994). In-service training in services integration can alter viewpoints about the nature of children's services and can provide valuable knowledge and skills to extend treatment options beyond single-discipline, single-setting services. Perhaps by clarifying one's own professional identity and knowledge within a context of comprehensive services, interprofessional training also may increase affiliation within one's discipline (Harbaugh, Casto, & Burgess-Ellison, 1987). Additionally, interprofessional training may provide effective solutions to professionals who face complex problems that are resistant to interventions available to any single discipline or setting.

Education for interprofessional practice progresses through stages of awareness. Casto (1994) proposed four levels, or stages, through which students pass as they advance toward interprofessional practice: sensitivity, openness, engagement, and cooperation. Early in their training, students become sensitized to a holistic conception of children and families and the advantage of addressing the needs of children and families through comprehensive, as opposed to fragmented, services. On the basis of this sensitivity, they learn to be open to expertise and perspectives of other agencies and professions in understanding clients' needs. As they become more aware of and open to holistic problem identification and comprehensive solutions, they become engaged in collaborative service delivery activities. At the final stage, students cooperate with other professionals and their associations to determine and influence policy for community service delivery. Casto suggests that students enter this sequence at different points, depending on their prior experiences and conceptualizations of problems and service delivery. Furthermore, curricula can be planned to promote movement through these stages toward true integrated service delivery.

Professional preparation for integrated services requires significant institutional support. Institutional commitment to interprofessional preparation, whether at the preservice or in-service level, should include allocations of space, personnel, and resources. Allocation of sufficient resources to maintain interpersonal preparation programs serves two purposes. First, it provides assurances of programmatic stability and quality. Second, it demonstrates the value that the supporting institution places on interprofessional training. In the absence of adequate institutional support, interprofessional programs are likely to remain ancillary to traditional within-discipline preparation and practice.

Elements of Successful Interprofessional Training Programs

Several writers have proposed necessary elements of successful service-integration training programs, typically based on their experiences in developing and maintaining such programs. Although these lists of components of effective programs presently are not based on outcome data, they represent the considered judgments of professionals with expertise in preparing interprofessional practitioners. In one case, the authors summarized the training literature from interdisciplinary training in adolescent health in order to distill important characteristics of these programs (Bearinger & Gephart, 1993). Casto (1994) proposed his necessary components of interprofessional training programs on the basis of his extensive experience with the National Consortium for Interprofessional Education

Table 1. Important Components and Characteristics of Education and
Training for Integrated Services

Authors	Characteristics
Bearinger & Gephart (1993)	A multidisciplinary team of faculty and learners
	Common educational goals and objectives, and core curricular requirements
	Discipline-specific educational goals and objectives, and curricular requirements
	Clinical practicum settings that provide integrated comprehensive health services
	Coursework that examines interdisciplinary processes and issues
	Faculty who demonstrate collaboration in clinical practice, teaching, and research
	Opportunities for learners to develop teaching skills adaptable to multiple audiences
	Collaboration of learners in research activities
Casto (1994)	Neutral base of operation
	Administrative support
	Shared interest and commitment
	Shared credit
	Shared resources
	Partnership with the community
	Training in collaborative skills
	Building horizontal bridges
	Rewards
Shepard, Yeo, & McGann (1985)	Emphasis on clinical science content
	Real or simulated clinical experiences
	Students with established professional identities
	Complex and thought-provoking materials rather than least-common-denominator approach
	Educators from many disciplines
	Interdisciplinary team experience
	Finance and health care regulations presented by exposure to real life problems
	Short, interspersed educational experiences
	Student–peer teaching
	Course scheduling responsive to difference in student schedules.

and Practice. Shepard, Yeo, and McGann (1985) apparently framed their task somewhat more broadly than Bearinger and Gephart, but arrived at a similar set of components. A summary of these sets of elements of successful interprofessional training is presented in Table 1.

Several general components of effective interprofessional preparation programs seem evident from examining Table 1. These include characteristics of faculty, applied experiences, training content, and student activ-

ities. Faculty in service-integration training programs should work collaboratively in teaching, research, and service delivery. Comprehensive
collaboration will establish patterns of interprofessional sharing and decision making in training programs, and will provide powerful models of
collaboration for students as they become practitioners themselves. Applied experiences in successful programs occur in settings where interprofessional and interagency collaboration is prominent. As with faculty collaboration, experiences in integrated-service settings provide models for
effective service delivery and help students build expertise in working with
other disciplines and settings. Training content in preparation programs
emphasizing interprofessional practice should stress both within-
discipline and between-discipline knowledge and skills, but should have
some common goals and objectives. Content that encompasses these two
facets of professional practice promotes within-discipline expertise and
identity while facilitating interprofessional competence and, perhaps as
important, a holistic view of children's functioning and children's services.
Finally, effective programs provide opportunities and training for students
in teaching and learning from other professionals—in this case, peer students from other disciplines.

Additional components may be important for successful programs.
Some items presented in Table 1 are unique to only one of the authors
cited, and a couple of additional areas may need to be included in a set of
components of effective programs. Casto (1994) noted the importance of a
neutral base of operations for successful programs. This component seems
quite important to avoid perceived and real power differences among professions, but may be difficult to implement within funding and organizational limitations of many training sites. Bearinger and Gephart (1993)
noted the importance of learner collaboration in research activities, which
may be more difficult in nonuniversity settings that do not emphasize
research activities. Shepard, Yeo, and McGann (1985) suggested that interprofessional programs should admit students with established professional identities. Although implementing this criterion would facilitate the
maintenance of within-discipline profession identity, it may not always be
practical in graduate programs. By building in strong within-discipline
training and identity, training programs may minimize the importance of
the Shepard et al. criterion. Although it is not included in Table 1, I believe
that training in interagency (as opposed to within-agency interprofessional) collaboration is necessary to deal with organizational variables in
integrated service delivery. Also, students need considerable exposure to
funding issues, which remain a crucial element of maintenance of interprofessional service delivery programs (Cohen & Ooms, 1993).

Obstacles to Education and Training in
Services Integration

Training in integrated services is a critical component of effective children's services (Holmes & Robertson, 1995; Koppich & Kirst, 1993). How-

ever, several obstacles to effective interprofessional training render such training difficult and often impossible. The persistence of narrowly focused university training programs and continued dependence on grant funds for training programs limits the development of effective preservice and in-service training in service integration (Gardner, 1993). Knapp and his colleagues (Knapp et al., 1993) have noted that particular challenges to sustained interprofessional preparation include accreditation and credentialing, conceptual bases of the professional disciplines, faculty roles in curriculum development, and applied learning experiences (practica and internships). Cohen and Ooms (1993) suggested that the traditional organizational structure and rewards associated with universities represent formidable barriers to implementation of training for integrated services. They further noted that state-certification requirements typically place little value on interprofessional training and may assign minimal weight to interprofessional courses and training experiences in such requirements.

Effectiveness of Education and Training for Service Integration

Given the complex nature of service-integration practice, evaluation of service integration is a difficult endeavor. Even a task as apparently simple as deciding on appropriate outcomes to measure may provoke conflict and lack of consensus. Teasing out important variables that relate to outcomes of integrated services is at least as difficult because of the multiple, heterogeneous factors that contribute to most significant problems of children and families. Though varied, coordinated interventions may be necessary to deal with difficult problems, ascertaining the relative contribution of individual interventions versus their aggregate is complicated and expensive. Accordingly, results of evaluations of integrated services often are difficult to interpret and subject to multiple interpretations. Nonetheless, evaluation of effectiveness may be critical to continued governmental funding and support.

Wang, Haertel, and Walberg (1995) recently surveyed studies of the effectiveness of collaborative school-linked programs. Although they did not include evaluations of education and training in collaboration, their conclusions may provide a context for interprofessional preparation and a guide for outcomes of training. Wang and her colleagues noted that overall results from collaborative school-linked projects are positive, but that data from evaluation studies of these programs should be interpreted cautiously. They reported that details about implementation of collaborative school-linked programs reported in the literature were sparse, which limited the interpretability of their findings.

Evidence for the effectiveness of training in promoting integrated practice remains meager and equivocal. In one of the few reported studies of outcomes of interprofessional preparation, Harbaugh, Casto, and Burgess-Ellison (1987) found that students that experienced interprofessional components in their training programs reported more positive attitudes toward integrated practice, perceptions of being better prepared for practice, and stronger identity with their own profession. Golan and Williamson (1994) studied in-service teachers' perceptions of their training in school-linked services. Teachers in their study reported having participated in about three types of school-linked-services training activities, typically consisting of information sessions or training in identification of students for referral. Although teachers reported increases in knowledge and involvement in services integration, they also reported little improvement in services available to students. Clearly, research on the effects and effectiveness of interprofessional preparation and practice is sorely needed.

Training for Integrated Services: Unresolved Issues

Even though it seems clear that interprofessional preparation may be necessary to meet modern conceptions of children's services, several major issues remain to be resolved before integrated training is the norm in professional education. The first and most prominent of these is organizational structure and associated funding. The organization of most training sites continues to be structured around discrete units such as departments and colleges, each of which maintains an independent budget and accounting system. Often, organizational units compete for resources in a zero-sum system: Increases in one program's budget require decreases in that of other programs. Providing funding for an interprofessional program may require pulling resources from other programs, resulting in fewer resources for within-discipline training. Interprofessional training programs often have avoided drawing resources from other programs by relying on grants and other short-term funding sources. Short-term solutions of this type may ultimately fail to institutionalize interprofessional preparation by allowing organizations to avoid long-term commitment to integrated programs.

Training for different types of practice represents another issue to be resolved. According to Bruner (1991), professional collaboration is appropriate for three types of problems: (a) improving services to families already being served by several systems, (b) ensuring that systems are available to identify and meet specific children's needs, and (c) reducing risks affecting all children in a neighborhood or community. These types of problems may be more readily addressed by practitioners in public service settings than by independent practitioners, who often provide treatment to individual clients on a fee-for-service basis. Interprofessional training is a valuable addition to any practitioner's armamentarium, but may be more applicable to public service providers than to private practitioners. Related to this, Cohen and Ooms (1993) have suggested that an emphasis on interprofessional preparation raises issues about the balance between generalist and specialist training. Generalist training may resemble case management, which characteristically is a public service role. Generalist training may require attention to issues of professional identity and concerns about the relevance and replacement of professions. On the other hand, specialist training may fail to address systemic variables in child and family functioning and may require bridge building to other specialists.

Another critical issue in integrated services training is evaluation of interprofessional preparation. As noted earlier, data on the effectiveness of interprofessional training is quite sparse and results are equivocal. Research is needed to address at least two major concerns. First, changes in students as a result of interprofessional training needs to be investigated. Important growth from integrated training could be hypothesized in areas of identity, competence, attitudes, problem identification and problem solving, and collaboration. Second, the relationship of these changes to community and client outcomes needs to be studied. Ultimately, some connection between interprofessional preparation and improvements in client functioning needs to be ascertained to justify the massive reorganization and reallocation of resources that probably will be needed to establish widespread, effective training.

Sanctioning is a final issue to be addressed in moving toward interprofessional preparation. Cohen and Ooms (1993) have noted that credentialing bodies typically have shown little interest in including interprofessional training and practice in certification and licensure requirements. Whenever interprofessional training is recognized in certification and licensure standards, it typically requires extra credit hours for certification. This lack of acknowledgment of training for integrated services limits desirability and accessibility of such training for practitioners in training. Accreditation of professional training programs also is problematic in implementation of training for integrated services. Accreditation guidelines often are quite conservative in adapting to new conceptualizations of professional training. Whereas this conservative approach ensures stability within professional preparation, it may limit incorporation of important new forms and ideas of training such as interprofessional preparation.

Conclusion

Education and training for integrated service delivery, or interprofessional education, may be a critical component in preparing professional practitioners to meet the complex needs of children and their families. Effective interprofessional education requires careful consideration of assumptions underlying such training, crucial components, and unresolved issues. Perhaps more important, successful interprofessional education must include a significant, long-term organizational commitment to the assumptions and implementation of integrated service training. Because interprofessional education is early in its development, major questions concerning content, procedures, structure, and effectiveness remain to be answered. However, considerable progress has been made in both understanding of and commitment to interprofessional education and training. Given the strong foundation that already has been laid, rapid progress in this area should occur.

References

Bearinger, L. H., & Gephart, J. (1993). Interdisciplinary education in adolescent health. *Journal of Paediatric Child Health, 29,* 10–15.

Bruner, C. (1991). *Thinking collaboratively: Ten questions and answers to help policy makers improve children's services.* Washington, DC: Education and Human Services Consortium.

Casto, R. M. (1987). Preservice courses for interprofessional practice. *Theory Into Practice, 26*(2), 103–109.

Casto, R. M. (1994). Education for interprofessional practice. In R. M. Casto & M. C. Julia (Eds.), *Interprofessional care and collaborative practice.* Pacific Grove, CA: Brooks-Cole.

Cohen, E., & Ooms, T. (1993). *Training and technical assistance to support family-centered, integrated services reform.* Policy seminar presented at Family Centered Social Policy: The Emerging Agenda. Family Impact Seminar, American Association for Marriage and Family Therapy Research and Education Foundation, Washington, DC.

Friedman, R. M. (1986). Major issues in mental health services for children. *Administration in Mental Health, 14*(1), 6–13.

Gardner, S. (1993). Afterword. *Journal of Education Policy, 8,* 189–199.

Golan, S., & Williamson, C. (1994, April). *Teachers make school-linked services work.* Paper presented at the Annual Meeting of the American Educational Research Association, New Orleans, LA.

Harbaugh, G. L., Casto, R. M., & Burgess-Ellison, J. A. (1987). Becoming a professional: How interprofessional training helps. *Theory into Practice, 26*(2), 141–145.

Holmes, M., & Robertson, B. (1995). Why Head Start and mental health associations should collaborate: Pathways to partnership. *National Health Services Administration Journal, 14,* 23, 25–28.

Knapp, M. S., et al. (1993). University-based preparation for collaborative interprofessional practice. In L. Adler & S. Gardner (Eds.), The politics of linking schools and social services: The 1993 politics of education association yearbook (theme issue). *Journal of Education Policy, 8*(5/6), 137–151.

Knitzer, J. (1984). Mental health services to children and adolescents: A national view of public policies. *American Psychologist, 39*(8), 905–911.

Koppich, J. E., & Kirst, M. W. (1993). Editors' introduction. In J. E. Koppich & M. W. Kirst (Eds.), Integrating services for children: Prospects and pitfalls (theme issue), *Education and Urban Society, 25,* 123–128.

McLinden, S. E., & Prasse, D. P. (1991). Providing services to infants and toddlers under PL 99-457: Training needs of school psychologists. *School Psychology Review, 20*(1), 37–48.

Saxe, L., Cross, T., & Silverman, N. (1988). Children's mental health: The gap between what we know and what we do. *American Psychologist, 43*(10), 800–807.

Schorr, L. B. (1993). Daring to learn from our successes. *Aspen Institute Quarterly, 5*(1), 78–107.

Shepard, K., Yeo, G., & McGann, L. (1985). Successful components of interdisciplinary education. *Journal of Allied Health, 14*(3), 297–303.

Short, R. J., Meadows, M. E., & Moracco, J. C. (1992). A project to meet the needs of rural at-risk children: Pilot At-Risk Interventions in Rural Schools (PAIRS). In R. C. Morris (Ed.), *Solving the problems of youth at risk: Involving parents and community resources* (pp. 176–180). Lancaster, PA: Technomic.

Short, R. J., Simeonsson, R. J., & Huntington, G. S. (1990). Early intervention: Implications of P. L. 99-457 for professional child psychology. *Professional Psychology: Research and Practice, 21*(2).

Wang, M. C., Haertel, G. D, & Walberg, H. J. (1995). *The effectiveness of collaborative school-linked services.* San Francisco: Jossey-Bass.

Afterword

On The Nature and Future of Practice

Robert J. Resnick

Collectively, the chapters in this book have pointed psychologists toward a new and more productive way of providing services to children and families in need. It is clear, however, that if this new paradigm is to become a reality, we as practicing psychologists will need to rethink our traditional role of independent service providers. Our apparent reluctance to do this can be traced back to the service model created after World War II, when psychological practice grew exponentially. Expanded services were primarily directed toward war veterans returning to civilian life with what was then called *battle fatigue*. The Veterans Administration health care system in the late 1940s and early 1950s had the largest number of training slots for psychologists. These trainees began a model that continues today, wherein the preponderance of psychological practitioners function in solo practice settings. Indeed, in 1996, a survey was completed by the practice directorate of the American Psychological Association indicating that 40% of all licensed psychologists continue sole practitioner practice (R. Newman, personal communication, May 3, 1996).

For decades this model served us well, but the advent of the health care reform initiatives in the early 1990s forced psychologists and other health care providers to reexamine the nature of their practice. Others heard the "wake up call" to reevaluate psychological training and practice paradigms also. It was clear for mental health, as it was for physical health, that truncated fee for service care was not efficient or cost-effective. Costs continued to skyrocket, exceeding one trillion dollars in 1995. If allowed to continue, such costs would bankrupt the U.S. economy.

Although it was true that most of the increases in mental health costs were traceable to inpatient psychiatric services for children and adolescents and the treatment of substance and alcohol abuse, powerful forces generated by the purchasers of health services clearly demonstrated that major change was imminent. Concepts like "one-stop shopping," "wraparound services," and continuity of care (all discussed in detail within this volume) were rapidly gaining acceptance by the purchasers of health insurance as well as state and federal publicly funded programs.

This shifting service paradigm emphasized high quality and accessibility. Such services need to be comprehensive (i.e., the one-stop shop phenomenon) and delivered at an appropriate level of intensity. Cost-effective outpatient care, some very intensive, is an alternative to more costly hospitalization and can be consistent with patient or consumer needs. As this book has emphasized repeatedly, services must be based on an individual's strengths as well as problems. Thus, patients are enabled to be a part of the treatment process rather than being "the victim" or passive recipient of their treatment. Developing a treatment plan with the patient rather than only for the patient has been of particular concern, as has the fact that health care plans are not being designed and implemented with measurable outcome and projected time lines. No longer will third-party payors routinely pay for unlimited long-term individual therapy without outcome measures and progress markers.

Additionally, the shift to an integrated care model for psychological services must include services that can be provided at multiple sites such as the provider's office, the school, the home, the workplace, and the community. This component of the health care revolution has been difficult both for the providers of services and the training programs to comprehend. Problems of inertia are frequently found in training programs in any discipline, and thus, there needs to be an ongoing dialogue with training programs to ensure that the training of psychologists is current and reflects practice as it exists as well as evolving practice. To obtain more and more of less and less (T. Boll, personal communication, April, 1994) is not in our economic best interest. Thus, it is not in our professional self-interest to be narrowly defined only as long-term therapists.

Psychology, therefore, must make this paradigm shift to incorporate the realities of the health care delivery system as it evolves into an integrated service delivery model. Even more important is the necessary shift away from identifying psychologists as mental health providers and establishing the profession as psychological health providers in primary care settings. This "new breed" of psychologists will need to not only provide psychotherapeutic services but will view themselves as psychologists with a wide variety of intervention and prevention skills in a wide variety of settings.

Psychologists are, by virtue of their training, the preeminent experts in behavior. One need not look very far to recognize that many of today's health problems, including those that are destroying the fabric of our society, are driven by behavior (e.g., AIDS, smoking, sedentary life styles, teen pregnancy). AIDS is entirely caused and transmitted by behavioral events and thus is 100% preventable by appropriate intervention that must occur outside the practitioner's office. Teen and unwanted pregnancy is another significant problem that can be aggressively addressed by early interventions by psychological practitioners as part of an overall health care delivery system. There is ample evidence that alcohol and drug abuse are genetically weighted, but it is also clear that if an individual does not drink or experiment with drugs, then the expression of the genetic load can never occur. Stated simplistically, if one never drinks, one will never become an alcoholic. Serious health problems affecting individuals and society can be ameliorated by aggressive prevention and wellness programs that exist out of the office and in the communities. Another example is the violence in our cities and the abuse of children, behaviors that can be vigorously intervened and modified with appropriate interventions in the community, the school, through the courts, or community mental health centers. Psychologists must be partners in this comprehensive health care delivery system.

Psychologists who work regularly with primary care physicians know the benefit of supporting patients through invasive tests and procedures, preparing them for surgery or transplantation, or increasing compliance to medical treatment. These are additional settings in which psychologists can and do to make a contribution. In an integrated service delivery model, not only will psychologists be part of primary care, they will be part of medical diagnostic and treatment teams. If programs continue to train psychologists in a single service paradigm, then for a number of our colleagues, the practice of psychology will go the way of the Dodo bird. Not all the Dodo birds became extinct in one day, but eventually the species disappeared because it could not adapt to the new environment. Let us take a lesson from them. The failure to adapt, not only to new market realities but to new societal realities, will ultimately relegate psychologists to an expensive and essentially irrelevant profession. For, if all we offer is psychotherapy, there are many other professions in a community that also provide the same service at a lower cost!

Psychologists must keep, then move from, our mental health origins and continue to evolve into primary care in all its ramifications. One need not look far to recognize how much psychology has evolved from its roots in philosophy to psychological assessment and testing to inpatient and outpatient services to services in nontraditional settings such as medical schools, corporate offices, and employee assistance plans to the current movement for prescription privileges for appropriately trained psychologists. Virtually all of these changes were in response to forces in society mandating change in the status quo.

Today's psychologist will likely benefit, too, from some entrepreneurial skills to help market psychological services and provide them in integrated service models. Indeed, both private and public sector systems are reexamining the one-on-one fee for service paradigm in all health care. Almost every state in the union and the federal government have demonstration projects with some form of capitation or managed care paradigm for the public sector for medical and mental health care recipients. Additionally, in many communities, services are interlocked and integrated for children and adolescents within the school, community-services board, social-service agencies, and juvenile courts—having learned that truncating their services is not in the youth's best interest. A collaborative effort is the more efficient and cost-effective system.

As health care continues to evolve, it appears that the next iteration of this evolution is capitation. In this system, providers assume some of the financial risk of seeing patients. Under capitation, a provider group agrees to meet all of the medical or psychological needs of a finite number of people at a fixed cost per person per month. Thus, the group knows exactly how much income is coming in and for that amount of money, must provide all of the necessary care for this "captive" population. Psychologists in many parts of the country have formed multidisciplinary practices and are actively seeking such business. Historically, psychologists have unfortunately had difficulty viewing themselves as a business people selling a service. It is, indeed, problematic for psychologists, for that is how purchasers of health care see us—just like other providers, a vendor of a product or service. This is the jargon of the business community. Recently, I was at a conference where managed care executives and individuals who market services were talking about their "new product"—a capitated system of care for the developmentally disabled. Again, this is the language of business. Psychologists must become, if not facile, then at least conversant.

In summary, there will always be a need (and those who can afford) long-term individual therapy, but it is likely that this solo form of practice will become more difficult to maintain for the vast majority of psychologists in most areas of the country. What is evolving is a system of integrated health care systems that will have psychologists work with traditional colleagues such as psychiatrists and social workers but also become a part of practice groups and sites that have been nontraditional for the profession. Psychologists will need to be trained in many modalities across divergent cultures and socioeconomic standing and have the knowledge base to work in primary health care settings. Fortunately, psychologists are ideally suited and trained for such an endeavor. As the most extensively trained and knowledgeable professionals in the area of human behavior and outcome research, psychologists can be on the cutting edge and help shape these new systems. In order to accomplish this, psychology will need to abandon outdated ideas of training and practice and develop new training systems with the expansion of intervention strategies and tools (such as the integration of mind–body phenomena in primary health care and acquisition of prescriptive authority to complement behavioral strategies). Last, psychologists can bring to these evolving systems a frame of reference that has emphasized competence rather than disease and dysfunction. Such a perspective allows for the empowerment of the individuals, subcultures, and society we serve.

Author Index

Numbers in italics refer to listings in the reference sections.

Patterson, G. R., 128, *134*, 164, 166, *188*
Peak, G., 30, *51*
Pease-Alvarez, L., 64, *72*
Pecora, P. J., 123, 125, *136*
Pentz, M. A., 151, *155*
Peters, T. J., 102, *118*
Peterson, D. R., 281, 289, *301*, 305, 306, 322
Petr, C. G., 77, 87, *88*
Phillips, E. A., *279*
Phillips, E. L., *279*
Philpot, C. L., 313, *322*
Pickrel, S. G., 129, 130, 131, *135*, *136*
Pierce, J. K., 313, *321*
Pierce, P. M., 175, *188*
Pinker, R., 59, *72*
Pires, S. A., 16, *20*, *188*
Poe, S., 9, *18*, 269, *278*
Poe, S. L., 160, 182, *185*
Poertner, J., 157, 173, *186*, *188*
Polite, K., *322*
Ponti, C. R., 153, *156*
Powell, D., 60, *72*
Prange, M. E., *185*
Prasse, D. P., 348, *357*
President's Commission on Mental Health, 263, *279*
Pritchard, E., 3, *19*, 112, *118*
Provus, M. M., 326, *346*

Quay, H. C., 128, *136*

Rabinowitz, V., 78, *88*, *90*
Radin, B. A., 6, *19*, 210, 214, *219*
Rapoff, M. A., 234, *253*
Rapp, C. A., 164, 177, *185*, *187*
Rappaport, J., 80, 81, 85, *90*, *91*
Reed, T., 3, *20*
Reid, J. B., 128, *134*, 164, 166, *188*
Rein, M., 16, *20*
Reisinger, K. S., 234, *254*
Report of the Task Force on Education of Young Adolescents, 140, *156*
Richards, P., 191, 193, 195, 196, *218*
Richman, H., 41, *50*
Richman, H. A., 56, 57, *71*
Riddle, D. B., 247, *254*
Rienzo, B., 37, 40, *52*
Riffle, D. W., 177, *187*
Rivara, F. P., 151, *155*
Rivera, V. R., *189*, 263, 267, *279*, 282
Roberts, M., 75, *90*
Roberts, M. C., 160, *185*, 223, 224, *254*, 281, *301*
Roberts, R. M., 75

Roberts, R. N., *90*
Roberts-DeGennaro, M., *219*
Roberts-DeGennero, M., 196
Robertson, B., 353, *357*
Rodrigue, J. R., 75
Rodrique, J. R., *90*
Rodway, M. R., 75, 86, *90*
Rogers, C. R., 305, *322*
Rome, L. P., 222, *255*
Ronneau, J., 162, 174, *189*
Rosenbaum, L., 63, *72*
Rosenblatt, A., 166, 178, *185*, *189*, *279*
Rosenstock, I. M., 143, *156*
Rosenthal, S. L., 248, *254*
Rossi, P. H., 124, 127, *136*, 336, *346*
Rossman, G. B., 325, *346*
Rothman, J., 157, 164, 177, *189*
Routh, D. K., 221, 222, 230, *254*
Rowland, M. D., 130, 131, *135*
Rozecki, T., 173, *188*
Ruffolo, M. C., 178, 180, *187*
Rugs, D., *279*
Rutherford, R. B., Jr., 9, *20*
Rutman, L., 326, *346*
Rutter, J., 162, *189*
Rutter, M., 7, *20*, 237, *254*
Ryan, C. S., 178, *189*
Rzepnicki, T. L., 124, 125, 127, *136*

Sagduyu, K., 177, *187*
Salazar, D. D., 4, *18*
Salk, L., 221, *254*
Salovey, P., 141, *156*
Sameroff, A. J., 7, *20*
Sanders, D., 160, 176, *187*, 287, 288, *301*
Sanders, D. S., 196, *219*
Sandfort, J., 11, *18*
Santelli, J., 37, *52*
Santos, A. B., 122, *136*
Santos de Barona, M., 62, *71*
Sarason, S., 213, *219*, 300, *301*
Sarason, S. B., 54, *72*, 305, *322*
Saxe, L., 348, *357*
Scherer, D. G., 126, 130, *136*
Scherz, F. H., 75, *90*
Schoen, J., 3, *18*
Schoenborn, C. A., 222, *255*
Schoenwald, S. K., 126, 129, 130, 131, 132, *134*, *135*, *136*
Schorr, D., 193, 218, *219*
Schorr, L. B., 16, *19*, 55, *72*, 94, 106, *118*, 147, *156*, 167, *189*, 193, 218, *219*, 348, 357
Schraeder, S. S., 304, *321*
Schroeder, C., 125, *136*
Schroeder, C. S., 222, 225, 228, 230, 231,

Subject Index

About the Editors

Robert J. Illback, PhD, is Executive Director of R.E.A.C.H. of Louisville, Inc., a human services agency that serves children and youth with serious emotional and behavioral disabilities. He holds a PsyD from the Graduate School of Applied and Professional Psychology at Rutgers University, and in 1990 was the inaugural recipient of the Donald R. Peterson Prize in recognition of career contributions in professional psychology by a PsyD graduate. A Fellow of the American Psychological Association, the American Psychological Society, and the American Association for Applied and Preventive Psychology, Dr. Illback has published extensively in areas of child psychology and education. He is principal investigator of a number of nationally recognized initiatives, including Kentucky's Family Resource and Youth Services Centers and the Kentucky IMPACT program. His professional and research interests include systems of care in child mental health, school-based and school-linked integrated service programs, community-based intervention, program planning and evaluation, and planned organizational change. Dr. Illback is active in professional association work, and is a member of the Kentucky State Board of Psychology.

Carolyn T. Cobb, PhD, is Section Chief for Evaluation Services in the North Carolina Department of Public Instruction (NCDPI). She has previously served as the Coordinator for School Psychology, Chief Consultant for Pupil Personnel Services, and Director for Innovation and Development in NCDPI. She holds a PhD in Psychology from North Carolina State University and was awarded the first Distinguished Alumni Award from the Department of Psychology in 1988. She also holds an MA in School Psychology from the University of North Carolina-Chapel Hill and has served as President of the National Association of School Psychologists and the North Carolina School Psychology Association. Her publications and professional interests include systemic change in education, the role of psychologists in educational reform, and the development of new service delivery models. In addition to her work in the NCDPI, she works with professional and nonprofit groups on strategic planning and organizational development.

Herbert M. Joseph, Jr., PhD, is the current Chief Psychologist and Director of the Center for Multicultural Training in Psychology (CMTP) in the Division of Psychiatry at the Boston Medical Center (a 1996 public–private merger between Boston City Hospital and Boston University Medical Center Hospital). CMTP's predecessor, the Minority Training Program in Clinical and Community Psychology at Boston City Hospital, was one of the first sites in the country devoted to training pre- and postdoctoral psychology trainees from racial, ethnic, and culturally diverse backgrounds to work in urban community-based settings in the public sector. Dr. Joseph, himself having completed an internship there, holds a PhD from the Boston University Clinical Psychology Program and in 1996 was awarded an MPH in Health Services from the Boston University School of Public Health. From 1991–1995, Dr. Joseph served as a member, and later as Vice-Chairperson, of the Massachusetts Board of Registration in Psychology. An Assistant Professor of Psychiatry at the Boston University School of Medicine, his professional interests include child mental health, multicultural training, and public health policy, interventions, and program development in communities of color.